# PHILOSOPHICAL PAPERS

# PHILOSOPHICAL PAPERS

Volume 1

Peter Unger

2006

# OXFORD
UNIVERSITY PRESS

Oxford University Press, Inc., publishes works that further
Oxford University's objective of excellence
in research, scholarship, and education.

Oxford   New York
Auckland   Cape Town   Dar es Salaam   Hong Kong   Karachi
Kuala Lumpur   Madrid   Melbourne   Mexico City   Nairobi
New Delhi   Shanghai   Taipei   Toronto

With offices in
Argentina   Austria   Brazil   Chile   Czech Republic   France   Greece
Guatemala   Hungary   Italy   Japan   Poland   Portugal   Singapore
South Korea   Switzerland   Thailand   Turkey   Ukraine   Vietnam

Copyright © 2006 by Peter Unger

Published by Oxford University Press, Inc.
198 Madison Avenue, New York, New York 10016

www.oup.com

Oxford is a registered trademark of Oxford University Press

All rights reserved. No part of this publication may be reproduced,
stored in a retrieval system, or transmitted, in any form or by any means,
electronic, mechanical, photocopying, recording, or otherwise,
without the prior permission of Oxford University Press.

Library of Congress Cataloging-in-Publication Data
Unger, Peter K.
Philosophical papers / Peter Unger.
p. cm.
Includes bibliographical references and index.
ISBN-13 978-0-19-515552-5 (vol. 1)

ISBN-13 978-0-19-530158-8 (vol. 2)

1. Philosophy.   I. Title.
B945.U543P48 2006
191—dc22         2005048843

Printed in the United States of America
on acid-free paper

For my wife, Susan
Our son, Andrew

And for my dear friend,
Stephen Bloom

# PREFACE TO VOLUME 1

Just a few months ago, I finally finished my *magnum opus*—well, my Really Big Book, anyway—a tome whose creation had been consuming me for eight very full years. With my so recently having relinquished any very vital connection with *All the Power in the World*, it's now hard, for me, to engage in substantial philosophical writing. But, that's hardly the whole story. Even years before completing that book, I decided I wouldn't try to supply this collection, already on the drawing boards, with any intellectually ambitious Introduction—even if that might be much in vogue nowadays, as it just might possibly be. At all events, and for each of several individually sufficient reasons, in this large collection's many pages, one thing you won't find is any Introduction—none that's intellectually ambitious and, of course, none that's just so much perfectly pedestrian padding. (As James Carville might say, if he'd been advising me, "It's the papers, stupid!" Or, as I've given the Democrats a fair sum of cash, over the years, while nary a cent to the Real Protector of the Powerful's Privileges, maybe he'd leave out the "stupid." Or, maybe he wouldn't leave it out; I don't know.)

Though there's a fair lot of my shortish philosophical publication that's not contained anywhere in *Philosophical Papers*, still, this is a very sizeable collection—too big to comfortably fit between the covers of a single volume. Or, maybe in better words, there's too much to be contained in a single volume that's comfortable for a typical human being to comfortably read, while holding the whole thing in her own two hands. Accordingly, the collection is presented as a two-volume set.

In allocating papers to the set's two Volumes, I've tried to present the material thematically, by contrast with, say, a chronological presentation. Following some such principle for allocation pretty consistently, I've been able to manage, it happily turns out, a nice balance, so far as the number of selected papers goes, for the pair of Volumes: Exactly eleven selections serve to constitute this First Volume, Volume 1, and, as well, precisely that many may be found in its complementary Volume, Volume 2.

For a rough idea as to which sorts of pieces are in each Volume—where sorts are determined by thematic topic area—you may think of Volume 1 as having the alliterative subtitle "Epistemology, Ethics, Etcetera," and you may think of Volume 2 as being subtitled, almost as alliteratively, "Metaphysics and More." As each would-be subtitle indicates, in neither Volume are the selected works very neatly compartmentalized. At any rate, they're not exhaustively covered by brief terms for topic areas, with each term's proper denotation excluding that of the other topic terms. As this isn't any big deal, I'll say no more about it.

As I've already intimated, to put the point very mildly, in neither Volume will you find any intellectually ambitious Introduction, to precede that Volume's selected offerings. Nor will you find, in any of this big collection's many pages, anything else that might be taken to be some new substantial philosophical effort, not previously published. For one thing, in each of the two Volumes, I'm leaving all of the published pieces collected therein perfectly intact, just as they first appeared in published print. (Well, very nearly so: Of course, the collection's publisher, the Oxford University Press, may see fit to correct however many typographical errors some Oxford editors might find in the originally published material. And, of course, I'll allow them to format the papers so that the present presentations appear most pleasingly consistent. But, of course, none of that amounts to anything that's philosophically substantial.)

Just so, another thing you won't find in *Philosophical Papers*, is this: Any remarks aimed at expressing my present views—or my later views, anyway—on questions addressed in any of the collection's published papers. (For that matter, you won't find any newly penned remarks, either, on any *other* philosophical issues.) As I'm thinking, there's little point in that. Why? Here's my thinking, about that question.

On the one hand, it may very well be, I think, that some of the presented papers grab you. In such a happy event, I'm quite sure, they'll serve to stimulate enjoyably disturbing thinking on your part. If anything much happens for you with my papers, or maybe even anything at all, it's that sort of experience that you'll enjoy. Now, in such a circumstance, you'll do far better to press on with your own responsive thoughts—prompted by my strangely challenging papers—than you'd do by gazing upon more words from me. For these further words of mine, they're likely to be more mature and mellow comments, far less happily stimulating than what's forcefully grabbed you and, accordingly, what's gotten you involved in your own enjoyable philosophic thinking. Well, that's what's on one hand.

Now, here's what's on the other hand: Unlikely though it may be, it just might happen, I fearfully allow, that my presented papers *don't* grab you—not even some very few among the twenty-two selected for the whole two-volume set. What's to be done in such a very different circumstance? Well, it's most unlikely that there's anything *I* can do to improve matters much. Do you think that, though I've entirely failed to light your fire, with all the very many presented attempts you've already seen me make toward such an end—well, somehow or other, I'll suddenly change things, very much for the better, by my heaping yet more words on you? Hardly likely, I'd say: Look, in such a sad circumstance as this, you'll be a (sort of) reader—a rather rare (sort of) reader, I hope—who's quite *dis*inclined to respond, in any very enjoyably active way, to the (sort of) sentences that a writer like *me* is so deeply disposed to produce. Let's face it; for happily active philosophical reading, I'm not your guy. Astonishing though the thought is, you'll likely do better by perusing the works of other contemporary philosophical writers. ("It's the papers, stupid!")

But, hey; let's be a little optimistic. You're a reasonably well-educated reader, I'm thinking, though you're not so very deeply steeped in recent philosophy as are most mainstream academic philosophers. So, as is then most likely, you'll be thinking that, since this collection comprises just so many papers produced by a worker in core analytic philosophy and, to boot, such a one as holds a very reputable academic post, these constituent papers are likely to be quite like those in each of just so many pretty similar collections—pretty much all of them published by academic presses (just as this present collection so obviously is). And, most likely, your related further thoughts will be a lot like these imminently upcoming ideas, even if they're not nearly so specific or detailed as what's coming right after my next colon: Except for a very few hundred other analytically-oriented metaphysicians, or epistemologists, or philosophers of language, and so on, well, there's scarcely anyone who'll find much enjoyable reading in anything even remotely like most such academical essays. Well, as you may be somewhat surprised to learn, I agree with this thinking of yours. (There's not absolute and complete agreement here, mind you. But, of course, that rarely happens among us opinionated human beings. More to the realistic point, there's agreement on the whole.) In fact, on the whole, I may have an ever dimmer view of the situation than you do. "Well, what's so optimistic about *that*?" you should now be thinking.

Nothing; nothing at all. But, as I'll remind you, the general situation isn't an all-encompassing situation. Happily for me—and for you, too, I imagine—this collection's papers were written by a very different sort of analytic metaphysician, and analytic epistemologist, and so on. Just so, the collection contains papers that, with almost every one of them, go smack against the grain of all the widely boring writing that you're so accustomed to dreading: In matters epistemological, I'm a radical skeptic, gosh-darned-it—leastways, most of the time I am. In matters metaphysical, I'm a self-styled nihilistic philosopher—very often, at least, that's my happily radical view. And so it goes. In the words of that delightfully wise cultural critic, Steve Martin, I'm a wild and crazy guy—not absolutely always, mind you, but—very much of the time, that's me.

For most browsers in any big Borders, say, or in any large Barnes and Noble store, just take a look at, say, "A Defense of Skepticism" (Paper number 1, in this Volume) and "Skepticism and Nihilism" (Paper number 4, in the Volume). Right there, you'll find far more enjoyable stimulation, I'm sure, than in any of the dozens upon dozens of mainstream collections that, quite understandably, indeed, you won't give even so much as a two-minute lookover.

Equally, this holds true with most viewers of, say, Web-pages of Amazon.com. Or, to give such Web-surfing folks equal space here, I'll say this: In Volume 2 of *Philosophical Papers*, they'll find quite a lot to enjoy in, say, just the readily readable short selection "I Do Not Exist" (Paper number 2, in that Volume) and, directly after that, in the same Second Volume, the short essay's more thoroughly exploratory companion, "Why There Are No People." Just in those two pieces, they'll find *far* more, to really enjoy, than in the whole of most any of the aforesaid analytically-oriented essay collections. I say *far* more to enjoy, and I mean just that. (Heck, if the difference was anything *much less* than that, most sensible book-buyers oughtn't give this present collection, either, so much as a two-minute lookover.)

Well, that's more than enough of such confident but self-serving comparisons. By this point, you've gotten my point, I'm sure. ("It's the papers, stupid!")

Now, even though it's just a rhetorical device, I'll again ask this question: Is there reason for you to be optimistic here, about what you'll find here, in this voluminous two-volume collection? Of course, you won't be at all surprised at the answer I provide: *Heck*, yeah! You'll become very happily embroiled, I'll bet you a quarter, in lots that's in *Philosophical Papers*.

Beyond what's in this Volume's reprinted papers, and beyond the Volume's Index, and, of course, beyond this happily humorous Preface, I'll supply you, in what's between the book's front cover and its back, little more than three lists: First, there's the (Table of) Contents for this very Volume, that is, for Volume 1 of *Philosophical Papers*. Second, there's the (Table of) Contents for this Volume's companion in the collection, that is, for Volume 2 of *Philosophical Papers*. Third, there's a lulu of a list, quickly called *Provenance of Papers*, that provides, in chronological order, quite full bibliographic information, for each of the twenty-two items reprinted in this entire two-volume collection. As with the two Contents lists, this list, too, will appear, identically the same, in both Volumes. Not obvious to sheer inspection, still, you'll soon see how very useful this list can be—especially for me!

With the next few paragraphs, you'll come to know more than enough, and more than you want, about how serviceable are the three lists provided in this Volume. ("It's the papers, stupid!")

Even while this little prefatory production's meant to comprise mostly prose that's remarkably entertaining, it's also meant to serve certain more serious purposes. While those purposes are pretty serious, there's nothing very profound, let me tell you, in any of that: Indeed, far from concerning anything that's deeply philosophical, the points the Preface has yet to cover lie along such sensibly superficial lines as these: Beyond making some serious use of the lists lately mentioned, including what may be some legally necessary use, I'll supply you, in this Preface, with a smidgeon of authorial autobiography, and also a bit of practical advice for prospective readers. And, to top all that off—what the heck—I'll provide some blatant advertising for much other published work of mine, specifically, for all my self-standing book-length philosophical productions.

First, the smidgeon of authorial autobiography: Though I'd never have guessed it when first I wrote philosophy for publication, it's turned out that I'm more of a book-writer than a paper-writer—though, as I trust this collection makes plain, I've been a pretty considerable paper-writer, too. In retrospect, insofar as it's been papers that I've been writing, many of them turned out to be studies for books, or ancestors of books, or something of the kind. But, even so, many haven't ever been anything much like that and, most likely, they never will be. This is reflected, pretty well, I think, in what's been selected for appearance in *Philosophical Papers*: While eight of this whole collection's papers may be rightly regarded as seeds of longer and later published works, almost twice that number, fully fourteen selections, can't be regarded as being, in that way, anything like so seminal. So, for your hard-earned money—or for your institutional library's money—I've given you a nice mix here, I think. It's sort of a happy sampler, I'll suggest, with quite a nice variety of Ungerian offerings. ("It's the papers, stupid!")

From that bit of authorial storytelling, I segue to remark on the chronological list that, briefly, I call *Provenance of Papers*: My Provenance list, as I've noted, supplies bibliographic information for each of the original publications represented in *Philosophical Papers*—all those in Volume 1 of the collection and, as well, all those in Volume 2. I'm not sure how useful that may be for you. But, for me, it certainly serves a very useful purpose: In one fell swoop, I hereby thank all the relevant entities duly associated with each and every one of the twenty-two pieces listed therein, including the past and present editors of the various volumes and journals listed, their past and present publishers, and even whatever conglomerates may have, at one time or another, acquired rights regarding reprinting of the listed pieces. And, as instructed by one of these publishers, both for the one paper first appearing in *Synthese*, and for the two first appearing in *Philosophical Studies*, I'll now give my thanks by adding these very words, specifically wanted by that outfit: with kind permission of Kluwer Academic Publishers. So, that's it, guys, or corporations, or whatever "you" may be— you're all thanked now, every last one of you—especially you sticklers at Kluwer Academic Publishers. All of you—and not just the Kluwer guys—should feel very much appreciated, by me, who does very much appreciate, in fact, your kind cooperation in the present project. Indeed, I ask that you take full notice of this fact: Not only do I thank all you folks, but—doubling everything up—I thank you all twice over: I thank you here, in this collection's First Volume, and I thank you, again, in the Second Volume of the set. For as happens with this most relevant part of my prefatory writing, the Provenance of Papers list also appears, in its entirety, in *both* Volumes of *Philosophical Papers*. (Surely, in the very bright light of all this clearly expressed appreciation, good fellows, all your lawyers should find useful work to do elsewhere— someplace far from me and my family.)

That said and done, I'll make some comments on two other lists I'm providing, each also appearing in both of the collection's two Volumes. These are the (Table of) Contents for Volume 1 and, complementing that, the (Table of) Contents for Volume 2: In each of these two (Tables of) Contents, I've grouped a Volume's eleven reprinted papers—including a self-styled paper wholly composed of Book

Symposium material—into four numbered Parts. Just so, the First Volume has four numbered Parts, numbered from 1 through 4, and, equally, the Second Volume has four numbered Parts, also numbered from 1 through 4. For your happy perusal, I've quite delightfully labeled each of these eight (two times four) Parts. With so many as six of the Parts, all told, in the Part's well-chosen title, there's cleverly embedded the title of one of my five already-existing, self-standing, solely-authored books. In each instance, there are several good reasons for doing that. But, for my money, the most operative reason is always this: All five of these self-standing works—the volumes with the cleverly embedded titles—they're all currently (2006) available for purchase. And, what's more, they're all readily available, for purchase, from this present collection's worldwide publisher, the Oxford University Press. ("It's the papers, stupid!")

Now, think about this, for a minute: If you like what's in any given one of these six Parts, or even just some of what's there, then there's a good chance, I'll bet, that you'll like the book whose title is embedded in that Part's title. Makes sense; doesn't it?

OK. So, then what?

Here's where I offer sound advice to prospective readers: In your "institutional" library—using that word for want of another that's better—you should, I'll suggest, go have a gander at the book (pretend there's just one) whose embedded title helped provide the title for the Part that contains the shorter writing, or shorter writings, that you've just so greatly enjoyed. As I just said, and as makes perfect sense, there's a good chance you'll then like what you see *there*—in the self-standing book whose embedded title is presently most salient. And, if you *do* like what you see—well, then, you should (try to) take that self-standing book home with you—along with both Volumes of *Philosophical Papers*—providing, of course, that it's perfectly legal for you to do all that. After some several days of actively living with all these legally borrowed books, it may very well happen, I'll just venture to guess, that you'll *still* like the philosophical productions that you've been perusing. Now, if you're enthralled with one of these books—or, as I hope, with many more than one—well, then you'll be happy that I've bothered to include, in this breezy Preface, some slickly effective advertisements for my writing. Anyway, at least by my lights, it's high time we encounter my Preface's main advertising section. ("It's the papers, stupid!")

Except for the very poorest among us, it's quite easy to permanently acquire, perfectly legally, a copy of any of my books, leastways any of them that's available as a paperback. For, among other convenient sources for the books I've authored, each is very readily available through the OUP's *Web-page*, whose address is, at the time of this prefatory writing, this Web-address: http://www.oup.com Now, once you're on this main OUP Web-page, you'll then have to search around there, it's true, to get onto a page where one of my books is featured, or where there's featured more than one—and this may involve rather a bit more clicking. But, for most decently well-educated Americans not yet on Medicare, that's a piece of cake. Or, as we perennial dieters prefer to say, it's a stroll in the park. ("It's the papers, stupid!")

Heck, if you're reading these words just a few years after I wrote them, you may easily be able to feast, for years and years, on a veritable banquet of my published philosophical food for thought, the whole shebang priced pretty reasonably: With a dozen or so well-placed clicks, you'll be able to acquire, for your private use and enjoyment, something that's far nicer than just some several philosophy books I've sent into the world. Very easily, but not very expensively, you'll be able to acquire a *complete* **matched** *set* of the books that feature nothing but Peter Unger's philosophical writing! (Well, if you acquire all the books within just a few years of my writing this sentence, your set will be as complete as then can be. Beyond that, well, who knows what more the still further future may bring?) Each of the seven volumes, I've certainly specified to the OUP—by now, maybe specified it some seven times over—each should be precisely the same trim size as all the others: the same height—I'm measuring that at some 24 centimeters, as near as I can tell; and the same width, too—I'm measuring *that* at some 16 centimeters, with my same cheap cloth tape. (Of course, the books won't have the same thickness, even as some will be longer works while others will be shorter volumes. But, of course, that's perfectly irrelevant to any presently sensible point.) What's more, the paper cover of each book should look, most especially right where there's the book's spine, just so nicely like all the other books look. {Right now, it's true, in early 2005, my thirty-year old, my *Ignorance*, has a distinctly smaller trim size than that. But, by the time you're ready to buy a matched set of my paperback works, that should all be correctly changed. Still, you've now been forewarned, very clearly, of a (barely?) possible even long-term danger.} (Of course, even spinally presented, the books won't look precisely alike. Far from that, thank goodness! Not only will some books be thicker than others, but, often much more conspicuous, the title of any one book will look very different from the titles of (at least most of) the others. What do you want, for goodness sakes, that each book's *title* should look the same? That would be perfectly absurd!)

While the lined-up spines certainly won't look *precisely* alike, then, still and all, they'll look plenty pretty enough: Each book's spine will have, as its visually dominant feature, the same clean white background as will be gracing all its companion volumes. And, with all seven books having the very same trim size, there'll be a clean white line formed not only by the bottoms of these seven books—to be placed, I'd recommend, on a clean white shelf—but, quite as well, there'll be a clean white line formed by the *tops* of the books, as well. Think about *that*, for a minute. Very clean, very slick, very nice—almost perfectly exquisite will be that avidly awaited paperback matched set of Ungeriana. Heck, with such a nice slick look as that, I'll bet even your interior designer will give you a big thumbs up. Indeed, with a few friendly words from you—no doubt, by then a most happily satisfied customer—he (or she) might order his (or her) very own set, to grace his (or her) own den, or study or, just maybe, grand foyer. ("It's the papers, stupid!")

As I'm vividly imagining, by this point you've had quite enough of what's fast becoming a Preface both crassly and crudely commercial. So, with a more public-spirited remark, I'll now call it quits: Even if you never buy any of my works, please do return *all* your borrowed library books, *whoever* may have written them. It's the right thing to do; and, you'll feel better for it. Heck, it's about as easy as eating a hotdog, and it's nowhere near as fattening.

*New York*  P. K. U.
*April 2005*

# PROVENANCE OF PAPERS REPRINTED IN *PHILOSOPHICAL PAPERS*

# A CHRONOLOGICAL LIST

"An Analysis of Factual Knowledge," *The Journal of Philosophy*, LXV (1968): 157–170. Reprinted in Volume 1.

"A Defense of Skepticism," *The Philosophical Review*, LXXX (1971): 198–219. Reprinted in Volume 1.

"An Argument for Skepticism," *Philosophic Exchange*, vol.1, no.5 (1974): 131–155. Reprinted in Volume 1.

"Two Types of Scepticism," *Philosophical Studies*, 25 (1974): 77–96. Reprinted in Volume 1.

"The Uniqueness in Causation," *American Philosophical Quarterly*, 14 (1977): 177–188. Reprinted in Volume 2.

"Impotence and Causal Determinism," *Philosophical Studies*, 31 (1977): 289–305. Reprinted in Volume 2.

"There Are No Ordinary Things," *Synthese*, 41 (1979): 117–154. Reprinted in Volume 2.

"I Do Not Exist," pp. 235–251 in *Perception and Identity*, G. F. MacDonald ed., London: The Macmillan Press, 1979. Reprinted in Volume 2.

"Why There Are No People," *Midwest Studies in Philosophy*, IV (1979): 177–222. Reprinted in Volume 2.

"Skepticism and Nihilism," *Nous*, 14 (1980): 517–545. Reprinted in Volume 1.

"The Problem of the Many," *Midwest Studies in Philosophy*, V (1980): 411–467. Reprinted in Volume 2.

"Toward A Psychology of Common Sense," *American Philosophical Quarterly*, 19 (1982): 117–129. Reprinted in Volume 1.

"The Causal Theory of Reference," *Philosophical Studies*, 43 (1983): 1–45. Reprinted in Volume 1.

"Minimizing Arbitrariness: Toward a Metaphysics of Infinitely Many Isolated Concrete Worlds," *Midwest Studies in Philosophy*, IX (1984): 29–51. Reprinted in Volume 1.

"The Cone Model of Knowledge," *Philosophical Topics*, XIV (1986): 125–178. Reprinted in Volume 1.

"Book Symposium on *Identity, Consciousness and Value*," Precis of the Book, Reply to Sydney Shoemaker, Reply to Peter Strawson, Reply to Richard Swinburne, Reply to Stephen White, *Philosophy and Phenomenological Research*, LII (1992): 133–137 and 159–176. Reprinted in Volume 2.

"Contextual Analysis in Ethics," *Philosophy and Phenomenological Research*, LV (1995): 1–26. Reprinted in Volume 1.

"The Mystery of the Physical and the Matter of Qualities," *Midwest Studies in Philosophy*, XXII (1999), 75–99. Reprinted in Volume 2.

"Book Symposium on *Living High and Letting Die: Our Illusion of Innocence*," Precis of the Book, Reply to Fred Feldman, Reply to Brad Hooker, Reply to Thomas Pogge, Reply to Peter Singer, *Philosophy and Phenomenological Research*, LIX (1999): 173–175 and 203–216. Reprinted in Volume 1.

"The Survival of the Sentient," *Philosophical Perspectives*, 14 (2000): 325–348. Reprinted in Volume 2.

"Free Will and Scientiphicalism," *Philosophy and Phenomenological Research*, 65 (2002): 1–25. Reprinted in Volume 2.

"The Mental Problems of the Many,"*Oxford Studies in Metaphysics*, Oxford: Clarendon Press, Volume I (2004): 195–222. Reprinted in Volume 2.

# CONTENTS OF VOLUME 1

PART I. SKEPTICISM, NIHILISM AND SCEPTICISM: BEFORE AND BEYOND *IGNORANCE*
    1. A Defense of Skepticism    3
    2. An Analysis of Factual Knowledge    22
    3. An Argument for Skepticism    37
    4. Skepticism and Nihilism    69
    5. Two Types of Scepticism    96

PART II. COMPREHENDING AND TRANSCENDING STULTIFYING COMMON SENSE
    6. The Causal Theory of Reference    117
    7. Toward a Psychology of Common Sense    161
    8. Minimizing Arbitrariness: Toward a Metaphysics of Infinitely Many Isolated Concrete Worlds    180

PART III. KNOWLEDGE, ETHICS, CONTEXTS: SHADES OF *PHILOSOPHICAL RELATIVITY*
    9. The Cone Model of Knowledge    211
    10. Contextual Analysis in Ethics    264

PART IV. DEFENDING AND TRANSCENDING *LIVING HIGH AND LETTING DIE*

11. From a Book Symposium on *Living High and Letting Die*: Precis of the Book, Reply to Brad Hooker, Reply to Peter Singer, Reply to Thomas Pogge, Reply to Fred Feldman   295

Index of Names   315

# CONTENTS OF VOLUME 2

PART I.  THREE STUDIES FOR A BOOK
          THAT WASN'T
    1. There Are No Ordinary Things   3
    2. I Do Not Exist   36
    3. Why There Are No People   53

PART II.  MANY MATERIAL MYSTERIES: WITHOUT
          *ALL THE POWER IN THE WORLD*
    4. The Problem of the Many   113
    5. The Mental Problems of the Many   183
    6. The Mystery of the Physical and the Matter
       of Qualities: A Paper for Professor Shaffer   209

PART III.  DEFENDING AND TRANSCENDING
           *IDENTITY, CONSCIOUSNESS
           AND VALUE*
    7. From a Book Symposium on *Identity,
       Consciousness and Value*: Precis of the Book,
       Reply to Sydney Shoemaker, Reply to Peter
       Strawson, Reply to Richard Swinburne,
       Reply to Stephen White   241
    8. The Survival of the Sentient   265

PART IV. TRUE CAUSES AND REAL CHOICES:
STILL WITHOUT *ALL THE POWER
IN THE WORLD*

    9. The Uniqueness in Causation  295
  10. Impotence and Causal Determinism  319
  11. Free Will and Scientiphicalism  336

Index of Names  365

# PART I

# Skepticism, Nihilism and Scepticism: Before and Beyond *Ignorance*

# 1

# A DEFENSE OF SKEPTICISM

The Skepticism that I will defend is a negative thesis concerning what we know. I happily accept the fact that there is much that many of us correctly and reasonably believe, but much more than that is needed for us to know even a fair amount. Here I will not argue that nobody knows anything about anything, though that would be quite consistent with the skeptical thesis for which I will argue. The somewhat less radical thesis which I will defend is this one: every human being knows, at best, hardly anything to be so. More specifically, I will argue that hardly anyone knows that 45 and 56 are equal to 101, if anyone at all. On this skeptical thesis, no one will know the thesis to be true. But this is all right. For I only want to argue that it may be reasonable for us to suppose the thesis to be true, not that we should ever know it to be true.

Few philosophers now take skepticism seriously. With philosophers, even the most powerful of traditional skeptical argument has little force to tempt them nowadays. Indeed, nowadays, philosophers tend to think skepticism interesting only as a formal challenge to which positive accounts of our common-sense knowledge are the gratifying responses. Consequently, I find it at least somewhat natural to offer a defense of skepticism.[1]

---

1. Among G.E. Moore's most influential papers against skepticism are "A Defense of Common Sense," "Four Forms of Scepticism," and "Certainty." These papers are now available in Moore's *Philosophical Papers* (New York, 1962). More recent representatives of the same anti-skeptical persuasion include A.J. Ayer's *The Problem of Knowledge* (Baltimore, 1956) and two books by Roderick M. Chisholm: *Perceiving* (Ithaca, 1957) and

My defense of skepticism will be quite unlike traditional arguments for this thesis. This is largely because I write at a time when there is a common faith that, so far as expressing truths is concerned, all is well with the language that we speak. Against this common, optimistic assumption, I shall illustrate how our language habits might serve us well in practical ways, even while they involve us in saying what is false rather than true. And this often does occur, I will maintain, when our positive assertions contain terms with special features of a certain kind, which I call *absolute* terms. Among these terms, "flat" and "certain" are *basic* ones. Due to these terms' characteristic features, and because the world is not so simple as it might be, we do not speak truly, at least as a rule, when we say of a real object, "That has a top which is flat" or when we say of a real person, "He is certain that it is raining." And just as basic absolute terms generally fail to apply to the world, so other absolute terms, which are at least partially defined by the basic ones, will fail to apply as well. Thus, we also speak falsely when we say of a real object or person, "That is a cube" or "He knows that it is raining." For an object is a cube only if it has surfaces which are flat, and, as I shall argue, a person knows something to be so only if he is certain of it.

## 1. Sophisticated Worries about What Skepticism Requires

The reason contemporary sophisticated philosophers do not take skepticism seriously can be stated broadly and simply. They think that skepticism implies certain things which are, upon a bit of reflection, quite impossible to accept. These unacceptable implications concern the functioning of our language.

Concerning our language and how it functions, the most obvious requirement of skepticism is that some common terms of our language

---

*Theory of Knowledge* (Englewood Cliffs, N.J., 1966). Among the many recent journal articles against skepticism are three papers of my own: "Experience and Factual Knowledge," *Journal of Philosophy*, vol. 64, no. 5 (1967), "An Analysis of Factual Knowledge," *Journal of Philosophy*, vol. 65, no. 6 (1968), and "Our Knowledge of the Material World," *Studies in the Theory of Knowledge, American Philosophical Quarterly Monograph* No. 4 (1970). At the same time, a survey of the recent journal literature reveals very few papers where skepticism is defended or favored. With recent papers which do favor skepticism, however, I can mention at least two. A fledgling skepticism is persuasively advanced by Brian Skyrms in his "The Explication of '$X$ Knows that $p$,'" *Journal of Philosophy*, vol. 64, no. 12 (1967). And in William W. Rozeboom's "Why I Know So Much More Than You Do," *American Philosophical Quarterly*, vol. 4, no. 4 (1967), we have a refreshingly strong statement of skepticism in the context of recent discussion.

will involve us in error systematically. These will be such terms as "know" and "knowledge," which may be called the "terms of knowledge." If skepticism is right, then while we go around saying "I know," "He knows," and so on, and while we believe what we say to be true, all the while what we say and believe will actually be false. If our beliefs to the effect that we know something or other are so consistently false, then the terms of knowledge lead us into error systematically. But if these beliefs really are false, should we not have experiences which force the realization of their falsity upon us, and indeed abandon these beliefs? Consequently, shouldn't our experiences get us to stop thinking in these terms which thus systematically involve us in error? So, as we continue to think in the terms of knowledge and to believe ourselves to know all sorts of things, this would seem to show that the beliefs are not false ones and the terms are responsible for no error. Isn't it only reasonable, then, to reject a view which requires that such helpful common terms as "knows" and "knowledge" lead us into error systematically?

So go some worrisome thoughts which might lead us to dismiss skepticism out of hand. But it seems to me that there is no real need for our false beliefs to clash with our experiences in any easily noticeable way. Suppose, for instance, that you falsely believe that a certain region of space is a vacuum. Suppose that, contrary to your belief, the region does contain some gaseous stuff, though only the slightest trace. Now, for practical purposes, we may suppose that, so far as gaseous contents go, it is not important whether that region really is a vacuum or whether it contains whatever gaseous stuff it does contain. Once this is supposed, then it is reasonable to suppose as well that, for practical purposes, it makes no important difference whether you falsely believe that the region is a vacuum or truly believe this last thing—namely, that, for practical purposes, it is not important whether the region is a vacuum or whether it contains that much gaseous stuff.

We may notice that this supposed truth is entailed by what you believe but does not entail it. In other words, a region's being a vacuum entails that, for practical purposes, there is no important difference between whether the region is a vacuum or whether it contains whatever gaseous stuff it does contain. For, if the region *is* a vacuum, whatever gas it contains is nil, and so there is no difference at all, for any sort of purpose, between the region's being a vacuum and its having that much gaseous stuff. But the entailment does not go the other way, and this is where we may take a special interest. For while a region may not be a vacuum, it may contain so little gaseous stuff that, so far as gaseous contents go, for practical purposes there is no important difference between the region's being a vacuum and its containing whatever gaseous stuff it does contain. So if this entailed truth lies behind the believed falsehood, your false belief, though false, may not be harmful. Indeed, generally, it may even be helpful for you to have this false belief rather than having none and rather than having almost any other belief about the matter that you might have. On this pattern, we may have many false beliefs about regions being vacuums even while these beliefs will suffer no important clash with the experiences of life.

More to our central topic, suppose that, as skepticism might have it, you falsely believe that you *know* that there are elephants. As before, there is a true thing which is entailed by what you falsely believe and which we should notice. The thing here, which presumably you do not actually believe, is this: that, with respect to the matter of whether there are elephants, for practical purposes there is no important difference between whether you know that there are elephants or whether you are in that position with respect to the matter that you actually are in. This latter, true thing is entailed by the false thing you believe—namely, that you know that there are elephants. For if you do know, then, with respect to the matter of the elephants, there is no difference at all, for any purpose of any sort, between your knowing and your being in the position you actually are in. On the other hand, the entailment does not go the other way and, again, this is where our pattern allows a false belief to be helpful. For even if you do not really know, still, it may be that for practical purposes you are in a position with respect to the matter (of the elephants) which is not importantly different from knowing. If this is so, then it may be better, practically speaking, for you to believe falsely that you know than to have no belief at all here. Thus, not only with beliefs to the effect that specified regions are vacuums, but also with beliefs to the effect that we know certain things, it may be that there are very many of them which, though false, it is helpful for us to have. In both cases, the beliefs will not noticeably clash with the experiences of life. Without some further reason for doing so, then, noting the smooth functioning of our "terms of knowledge" gives us no powerful reason for dismissing the thesis of skepticism.

There is, however, a second worry which will tend to keep sophisticates far from embracing skepticism, and this worry is, I think, rather more profound than the first. Consequently, I shall devote most of the remainder to treating this second worry. The worry to which I shall be so devoted is this: that, if skepticism is right, then the terms of knowledge, unlike other terms of our language, will never or hardly ever be used to make simple, positive assertions that are true. In other words, skepticism will require the terms of knowledge to be isolated freaks of our language. But even with familiar, persuasive arguments for skepticism, it is implausible to think that our language is plagued by an isolated little group of troublesome freaks. So, by being so hard on knowledge alone, skepticism seems implausible once one reflects on the exclusiveness of its persecution.

## 2. Absolute Terms and Relative Terms

Against the worry that skepticism will require the terms of knowledge to be isolated freaks, I shall argue that, on the contrary, a variety of other terms is similarly troublesome. As skepticism becomes more plausible with an examination of the terms of knowledge, so other originally surprising theses become more plausible once their key terms are critically examined. When all of the key terms are understood to have essential features in common, the truth of any of these theses need not be felt as such a surprise.

The terms of knowledge, along with many other troublesome terms, belong to a class of terms that is quite pervasive in our language. I call these terms *absolute terms*. The term "flat," in its central, literal meaning, is an absolute term. (With other meanings, as in "His voice is flat" and "The beer is flat," I have no direct interest.) To say that something is flat is no different from saying that it is absolutely, or perfectly, flat. To say that a surface is flat is to say that some things or properties *which are matters of degree* are *not* instanced in the surface *to any degree at all*. Thus, something which is flat is not at all bumpy, and not at all curved. Bumpiness and curvature are matters of degree. When we say of a surface that it is bumpy, or that it is curved, we use the *relative terms* "bumpy" and "curved" to talk about the surface. Thus, absolute terms and relative terms go together, in at least one important way, while other terms, like "unmarried," have only the most distant connections with terms of either of these two sorts.

There seems to be a syntactic feature which is common to relative terms and to certain absolute terms, while it is found with no other terms. This feature is that each of these terms may be modified by a variety of terms that serve to indicate (matters of) degree. Thus, we find "The table is *very* bumpy" and "The table is *very* flat" but not "The lawyer is *very* unmarried." Among those absolute terms which admit such qualification are all those absolute terms which are *basic* ones. A basic absolute term is an absolute term which is not (naturally) defined in terms of some other absolute term, not even partially so. I suspect that "straight" is such a term, and perhaps "flat" is as well. But in its central (geometrical) meaning, "cube" quite clearly is not a basic absolute term even though it is an absolute term. For "cube" means, among other things, "having edges that are *straight* and surfaces which are *flat*": and "straight" and "flat" are absolute terms. While "cube" does not admit of qualification of degree, "flat" and "straight" do admit of such qualification. Thus, all relative terms and all basic absolute terms admit of constructions of degree. While this is another way in which these two sorts of terms go together, we must now ask: how may we distinguish terms of the one sort from those of the other?

But is there now anything to distinguish here? For if absolute terms admit of degree construction, why think that any of these terms is not a relative term, why think that they do not purport to predicate things or properties which are, as they now look to be, matters of degree? If we may say that a table is very flat, then why not think flatness a matter of degree? Isn't this essentially the same as our saying of a table that it is very bumpy, with bumpiness being a matter of degree? So perhaps "flat," like "bumpy" and like all terms that take degree constructions, is, fittingly, a relative term. But basic absolute terms may be distinguished from relatives even where degree constructions conspire to make things look otherwise.

To advance the wanted distinction, we may look to a procedure for paraphrase. Now, we have granted that it is common for us to say of a surface that it is pretty, or very, or extremely, flat. And it is also common for us to say that, in saying such things of surfaces, we are saying *how* flat the surfaces are. What we say here seems of a piece with our saying of a surface that it is pretty, or very, or extremely, bumpy, and our then saying that, in doing this, we are saying *how* bumpy the surface is. But, even intuitively, we may notice a difference here. For only with our talk about "flat," we have the idea that these locutions are only convenient means for saying how closely a surface approximates, or *how close it comes to being*, a surface which is (absolutely) flat. Thus, it is intuitively plausible, and far from being a nonsensical interpretation, to paraphrase things so our result with our "flat" locutions is this: what we have said of a surface is that it is pretty *nearly* flat, or very *nearly* flat, or extremely *close to being* flat and, in doing that, we have said, not simply how flat the surface is, but rather *how close* the surface is *to being* flat. This form of paraphrase gives a plausible interpretation of our talk of flatness while allowing the term "flat" to lose its appearance of being a relative term. How will this form of paraphrase work with "bumpy," where, presumably, a genuine relative term occurs in our locutions?

What do we say when we say of a surface that it is pretty bumpy, or very bumpy, or extremely so? Of course, it at least appears that we say *how* bumpy the surface is. The paraphrase has it that what we are saying is that the surface is pretty *nearly* bumpy, or very *nearly* bumpy, or extremely *close to being* bumpy. In other words, according to the paraphrase, we are saying *how close* the surface is *to being* bumpy. But anything of this sort is, quite obviously, a terribly poor interpretation of what we are saying about the surface. Unfortunately for the paraphrase, if we say that a surface is very bumpy it is entailed by what we say that the surface is bumpy, while if we say that the surface is very close to being bumpy it is entailed that the surface is *not* bumpy. Thus, unlike the case with "flat," our paraphrase cannot apply with "bumpy." Consequently, by means of our paraphrase we may distinguish between absolute terms and relative ones.

Another way of noticing how our paraphrase lends support to the distinction between absolute and relative terms is this: the initial data are that such terms as "very," which standardly serve to indicate that there is a great deal of something, serve with opposite effect when they modify terms like "flat"—terms which I have called basic absolute terms. That is, when we say, for example, that something is (really) very flat, then, so far as flatness is concerned, we seem to say less of the thing than when we say, simply, that it is (really) flat. The augmenting function of "very" is turned on its head so that the term serves to diminish. What can resolve this conflict? It seems that our paraphrase can. For on the paraphrase, what we are saying of the thing is that it is very *nearly* flat, and so, by implication, that it is *not* flat (but only very nearly so). Once the paraphrase is exploited, the term "very" may be understood to have its standard augmenting function. At the same time, "very" functions without conflict with "bumpy." Happily, the term "very" is far from being unique here; we get the same results with other augmenting modifiers: "extremely," "especially," and so on.

For our paraphrastic procedure to be comprehensive, it must work with contexts containing explicitly comparative locutions. Indeed, with these contexts, we have a common form of talk where the appearance of relativeness is most striking of all. What shall we think of our saying, for example, that one surface is not *as* flat as another, where things strikingly look to be a matter of degree? It seems that we must allow that in such a suggested comparison, the surface which is said to be the *flatter* of the two may be, so far as logic goes, (absolutely) flat. Thus, we should *not* paraphrase this comparative context as "the one surface is not as *nearly* flat as the other." For this form of paraphrase would imply that the second surface is not flat, and so it gives us a poor interpretation of the original, which has no such implication. But then, a paraphrase with no bad implications is not far removed. Instead of simply inserting our "nearly" or our "close to being," we may allow for the possibility of (absolute) flatness by putting things in a way which is only somewhat more complex. For we may paraphrase our original by saying: the first surface is *either not flat though the second is, or else it is* not as *nearly* flat as the second. Similarly, where we say that one surface is flatter than another, we may paraphrase things like this: the first surface is *either flat though the second is not or else it is closer to being flat* than the second. But in contrast to all this, with comparisons of bumpiness, no paraphrase is available. To say that one surface is not as bumpy as another is not to say either that the first surface is not bumpy though the second is, or else that it is not as nearly bumpy as the second one.

Our noting the availability of degree constructions allows us to class together relative terms and basic absolute terms, as against any other terms. And our noting that only with the absolute terms do our constructions admit of our paraphrase allows us to distinguish between the relative terms and the basic absolute terms. Now that these terms may be quite clearly distinguished, we may restate without pain of vacuity those ideas on which we relied to introduce our terminology. Thus, to draw the *connection* between terms of the two sorts we may now say this: every basic absolute term, and so every absolute term whatever, may be defined, at least partially, by means of certain relative terms. The defining conditions presented by means of the relative terms are negative ones; they say that what the relative term purports to denote is *not* present *at all*, or *in the least*, where the absolute term correctly applies. Thus, these negative conditions are logically necessary ones for basic absolute terms, and so for absolute terms which are defined by means of the basic ones. Thus, something is flat, in the central, literal sense of "flat," only if it is not at all, or not in the least, curved or bumpy. And similarly, something is a cube, in the central, literal sense of "cube," only if it has surfaces which are not at all, or not in the least, bumpy or curved. In noting these demanding *negative relative requirements*, we may begin to appreciate, I think, that a variety of absolute terms, if not all of them, might well be quite troublesome to apply, perhaps even failing consistently in application to real things.

In a final general remark about these terms, I should like to motivate my choice of terminology for them. A reason I call terms of the one sort "absolute" is that, at least in the case of the basic ones, the term may always be modified, grammatically, with the term "absolutely." And indeed, this modification fits so well that it is, I think, always redundant. Thus, something is flat if and only if it is absolutely flat. In contrast, the term "absolutely" never gives a standard, grammatical modification for any of our relative terms: nothing which is bumpy is absolutely bumpy. On the other hand, each of the relative terms takes "relatively" quite smoothly as a grammatical modifier. (And, though it is far from being clear, it is at least arguable, I think, that this modifier is redundant for these terms. Thus, it is at least arguable that something is bumpy if and only if it is relatively bumpy.) In any event, with absolute terms, while "relatively" is grammatically quite all right as a modifier, the construction thus obtained must be understood in terms of our paraphrase. Thus, as before, something is relatively flat if and only if it is relatively close to being (absolutely) flat, and so only if it is not flat.

In this terminology, and in line with our linguistic tests, I think that the first term of each of the following pairs is a relative term while the second is an absolute one: "wet" and "dry," "crooked" and "straight," "important" and "crucial," "incomplete" and "complete," "useful" and "useless," and so on. I think that both "empty" and "full" are absolute terms, while "good" and "bad," "rich" and "poor," and "happy" and "unhappy" are all relative terms. Finally, I think that, in the sense defined by our tests, each of the following is neither an absolute term nor a relative one: "married" and "unmarried," "true" and "false," and "right" and "wrong." In other plausible senses, though, some or all of this last group might be called "absolute."

## 3. On Certainty and Certain Related Things

Certain terms of our language are standardly followed by propositional clauses, and, indeed, it is plausible to think that wherever they occur they *must* be followed by such clauses on pain of otherwise occurring in a sentence which is elliptical or incomplete. We may call terms which take these clauses *propositional terms* and we may then ask: are some propositional terms absolute ones, while others are relative terms? By means of our tests, I will argue that "certain" is an absolute term, while "confident," "doubtful," and "uncertain" are all relative terms.

With regard to being certain, there are two ideas which are important: first, the idea of something's being certain, where that which is certain is *not* certain *of* anything, and, second, the idea of a being's being certain, where that which is certain *is* certain *of* something. A paradigm context for the first idea is the context "It is certain that it is raining" where the term "it" has no apparent reference. I will call such contexts *impersonal* contexts, and the idea of certainty which they serve to express, thus, the impersonal idea of certainty. In contrast, a paradigm context for the second idea is this one: "He is certain that it is raining"—where, of course, the term "he" purports to refer as clearly as one might like. In the latter context, which we may call the *personal* context, we express the personal idea of certainty. This last may be allowed, I think, even though in ordinary conversations we may speak of dogs as being certain; presumably, we treat dogs there the way we typically treat persons.

Though there are these two important sorts of context, I think that "certain" must mean the same in both. In both cases, we must be struck by the thought that the presence of certainty amounts to the complete absence of doubt, or doubtfulness. This thought leads me to say that "It is certain that $p$" means, within the bounds of nuance, "It is not at all doubtful that $p$." The idea of personal certainty may then be defined accordingly; we relate what is said in the impersonal form to the mind of the person, or subject, who is said to be certain of something. Thus, "He is certain that $p$" means, within the bounds of nuance, "*In his mind*, it is not at all doubtful that $p$." Where a man is certain of something, then, concerning that thing, all doubt is absent in that man's mind. With these definitions available, we may now say this: connected negative definitions of certainty suggest that, in its central, literal meaning, "certain" is an absolute term.

But we should like firmer evidence for thinking that "certain" is an absolute term. To be consistent, we turn to our procedure for paraphrase. I will exhibit the evidence for personal contexts and then say a word about impersonal ones. In any event, we want contrasting results for "certain" as against some related relative terms. One term which now suggests itself for contrast is, of course, "doubtful." Another is, of course, "uncertain." And we will get the desired results with these terms. But it is, I think, more interesting to consider the term "confident."

In quick discussions of these matters, one might speak indifferently of a man's being confident of something and of his being certain of it. But on reflection there is a difference between confidence and certainty. Indeed, when I say that I am certain of something, I tell you that I am not confident of it but that I am *more than* that. And if I say that I am confident that so-and-so, I tell you that I am *not so much as* certain of the thing. Thus, there is an important difference between the two. At least part of this difference is, I suggest, reflected by our procedure for paraphrase.

We may begin to apply our procedure by resolving the problem of augmenting modifiers. Paradoxically, when I say that I am (really) very certain of something, I say *less* of myself, so far as certainty is concerned, than I do when I say, simply, that I am (really) certain of the thing. How may we resolve this paradox? Our paraphrase explains things as before. In the first case, what I am really saying is that I am very *nearly* certain, and so, in effect, that I am not really certain. But in the second case, I say that I really am. Further, we may notice that, in contrast, in the case of "confident" and "uncertain," and "doubtful" as well, no problem with augmenting arises in the first place. For when I say that I am very confident of something, I say more of myself, so far as confidence is concerned, than I do when I simply say that I am confident of the thing. And again our paraphrastic procedure yields us the lack of any problems here. For the augmented statement cannot be sensibly interpreted as saying that I am very nearly confident of the thing. Indeed, with any modifier weaker than "absolutely," our paraphrase works well with "certain" but produces only a nonsensical interpretation with "confident" and other contrasting terms. For example, what might it mean to say of someone that he was rather confident of something? Would this be to say that he was rather close to being confident of the thing? Surely not.

Turning to comparative constructions, our paraphrase separates things just as we should expect. For example, from "He is more certain that $p$ than he is that $q$" we get "He is either certain that $p$ while not certain that $q$, or else he is more nearly certain that $p$ than he is that $q$." But from "He is more confident that $p$ than he is that $q$" we do *not* get "He is either confident that $p$ while not confident that $q$, or else he is more nearly confident that $p$ than he is that $q$." For he may well already be confident of both things. Further comparative constructions are similarly distinguished when subjected to our paraphrase. And no matter what locutions we try, the separation is as convincing with impersonal contexts as it is with personal ones, so long as there are contexts which are comparable. Of course, "confident" has no impersonal contexts; we cannot say "It is confident that $p$," where the "it" has no purported reference. But where comparable contexts do exist, as with "doubtful" and "uncertain," further evidence is available. Thus, we may reasonably assert that "certain" is an absolute term while "confident," "doubtful," and "uncertain" are relative terms.

## 4. The Doubtful Applicability of Some Absolute Terms

If my account of absolute terms is essentially correct, then, at least in the case of some of these terms, fairly reasonable suppositions about the world make it somewhat doubtful that the terms properly apply. (In certain contexts, generally where what we are talking about divides into discrete units, the presence of an absolute term need cause no doubts. Thus, considering the absolute term "complete," the truth of "His set of steins is now complete" may be allowed without hesitation, but the truth of "His explanation is now complete" may well be doubted. It is with the latter, more interesting contexts, I think, that we shall be concerned in what follows.) For example, while we say of many surfaces of physical things that they are flat, a rather reasonable interpretation of what we do observe makes it at least somewhat doubtful that these surfaces actually *are* flat. When we look at a rather smooth block of stone through a powerful microscope, the observed surface appears to us to be rife with irregularities. And this irregular appearance seems best explained, not by being taken as an illusory optical phenomenon, but by taking it to be a finer, more revealing look of a surface which is, in fact, rife with smallish bumps and crevices. Further, we account for bumps and crevices by supposing that the stone is composed of much smaller things, molecules and so on, which are in such a combination that, while a large and sturdy stone is the upshot, no stone with a flat surface is found to obtain.

Indeed, what follows from my account of "flat" is this: that, as a matter of logical necessity, if a surface is flat, then there never is any surface which is flatter than it is. For on our paraphrase, if the second surface is flatter than the first, then either the second surface is flat while the first is not, or else the second is more nearly flat than the first, neither surface being flat. So if there is such a second, flatter surface, then the first surface is not flat after all, contrary to our supposition. Thus there cannot be any second, flatter surface. Or in other words, if it is logically possible that there be a surface which is flatter than a given one, then that given surface is not really a flat one. Now, in the case of the observed surface of the stone, owing to the stone's irregular composition, the surface is *not* one such that it is logically impossible that there be a flatter one. (For example, we might veridically observe a surface through a microscope of the same power which did not appear to have any bumps or crevices.) Thus it is only reasonable to suppose that the surface of this stone is not really flat.

Our understanding of the stone's composition, that it is composed of molecules and so on, makes it reasonable for us to suppose as well that any similarly sized or larger surfaces will fail to be flat just as the observed surface fails to be flat. At the same time, it would be perhaps a bit rash to suppose that much smaller surfaces would fail to be flat as well. Beneath the level of our observation perhaps there are small areas of the stone's surface which are flat. If so, then perhaps there are small objects that have surfaces which are flat, like this area of the stone's surface: for instance, chipping off a small part of the stone might yield such a small object. So perhaps there are physical objects with surfaces which are flat, and perhaps it is not now reasonable for us to assume that there are no such objects. But even if this strong assumption is not now reasonable, one thing which does seem quite reasonable for us now to assume is this: we should at least suspend judgment on the matter of whether there are any physical objects with flat surfaces. That there are such objects is something it is not now reasonable for us to believe.

It is at least somewhat doubtful, then, that "flat" ever applies to actual physical objects or to their surfaces. And the thought must strike us that if "flat" has no such application, this must be due in part to the fact that "flat" is an absolute term. We may then do well to be a bit doubtful about the applicability of any other given absolute term and, in particular, about the applicability of the term "certain." As in the case of "flat," our paraphrase highlights the absolute character of "certain." As a matter of logical necessity, if someone is certain of something, then there never is anything of which he is more certain. For on our paraphrase, if the person is more certain of any other thing, then either he is certain of the other thing while not being certain of the first, or else he is more nearly certain of the other thing than he is of the first; that is, he is certain of neither. Thus, if it is logically possible that there be something of which a person might be more certain than he now is of a given thing, then he is not really certain of that given thing.

Thus it is reasonable to suppose, I think, that hardly anyone, if anyone at all, is certain that 45 and 56 are 101. For it is reasonable to suppose that hardly anyone, if anyone at all, is so certain of that particular calculation that it is impossible for there to be anything of which he might be yet more certain. But this is not surprising; for hardly anyone *feels* certain that those two numbers have that sum. What, then, about something of which people commonly do feel absolutely certain—say, of the existence of automobiles?

Is it reasonable for us now actually to believe that many people are certain that there are automobiles? If it is, then it is reasonable for us to believe as well that for each of them it is not possible for there to be anything of which he might be more certain than he now is of there being automobiles. In particular, we must then believe of these people that it is impossible for any of them ever to be more certain of his own existence than all of them now are of the existence of automobiles. While these people *might* all actually be as certain of the automobiles as this, just as each of them *feels* himself to be, I think it somewhat rash for us actually to believe that they *are* all so certain. Certainty being an absolute and our understanding of people being rather rudimentary and incomplete, I think it more reasonable for us now to suspend judgment on the matter. And, since there is nothing importantly peculiar about the matter of the automobiles, the same cautious position recommends itself quite generally: so far as actual human beings go, the most reasonable course for us now is to suspend judgment as to whether any of them is certain of more than hardly anything, if anything at all.[2]

## 5. Does Knowing Require Being Certain?

One tradition in philosophy holds that knowing requires being certain. As a matter of logical necessity, a man knows something only if he is certain of the thing. In this tradition, certainty is not taken lightly; rather, it is equated with absolute certainty. Even that most famous contemporary defender of common sense, G. E. Moore, is willing to equate knowing something with knowing the thing with absolute certainty.[3] I am rather inclined to hold with this traditional view, and it is now my purpose to argue that this view is at least a fairly reasonable one.

To a philosopher like Moore, I would have nothing left to say in my defense of skepticism. But recently some philosophers have contended that not certainty, but only belief, is required for knowing.[4] According to these thinkers, if a man's belief meets certain conditions not connected with his being certain, that mere belief may properly be counted as an instance or a bit of knowledge. And even more recently some philosophers have held that not even so much as belief is required for a man to know that something is so.[5] Thus, I must argue for

---

2. For an interesting discussion of impersonal certainty, which in some ways is rather in line with my own discussion while in other ways against it, one might see Michael Anthony Slote's "Empirical Certainty and the Theory of Important Criteria," *Inquiry*, vol. 10 (1967). Also, Slote makes helpful references to other writers in the philosophy of certainty.

3. See Moore's cited papers, especially "Certainty," p. 232.

4. An influential statement of this view is Roderick M. Chisholm's, to be found in the first chapter of each of his cited books. In "Experience and Factual Knowledge," I suggest a very similar view.

5. This view is advanced influentially by Colin Radford in "Knowledge by Examples," *Analysis*, 27 (October, 1966). In "An Analysis of Factual Knowledge," and especially in "Our Knowledge of The Material World," I suggest this view.

the traditional view of knowing. But then what has led philosophers to move further and further away from the traditional strong assertion that knowing something requires being certain of the thing?

My diagnosis of the situation is this. In everyday affairs we often speak loosely, charitably, and casually; we tend to let what we say pass as being true. I want to suggest that it is by being wrongly serious about this casual talk that philosophers (myself included) have come to think it rather easy to know things to be so. In particular, they have come to think that certainty is not needed. Thus typical in the contemporary literature is this sort of exchange. An examiner asks a student when a certain battle was fought. The student fumbles about and, eventually, unconfidently says what is true: "The Battle of Hastings was fought in 1066." It is supposed, quite properly, that this correct answer is a result of the student's reading. The examiner, being an ordinary mortal, allows that the student knows the answer; he judges that the student knows that the Battle of Hastings was fought in 1066. Surely, it is suggested, the examiner is correct in his judgment even though this student clearly is not certain of the thing; therefore, knowing does not require being certain. But is the examiner really correct in asserting that the student knows the date of this battle? That is, do such exchanges give us good reason to think that knowing does not require certainty?

My recommendation is this. Let us try focusing on just those words most directly employed in expressing the concept whose conditions are our object of inquiry. This principle is quite generally applicable and, I think, quite easily applied. We may apply it by suitably juxtaposing certain terms, like "really" and "actually," with the terms most in question (here, the term "knows"). More strikingly, we may *emphasize* the terms in question. Thus, instead of looking at something as innocent as "He knows that they are alive," let us consider the more relevant "He (really) *knows* that they are alive."

Let us build some confidence that this principle is quite generally applicable, and that it will give us trustworthy results. Toward this end, we may focus on some thoughts about definite descriptions—that is, about expressions of the form "the so-and-so." About these expressions, it is a tradition to hold that they require uniqueness, or unique satisfaction, for their proper application. Thus, just as it is traditional to hold that a man knows something only if he is certain of it, so it is also traditional to hold that there is something which is the chair with seventeen legs only if there is exactly one chair with just that many legs. But, again, by being wrongly serious about our casual everyday talk, philosophers may come to deny the traditional view. They may do this by being wrongly serious, I think, about the following sort of ordinary exchange. Suppose an examiner asks a student, "Who is the father of Nelson Rockefeller, the present Governor of New York State?" The student replies, "Nelson Rockefeller is the son of John D. Rockefeller, Jr." No doubt, the examiner will allow that, by implication, the student got the right answer; he will judge that what the student said is true even though the examiner is correctly confident that the elder Rockefeller sired other sons. Just so, one might well argue that definite descriptions, like "the son of X," do not require uniqueness. But against this argument from the everyday flow of talk, let us insist that we focus on the relevant conception by employing our standard means for emphasizing the most directly relevant term. Thus, while we might feel nothing contradictory at first in saying, "Nelson Rockefeller is the son of John D. Rockefeller, Jr., and so is Winthrop Rockefeller," we must confess that even initially we would have quite different feelings about our saying "Nelson Rockefeller is actually *the* son of John D. Rockefeller, Jr., and so is Winthrop Rockefeller." With the latter, where emphasis is brought to bear, we cannot help but feel that what is asserted is inconsistent. And, with this, we feel differently about the original remark, feeling it to be essentially the same assertion and so inconsistent as well. Thus, it seems that when we focus on things properly, we may assume that definite descriptions do require uniqueness.

Let us now apply our principle to the question of knowing. Here, while we might feel nothing contradictory at first in saying "He knows that it is raining, but he isn't certain of it," we would feel differently about our saying "He really *knows* that it is raining, but he isn't certain of it." And, if anything, this feeling of contradiction is only enhanced when we further emphasize, "He really *knows* that it is raining, but he isn't actually *certain* of it." Thus it is plausible to suppose that what we said at first is actually inconsistent, and so that knowing does require being certain.

For my defense of skepticism, it now remains only to combine the result we have just reached with that at which we arrived in the previous section. Now, I have argued that each of two propositions deserves, if not our acceptance, at least the suspension of our judgment:

> That, in the case of every human being, there is hardly anything, if anything at all, of which he is certain.

> That (as a matter of necessity), in the case of every human being, the person knows something to be so only if he is certain of it.

But I think I have done more than just that. For the strength of the arguments given for this position on each of these two propositions is,

I think, sufficient for warranting a similar position on propositions which are quite obvious consequences of the two of them together. One such consequential proposition is this:

> That, in the case of every human being, there is hardly anything, if anything at all, which the person knows to be so.

And so this third proposition, which is just the thesis of skepticism, also deserves, if not our acceptance, at least the suspension of our judgment. If this thesis is not reasonable to accept, then neither is its negation, the thesis of "common sense."

## 6. A Prospectus and a Retrospective

I have argued that we know hardly anything, if anything, because we are certain of hardly anything, if anything. My offering this argument will strike many philosophers as peculiar, even many who have some sympathy with skepticism. For it is natural to think that, except for the requirement of the truth of what is known, the requirement of "attitude," in this case of personal certainty, is the *least* problematic requirement of knowing. Much more difficult to fulfill, one would think, would be requirements about one's justification, about one's grounds, and so on. And, quite candidly, I am inclined to agree with these thoughts. Why, then, have I chosen to defend skepticism by picking on what is just about the easiest requirement of knowledge? My thinking has been this: the requirement of being certain will, most likely, not be independent of more difficult requirements; indeed, any more difficult requirement will entail this simpler one. Thus one more difficult requirement might be that the knower be completely *justified* in being certain, which entails the requirement that the man be certain. And, in any case, for purposes of establishing some clarity, I wanted this defense to avoid the more difficult requirements because they rely on normative terms—for example, the term "justified." The application of normative terms presents problems which, while worked over by many philosophers, are still too difficult to handle at all adequately. By staying away from more difficult requirements, and so from normative terms, I hoped to raise doubts in a simpler, clearer context. When the time comes for a more powerful defense of skepticism, the more difficult requirements will be pressed. Then normative conditions will be examined and, for this examination, declared inapplicable. But these normative conditions will, most likely, concern one's being certain; no justification of mere belief or confidence will be the issue in the more powerful defenses. By offering my defense, I hoped to lay part of the groundwork for more powerful defenses of skepticism.

I would end with this explanation but for the fact that my present views contradict claims I made previously, and others have discussed critically these earlier claims about knowledge.[6] Before, I strove to show that knowledge was rather easy to come by, that the conditions of knowledge could be met rather easily. To connect my arguments, I offered a unified analysis:

> For any sentential value of $p$, (at a time $t$) a man knows that $p$ if and only if (at $t$) it is not at all accidental that the man is right about its being the case that $p$.

And, in arguing for the analysis, I tried to understand its defining condition just so liberally that it would allow men to know things rather easily. Because I did this, I used the analysis to argue against skepticism—that is, against the thesis which I have just defended.

Given my present views, while I must find the criticisms of my earlier claims more interesting than convincing, I must find my analysis to be more accurate than I was in my too liberal application of it. For, however bad the analysis might be in various respects, it does assert that knowledge is an absolute. In terms of my currently favored distinctions, "accidental" is quite clearly a relative term, as are other terms which I might have selected in its stead: "coincidental," "matter of luck," "lucky," and so on. Operating on these terms with expressions such as "not at all" and "not in the least degree" will yield us absolute expressions, the equivalent of absolute terms. Thus, the condition that I offered is not at all likely to be one that is easily met. My main error, then, was not that of giving too vague or liberal a defining condition, but rather that of too liberally interpreting a condition which is in fact strict.

But I am quite uncertain that my analysis is correct in any case, and even that one can analyze knowledge. Still, so far as analyzing knowledge goes, the main plea of this paper must be this: whatever analysis

---

6. See my cited papers and these interesting discussions of them: Gilbert H. Harman, "Unger on Knowledge," *Journal of Philosophy*, 64 (1967), 353–359; Ruth Anna Putnam, "On Empirical Knowledge," *Boston Studies in the Philosophy of Science*, IV, 392–410; Arthur C. Danto, *Analytical Philosophy of Knowledge* (Cambridge, 1968), pp. 130 ff. and 144 ff.; Keith Lehrer and Thomas Paxson, Jr., "Knowledge: Undefeated Justified True Belief," *Journal of Philosophy*, 66 (1969), 225–237; J.L. Mackie, "The Possibility of Innate Knowledge," *Proceedings of the Aristotelian Society* (1970), pp. 245–257.

of knowledge is adequate, if any such there be, it must allow that the thesis of skepticism be at least fairly plausible. For this plea only follows from my broader one: that philosophers take skepticism seriously and not casually suppose, as I have often done, that this unpopular thesis simply must be false.[7]

---

7. Ancestors of the present paper were discussed in philosophy colloquia at the following schools: Brooklyn College of The City University of New York, The University of California at Berkeley, Columbia University, The University of Illinois at Chicago Circle, The Rockefeller University, Stanford University, and The University of Wisconsin at Madison. I am thankful to those who participated in the discussion. I would also like to thank each of these many people for help in getting to the present defense: Peter M. Brown, Richard Cartwright, Fred I. Dretske, Hartry Field, Bruce Freed, H.P. Grice, Robert Hambourger, Saul A. Kripke, Stephen Schiffer, Michael A. Slote, Sydney S. Shoemaker, Dennis W. Stampe, Julius Weinberg, and Margaret Wilson, *all* of whom remain at least somewhat skeptical. Finally, I would like to thank the Graduate School of The University of Wisconsin at Madison for financial assistance during the preparation of this defense.

# 2

# AN ANALYSIS OF FACTUAL KNOWLEDGE

I intend to provide an analysis of human factual knowledge, in other words, an analysis of what it is for a man to know that something is the case. I try to capture the conception of human factual knowledge that ordinary knowledgeable humans do in fact employ in making commonsensical judgments about the presence or absence of such knowledge. My analysis will depart most radically from all previously offered analyses and will, I think, be all the better for this departure.

## 1. The Presence of Knowledge and the Absence of Accident

In a recent critical paper,[1] after arguing to refute the idea that knowledge of most contingent matters must be based on experience,

---

I thank The University of Wisconsin for providing me with generous financial support during the summer of 1966, when I wrote much of this paper, and for providing me, during the spring of 1966, with the students in my Problems of Knowledge course, about half of whom made helpful contributions to my thinking on the matters with which the paper is concerned. Additional support (not of a financial kind) was provided, not unusually, by Saul A. Kripke and Michael A. Slote, in this case, especially by Mr. Slote; I thank them both for their helpful criticism and guarded approval, retaining full responsibility for that on which I made them spend their valuable time and efforts.

1. "Experience and Factual Knowledge," *Journal of Philosophy*, LXIV, 5 (March 16, 1967): 152–173.

I put forward the following (there numbered 12.1, page 172) as providing a logically necessary condition of when a man's belief is an instance of knowledge:

(0) For any sentential value of $p$, a man's belief that $p$ is an instance of knowledge only if it is not an accident that the man's belief is true.

Speaking of a man's belief as being an instance of knowledge may be too unnatural; at any rate it is not a very ordinary sort of thing to do. And, in the end, we are not so interested in when a man's belief might be an instance of knowledge, as we are in when a man might know that something is so. Thus, motivated by a consideration of (0), I now assert as a unified and univocal analysis of human factual knowledge:

(1) For any sentential value of $p$, (at a time $t$) a man knows that $p$ if and only if (at $t$) it is not at all accidental that the man is right about its being the case that $p$.

To speak most clearly and correctly, a reference to specific times should be an explicit part of any adequate analysis of human knowledge. At one time it may be at least somewhat accidental that a man is right about a certain matter, although at another time it is not at all accidental that he is right. Thus, a man may believe that there is a rosebush on his vast estate simply because a servant told him so and convinced him of that. The servant did not know of the existence of any rosebush and only convinced the man for amusement, thinking, indeed, that he had got his employer to believe something false. However, unbeknownst to the servant there was a rosebush in a far corner of the estate. One day the man may ride into that corner of the estate. We may suppose that he sees the rosebush. Before he sees the bush, it is entirely accidental that the estate owner has been right about there being a rosebush on his estate; when he sees the bush, it first becomes the case that it is not at all accidental that he is right about the matter. This is when the man first knows that his estate is so blessed. Again, and in contrast, a man who holds no opinion on the matter may see a rosebush and so first come to know and to be right that it is in a certain place. While he still has some but no very strong memory of the matter, he may believe that the rosebush is there and may have this belief as a result of his remembering that it is there. While he has this belief, a friend who has no knowledge of the rosebush, who simply wants to convince the man that there is a rosebush in the aforementioned place, may tell the man in most convincing and memorable terms that he, the friend, saw the rosebush there. When he hears the friend's story the man holds his belief about the rosebush both because he has seen it and remembers that it is there, and also because of the friend's story; either then being sufficient to ensure his then holding that belief. At this time the man does know; for, because he originally saw the bush, it is then not at all accidental that he is right about the location of the bush. Still later, the man may still believe that the rosebush is in the proper location but only because his friend so convincingly told him so. His originally seeing the bush will then be not at all responsible for his holding the (correct) belief. At this point, the man no longer knows; for at the time in question it is false that it is not at all accidental that the man is right about the matter. Indeed, at this time it is very much an accident that he is right about its being the case that the rosebush is in the place in question, and thus it is clear that at the time in question the man does not know the location of the bush.

It is essential, then, that we think of a man as knowing something *at a certain time* and say that *at that time* it is not at all accidental that he is right. With this understanding firmly in mind, we need not always refer to times in our subsequent discussion, and, to make matters easier, we often will not do so.

## 2. Irrelevant Accidents

What we properly regard as an accident, or as accidental, does appear to depend upon our various interests, as well as upon other things. Thus, even in the most physically deterministic universe imaginable, automobile accidents may occur, and it may be largely accidental that one man, rather than another, is successful in his competitive business enterprise. To provide an analysis of when something is an accident, or somewhat accidental, is more than I am (now) capable of doing. Nor can I show in any helpful detail how our notion of an accident, or of something's being accidental, may be used to express or reflect the various interests we might have. Thus, I will rely on a shared intuitive understanding of these notions.

In my analysis of human factual knowledge, a complete absence of the accidental is claimed, not regarding the occurrence or existence of the fact known nor regarding the existence or abilities of the man who knows, but only as regards a certain relation concerning the man and the fact. Thus, it may be accidental that $p$ and a man may know that $p$, for it may nevertheless be that it is not at all accidental that the man is right about its being the case that *p*. In other words, a man may know about an auto accident: when the car accidentally crashes into the truck, a bystander who observes what is going on may well know that the car crashed into the truck and accidentally did so. He will know just in case it is not at all accidental that he is right about its being the case that the car crashed into the truck and accidentally did so. Nor do I claim that there must be nothing accidental in the way that a man comes to know that *p*. Thus, a man may overhear his employer say that he will be fired and he may do so quite by accident, not intending to be near his employer's office or to gain any information from his employer. Though it may be an accident that the man came to know that he will be fired, and it may be somewhat accidental that he knows this to be so, nevertheless, from the time that he hears and onward, it may well be not at all accidental that the man is right about its being the case that he will be fired. Thus, he may know, whether by accident or not.

Of all the things that a man knows, none is more certainly known by him than the fact of his own existence. Thus, it must be most obvious that a man who, at a certain time, exists or is alive only as a matter of fact; he may, for instance, most certainly know that he matter of some accident may, even at that time, know about various exists. Though it may be largely accidental that he exists or is alive, it may be not at all accidental that he is right about various matters of fact; (indeed, necessarily, should he sincerely hold that he then existed, it would be not at all accidental that he was right about that matter). These points can perhaps be made more clear by our considering the following simple story: Suppose that a man is looking at a turtle and even seeing that the turtle is crawling on the ground. This man may know that the turtle is crawling on the ground (and will in that he sees that it is); for because he is using his eyes (and because of other things as well), it may be that at that time it is not at all accidental that the man is right about its being the case that the turtle is crawling on the ground. However, suppose further that just at this time, or immediately before it, a heavy rock would have fallen on the man and would have killed him then and there, smashing him to smithereens, but for the occurrence of an accidental happening which prevents the rock from falling and allows him to remain alive. Say, all of three terrible people who were pushing the rock that was to fall were themselves, coincidently and simultaneously, hit on the head by three independently falling bricks and were killed upon impact. Each of the bricks, quite independently of the others, just happened to fall loose from an ancient wall of which they all were a part. Thus, quite by accident, all three of the terrible rock pushers were killed, and the turtle watcher's life was spared, perhaps only until some later time. On these suppositions, it is indeed quite an accident that the turtle watcher is alive at the time he sees the turtle crawling on the ground before him. Yet, at that time, it is not at all accidental that he is right about its being the case that there is a turtle on the ground. And at that time, as we have supposed, the turtle watcher knows that there is a turtle crawling there upon the ground. These are the judgments that common sense and good sense would make about our case. Thus, it may be not at all accidental that a man is right about a certain matter, even though it is very much an accident that he then exists or is alive. Once we are clear about this, we can more fully appreciate the ability of my analysis to explain the cogency of Cartesian examples. Though it be accidental that a certain man exist, yet necessarily if he thinks that he exists, it is not at all accidental that he is right about the matter. An unwanted and accidental child, pursued by hapless rock pushers all his life, may grow up to know more than any of his brothers or sisters. He may do so even on my analysis of human factual knowledge, whether he fancy himself a Cartesian skeptic or whether he be entirely unconcerned with such philosophical profundities.

## 3. Accidents and Phenomena of Chance

The condition of my analysis is stronger than the necessary condition most naturally suggested by my earlier statement (0) and explicitly given by the following:

> (2) For any sentential value of $p$, a man knows that $p$ if and only if it is not an accident that the man is right about its being the case that $p$.

That such strength is required, that the weaker condition of (2) is not sufficient, can be most readily seen by considering our thought about phenomena of chance. Such a consideration will show, I think, how only our stronger condition, and none such as that of (2), adequately reflects tensions that often exist in the application of the concept of knowledge.

Let us, then, suppose a standard and simple sort of example: a man knows that a deck of cards contains ninety-nine white cards, one black card, and no others. He also knows that the cards have just been well shuffled and fairly so. On the basis of this knowledge, he concludes, as is his custom, that it is likely that the top card is white. Thus he may come to believe that the top card is white, and we may suppose him to do so. Let us further suppose that the top card is white: we are supposing that the man's belief is correct, that he is right about its being the case that the top card is white. The only reason that he has this (correct) belief is that he has reasoned in a certain way on the basis of the knowledge that we have supposed him to have. Now once we have made all these suppositions, we have supposed, not only that the man is right, but also, and with equal clarity, that it is not an accident that he is right about the matter. But, in contrast, it is *not* entirely clear that it is not at all accidental that the man is right. But, equally, it is *not* clear that it is *false* that it is not at all accidental that he is. In other words, there is a tension in the application of our analytic condition to the probabilistic case presented. This same tension is also in evidence when we consider the application of our concept of factual knowledge. For in the simple case presented, it is *neither* clear that the man does know *nor* clear that he does not. The suppositions neither allow nor yield any decisive answer as to whether the man knows the color of the top card.

The magnitude of the numbers involved may help to further our willingness to say that the man knows, to apply our concept of knowledge. But sheer consideration of number will not remove the tension entirely. Thus, were there a billion white cards, and only one of another color, we are more ready to say that the man who bets that the top card is white knows full well that he will win (assuming of course that he will win). Still, we may also find ourselves saying that he cannot really know that he has won until the color of the card is actually revealed. Similarly, such an increase in the chances furthers our readiness to apply our analytic condition, to say that it is not at all accidental that the man is right (assuming of course that he is right). But again, and equally I think, our willingness here is not so complete as it might be. Perhaps it is not really true, after all, that it is not at all accidental that he is right, even when such large numbers are involved. Thus, a consideration of our thought about such simple probabilistic cases gives some further support to the claim that our analytic condition mirrors well our concept of factual knowledge.

We may gain yet further support, I think, by considering the way in which our thought about more highly structured cases compares with what we think about such unstructured cases of the most simple probabilistic kind. In contrast to the first case of the card deck, let us consider the following, more structured sort of case, where considerations of probability enter rather less directly: a man is performing a hundred problems in addition and checking his answers by an independent arithmetic method. These problems each involve his adding three different numbers, each between 10 and 100. There is nothing mysterious here: the man uses the normal paper-and-pencil methods for both adding and checking. He always expresses the numbers in the decimal system, in the familiar arabic notation. Suppose the man, like most other men, characteristically to make only one mistake unspotted, and eventually to add and check correctly in ninety-nine of the hundred cases. And suppose him in *each* case to think the answer correct (though we may allow that he may not think he has been correct in *all* cases). Then, with respect to each problem that he worked and checked correctly, our common-sense judgment would be that he knew what the answer was. Having worked the problem correctly, he would know, for example, that 134 is the sum of 32 and 49 and 53. And equally, the common-sense attitude still prevailing, there is no doubt but that we should say that it is not at all accidental that the man is right about the sum. Such tension as was present in the purely probabilitistic case of the card deck, is now absent from our judgment—both as regards our concept of knowledge and as regards our analytic condition. Exactly why cases like that involving fallible addition should differ so markedly from cases of pure probability is a deep question that cries out for further analysis and greater understanding. But though our understanding of these matters is presently quite limited, we may recognize that there are between the two sorts of cases just considered, notable differences in our willingness to apply our concept of factual knowledge. Even here, where my analysis leads us to no very important increase in our understanding of the relevant matters, we may say that the analysis has received some notable support.[2]

## 4. Justification, Evidence, and Knowledge

My analysis of human factual knowledge differs markedly from those analyses in which an attempt is made to consider such knowledge as some sort of justified true belief. Indeed, according to my analysis a man may know something without his being in any way justified in believing that it is so. And my analysis does not require, as does that of A. J. Ayer,[3] that

---

2. I have been much influenced on these matters and others that I have been writing about, by discussions with Robert Nozick and Michael Anthony Slote.

3. *The Problem of Knowledge* (London: Macmillan, 1956), ch. 1, "Philosophy and Knowledge," pp. 31–35, esp. p. 35.

(3) For any sentential value of *p*, a man knows that *p* only if the man has the right to be sure that *p*.

It also disagrees with Roderick Chisholm's claim[4] that

(4) For any sentential value of *p*, a man knows that *p* only if the man has adequate evidence that *p*.

Let us consider a straightforward example which upsets these claims most decisively, and shows that no sort of justification is ever a necessary condition for knowledge. Thus, we may better understand my analysis by seeing how it conflicts with this other, more traditional view.

The example, which I first adduced in my aforementioned essay against empiricism, concerns a certain gypsy, one who, we must conclude, knows things of which others are ignorant. Our gypsy has been brought up to accept the messages of a certain crystal ball that he inherited from his family. Owing to forces in nature which no one understands, the ball always gives a correct report on any matter on which it provides a message. And, because of certain loyalties and beliefs instilled by his upbringing, the gypsy never checks up on the ball in any way whatever. We shall, indeed, suppose the gypsy to believe, what he inferred from what he learned later in life, that the ball will almost never give a correct report. But though the gypsy has this (false) general belief, which we may suppose him to be justified in having, when it comes to any particular matter, he cannot help but believe the message of the ball. Moreover, these acquired beliefs he holds most insistently though he is unable to provide any reasonable defense of these beliefs when challenged and is even wholly unconcerned with whether he is reasonable or not in holding them. We may even suppose that, despite his unreasonable attitudes and the lack of adequate evidence for his beliefs, the gypsy is entirely confident about the truth of each report despite his knowledge of its source and his belief about the general unreliability of the source. Where the fact that *p* is reported by the ball, on these suppositions, the gypsy does not have adequate evidence that *p*, and especially so when we further suppose him to have a wealth of evidence for thinking it false that *p*. Does the gypsy then have the right to be sure that *p*? Plainly not, unless everyone has the

---

4. *Perceiving: A Philosophical Study* (Ithaca, N.Y.: Cornell, 1957), ch. I, "Epistemic Terms," esp. p. 16.

right to be sure of anything that is true. Such are the effects of the gypsy's early upbringing and certain later happenings.

But it does appear that, in the present case, the effects are not wholly and simply unfortunate ones. Owing to the gypsy's early upbringing and the operation of the crystal ball, the gypsy does have knowledge of those matters on which the ball delivers a report. This fact may be made especially clear by supposing that the gypsy's parents knew, by observational check or by some other means, that the ball gave only correct reports. On this basis they raised their gypsy child to accept unquestioningly the reports of the ball, whether these be of a pictorial sort or whether expressed in some sort of unusual writing. Thus, this gypsy, though he is only unreasonable in believing that $p$, knows that $p$, where the report that $p$ is a report of the ball that the gypsy accepts. Though our gypsy does not satisfy the conditions of (3) or (4), he does have factual knowledge. For it is, after all, not at all accidental that he is right about the relevant matters. Thus we can see how my analysis conflicts with the fundamental claims of leading contemporary analysts, and how only my analysis survives this conflict intact.

As my analysis dictates, we must give up the idea that factual knowledge is any sort of justified true belief, or anything of the like. But even so, we may obtain both a better understanding of and further support for the analysis by examining another idea, one that derives from the attempt to understand our knowledge in this traditional way. This derivative idea is that a belief that represents knowledge on someone's part cannot be based on grounds that are entirely false. This derivative idea comes from a consideration of the standard sort of argument to show that epistemically justified true belief is not logically *sufficient* for factual knowledge. According to this standard argument, a man justifiedly deduces from justified beliefs of his that are entirely false, a true conclusion which he accepts on the basis of the deduction. Thus, by believing the conclusion, the man has an epistemically justified belief which, though true, represents no knowledge on his part.[5] It may be thought, then, that this justified true belief fails to be knowledge simply because it is based on grounds that are false. We might then require of a belief that some of its grounds be true, if the belief represent knowledge.

---

5. This standard argument is most influentially stated by Edmund L. Gettier in his "Is Justified True Belief Knowledge?," *Analysis*, XXIII.6, n.s. 96 (June 1963): 121–123, and it is earlier suggested by Bertrand Russell in *The Problems of Philosophy* (New York: Oxford, 1912), ch. XIII, "Knowledge, Error, and Probable Opinion," esp. p. 131 ff.

But such a requirement would be too strong. There are various examples in terms of which this may be seen. I should most like to adduce the main example of my aforementioned essay. In this example, knowledgeable scientists successfully duplicate a person who the scientists know to have a lot of important factual knowledge. They do this in order that there be more people who have this knowledge. The duplicate knows various things, say, various facts of physics. And we can now better say why he does: he knows because it is not at all accidental that the duplicate is right about these physical matters. But the beliefs that represent this knowledge on the part of the duplicate, all have as grounds beliefs that are entirely false. The duplicate, just like a normal scientist, bases his beliefs about the physical world on beliefs about his own personal history and experience: about what he has seen and read, about the experiments he has performed and heard about, and so on. But the duplicate has not done any of these things. Thus, these constructed duplicates, which satisfy the condition of my analysis, show that a belief may represent knowledge though it be based on grounds that are themselves entirely false.

Why, then, is there a lack of knowledge on the part of the man whose justified true belief is, in a simple and straightforward way, deduced from and based on grounds that are entirely false? The answer is, I think, that given by my analysis. Generally, with such a man, it is entirely accidental that he is right about the matter in question, whereas, for him to know, it must be quite the opposite. It must be not at all accidental that he is right about the matter.

In connection with our simple answer, we may note that there are other ways of seeing that justified true belief need not ensure factual knowledge. With such ways, no false belief is attributed to the man in question, and thus his failure to know is most clearly unrelated to his having any false grounds. One such way, it is interesting to note, is suggested by the card-deck examples we examined in the previous section. There, we noted that, with a very high proportion of white cards to black, it is not easy to tell or decide whether the man knows the top card to be white. But where we have, say, eighty-five white cards and fifteen black ones, it is *clear* that the man who reasons to the belief that the top card is white does not know the card to be white. On the other hand, it is also clear that the man is epistemically justified in believing the card to be white. Thus, though this man has no relevant false beliefs and though he reasons in no faulty manner, his epistemically justified true belief fails to represent knowledge. Again, the result is explained by my analysis: this man does not know because it is false that it is not at all accidental that he is right. So it is of interest that, in yet another way, a consideration of purely probabilistic cases lends support to my analysis while rendering it still more implausible that factual knowledge be some sort of justified true belief or, for that matter, anything of the like.

## 5. The Imprecision of the Concept of Knowledge

No doubt, any attempted analysis of factual knowledge will fail to take account of every imaginable case and example as nicely as one might wish. But, then, our concept of knowledge is itself not so exact with every imaginable case as one might wish it to be. Primarily in connection with certain matters peculiar to his own account of factual knowledge, Bertrand Russell warns against our having unrealistic expectations:

> But in fact 'knowledge' is not a precise conception:...A very precise definition, therefore, should not be sought, since any such definition must be more or less misleading (*op. cit.*, 134).

Thus, though various examples may be brought to refute a putatively adequate analysis, whether such examples show the analysis to be inadequate is not always a very easy matter to decide.

Having expressed these thoughts, I will now put forward what has occurred to me as the example most likely to incline someone to reject the analysis that I offer. As might be expected, the example apparently could be used to show that the condition of my analysis is too weak, to show, that is, that at a certain time it might be not at all accidental that a man is right about its being the case that $p$ and, even so, at that time he may not know that $p$. But I think that when this example is judged with impartiality and care, it is seen not to present any problem for my analysis of human factual knowledge. Indeed, such careful scrutiny, if anything, reveals that, when most clearly understood, the apparently damaging example actually may lend support to my analysis.

The example that I offer involves what might be called the fulfillment of a man's expectation about the future being brought about as a result of the man's having that expectation. Such happenings can, of course, occur in various ways, but rather than attempt to consider the entire variety, let us turn directly to the most bizarre sort of example, which is apparently most troublesome. Let us think, then, of a man who has a dream, and dreams that a certain horse will win a certain race. The man that I imagine generally believes only some of the things that he dreams will happen, and those that he believes simply as a result of a dream, he mumbles audibly upon awakening. Upon awakening from his dream about the horse race, the man mumbled that Schimmelpenninck, one of the horses to run in the 1965 Kentucky Derby, would be the winner of that race. Now, whenever our man awakes, he is wakened by his friend, who sees to it that the man has time to do his morning exercises. The friend knows that whatever the man mumbles upon awakening is what he has just dreamed about the future and thus believes will happen. The friend thus knows each of the man's beliefs that come to him simply as a result of dreaming, and he knows of each of these that it is the product of a dream. Hence, in particular, the friend knows that the man believes that Schimmelpenninck will win the 1965 Kentucky Derby, and he knows that the man acquired this belief simply as a result of his having an appropriate dream about that horse race. The friend, that morning, immediately decides to ensure the truth (or correctness) of his friend's belief; he resolves that the dreamer's belief be true. Now, the friend is an eminent veterinarian with access to all racing stables, and so he drugs all of Schimmelpenninck's competitors, endeavoring to fulfill the resolution that he made. I suppose that in this way the friend ensures that Schimmelpenninck is the winner of the 1965 Kentucky Derby; among other things, I here assume that Schimmelpenninck does finish first and that the veterinarian's activites are not detected. We may even suppose that once the veterinarian had made up his mind, it was no longer a matter of any chance which horse would win the race. In short, we may even suppose that the veterinarian knows that Schimmelpenninck will win. It is not very important here whether we suppose that without the doctor's intervention the horse would have not won, or whether we suppose the opposite, that the horse would have won anyway. In either case, the veterinarian knows the winner of the race. But the dreamer has no knowledge of the winner, for he always believes that Schimmelpenninck will win simply because he has a dream, a dream relevantly unconnected with the race to be run, and he never does in any way gain any relevant information.

It is clear that, on our suppositions, the dreamer does not know at any time. Yet, it may appear that, after the veterinarian makes his resolve or after he drugs the horse's competitors, it is not at all accidental that the dreamer is right about its being the case that Schimmelpenninck is the winner. But such appearances, I fear, would be most deceptive. Were it truly the case that at the relevant times it is not at all accidental that the dreamer is right, then we should have to make much stronger suppositions about our case than those we have made.

Indeed, we should then have to make just such suppositions as render the case one most plausibly described as one in which the dreamer does know. To see that all of this is so, let us ask some questions of the presented case, questions which make it most dubious to suppose that the case is one which is correctly described by saying that it is not at all accidental that the dreamer is right about the outcome of the race.

The essential accidentality will not be fully brought out by asking what we should say were the veterinarian to make his resolve, not after his learning of the dreamer's acquisition of belief, but in advance of such information. To see this clearly, we may suppose the contrasting situation, that the doctor does make his resolve in advance, even long before the dreamer has the appropriate dream, and that he resolves that should his friend ever dream that a certain horse would win a certain running of the Kentucky Derby, he, the veterinarian, would ensure that his friend's belief be true. For even with such a supposition, the circumstances of which are unknown to the dreamer, we may ask: First, why did the veterinarian make just that particular resolve, which is still a rather specific one, and not some other one, or, better, some very general resolve whose fulfillment would entail the fulfillment of many particular resolves he might well make? And second, would the doctor be able to ensure the truth of other sorts of dream-produced beliefs that his friend might have, beliefs about future fluctuations of the stock market, future moon-rocket launchings, earthquakes, elections, and eclipses? These questions do, I think, bring out the large amount of accidentality that remains concerning the relevant matter, even after we have supposed that the veterinarian made his resolve long in advance of the particular dream or in advance of information of it. But, in contrast to the case so far considered, we may make suppositions that are quite extreme, and so rule out rather clearly any accidentality about the dreamer's being right about the subject of his opinion: We will imagine that the earth and all the life upon it were originally created by an extremely powerful and knowledgeable being. This being's chief fascination was with ensuring that a man's beliefs be true in case he acquired those beliefs simply as a result of a dream. In line with his most important desires, the being so created everyone that no man would ever have a dream-produced belief that conflicted with that of any other man; thus the being ensured that it be possible that he ensure the truth of every man's dream-produced belief about the future, for he also saw to it that no man would come to have any inconsistent beliefs simply as the result of a dream. Further, as the being well knew, it was well within his power to ensure the truth of any such belief that would ever actually be held. And the being, acting reasonably with respect to his chief fascination, proceeded to do what he knew to be well within his power. Now, though some philosophers might think otherwise, it strikes me as rather clear that a fair employment of our shared conception of factual knowledge dictates that, in such a world as this, the being has ensured that a man's dreams are a source of knowledge for the man (just in case the man believes that what he dreams about the future is the way that things will be). We have, then, presented a rather clear case of knowledge of the future which is of the relevant kind, enabling us to give an answer to what appeared to be the gravest problem that would befall my analysis of human factual knowledge. Happily, this example is quite in accord with that analysis, for it is on such extreme suppositions as those we have just made that it is most clear that, at the relevant time, it is not at all accidental that the man is right about the subject of his opinion.

Complete satisfaction with our extreme case allows us better to understand cases that are not so extreme, and thus not so clear. For example, we can now better understand and appreciate the following sort of case, one that lies somewhere between the last two we have considered: We suppose that a powerful and knowledgeable man makes a longstanding resolve that all of his dreaming friend's appropriate beliefs about the outcomes of all sporting events would be correct, and that the man succeeds in fulfilling this resolve, just as he knew that he would. About such a situation, we should not be so very disinclined to judge that the powerful man ensured that his friend's dreams were a source of knowledge for that man (just when he believes that what he dreams about the future is the way that things will be). Just so, about such a situation, we should be equally and not so very disinclined to judge that the powerful man ensured that at the relevant times it was not at all accidental that the dreamer was right about the subjects of his dream-produced beliefs.

Our putative counterexample, about the dreamer and his friend the veterinarian, has been shown to present problems that are only apparent. Indeed, by pursuing further these merely apparent difficulties, we have encountered relevantly similar cases that lend support to my analysis of human factual knowledge. Now, in all such cases of knowledge, as we suppose that the knower is wholly unaware both of the agent who makes it happen that he knows and of any happenings that help explain his knowledge, we may say that he does not know why he knows various things about the future, or at least that he knows almost nothing about why he knows. But still, should the man in such an example believe that he knows, this belief having as its source the same process of dreaming as does the belief that is supposed to represent knowledge on the part of the man, then, so far as I can see, there is no good reason for denying that the man knows *that* he knows, though he may lack completely knowledge of why he knows. Of course, we do know why the man knows; we know that a powerful agent makes it happen that at the relevant time it is not at all accidental that the man is right.

Apparent problems now appear to be resolved entirely, this resolution affording further support for my analysis of human factual knowledge.

# 3

# AN ARGUMENT FOR SKEPTICISM

I mean to offer a positive argument for skepticism about knowledge; I do not mean just to raise some doubts, however general, about statements to the effect that people know. The argument to be offered has as its conclusion the universal form of the skeptical thesis, that is, the proposition that nobody ever knows *anything* to be so. If this argument is sound, as I am inclined to think, then it will follow in particular that nobody ever knows anything about the past or future or even the present, about others or even about himself, about external objects or even about his own experiences, about complicated contingencies or even the simplest mathematical necessities. This, then, is an argument for an extremely strong and sweeping conclusion indeed.

The opposite of skepticism is often called dogmatism. In these terms, dogmatism is the view that certain things are known to be so. The stronger the form of dogmatism, the more sorts of things would be claimed to be known and, so, the weaker the form of skepticism which might still be allowed to hold. Thus, one might be a dogmatist about the past but a skeptic about the future in the sense that one might hold that we know a fair amount about the past but know nothing of the future. But typical arguments to the effect that we know things about the past do not *look* dogmatic in any usual sense. And, arguments to the effect that we know nothing of the future do not in any standard sense *look* particularly undogmatic; they do not *look* particularly indicative of an open-minded approach to things. Going by the typical arguments, then, the label "dogmatist" is unfairly prejudicial and there is no force in the claim that skepticism is to be preferred because the alternative is dogmatism. Unlike such typical arguments, the argument I mean to offer gives substance to the claim that the alternative to skepticism is a view which sanctions a dogmatic attitude. In that one may well not appreciate that this is indeed skepticism's only alternative, one might, perhaps, innocently believe that one knows things without being dogmatic in the process. But once the implications of that belief are brought out, as my argument means to do, the persistence in such a belief may itself be considered dogmatic. Of course, I do not want to be dogmatic in asserting any of this and, indeed, confess to only a moderate amount of confidence in what I have to offer. But, as I am inclined to think it true, I offer it in a spirit which I hope may be taken as quite undogmatic and open-minded.

## 1. A Preliminary Statement of the Argument

I begin by giving a statement of the argument which, while correct in all essentials, does not account for certain complications. On this statement, the argument is exceedingly simple and straightforward. It has but two premises and each of them makes no exceptions whatsoever. The first of these is the proposition:

(1) If someone *knows* something to be so, then it is all right for the person to be absolutely *certain* that it is so.

For example, if it is true that Knute *knows* that there was a general called "Napoleon", then it is (perfectly) all right for him to be absolutely *certain* that there was. And, if Rene really *knows* that he exists, then it is (perfectly) all right for Rene to be absolutely certain that he does.

Our second and final premise, then, is this categorical proposition:

(2) It is never all right for anyone to be absolutely *certain* that anything is so.

According to this premise, it is not all right for Knute to be absolutely certain that there was a general called "Napoleon", nor is it even all right for Rene to be absolutely certain that he exists. No matter what their situations, these people should not have this "attitude of absolute certainty". When one understands what is involved in having this attitude, or in being absolutely certain of something, one will presumably understand why it is never all right to be absolutely certain.

These two premises together entail our conclusion of universal skepticism:

(3) Nobody ever *knows* that anything is so.

In particular, Knute does not really *know* that there was a general called "Napoleon", nor does Rene really *know* that he exists.

The first of these premises is hardly novel unless novelty may be gained by any slight change in the words one chooses. Words to the same effect are prominent in the philosophical literature; one might mention Moore, Ayer, Malcolm and Hintikka as a few significant examples.[1] To my own way of thinking any such words are in need of some small qualification to get things right. But the essential idea of this premise can hardly be faulted without doing violence to the concept of knowing.

The second premise is, I think, also in need of a small qualification, one which matches that needed for the first. But even with a qualification, it is difficult to find such a proposition put forward in the literature. Indeed, the philosophers we just mentioned seem all too typical in denying it, at least by implication. It is this premise which is most crucial, and I will argue that denying it amounts to embracing dogmatism. Given the truth of the first premise, it is for this reason that skepticism is indeed the alternative to dogmatism.

The force of these remarks will be better appreciated, I think, when we understand more fully what the premises really amount to. That will also help us appreciate how the premises must be qualified in order that the argument may actually be sound. Accordingly, I will now discuss each of the premises in turn, beginning with the first.

## 2. The First Premise: The Idea That If One Knows It Is All Right for One to Be Certain

We often have the idea that someone is certain of something but he shouldn't be. Perhaps from his expressive behavior, perhaps from

---

1. G. E. Moore, "Certainty" in *Philosophical Papers*, New York: 1962, p. 223, Sir A. J. Ayer, *The Problem of Knowledge*, Baltimore: 1956, pp. 33–35, Norman Malcolm, "Knowledge and Belief" in *Knowledge and Certainty*, Englewood Cliffs, New Jersey: 1963, pp. 67–68, and Jaakko Hintikka, *Knowledge and Belief*, Ithaca, New York: 1962, pp. 20–21.

something else, we *take* it that he is certain of something—whether or not he really is certain of it. We ask him, if we are so inclined, "How can you be *certain* of that?" In asking this question, we manage to imply that it might not be all right for him to be certain and imply, further, that this is because he might not really *know* the thing. If the man could show us that he does know, then we should withdraw the question and, perhaps, even apologize for implying what we did by raising it. But, then, how do we manage to imply so much just by asking this question in the first place? Neither 'know' nor any cognate expression ever crosses our lips in the asking. We are able to imply so much, I suggest, because we all accept the idea that, at least generally, if one does know something then it is all right for one to be certain of it—but if one doesn't then it isn't. This suggests that there is some analytic connection between knowing, on the one hand, and on the other, it's being all right to be certain.

The very particular idea that knowing *entails* it's being all right to be certain is suggested, further, by the fact that knowing entails, at least, that one *is* certain. That this is a fact is made quite plain by the inconsistency expressed by sentences like "He really *knew* that it was raining, but he *wasn't* absolutely *certain* that it was". Such a sentence can express no truth: if he wasn't certain, then he didn't know. We get further confirmation here from considering transitivity. The sentences "He was *sad that* it was raining, but he *didn't know* it was" and "He was really *sad that* it was raining, but he *wasn't* absolutely *certain* it was" are likewise inconsistent. Their inconsistency means an entailment from being sad that to knowing, in the first case, and to being certain in the second. This can be best explained, it would seem, by the entailment from knowing to being certain is convincingly clinched, I think, by appreciating the equivalence between someone's knowing something and his knowing it for certain, or with absolute certainty. To be sure, we may describe cases which we would more naturally react to with the words "He knew it" than "He knew it for certain": Consider a man who, looking for his cuff links, unerringly went to the very spot they were while doubts went through his mind. Did he know that they were in that spot? But our readiness to say he knew might only indicate loose usage of those words by us, while we are more strict in our use when the word "certain" enters the picture. That this is much the more plausible hypothesis than thinking there to be an inequivalence here is evidenced by the inconsistency of the relevant sentences: "He *knew* it, but he *didn't* know it for certain", "He really *knew* it, but he *didn't* know it *with absolute certainty*", "He knew it was there, but he didn't *really know* it", and so on. No truth can be found in these words no matter when they might be uttered. Even if they are put forth at the end of stories like that of the cuff-link finder, where we are inclined at first to say he knows, we realize that they must express what is false. Accordingly, we are forced to be unswayed by our tendency to loose usage and to admit the equivalence between knowing with absolute certainty and just plain knowing to be so. Admitting this equivalence, we can be quite confident that knowing does indeed entail being absolutely certain.

Now, our intuitive thought about knowledge or knowing is that it is something good, of value, which ought to be sought, and prized when attained. But, if knowing always entails being certain, and the latter may so often be bad, as our questions often imply, how might it be that knowing is so often good? The situation here is very unlike others that are only superficially alike, e.g., the case of helping someone in trouble which entails someone's being in trouble. These latter cases involve the righting of a wrong, or the improvement of a situation which starts off bad. But our idea is not that being certain is bad, or generally bad, like being in trouble. Rather, it is bad *unless* one knows, but if one does know then there's nothing wrong at all with being certain. This is the reason that there is no conflict between the supposed value of knowing and its entailing that one is absolutely certain.

All of these ideas suggest the universal and unqualified proposition that if one knows, it is always all right for one to be certain. And, quite surely, at least something like this must be right. But a qualification must be made if we are to arrive at a statement which actually is correct. Everyday life provides cases where it is bad that one knows, and these are also cases where it is bad for one to be certain even if one does in fact know. For example, one shouldn't know too much about the private lives of others. If one's neighbor sleeps in the nude and doesn't want others to know it, it may well be no good thing for one to know that he sleeps this way. In such a case as this, even if one knows that the neighbor sleeps in the nude, it is neither all right for one to know it nor all right for one to know it nor all right for one to be absolutely certain that he does. A more unrealistic case but in some ways a clearer one is as follows. Here one's being certain of a particular thing is so bad that it is quite clear that one should not be certain of it even if one in fact knows the thing. We may suppose, for example, that a powerful god makes it plain that he will bring fruitful times for the multitude just in case a particular individual is *not certain* of a particular thing: just in case Max is not certain that frogs are animals. Otherwise, years of *pain* are all that lie in store. Even if Max knows that frogs are animals it is not all right for him to be certain of this thing. If this means tampering with himself so that he no longer knows it, then Max had better go to a hypnotist or whatever: The price is too high and the knowledge too trivial. As in more realistic cases, a man's knowing something is not enough to entail that it is all right for him to be certain of it.

Cases like these, both ordinary and bizarre, show that our first premise must be qualified if we are to have any sound argument. They also show that a qualification is needed for Ayer's dictum that if one knows something one has the right to be sure of it, and for any other proposition which involves our basic idea, e.g., that if one knows something, then one is justified in being certain of the thing. There is no doubt much truth in these propositions, as we have argued and as is evidenced by the inconsistent appearance of sentences to the contrary: "He *knows* that it's raining, but he *shouldn't* be *sure* of it", "He really *knew* they were fools, but it was *wrong* for him to be absolutely *certain* that they were", and so on. But, this inconsistent appearance, while important to notice, is not due to any actual inconsistency in what is expressed. It is due, rather, to the fact that when one attends to these sentences one is liable to think only of evidential or epistemic considerations. One is not likely to think in terms of possibilities that have little or nothing to do with sad matters—but of course those are the only ones which might falsify the statement. These upsetting cases present no interesting relation between knowing something and being certain of it.

The sorts of cases which make us qualify our premise present considerations which are not entailed by the person's being certain or by his knowing. They involve the contingencies of bad consequences, or similar external factors which must be given their due weight. Thus, the upsetting cases present unusual considerations which *override* any consideration that one knows. An adequate premise must take care to allow for these considerations, and we modify (1) to take care of just that:

(1q)  If someone *knows* something to be so, then it is all right for the person to be absolutely certain that it is so providing only that no overriding consideration (or considerations) make it not all right.

Such a qualification was to be expected anyway. Few things, if any, are so important that some others might not sometimes take precedence. And anything which might be involved in knowing, unlike avoiding punishing the innocent, is quite surely no such absolutely important a thing. Once we make this qualification, however, it seems impossible to deny our first premise. Indeed, it is no doubt just what this premise says which is indicated by the words "for certain" and "with absolute certainty" in the sentences "He knew it for certain" and "He knew it with absolute certainty". It is not just the idea that the knower is certain to which these merely emphatic words here point. Rather, it is to the idea his knowing means that, pending no overriding considerations to the contrary, his being certain of the thing is perfectly all right.

Now, it cannot be too strongly emphasized that everything I said is meant to be compatible with the sense which the ordinary word 'know' actually has. Indeed, it fairly relies on this word's having only one ("strong") sense as it occurs in sentences of the forms 'S knows that p' and 'S knows about X'. Some philosophers have suggested 'weak' senses of 'know' in which it does not even have an entailment to absolute certainty.[2] But though there is some reason to suppose that 'know' has different meanings in 'John knows that Jim is his friend' and 'John knows Jim',[3] there appears no reason at all to suppose that 'knows' may mean different things as it occurs in the former sentence. Indeed, reason seems to favor the opposite view. If a genuine ambiguous sentence has a meaning on which it is inconsistent, there will generally be one also on which it is consistent. Once the latter meaning is pointed out, this difference is appreciated and felt to be quite striking. Thus, the sentence 'John really *types* many things, but he produces symbols *only orally*' has an obvious meaning on which it is inconsistent. But, it may be pointed out that 'types' has another sense, which it shares (roughly) with 'classifies'. Once this is pointed out, the consistent meaning is appreciated, and the effect is a striking one. No similar phenomenon is ever found with the sentence 'John really *knows* that he types things, but he *isn't* absolutely *certain* that he does'. There may be many *ad hoc* explanations of this fact. But the only plausible explanation is, I think, that 'know' doesn't have a weak sense with no entailment to absolute certainty.[4]

To deny our first premise, then, is to do violence to the meaning of 'know' and to our concept of knowledge. If our argument is to be stopped, it must be with the consideration of the second premise. In

---

2. For examples, see Malcolm, *op. cit.*, p. 62ff. and Hintikka, *op. cit.*, p. 18ff.

3. For example, Spanish uses the verb 'saber' to translate the first of these sentences and 'conocer' to translate the second, and so for various other languages. This evidence is both indirect and inconclusive, but it is *some* evidence anyway.

4. Perhaps philosophers who seem to see more senses than I do are using 'sense' in a different sense. Or, perhaps more likely, they are inventing a new sense for 'sense', so as to use the word to make important distinctions about the meaning of our expressions. But, without being impertinent, I can only request to see some reason for supposing that, even in such a new sense of 'sense', our verb 'know' has two senses.

any case, it is with that premise that the *substantive* claim of the argument is made: It is not only with mere questions of logical relations with which we must now contend. Accordingly, we now come to the largest and most important part of our discussion.

## 3. The Second Premise: The Idea That It Is Never All Right to Be Absolutely Certain

As I have stated it, the second premise of our argument is a triply universal proposition:

(2) It is *never* all right for *anyone* to be absolutely certain that *anything* is so.

It is universal, first, in that it applies to all beings without fear or favor, the most almighty of gods as well as the humblest of creatures. Second, it is also universal in that it applies to all propositions or things (of which one might or might not be certain). It is to hold no matter how simple and certain a thing may seem to a being: that one exists right now, that there is an experience of phenomenal blueness, and so on. We want a premise which is universal in both of these respects, and I will argue that we may have one. But there is a third way in which this premise is universal, and this aspect of it may be doubted: It says that no matter what the circumstances, being certain is not all right. In other words, it says that it is not all right in *any* circumstances whatsoever.[5]

This third point of universality was needed for the second premise to match up with the first in our original statement of our argument. For if there were some circumstances when it is all right to be certain, then according to our original first premise (1), we might know in just those circumstances. Then it would not be true that nobody ever knows anything. But, we have found it necessary to alter our first premise, from (1) to (1q). So, we no longer require a second premise which, like (2), is universal with respect to circumstances as well as with respect to beings and propositions. Is this universality of circumstances fatal to the truth of (2), so that we *must* reformulate the premise now that we *may* do so?

---

5. By 'any circumstance', I mean 'any logically possible circumstance', or 'any consistently describable circumstance'. This only means that we are willing to treat our premise as open to any counter-examples even purely hypothetical, unrealistic ones so long as they may be consistently described.

As we have been at pains to make clear, no one's being certain of any particular thing is all that important apart from the consequences it might have. Neither is one's knowing something—supposing that one knows—of any such great moment. Just as knowing is not so importantly good that it cannot sometimes be bad, so being certain is not so importantly bad that it might not sometimes be all right and even good. It may be in fact necessary for a researcher to find a cure for a dread disease that that man be absolutely certain that there is a cure to be found. Even if he is dogmatic about the cure's existence, this may prove to be all right, I think, if he discovers the cure. As before, a more bizarre case may serve to clarify. We may suppose that this time our powerful god wants Max to be absolutely certain that tulips are animals. Now, the god makes it quite plain that the multitude will have fruitful times just in case Max is certain of this thing and that otherwise excruciating pain and suffering will be all. In such a case, Max had better be absolutely certain no matter what negative feature might be inherent in his being so. Even if it takes hypnotism or drugs, Max ought to get himself into the state desired by the eccentric but effective deity. In such circumstances as these, it is perfectly all right for him to be certain that tulips are animals. These cases and others force us to qualify our premise. The situation is much as before with premise (1). This time, however, we have overriding considerations which—supposing that it is not otherwise all right—make being certain perfectly all right. Accordingly, we may reformulate (2) so that it matches up with (1q):

(2q)  It is *not* the case that it is all right for someone to be absolutely *certain* that something is so providing only that no overriding (consideration or) considerations make it all right.

This premise says that there is something wrong with being certain but allows that this may be outweighed by external factors. These factors have nothing much to do with evidence, or with any other epistemic criteria. It is for this qualified proposition that I shall make a case. If it may be accepted, then we may deduce the conclusion of universal skepticism.

## 4. What Attitude Is Involved in One's Being Absolutely Certain?

I will now, at last, begin to argue for the idea that to be absolutely certain of something is, owing to a certain feature of personal certainty, to be *dogmatic* in the matter of whether that thing is so. It is because of this dogmatic feature that there is always *something* wrong with being absolutely certain. In other words, it is because of this feature that our second premise, (2q), is correct. My argument for the idea that this feature ensures this dogmatism falls naturally into two parts. The first part, which will occupy us in this present section, is aimed at specifying the feature. Thus, we will argue here that one's being absolutely certain of something involves one in having a certain severely negative *attitude* in the matter of whether that thing is so: the attitude that *no* new information, evidence or experience which one might ever have will be seriously considered by one to be *at all* relevant to *any possible* change in one's thinking in the matter. The second part is aimed at showing this attitude to be wrongly dogmatic even in matters which may appear to be quite simple and certain. That more normative segment will be reserved for the section immediately to follow.

That such an absolutely severe attitude should be essential to one's knowing is hardly novel with me. Indeed, philosophers who are quite plainly anti-skeptical proclaim just this attitude as essential to one's knowing. Thus Norman Malcolm thinks himself to know that there is an ink-bottle before him, and describes what he takes to be implicit in this knowledge of his:

> Not only do I not *have* to admit that (those) extraordinary occurrences would be evidence that there is no ink-bottle here; the fact is that I *do not* admit it. There is nothing whatever that could happen in the next moment that would by me be called *evidence* that there is not an ink-bottle here now. No future experience or investigation could prove to me that I am mistaken....
>
> It will appear to some that I have adopted an *unreasonable* attitude towards that statement. There is, however, nothing unreasonable about it.
>
> In saying that I should regard nothing as evidence that there is no ink-bottle here now, I am not *predicting* what I should do if various astonishing things happened....
>
> That assertion describes my *present* attitude towards the statement that here is an ink bottle....[6]

Now, Malcolm, it is true, aligns himself with the idea that there are two (or more) senses of 'know' to be found in sentences like 'John *knows* that there is an ink-bottle before him'. This idea is neither correct nor essential to his position in those passages. We have already argued, in

---

6. Malcolm, *op. cit.*, pp. 67–68.

section 2, that this idea is not correct. That this incorrect idea is not essential to the main thrust of his quoted remarks is, I think, equally clear. For he allows that there is at least *a* sense of 'know' where knowing entails one's having the extreme attitude they characterize. Presumably, that sense, at least, is just the sense where knowing entails being absolutely certain, and the extreme attitude is just the one which is necessarily involved in absolute certainty. In that such philosophers think that when one knows the attitude of certainty is not only present but quite all right, their thinking that the attitude is to be characterized in such severe negative terms is some indirect evidence for thinking so. An attitude which is so *severely* negative as this might well *not* be one which is very often justified. However, even if one wants to avoid skepticism, a concern for the truth about this attitude makes a severe characterization of it quite unavoidable.

The attitude of certainty concerns *any* sequence of experience or events which could consistently be presented to a sentient subject, without its description prejudging the issue on which it might supposedly bear. Thus, one is certain that there is an ink-bottle before one only if one's attitude is this: Insofar as I care about being right about whether an ink-bottle is or was before me, no matter how things may seem to appear, *I will not count* as contrary evidence even such extraordinary sequences as these:

> ...when I next reach for this ink-bottle my hand should seem to pass *through* it and I should not feel the contact of any object...in the next moment the ink-bottle will suddenly vanish from sight...I should find myself under a tree in the garden with no ink-bottle about...one or more persons should enter this room and declare that they see no ink-bottle on this desk...a photograph taken now of the top of the desk should clearly show all of the objects on it except the ink-bottle.[7]

Now, however (nearly) certain one may be that some or all of these sequences will not occur, that is of course not the same thing as being (at all) certain that there is an ink-bottle before one. But, though there are many differences between the two, perhaps the one which should most clearly be focused on is this: If one is really certain of the ink-bottle, and not just of other things however related, then one's attitude is that *even if one should* seem to find oneself in *a* contrary garden, one

---

7. *Ibid.*, p. 67. The introductory clause "Insofar as I care about being right about...." is left out by Malcolm. I think it may be necessary for ruling out certain counterexamples concerning untoward motivations. As it plays no important part in our argument however, I will leave it out from now on.

*would disregard* this experience as irrelevant to the question of whether, at the time in question, there is or was an ink-bottle before one. One might resist this characterization, but then, I think, one would lose one's proper focus on what it is of which one is certain.

Here is a line of resistance to our characterization of being certain. Suppose, in contrast, one's attitudes were these: *If* strange things seemed to happen, then perhaps I would change my mind, I just might. But, I am absolutely certain that no strange things will ever happen to speak against there being an ink-bottle. Might not these attitudes be those of a man who was *absolutely* certain that *there is an ink-bottle before him*? Might not he be certain of the ink-bottle, not in or by having a completely exclusionary attitude on that matter itself but, rather, indirectly, so to speak, in or by having just such an attitude toward the possibility of apparently contrary appearances?[8]

This suggestion, this line of resistance, is an interesting one, but it is neither correct nor of any use even if it were correct. First, let us notice that *at least almost* invariably when one is even very close to being absolutely certain of something, one is not nearly so certain that no contrary appearances will turn up. For example, you may be quite sure that I am married. But, you will not be quite so sure that no appearances to the contrary might show up: I may be married but say to you "No, I'm not really married. Mary and I don't believe in such institutions. We only sent out announcements to see the effect—and it's easier to have most people believe that we are." I might, at a certain point, say these things to you and get a few other people to say apparently confirmatory things. All of this, and some more if need be, should and would, I think incline you to be at least a bit less certain that I am married. Thus, at least with things where one is *quite* certain, the matter seems to be quite the *opposite* of what was suggested: One will not be so certain that nothing strangely contradictory will turn up—but one will be inclined to reject any such thing even if it does turn up. We may plausibly project that things work quite the same in situations where someone is absolutely certain (if there really are any such).[9]

Let us now take something of which you are as certain as anything, say, that one and one are two. Suppose that you are very sure that your favorite mathematician will never say something false to you about any

---

8. Some such line of resistance was suggested to me by Gilbert Harman and also by Michael Lockwood.

9. I owe to Saul Kripke the idea that these observations are important to consider for such matters.

simple sum. Imagine that he, or God, tells you and insists that one and one are three, and not two. If your attitude is that he is still to be trusted or, at least, that you would no longer be quite so sure of the sum, then you are not absolutely certain that one and one are two. If you think you *are absolutely certain* of this sum, then, I submit, you should think also that your attitude will be to reject entirely the message from the mathematician or God. In this simple arithmetical matter, you are to give it, perhaps unlike other messages from the same source, no weight at all in your thinking. It seems, then, that this line of resistance is not faithful to the idea of being certain of a particular thing. But would it be of any use in countering skepticism, or the skeptic's charge of dogmatism, even if it were right?

It seems to me that it is at least as dogmatic to have the position that it is absolutely certain that nothing will ever even appear to speak against one's position than to have the attitude that any such appearances which might show up should be entirely rejected. What about appearances to the effect that some contrary appearances, their precise nature left open as yet, are likely to show up in the future? If one is absolutely certain that the latter sort of appearances won't ever show up, one would, presumably, have the attitude of rejecting entirely the indication of the former appearances. One's attitude of rejection gets pushed farther back from the matter itself. Perhaps, on our line of resistance, this may go on indefinitely. But each retreat, and the consequent new place for rejection, only makes a man look more and more obvious in his dogmatism and unreasonableness about the whole affair. Even going back no farther than the second level, so to speak, only a quite foolhardy man would, it seems to me, reject out of hand any suggestion that some things might be brought forth to speak against his position. If anything, it is better for him to allow that they may and to be ready to reject them. So, even if our line of resistance had presented us with a case of being certain, the "indirect" way of being certain would hardly help us to avoid the skeptical charge. That is quite surely no way for being perfectly certain to be perfectly all right.

It is important to stress very hard that a clause like 'I should regard nothing as evidence that there is no ink-bottle now' must be regarded as the expression of a man's *current attitude*, and not as any prediction of what he will do under certain future circumstances.[10] Thus, one may allow that a sentence like the following is indeed consistent: "He is

---

10. In a footnote on p. 68 of "Knowledge and Belief", Malcolm says that he doesn't think the word 'attitude' is very satisfactory. He would rather put things, he says there, in

absolutely *certain* that there are automobiles, but he *may* change his mind should certain evidence come up". That is because even if his present attitude is that he will not, things may not happen in accordance with his attitude. For example, things might happen to him which *cause* him to become uncertain. Or, his attitude might just evaporate, so to speak, the new evidence then effecting him in the unwanted way; and so on. Such conditions as these give us a consistent interpretation for the foregoing sentence, even if not a very ordinary one. A sentence which will always express an inconsistency, on the other hand, is obtained once we make sure that our severely negative clause is embedded so that it is clear that the man's current attitude is the point. Thus, in contrast with the foregoing, it is always inconsistent to say "He is absolutely *certain* that there are automobiles, but *his attitude* is that he *may* change his mind should certain evidence come up". A proper assessment of the direct linguistic evidence supports the idea that the attitude of certainty is thus absolutely severe.

This direct linguistic evidence cannot be enough to satisfy one that being certain, or the attitude in knowing, demands so much as we claim. And, it is not enough to add the indirect evidence from antiskeptical authors. What we want is to fit a severe characterization of this attitude into some more general account of things. Toward this end, I now recall my account of absolute terms.[11] On this account, *absolute adjectives* like 'flat', 'useless' and 'certain' purport to denote a limiting state or situation to which things may approximate more or less closely. Thus, in the case of these adjectives, the modifier 'absolutely', as well as 'completely' and 'perfectly', is redundant apart from points of emphasis. Now, various locutions with 'certain' may appear to indicate matters of degree. But they will always admit of a paraphrase where this appearance is dispelled in favor of a more explicit reference to an *absolute limit*: "That's pretty certain" goes into "That's pretty *close to being absolutely* certain"; "He is more certain of this than of that" goes into "He is *absolutely* certain of this but not of that or else he is *closer*

---

terms of some conditional statements about what he would say or think right now if or when he imagines things now as happening. But, actually, this latter suggestion is much the poorer and, indeed, Malcolm's choice of the word 'attitude' is quite apt and satisfactory.

11. Peter Unger, "A Defense of Skepticism", *The Philosophical Review*, Vol. LXXX, No. 2, (April, 1971), Sections II–IV. In a later issue of this journal, James Cargile replied to the skeptical suggestions in that paper of mine: "In Reply to a Defense of Skepticism", *The Philosophical Review*, Vol. LXXXI, No. 2, (April, 1972). Perhaps the present paper may be taken as deepening the debate between myself and this critic in a way that would not be possible in a brief and direct rejoinder on my part.

*to being absolutely* certain of this than of that", and so on. None of this is peculiar to 'certain'; the same happens with locutions containing other absolute adjectives. Thus, these sentences seem to denote matters of degree, but their paraphrases dispel the illusory appearance: "That's the flattest (most useless) thing I've ever seen" goes into "That's the only *absolutely* flat (useless) thing I've ever seen or else that's *closer to being absolutely* flat (useless) than anything else I've seen". In light of these paraphrases, we may repose some confidence in the following formula as saying what it is for something to be x where that is the same as being absolutely x: Something or someone is x (flat, useless, certain, etc.) just in case nothing *could possibly* ever be more x, or x-er, than that thing or person is right now. It is in this strict sense, then, that being certain, and a *fortiori* being absolutely certain, is being at an absolute limit. Now, absolute adjectives typically have contrasting terms which are *relative adjectives*: 'certain' has 'confident' and 'doubtful', 'flat' has 'bumpy' and 'curved', 'useless' has 'useful' and 'serviceable', and so on. Because matters of degree *are* concerned, there is nothing which is deceptive about the locutions with *these* terms: The sentence "He is pretty confident" does not go into the apparently senseless ?? "He is pretty close to being absolutely confident"; nor does "That is very useful" go into ?? "That is very close to being absolutely useful". These relative terms really do denote matters of degree and not any state or situation which is an absolute limit. If something is bumpy, it is *not* true that nothing could possibly be more bumpy or bumpier. And if someone is confident of something, it does not follow that no one could ever be more confident. Now, a necessary condition for the correct application of an absolute adjective is, at least generally, that certain things denoted by relative adjectives be entirely absent. Thus, it is a necessary condition of something's being flat that it be *not at all* bumpy, that is, that bumpiness not be present even in the least degree. Also, it is a necessary condition of being flat that the thing be *not at all* curved, or that curvature or curvedness not be present at all. We might expect the same sort of thing to hold in the case of someone's being certain of something, and indeed it does: If someone is certain of something, then that thing is *not at all* doubtful so far as he is concerned, that is, doubt or doubtfulness is not present at all in that man with respect to that thing. I have already argued this before, but there are other things which must also be entirely absent if a man is to be certain, though their absence may be included, I suggest, in the absence of all doubt.

One thing which must be entirely absent, and which is, I think, implicit in the absence of all doubt, is this: any *openness* on the part of the man to consider new experience or information as seriously relevant to the truth or falsity of the thing. In other words, if S is certain that $p$, then it follows that S is *not at all* open to consider any new experience or information as relevant to his thinking in the matter of whether $p$. Of course, our saying that the complete absence of openness is a necessary condition of personal certainty by no means commits us to the idea that it is a sufficient condition. Indeed, it is not. Someone may be fixedly attached to a proposition even if he is not certain of it. He might, for example, refuse ever to reconsider his belief in it even though, in any circumstances of choice, there will be other propositions on whose truth he would prefer to risk inferences, actions, goals and goods. Indeed, another necessary condition of being certain of something is, at least roughly this, that one is not at all hesitant or reluctant to risk what he deems valuable or of worth on the truth of that thing. I say, 'at least roughly', because one might have an adversion, moral, aesthetic, religious or otherwise, to risking anything, or to risking too much, or to risking too much on certain sorts of propositions. This might cause one to be somewhat hesitant or reluctant to take the called for risk despite one's being absolutely certain of the thing involved. But the complete absence of reluctance will still be a condition for certainty, provided that it is suitably relativized to the entire outlook of the person in question.[12] Accordingly, in parallel with our condition of no openness, this condition will be necessary but not sufficient: One might be entirely willing to risk everything on the truth of a certain proposition and yet be willing to abandon it, or at least risk much less on it, should even rather slight experience to the contrary present itself.

One may liken these two conditions to the two independently necessary conditions of being flat which we mentioned earlier, namely, being not at all curved and being not at all bumpy. In the case of being flat, we deal with matters which we may picture. So, there we may get pictures of the different ways things may meet a necessary condition and yet fail to be flat. Here, then, is a view of a surface which, while not at all bumpy, is not flat:

---

12. A vivid characterization and illustration of this necessary condition of being certain, involving both himself and his wife, is given by Harry G. Frankfurt in "Philosophical Certainty" *The Philosophical Review*, Vol. LXXI, No. 3 (July, 1962), sections IV and V. The main difference here between Frankfurt and myself is that he thinks this complete willingness to risk is not implied by a meaning of 'certain' or even 'absolutely certain' but is only a philosopher's idea; which deserves a new expression, 'philosophically certain'. My own view of course is that no new expression is needed here.

 (Infinite smooth hyperbola)

The problem with this surface is that it is curved, though perhaps ever so slightly or gently so. On the other hand, we may have a surface which is not at all curved (though some technical usages might call it so), but which fails to be flat for failing to be not at all bumpy:

 (Right-angled sawtooth)

(Of course, things which are not surfaces and which have none may meet both of these necessary conditions while easily failing to be flat. Thus, numbers and treaties are not at all bumpy and not at all curved, but neither are they flat.) In the case of being certain, we do not of course have the aid of pictorial representation. We cannot use our eyes or our mind's eye to see how being not at all open differs from being not at all hesitant to risk. But, we may understand that the logical relation of these two being certain is just the same as that of pictorially understood conditions to being flat. (Again, other things, like stones, may easily fail to be certain of something though they are not at all open and not at all hesitant in the relevant respects. This parallels a number's meeting the necessary conditions but failing to be flat. The parallel holds because in both cases the conditions are just negative ones.)

It should be quite clear from this discussion that we do not identify being certain with being not at all open to new experience, or even to what we may call the attitude of certainty. Rather, we only claim that the latter is a *necessary* condition of one's being certain, or a logically *essential* feature of one's personal certainty in a matter. It is in just this way that the attitude described by Malcolm and Hintikka fits into our general account of absolute terms. But, of course, it is just in this way that the attitude they describe is needed for our skeptical argument.

## 5. Why Is There Always Something Wrong with Having This Absolute Attitude?

At the beginning of his brilliant paper, "Certainty", G. E. Moore, perhaps the most influential opponent of skepticism in this century, makes some assertions and, as he points out, does so in a very positive and definite way. In just this way, he says, for example, that he had clothes on and was not absolutely naked. Moore goes on to note that although he did not expressly *say* of the things which he asserted that he *knew* them to be true, he implied as much by asserting them in the way he did. His words are these:

> .... I *implied* ... that I myself knew for certain, in each case, that what I asserted to be the case was, at the time I asserted it, in fact the case. And I do not think that I can be justly accused of dogmatism or overconfidence for having asserted these things positively in the way that I did. In the case of some kinds of assertions, and under some circumstances, a man can be justly accused of dogmatism for asserting something positively. But in the case of assertions such as I made, made under the circumstances under which I made them, the charge would be absurd.[13]

I think that we may take it that, according to Moore, the reason he could not so be accused is that he was *not* dogmatic here. And the reason for that is that he *knew* these things, e.g., that he was not naked, so that he was *justified* in being absolutely *certain* of them. And, so, in those innocuous circumstances of speech, he was justified in acting out of, or in accord with, his position or attitude of personal certainty. Moore was saying, in effect, that one could have this by now familiarly characterized attitude without any pain of being at all dogmatic in the matter: That no new experience or information will have any effect at all on one's thinking in the matter at hand, in this case, in the matter of whether at the then present time one is absolutely naked or not. Moore's position here is, then, quite of a piece with Malcolm's thought that it is *not at all unreasonable* of him to allow nothing to count as contrary evidence in the matter of whether an ink-bottle is before him. But Moore's point is more particular than Malcolm's, for he notes the *particular way* in which one who is certain might be thought to be unreasonable, or not justified, in his attitude: He might be thought to be such *in that* he is *dogmatic* in the matter. Moore similarly foreshadows, while focusing more clearly on the form of the opposite view, Hintikka's implication that in many matters one is *justified* in disregarding any further information: In situations where one knows, Moore says or implies, one is not at all dogmatic in having just such an absolutely negative position or attitude. It seems, then, that Moore was more sensitive than these other authors to the possibility that *dogmatism* might (almost) always be charged of one who was absolutely certain, even when he might rather plausibly claim to know. Now, it strikes me as oddly unfortunate, in a way, that others who actually spelled out

---

13. Moore, *loc. cit.*

what was involved in being certain, were not so sensitive to this particular charge. For it is, I think, precisely the feature they spell out which makes the charge of dogmatism live and convincing. By the same token however, it is to Moore's credit that, without articulating the key idea, he was able to sense the charge of *dogmatism* as a particular threat to his position, perhaps as the key one. Indeed, in the three full sentences I quoted, he refers to this charge as many times. We may put the substantial question, then, in these words: Was Moore referring to a charge of some real substance, or was he right in contending that (because he knew) there was really nothing to be feared?

Controversy being what it is, dogmatism is most often associated with questions or matters where there does not seem to be a clear-cut answer either way. For example, someone might commonly be called dogmatic about whether some form of socialism is the most efficient form of government for the economic growth of a certain country now. Or one might well be called dogmatic about whether the old-time baseball stars were better hitters than their modern counterparts. Perhaps, one might be recognizably dogmatic in the matter of whether Germany would have been defeated eventually had the United States not entered World War II. During a discussion of such matters as these, people commonly refuse to be moved *at all* by apparently forceful evidence for the other side; instead, they belittle that evidence as misleading or irrelevant. It is at these times that we say people are just being dogmatic and that, if they continue to have such an attitude, there can be no point in discussing the matter with them.

People may, of course, be more or less dogmatic in various matters: The more dogmatic someone is, the less the evidence he would admit as relevant and possibly damaging. When *nothing* is allowed to count, the person is completely dogmatic about the matter. Now, it may be that some people who are dogmatic, even completely dogmatic, about a certain thing are not absolutely certain of that thing. Perhaps they would not bet so much on its truth; perhaps they would not be so ready to draw inferences from it, and so on. Thus, their exclusionary attitude toward new experience is not on a par with certain other things, as it might be in cases where matters seem clear-cut, e.g., where the matter is whether one is absolutely naked, or whether there is an inkbottle before one. This may make people's dogmatism more obvious in controversial cases than in clear-cut ones. There are a number of reasons for this, some themselves quite obvious and some not quite so obvious. In apparently clear-cut cases, there is, first of all, likely to be no disagreement on the matter, so no one is apt to question anyone else's view in the matter. But, more than that, each person is likely to be at least quite close to being perfectly certain of his position, at least if he has about as much experience or involvement in the matter as other parties present. So, no one is apt to question either the degree of strength of anyone's position, since anyone else's is quite close on that score to his own. These are quite obvious reasons for there being no apparent dogmatism in matters where things appear to be certain, e.g., where people agree that it is quite plain that there is a rug on the floor where they are standing. But, here are some reasons which, though less obvious, may operate as well. In the first place, it may be that in many matters which seem certain, people are not really absolutely certain of things. This is what I suggested before, in preparing the way for skepticism.[14] If this is correct then, as people will not be absolutely certain even, e.g., that there is a rug on the floor, any dogmatic feature of being certain will not be there to be noticed even in such cases, and so for this most elementary reason must of course not be noticed. All that will be noticed then might be everyone's agreement in the matter. But if this is not so and people are certain, there will be further factors unobviously masking possible dogmatism anyway. And these may be at work as well when people are quite close to being absolutely certain of something. Whether people are perfectly certain or only nearly so, the sorts of experiences which might be pertinent to their becoming less certain, whether in actuality or only in description, are not likely to present themselves. They will likely range from very unusual to utterly bizarre. Thus, tests for spotting too great an adherence on someone's part, that is, too exclusionary an attitude to contrary experience, are not likely to arise in such matters. With people being thus untested, any dogmatic feature on this score will go unnoticed in the normal course of life and conversation.

Still another reason for the masking of dogmatism here might be the lack of a relevant inconsistency in such matters. This is suggested from our previous discussion, where we saw that personal certainty has several independent necessary conditions or, so to speak, essential dimensions. In a controversial case, the following sort of inconsistency often arises: a man who is very exclusionary in his attitude regarding a particular proposition may, at the same time, not be so willing to risk stakes or base inferences in it as on several other less controversial propositions. In other words, in such matters, people often are not even very close to being certain—mainly, at least, for failing to be close along dimensions other than the one of tenacity. Thus, their tenacity in

---

14. Unger, *op. cit.*, sec. IV.

debate or discussion bespeaks an inconsistency on their part which is unreasonable and, in a way at least, dogmatic. This sort of dogmatism will not be present when people are even very nearly certain, or at least it will never be obviously present then. For, in such cases, the disparity involved will be, of analytic necessity, nothing or very small. Thus, in apparently clear-cut cases, it may be that the only way that one might be thought dogmatic is through the appreciation of an overly exclusionary attitude. No significant inconsistency, at any rate, is likely to bring such a charge.

There are quite enough reasons, for our not noticing dogmatism in cases where matters are, not controversial but, clear-cut. Accordingly, we should suspect that in quite clear-cut cases, one might well be at least very nearly certain of something and dogmatic for having too exclusionary an attitude in the case. For one's dogmatic feature is not likely to be brought to one's attention. In consequence, we ought to be careful to guard against being prejudiced against the possibility that in apparently clear-cut cases people may often be dogmatic.

We may now, I think, more fairly assess the question of whether in cases where one is absolutely certain, supposing there are any such, one's attitude is dogmatic at least in some degree. In such a case, there may be no relevant inconsistency, there being no disparity between one's tenacity and willingness to risk and infer. And, it may well be that no one will ever disagree with one, or even be much less certain of the thing. For, when one is absolutely certain, as we are supposing, the matter is likely to be clear-cut. But, even if nothing rubs the wrong way, from within oneself or without, one's attitude in the matter is this: I will not allow *anything at all* to count as evidence against my present view in the matter. The case being clear-cut, this attitude will cause one no trouble nor bring any challenge. But, what is one to think of it anyway, even if no penalty or embarrassment is liable ever to occur. I think that any reflection at all makes it pretty plain that, no matter how certain things may seem, *this* attitude is always dogmatic and one who has it will always be open to that charge even if circumstances mean that he will never be exposed to it.

Now, in order to see more clearly why, even in the apparently most clear-cut and certain matters, there is something wrong with letting nothing count against one's being right, it will *help* to describe some sequences of experience. I do *not* think that such an appreciation of detail is really necessary to gaining conviction that the attitude of certainty is always dogmatic and, providing there are no other considerations in its favor, to be foregone in favor of a more open minded position. One must favor such an attitude in any case, no matter how certain something seems and no matter how little one is able to imagine what experiences there might be which, should they ever occur, one had best consider seriously and not just disregard. This is the right view in the matter however poor our own imaginations might be. But, the strength of habits to the contrary being so great, it will be a big help if we can succeed in imagining sequences of experience which seem to cry out for serious thought. Even in the cases of things which at first seem quite certain, then, and beyond any possibility of questioning at all, I will strive to be of service by imagining experiences. These described experiences should help one grasp firmly the idea that the attitude of certainty is always dogmatic.

## 6. Helpful Experiences for Rejecting the Attitude of Certainty

In quoting Malcolm's meditations on himself and his ink-bottle, we looked at some sequences of experiences which, if they occurred, might rightly be considered to have some weight and, accordingly, result in one's not being quite so certain as before that there is or was an ink-bottle before one. Malcolm says he wouldn't take those experiences as relevant here, that that is his attitude and that all of that is perfectly all right. I would disagree. But, in any event, it seems that one can easily imagine experiences which are more telling in this regard. And, also, with only more difficulty, one can imagine others which are easily more telling.

In respect of the matter of that ink-bottle, there are, it seems to me, all sorts of possible experiences which might cast some doubt. For example, one may be approached by government officials who seem to demonstrate that the object on one's desk is a container of a material to poison the water supply, which somehow found its way out of government hands and into one's home. It was disguised to look like an ink-bottle, but it is seen to have many small structural features essential to such a container of poison but which no ink-bottles have. One might well think, then, that though this object holds ink it is not an ink-bottle but, rather is something else. Perhaps, then, there never was *an ink-bottle* before one, but only some such other object. It seems, at any rate, that such an experience as this should not be disregarded out of hand no matter what one eventually should come to think about whether an ink-bottle was before one. An attitude which would thus disregard it seems, then, to be a dogmatic one.

The experience just described is, I suppose, less than completely convincing. And, even if it is admitted that the experience does have some weight, it seems easy enough to retreat to other statements which are not thus susceptible to experimental challenge. For example, one may be, instead, absolutely certain that there is before one something which looks like an ink-bottle, or that there is something with a circular top, or whatever the favored things turn out to be. Though the sort of experience just imagined might go against one's being certain that *an ink-bottle* is before one, such a sequence of experience will not go against one's certainty about many other things: that there are automobiles, that there have been automobiles for quite some time now, and that one is not now absolutely naked. To get a more completely convincing case about one ink-bottle, and to begin to get a convincing case for these less susceptible things, one's imagination must work more radically. Descartes was quite well aware of the problem when he imagined his evil demon. We may do well to follow suit, though in a more modern and scientific vein.[15]

I begin to imagine a more radical sequence of experience by supposing myself to experience a voice, coming from no definite location, which tells me this, in no uncertain terms: All the experiences I am having, including that of the voice, are artificially induced. Indeed, this has been going on for all of my conscious life and it will continue to do so. The voice tells me of various experiences I have had, some of which I had myself forgotten almost entirely. It then says that scientists accomplish all of this with me; it seems to tell me what they are like, what I am really like and, in great detail, how they manage to bring about these effects in me. To make its case most convincing, the voice says what experiences I will next have, and next after that and, then, after that. First, I will seem to fly off the face of the earth to a planet where the inhabitants worship me because I have only one mouth. After that, I am to come back to earth and seem to find that I have been elected Secretary-Treasurer of the International Brotherhood of Electricians. Finally, if that is not preposterous enough, I will seem to open up my body and find myself stuffed with fried shrimps, even unto the inner reaches of my thighs. Miraculously enough, I experience just these to happen. The experiences are not as in a dream but indistinguishable from what I call the most ordinary waking

---

15. For a rather different but quite congenial description of unsettling experiences, see Edward Erwin's "The Confirmation Machine", in *Boston Studies in the Philosophy of Science*, Vol. VIII, Roger C. Buck and Robert S. Cohen, eds.

experiences—except, of course, for the extraordinary content. Nor does this predicted sequence seem to take place in a flash, or in any very brief interval. To mirror what I take as reality, it seems to take a couple of months. After a convincing talk with the voice at the end of this experiential journey, I am left in a blue homogenous field of visual experience, feeling little but wonder, to think over whether an inkbottle was ever before me, whether there are now or ever were any automobiles, and so on. Of course, the voice has told me that none of these things ever were, and told me why I thought otherwise. What am I to think now?

My attitude toward these imagined experiences is that if they should occur I would be at least somewhat less certain than I now am about these matters. I would be at least somewhat unconfident, even, that I was not naked at the time in question. This is my present attitude. If things would not develop in accord with it, that would be something I can now only hope will not happen. Moreover, I think it pretty plain that this is the attitude which I ought to have and that anyone who held an opposite one would have a dogmatic attitude in these matters. That is, if one's attitude is that these experiences will not be counted as having any weight at all, one would be dogmatic in these matters.

Now, some people might have the attitude that if these experiences occurred one should think himself to be quite mad or, at least, to have had his capacity for judgement impaired in some damaging way.[16] My own attitude is more open than this. But it should be pointed out that even this attitude of prospective self-defeat is quite compatible with that of lessening one's confidence. One's total attitude, that is, might be that if the imagined experiences really came to pass one would both be less certain that there ever were automobiles and also be inclined to think that one must have become quite mad. All that I am claiming or need to claim is that one ought to have at least the first part of this total attitude or, more precisely, that one ought not to have the opposite attitude that any such experiences will be completely disregarded.

It is easy to suppose that I am claiming quite a lot for these imagined experiences no matter how hard I try to make it clear that all I claim is rather little. One might suppose that, according to what I am saying, if the appropriate experiences turned up one ought to believe

---

16. Malcolm suggests this sort of view in his lecture "Memory and The Past", *Knowledge and Certainty*, p. 201. He considers it in a somewhat different context, being most concerned there with the proposition that the earth has existed for no more than five minutes. I will treat such propositions as that in the section following this one. My thoughts on this view owe something to conversation with Michael Slote.

the opposite of what now seems to one to be absolutely certain—or that the proper attitude is one to this effect. But I am, in fact, saying no such thing. All I am saying is that one's attitude should be that one will be less certain of those things than one formerly was. If one is now just as certain that there are automobiles as that ten and ten are twenty, then towards the experience of our voice denying the first while affirming the second one's attitude ought to be that a difference will emerge: one will then be less certain that there are or were automobiles than that ten and ten are twenty. At least this much must be admitted, I think, even if one may properly be set never actually to believe that there are no automobiles. Again, one might suppose that I have it that one must be prepared, in the face of such experiences, to abandon one's position or view in, say, the matter of automobiles. But I am not saying even this. One might just as well, so far as what I say goes, continue to believe that there are automobiles. That one's attitude should be to this effect might be quite all right according to my argument here. What is not all right, I say, is to hold it *as certainly as ever* that there are automobiles. Now, my *own* attitude is that should such experiences as these actually occur and persist, I *would* consider my present experiences to be an induced illusion, just as the voice would say. And I would *believe* the opposite of what now seems so certain to me. I think that there is nothing wrong with this attitude and I suspect that there is something wrong with any which is grossly incompatible with it. These points will, however, strike some as being rather more controversial. It is for this reason that I have taken pains to put forward a much weaker and, I think, quite uncontroversial claim about attitudes toward experiences. And, for just this reason, I have been careful to point out the difference between this safer claim and these others which I also believe to be true. Since only the safer claim is needed to establish that the attitude of certainty is, even in these simple matters, dogmatic, it is hard to deny that this attitude is indeed just that.

## 7. Helpful Experiences for the Hardest Cases

In respect of almost any matter, the possibility of certain imagined sequences of experience makes quite a convincing case that one ought not, on pain of dogmatism, have the attitude of absolute certainty. There are, however, two sorts of matters where something more must be said to explain how such experience might help us to appreciate the wrongness of this severe attitude. I treat them in turn, proceeding from the less to the more difficult.

The first and lesser difficulty concerns certain sorts of matters about the past. The most famous of these due to Russell,[17] is the matter of whether the world sprang into existence five minutes ago. But the matter of whether oneself has existed for more than a brief moment will pose the problem more clearly so far as sequences of convincing experiences are concerned. The problem may be put like this: If any sequence of experience is to be convincing, it must itself endure for much more than a brief moment. Even in advance of any experiences which might look to show that one has been in existence only for a brief moment, one can and ought to appreciate this fact about the conditions of convincing. Therefore, it is in any case quite all right to have the attitude that no possible experience will be counted as convincing evidence for the claim that one has existed only for a brief moment. Rather, one may disregard any new experience which purports to be to this effect.

The difficulty with this reasoning is that it doesn't take into account how new experiences might make us view time differently. If our voice told us new things about time, we might not be able to disregard it without ourselves being dogmatic. Suppose that the voice says that one has been brought into existence only a brief moment ago complete with an accurate understanding of how long temporal intervals are. But one is also provided, the voice says, with an appealing consistent web of ostensible memories: to believe that one has experienced the things it seems to one that one has will be, then, only to believe what is false. Now, the recent experiences one indeed has had are, according to the voice, part of a sequence which has gone on only for a brief moment, a billionth of a second, to be quite precise. And, this includes these very messages that even now are coming to one. Though it seems to one that the experiences have been going on for some months, one has in fact been alive for only a brief moment and, indeed, the world of concrete things, including the source of the voice, has existed for less than a minute. In response to these vocal claims one might put forward some relativistic theory of time on which the claims would make no sense and, at any rate, on which they could not possibly be true. But, that would only be to adduce some theory. And, if there is anything scientific about science it is that one should never be too certain of any theory, no matter how beautiful, comprehensive and

---

17. Bertrand Russell, *The Analysis of Mind*, New York: The Macmillan Company, 1921, pp. 159–160.

powerful it may seem. So it seems that, no matter how one might wish to reply, one would do well to allow some influence for such a sequence of experience as the one just imagined. One should have the attitude, at least, that should it occur one will be not quite *so* certain, as one otherwise might be, that one has been alive for more than a brief moment.

The greatest difficulty in finding possible experience a help in abandoning the attitude of certainty comes, I think, in matters where we think that the only possible error must be a "purely verbal" one. This occurs, I take it, with matters of "immediate experience", e.g., with whether one is now experiencing phenomenal blueness or pain. And, it occurs with the "simplest matters of logical necessity", e.g., with whether two is the sum of one and one. Perhaps the most famous case, due to Descartes, is that concerning one's own present moment thinking and existence, e.g., whether one now exists. Now, some philosophers have found it quite an article of faith to suppose that there might be anything to answer to the word "I". They would think, I suppose, that what one ought to be sure of is that *something* now exists, leaving it quite open, what that thing might be. Even if it is true that in such matters as these, any error must be purely verbal, why shouldn't the possibility of just such an error make the attitude of absolute certainty dogmatic in these very matters? I have never heard anything to convince me of the opposite. It is said that what one believes or is certain of are propositions or, at least, some things that are too abstract to have uncertainty over words interfere with their status. Let us agree at the outset that we understand such attempts to downgrade the effect that words might have. But, nevertheless, ought not the following story about possible experience cause at least some very small doubts to enter one's mind? Again, we have our voice. After going through the sequence of experiences I described before, the voice tells me that I become easily confused about the meanings of certain terms. It says that on occasions, and now is one of them, I confuse the meaning of "exist", a word which means, roughly, "to continue on in the face of obstacles", with the meaning of "persist", a word which, roughly shares a meaning with the verb "to be". Consequently, in philosophizing, I often say to myself "I exist" and "It seems certain to me that I *exist* now". And, I then seem to remember that I have never thought otherwise. But, in fact, of course, I am quite a changeable fellow and, so I rarely if ever *exist*. It is true that I *persist*, as everyone does, and I *should* say *this* when I do that philosophizing. No doubt, I will soon change once again and say and think, rightly, that what I do is persist. This will then seem certain to me, which is better than it's seeming certain to me that what I do is exist, since at least the former is something which is *true*. But, it would be far better still if *neither* ever even *seemed* to be absolutely certain. At the very least, the voice concludes, I ought never to *be* certain of these things, no matter how tempting that might be. This is especially true in my case because I am so changeable and, as a consequence, so often and so easily confused.

I have no doubt that many would want to protest to this voice. Some might say that the matter of whether the words "I exist now" express a truth and that of whether I exist now are two utterly different matters. Now, it is very true that these matters are very different. But, why should that lead anyone to protest what I am saying? What I am saying is just that under certain conditions of experience one ought to become less certain than before that one indeed *exists*, that one thing one does is exist. Indeed, one may be in just such an experiential situation even while being quite confident that the words "I exist now" do indeed express a truth. We may suppose, after all, that the voice tells one that one *does* continue on in the face of obstacles, and so one ought to be confident that one exists, as well as that one persists. Now, it *may* be that there is something deeply wrong with any of these vocal suggestions and, so, that one ought never to allow any to effect one's beliefs or attitudes even in the most minimal way. But I can't see how anyone can be absolutely certain that *this* is so. And, suppose that the *voice itself* went through all those matters with you and told you to rest assured that such verbal confusions can get you, and are now getting you, into error here. In that one might experience even this, so far as I can see, one's attitude in any of these matters ought not to be that of absolute certainty. Thus, one ought not, really, be absolutely certain that one now exists, or that something exists, or that one now feels pain, or whatever. Of course, the source of uncertainty we have just uncovered is present in matters which are not so apparently certain or simple. Thus, we may now appreciate a bit more fully why it is at least a bit dogmatic to be certain that there is an ink-bottle before one, that there ever are any automobiles, or that one has existed for more than a brief moment.

As I said earlier, these imagined sequences of experience are only meant to be a help in coming to the idea that being certain involves being dogmatic. Their role is to exemplify some situations where this feature of dogmatism might be brought out. I hope that the sequences I have described have been thus revealing and, so, convincing. But that they be so is hardly essential to making good our claim.

For even if the particular experience one is able to imagine does not seem to jeopardize some statement which seems quite certain, one shouldn't be *sure* that there isn't any such sequence—possibly, even one which a human imagination just can't grasp in advance. And, even if there is no sequence of *experience* which ought to make one less certain, *mightn't* there be some other factor information about which ought to give one pause? Perhaps, there are some currently obscure conceptual truths about the nature of thought and reason, which show how any thinking at all is parasitic on the possibility of error in the case. No matter how comfortable one feels in his philosophy and his view of the world, I can't see how he might properly be *certain* that there is no way that he could possibly be wrong. He cannot properly be certain that he has given a complete accounting of every sort of experience, evidence and information which might possibly exist. For this reason, if for no other, it will be dogmatic of him ever to have the attitude that he will disregard *any* new experience, evidence and information which runs counter to what he holds.

This is our case, then, that being certain involves being dogmatic and, so, that there is always at least *something* wrong with being certain. As we noticed, whatever is wrong with this dogmatism may be overridden by other considerations, considerations which are not properly epistemological ones. But, the fact that there is always some dogmatism, whether overridden or not, means that nobody ever knows anything about anything. In this sense, then, dogmatism is the opposite of skepticism, and the necessary presence of dogmatism means that skepticism is really true.

## 8. Some Concluding Remarks

Having argued for its premises at some length, there is not much left for me to say in support of our argument. As regards the first premise, one can keep checking for entailments that it would predict—especially when we conjoin it with our rigid condition for being certain: that one's attitude is that *nothing* will be allowed to change one's mind. Is it consistent to say, for example, "He regrets that he quit school, but his attitude is that he may yet change his mind about whether he did"? It seems that it is not. If that is right, then it speaks strongly for the idea that knowing entails having the attitude that nothing will change one's mind. And, given the purported value and justifying power of knowing, it speaks also for the idea that knowing entails that it's all right for one to have this attitude, providing that there are no overriding reasons to the contrary. So, we trade on no equivocation in our first premise—on some "weak sense" of 'certain' to get it accepted and some "strong sense" to get it to connect with the second. The evidence for accepting it in the first place itself connects with what serves to make the second premise acceptable.

As regards the second premise, one may be in sympathy with its spirit, but may think that it takes things too far. Philosophy has traditionally distinguished between statements about one's own present moment existence and experience, on the one hand, and on the other, statements about things further removed from one's momentary consciousness. It has also separated the simplest or most intuitive logical truths and those which might better be called derivative. One might feel that as regards statements of these first two classes there is no real possibility of error, and only some confused argumentation might look to show otherwise. If one takes this position, which is not an entirely implausible one, one may restrict our argument and, accordingly, accept the skeptical thesis in a restricted form. First, he may accept our first premise

(1q) If someone *knows* something to be so, then it is all right for the person to be absolutely certain that it is so providing only that no overriding (consideration or) considerations make it not all right,

for he has voiced no cause for denying it. And, then, he may restrict the matters on which the second will be taken to hold true. Let us call the statements which he favors, "statements of type x", and the correlative matters, "matters of type x". Thus, the statement that something now looks blue to one might be allowed as a statement of type x, and the matter of whether something now looks blue to one would then be a matter of type x. Our restrictor may then say that he thinks it quite all right for one to be certain that something is so, provided that it is in a matter of type x. But then he may accept this restriction of our second premise:

(2qR) In respect of any matter which is not of type x, it is *not* the case that it is all right for someone to be absolutely *certain* that something is so providing only that no overriding (consideration or) considerations make it all right.

From these two premises, he will deduce the correlatively restricted form of skepticism:

(3R)   In respect of any matter which is not of type x, nobody ever *knows* that anything is so.

Thus, we have a quite obvious refuge for one who thinks that some confusion must have come upon me when I claimed the attitude of certainty to be *everywhere* dogmatic. He need not abandon skepticism about knowledge entirely. All he need refuse is a small part of what that thesis claims. He will accept the idea that, while a few simple sorts of things might be known, almost all the sorts of things which people claim to know to be so are never really known by anyone at all.

My final passage must emphasize again that I have nowhere in this essay used any key terms, neither 'certain' nor 'know', in any special or technical or philosophical sense. I have used them in the ordinary sense of these words and, so far as I can discern, their *only* ordinary sense in the relevant sentences of philosophic interest. It is in virtue of certain shared aspects of their sense or meaning that these words do not allow for simple positive sentences which express anything true. Now, a fairly standard attitude for a philosopher to take at this last juncture is the one of being gracious in defeat toward the skeptic's empty victory: "I will give you the words 'know' and 'certain', and never use them in the sorts of sentences and claims to which you have objected. Nor will I ever believe any such to be true. But, this still allows me to say and think almost everything I formerly did, for hardly any of our statements or beliefs are, in fact about whether people know or are properly certain of things. So, though skepticism may be right, it need not have much consequence even so far as the truth or falsity of things goes, much less regarding practical problems. The victory of skepticism about knowledge is as unimportant as it is isolated." What are we to say to this response? We must agree with at least the last remarks, that insofar as it is isolated skepticism's victory is bound to lack much significance. But, our objector has produced no evidence that any such isolation must be accepted as a consequence of victory. Surely, nothing which we have said in skeptical argument entails as much and, indeed, some things, like our experience with 'regret' and 'happy' point quite the opposite way. We need not, then, acquiesce to this hopefully disarming agreement from the former dogmatist. On the contrary, we may look forward with open minds toward looking into the question of what consequences our newly won skepticism might have.[18] Perhaps, practical matters will not be much affected. But for those of us for whom truth matters, we may wonder at least that the consequences of skepticism might be quite material.[19]

18. I look into this question, or part of it, in the following two companion papers: "The Wages of Scepticism", *American Philosophical Quarterly*, Vol. 10, No. 3, (July, 1973) and "Two Types of Scepticism", (forthcoming in) *Philosophical Studies*.

19. The main points of this paper were presented as part of a Symposium entitled "Perception, Observation and Skepticism" on March 30, 1973 in Seattle, Washington to the Pacific Division of the American Philosophical Association. My fellow symposiasts were Gilbert Harman and William P. Alston. Switching gears, I would like to thank the many people who have conversed helpfully with me about the ideas of this paper, and to give special thanks to Gilbert Harman, Saul Kripke and Michael Slote for their very great assistance in that regard.

# 4

# SKEPTICISM AND NIHILISM

My main aim in this paper is to help foster a positive attitude toward a thesis of *radical nihilism.* According to this thesis, none of the things which, it seems, are most commonly alleged to exist do in fact exist: neither rocks nor stones, not tables nor chairs nor even people; perhaps most importantly, neither you nor I exist. The positive attitude toward this thesis is that it is worthy of serious consideration. The recommended attitude is that it should be seriously considered, at least, whether this thesis may not be perferable to its denial. Thus taken as a "working hypothesis", this attitude continues, the thesis may provide a first step to developing a more adequate way of thinking. To be sure, if we stay within our ordinary thinking, the nihilistic thesis means commitment to paradox for us. Thus the paradoxical character of some things just said. But that may mean no relevant refutation of the thesis, or of our arguments on its behalf. Rather, it might direct us to abandon common sense entirely, in our philosophical thinking. Perhaps new beginnings for understanding may then be sought so that such paradox may be properly avoided.

But problems of paradox, while offering a quick reply for some, will not be the main obstacle to nihilism. Rather, that obstacle will be a general trust of common sense. To undermine this trust, I shall develop a *complex of reasoning.* This complex will consist of *cycles of argument*: first, two quite specific ones and, finally, an entirely comprehensive cycle. Each cycle may be regarded as consisting of four steps; so regarded, what is distinctive in each cycle is its *first step*, for the cycles are otherwise quite the same. In each first step, there are offered dinstinctive arguments against one's own existence.

My first cycle begins with *sorites arguments* against myself. These are extensions of, or adaptations of, the original sorites argument of Eubulides, that is, the argument of the heap.[1] My second cycle begins with an *Argument from Invented Expressions*. There, I invent an expression which is, I think, quiet clearly an inconsistent one, whose inconsistency is revealed by the stepwise reasoning familiar from sorites arguments. So, the concocted expression applies to nothing, even while it may prove a very useful expression. But, so far as logical features go, the invented expression is quite on a par with ordinary terms, including "person". Hence, these too are inconsistent; there are no people; I do not exist.

Each cycle then proceeds as follows: while one may not be *very* convinced of the nihilistic reasonings offered in the first step, it is *not* that they are of *no* moment at all. Rather, in light of these arguments, it may be argued that there is no human person who now *knows for certain* that he exists. But then, there is no one who now knows *anything* for certain. Thus, the *second* step is a dependent epistemological argument for a skeptical thesis. Is this thesis a very interesting one? While it does go against trusted common sense, it may seem to do so only mildly. But, as I argue in my *third* step, that is not the case. In that we know nothing for certain, none of us now is *even the least bit reasonable in believing anything*. Our nihilistic arguments, it will be seen, indirectly yield a thesis of *radical skepticism*. It is the second aim of this paper to argue, in a somewhat novel fashion, for this second radical thesis, which of course is implied by, but does not imply, the thesis of radical nihilism.

While it does not imply our thesis of nihilism, our radical skepticism does imply that our common sense thinking is badly false and not nearly as good and true as it appears. Accordingly, as I shall note in my *fourth* step, our argument for radical skepticism undermines the chief and most persistent obstacle to nihilism. So, this forth step brings us full circle; a cycle is completed.

---

1. Apparently, there is no written work of Eubulides available. But scholars have attributed to him, in addition to the sorites, the discovery of the Liar, and what may be the first problems of intentionality and of presupposition. See [2]: 114 ff. For some recent research on Eubulides and the sorites, see [3]. It is my belief that this radical Megarian thinker was one of the greatest, and most neglected, philosophers in history; it is my hope that this present paper will do something to help rectify the matter.

## 1. A First Step for Nihilism: Adapting the Sorites

I begin by developing the first step of my first cycle. The arguments here, as remarked, derive from the original argument of the heap.

The argument of the heap, or the sorites, may be given in two main forms. As a *direct* argument, it goes like this. A single bean is not a heap. And, if you add a single bean to something which is not a heap, while making no other change in the situation, there will still be no heap, no matter how you place the new bean. Hence, no matter how many beans you thus place in a situation, and no matter how arranged, there will not be any heap there. But, if that is so, then there never are heaps at all, for any difference with other cases will not relevantly favor them. Therefore, there never are any heaps. As an *indirect* argument, it runs this way. If there are any heaps, then a million beans nicely arranged gives us a heap of beans. Let's suppose it does. Well, then, gently removing a peripheral bean will not mean the difference between having a heap there and having none. Hence, after sufficient removals, even with one bean, or none, we still have a heap of beans. But that is absurd. Therefore, there are no heaps. Discounting minor matters of formulation, it is hard to see how these arguments might fail of their purpose. Mightn't they be adequate, and our idea of a heap devoid of application? "Perhaps," you may say, "but how important is the thought, anyway, that heaps are genuine entities?" Problems quickly get more important, though, as we adapt the sorites to putative 'more cohesive' things.

Here is an indirect argument to deny alleged swizzle sticks, those supposedly popular swizzle stirrers. We note that the existential supposition:

(1) There is at least one swizzle stick,

is inconsistent with the propositions we mean to express as follows:

(2) if anything is a swizzle stick, then it consists of more than one atom, but of only a finite number.
(3) If anything is a swizzle stick, then the net removal from it of one atom, or only a few, in a manner most innocuous and favorable, will not mean the difference as to whether or not there is a swizzle stick there still.

Supposing (1) and (2), by (3) we get down below two atoms and still say that a swizzle stick is there. That contradicts (2). The only way to maintain both (2) and (3), while being consistent, is to deny existence for those sticks.

The reasoning may, of course, be presented in a wide variety of ways. Instead of an atom, we could have talked in terms of a speck of dust's worth of stuff, or a tiny visible chip. No matter how we put it, however, for our sorites to fail, it appears that a miracle must obtain. Perhaps the sticks may be saved through a *miracle of metaphysical illusion*. Here, even supposing that things proceed as gradually as nature allows, sharp breaks in nature, perhaps indicating the actions of suitable souls, might possibly serve to preserve our sticks. For examples: with even the most cooperative putative swizzle sticks, after seven small units are removed, it may be impossible to take away any more. Or, if not that, then taking away the next may see what remains suddenly crumble or disappear, no matter how gentle we are. Or, again, the removal of an atom may turn the whole business into a frog, or a spitoon. But we do not expect any such miracle. Our soullessly gradual world is most uncooperative here. (Moreover, even if there were such miracles, it would not seem to help our sticks exist. For a relevant counter-factual premise could then serve: if anything is a swizzle stick, then providing that things *were* to proceed gradually, the net removal from it of one atom *would* leave a swizzle stick there still.) It seems, then, that we must turn to our own words to save our sticks.

In this direction, we might hope for a *miracle of conceptual comprehension*. For this, we must suppose that, while nothing much seems to be going on, a single speck, and even a single atom, will take us from having a swizzle stick to having none. And presumably, such an atomic removal will occur when there are still *millions* of peripheral atoms to choose from, so that, assuming there are no replacements, *every one of them* is essential to our having a swizzle stick! But we do not believe that our expression "swizzle stick" is all *that* sensitive or discriminating. With an expression like "has a greatest thickness of at least one inch", we might expect such sensitivity, holding our problems there to be "only epistemological". But this apparent contrast only underscores the miracle needed by swizzle sticks.

Now, many people will only begin to comprehend what I am saying, and they will object that all of this just goes to show that "swizzle stick" is a vague expression, which may have been expected anyway. But if we look at the matter closely, it is even unclear in what sense my argument does show the expression to be vague. An argument of this sort will *not* work well against the existence of *physical objects*; for that a more complex sorites will be required, perhaps involving considerations of identity which my argument here does not employ. And so far as I can discern, there is no sorites which will work directly to refute the idea that some *entities* exist. But I should think that, in certain regards at least, "physical object" is more vague that "swizzle stick", and the term "entity" is still more vague than that. So, it is not simply vagueness upon which these apparently effective arguments turn.

Let us suppose, however, that we may distinguish a sense of "vague", or a kind of vagueness, suitable to demarcate the expressions, and thus there putative referents, to which sorites arguments may directly apply. Then noting such vagueness will do nothing whatever to rebut the arguments. Unless such a suggestion of vagueness proves the basis for a counter-argument, noting it is no more important than saying that "swizzle stick" is an expression consisting of two words, or noting that it has a certain etymology. But for there ever to be such a counter-argument, we have argued, it will require there to be our miracle of conceptual comprehension. As this latter is not to be expected, neither is any refutation of our reasoning to be expected from remarks about how certain expressions are vague.

Another common objection to our argument will be that we have overlooked the linguistic resources available to describe the *range* of cases beginning at one end with swizzle sticks, or even paradigm swizzle sticks, and gradually extending to the other, where we first find no swizzle sticks of any sort. In between, it might thus be objected, we find such items as broken swizzle sticks, parts of swizzle sticks, and so on. By overlooking these linguistic resources, and so these intermediary entities which they denote, we have made it appear that an implausible big jump will always be upon us. For when we ignore these resources, and so these cases they denote, it looks like we must move from cases where "swizzle stick" applies, at one end of a spectrum, to cases where there are no swizzle sticks at the other end. Or else it looks like we *treat* swizzles as *though* they are on one end, and things which are not swizzles as though they are on the other. But without overlooking things, no such jump can plausibly be claimed. And so, our sticks can be saved, along with broken swizzle sticks, parts of sticks, and all sorts of other things.

But this objection fails on various counts. In the first place, we may point out that each of these terms, to apply, either presupposes the application of "swizzle stick" or it does not. If it does, then the argument against swizzle sticks, with one obvious step added, argues as well that the new term has no application either, that the things it purports to denote do not exist. An example here would be "broken swizzle sticks": if there are no swizzle sticks, then, it follows, there are no broken ones. If, on the other hand, the candidate expression has no such requirement, then it is quite irrelevant to our question. For there might, then, be no swizzle sticks at all, but plenty of these other things around. Thus, they will *not* be *intermediary* entities, sufficient to establish a helpful *range* of cases. An example of this is "skinny plastic object". So far as the considered issues go, there might be plenty of skinny plastic objects but no swizzle sticks at all. Much to the same effect is this logical consideration: some candidate intermediary terms would stop our sorites argument only if they provided a range of cases where one could neither properly apply nor properly withhold "swizzle stick"; but there can be no such case as that, much less a range of such cases.

In the second place, we may notice that any of the candidates which give this objection even a shred of initial plausibility, are as susceptible to our sorites arguments as are our sticks. Consider, for example, a broken swizzle stick or, in contrast, a skinny plastic object. Either of these will consist of more than two atoms but of only a finite number, and in either case, the appropriate removal of a single peripheral atom will not mean the difference between having such an object there and having none. So, by familiar stepwise reasoning, in a parallel with our sorites against swizzle sticks, we may argue that there are no broken swizzle sticks, and no skinny plastic objects either. Of course, these parallel arguments are no better than our reasoning against the swizzle sticks themselves. But, then, they are no worse, which is here the relevant matter. For in this case, our sorites against swizzles, to prove inadequate, must encounter a better objection than this one from an alleged range of genuine intermediary cases.

Still another common objection is that our nihilistic reasoning appears sound, but only through my becoming involved in an "unwarranted use of classical logic". It is hard to know what this might coherently mean. But let us suppose that part of the intended message, whether actually coherent or not, is that some unusual new logic, perhaps with "suitable restrictions specified by it", is more appropriate to reasoning about such ordinary things as swizzle sticks, while classical logic, that pure, simple, unrestricted mode of reasoning, had best be used only in regard to such things as the precise mathematical properties of the natural numbers. My using "the wrong logic", then, has made it appear that one of our alleged miracles is required to preserve our sticks, while if one uses "the right logic", this appearance may be seen as illusory. But even if we allow these remarks to have coherence, which seems somewhat doubtful, they would seem to have no relevance to the matter at hand; the "new logic" would appear to affect the situation not one jot. For no matter "what logic we use", and no matter how complex a construction we tie to "swizzle stick", the whole business must be presumed to leave off at some definite point, atomically counted, and so neither before nor after it. Whether our chosen sentence, say, "There is a swizzle stick here", then goes from expressing a truth to expressing a falsity, or whether to expressing a statement with some exotic new value, say indefiniteness, or a numerical one, is all immaterial. Whether that sentence goes from expressing a truth to expressing no proper statement at all is not the issue either, and so on. Any such attempts at manipulation only serve to make the needed miracle look smaller, and further away; they no more decrease it than a "wrong-way" look through a telescope serves actually to reduce an object viewed through it. For at the other end of all the logical apparatus, an enormous sensitivity of "swizzle stick" must always be expected.

So far as the more obvious objections to it go, our argument against swizzle sticks looks to be adequate. And in this paper, where the main points concern the *relation of* such nihilistic arguments *to* skeptical reasonings in epistemology, the more esoteric, or far-fetched, objections to the sorites need not be discussed. In any case, many of them have been dealt with at length elsewhere,[2] and what space I might be fairly allotted here can be better used in ways more directly related to my present topic.

Accordingly, with the sorites pattern of reasoning in mind, let's now turn from swizzle sticks to human persons. To begin our new topic, I will advance a direct argument against their existence. To avoid speculative matters, let's consider the widely supposed biological development of a human person from a fertilized egg. Now, as a matter of fact, we may agree, (a) if any human person now does or ever did exist, then such an entity will have developed from a fertilized egg, and will have done so in less than fifty years. Now, (b) such an egg is not itself a human person. For, lacking the capacity for thought and experience, it is not a person of *any* sort. But (c) no such developmental process will exhibit a human person during one second and at least one during the next. As there will be no human person during the first second, there will be none after the next, nor the third, nor even after fifty years of development. Hence, (d) there aren't any human persons now, and there never have been any. For this argument substantially to fail, there must be some important change which occurs during a certain second, beside which all the other changes are trivial, for example, the sudden emergence of an incorporeal soul. The only other chance for

---

2. I deal with them in [5] at some length, and still more in [6]. Wheeler deals with various objections in [8].

failure, discounting formulational details, will be for our expression "human person" to be far more sensitive than we have any reason to suppose.

It should be clear that "time itself" is not important to this argument. Rather, given the very gradual nature of the alleged process under consideration, intervals of a second will divide the relevant differences, whatever they are, finely enough that it is quite implausible to suppose our expression, "human person", is up to making the required discrimination. (Of course, for those who might doubt this, shorter intervals will, given the nature of the process, yield still finer discriminations for our apparently gross locution to have to make: in any such real situation, how much that is relevant changes in a trillionth of a second?) In my argument, I am using units of time only as points of reference for finely dividing, or considering, the allegedly important processes. If cells got added one at a time, then we would have a realistic sorites with increments of a single cell; in a sense, that would be a somewhat more direct argument. But, as things don't really seem to happen that way, we employ our timely device.[3]

As my final topic in this section, I shall argue against my own existence. Two routes suggest themselves. On the first, we make use of the proceeding argument, adding only the premise that (e) if I exist, then I am a human person. As a factually true conditional, this premise would seem to be in pretty good shape; not so, then, myself. On the second route, we begin again and this time we focus on me throughout. For the first time now, we shall be employing the notion of identity in a sorites argument; with such powerful reasonings as these, it's just a logical luxury. On this luxurious route, we may employ an obvious version of the direct argument given for human persons. Instead, for variety's sake, I shall offer an indirect one, somewhat reminiscent of our experiences with swizzle sticks. I wish to reduce to an absurdity the statement:

(1) I exist.

To do so, we employ these two likely premises:

(2) If I exist, then I consist of many cells, more than ten of them, but of only a finite number.

---

3. In [1], Cargile seems to place great weight on time itself, and so to miss the point of such sorites arguments as we are now considering. Though his view of the sorites is, generally, quite different from mine, I think he has useful things to say on the irrelevance of various logical manoeuvers which some might try against sorites arguments:

(3) If I exist, then the net removal from me of a single cell, in a manner that would most tend to preserve me, will not mean the difference as to whether or not I exist.

Our previous discussion has familiarized us with the reasoning. The following short sketch will help clarify the import of the expression "in a manner that would most tend to preserve me". In so doing, I think, it will render the key premise, where that expression occurs, difficult to deny.

We do not want anything relevant to die soon in our removal process, or abruptly to lose an "important property", for that might provide a quick halt to our argument. Accordingly, we opportunely bring in life-support systems and devices to keep things going at "the highest level of functioning". *None* of these devices would be considered *replacements* for the cells in me; in certain other cases such a consideration might be apt, but not here. Here, the supports are no more integral to me than a cardiac pace-maker, or a kidney machine. Indeed, here, there is never any question of there being present *any* person composed largely or wholly of artificial parts. In all events, I may be placed in a nutrient bath, in which I remain as cells are peeled away. At a certain point, or so we say, there is a brain floating in a vat, later we are down to half a brain, then a third, then a quarter, and so on. Rather far along, we have but fourteen connected floating neurons, perhaps artificially allowed to fire away. Farther still, there's only one; finally, there's none. When did I cease to be? Can a single cell here mean the difference between me and no me? That's almost an affront to my dignity! But I'm not around at the end. So, I really wasn't there at the start.

Adapted sorites arguments seem to further a view of radical nihilism. But the hold of common sense is great. We suspend nihilistic judgment, then, and turn to consider the epistemological situation which these reasonings create.[4]

## 2. The Second Step: From Nihilism to Skepticism; Adapting the Evil Demon to the Sorites

So powerful is Eubulides' insight, I imagine, that we should look to the best of the modern era to provide fitting company for that ancient

---

4. In preparing the foregoing section, I have been helped by discussion and correspondence with David Lewis, and with David Sanford.

idea. Descartes' evil demon argument would seem to suit. In brief, my idea is to give the demon's place to relevant sorites arguments. For it appears that they might do better than the demon in undermining even the *cogito*, or any other thoughts as to one's own present existence.

The first thing to do in implementing this strategy is to put the Cartesian idea in a relevantly explicit form. I attempt this in my book, *Ignorance*; I think with some success ([4]: 7–24).[5] I'll now advance a somewhat simplified version of that attempt, for the simplification will be more useful than harmful to us now. Accordingly, we shall exhibit the Cartesian argument in two premises, the first of which I put with the conditional sentence:

(I) In respect of any suitable thing, say, that p, if someone knows for certain that p, then, either he already knows for certain that there is no evil demon who is deceiving him into falsely believing that p, or should he engage in suitable simple reasoning, he could come to know for certain that this is so.

Suppose our person doesn't yet know for certain that there is no demon doing that. Then, providing he knows that *p*, he can simply reason like this from what he knows for certain: since it is the case that p, it is *not false* that *p*. Thus, *no one* will *falsely* believe that p, myself included. Thus, *nobody*, the demon included, will deceive me, or anyone else, into believing *falsely* that p. So, there can be no evil demon who is doing *that* deception. By repeating this reasoning, and perhaps discussing it with others, our putative knower can make this premise exceedingly difficult to deny.

It remains for us now only to advance a suitable denial of the consequent of our exhibited premise. There will be little force toward accepting a denial which is universal in scope, concerning any conceivable matter, as Descartes himself recognized. For consider the matter of one's own present existence. Can a demon be deceiving you into falsely believing that you now exist? Suitable simple reasoning appears to show not: if there is such a deception, then you must exist, if only to believe that you do. But, then you cannot *falsely* believe that you do, for it is *not* false that you exist. So, there is no evil demon doing *this* deception. But, we may say, there are very few (sorts of) matters, by a

---

5. See [4]. In what follows, I shall have occasion to refer repeatedly to this work. As in this case, above, I shall cite the relevant portion of the work in the body of this paper, in brackets. Where this occurs in what follows I shall not bother to cite the book explicitly.

reasonable reckoning, for which such reasoning can do so much. And, thus, we may quite forcefully advance.

(II) In respect of all but a few matters as regards whether or not $p$, there is no one who knows for certain that there is no evil demon who is deceiving him into falsely believing that $p$, nor is there anyone who could, by simple reasoning, come to know for certain that this is so,

from which we may now deduce:

(III) In respect of all but a few matters as regards whether or not $p$, there is no one who knows for certain that $p$.

While it is not obvious that this Cartesian argument is an adequate one, it is pretty clear that it is at least quite compelling, and worthy of much serious thought. A large part of the business of *Ignorance* is to supply a good deal of that thought, and the upshot of it is that, with small qualifications, the argument is indeed an adequate one. But that business is not our business here. For what we now must do is adapt this evil demon argument to accomodate our nihilistic sorites reasoning.

Following this idea, a suitable first premise for our adaptation may be given by some such sentence as:

(I) In respect of any suitable thing, say, that $p$, if someone knows for certain that $p$, then, either he already knows for certain that any (putative) sorites argument to opposite effect fails of its purpose, or should he engage in suitable simple reasoning, he could come to know for certain that this is so.

There cannot, I believe, be any substantial objection to this conditional premise. For if the person does not already know for certain that the indicated arguments fail, what need he do? He need only reflect that as it is indeed the case that $p$, *any* considerations to opposite effect will fail of their purpose. Hence, in particular, sorites arguments to such an opposite effect will fail. This simple reasoning may be gone through several times, discussed with friends and so on. Eventually, it will be hard to maintain that the person may know for certain that $p$ and yet still fail to thus know that any opposing sorites is relevantly ineffectual. But I doubt that many would wish to deny this conditional premise.

The main thrust of our argument will generally, and I suppose quite rightly, be taken to come with our second premise, which is our only other one. It may be put with some such negatively assertive sentence as this:

(II) There is no human person who now knows for certain that all (putative) sorites arguments against his own alleged existence fail of their purpose, nor is there any who could now, by simple reasoning, come to know for certain that this is so.

With our apparently acceptable conditional proposition, (I), there can be little serious question that (II) suitably yields the skeptical conclusion:

(III) There is no human person who now knows for certain that he himself exists.

As many will wish to deny this conclusion, they will, presumably, wish to reject (II), our second premise. But given the arguments exhibited in our first section, how might that reasonably be done? Let us consider the matter.

This second premise denies that either of two situations obtains. But we need not think much about both. For we have already exhibited the simple reasoning which is most relevant. If *it* hasn't *already* gotten *us* to know for certain that all the relevant sorites fail, it's quite doubtful that *any* such simple reasoning will soon enable any human person to be in that happy position. Accordingly, our discussion may be quite safely limited to this simplifying question: "Is there any human person who now knows for certain that all relevant sorites arguments fail?" It seems almost certain to me that the answer here is "No".

For a relevant sorites argument to succeed, perhaps it need not establish that there is a true statement to the effect that the person in question does not exist. An appropriate sorites will, at first glance, have the look of such a demonstration. But a wider perspective may let us view the true import of such arguments to be more radical. In addition to allegations as to our own existence, these reasonings may undermine themselves: they may "indicate", incoherently but in a manner which is "psychologically adequate", that there are no currently available concepts or terms. Our very notions of language, word, sentence, statement, thought and argument may themselves all be suitably undermined. If this is how matters stand, as I am often inclined to think, then we may say that for such an argument "to succeed in its purpose", it need not be sound in the restricted sense of the logic texts. On the other hand, perhaps there are, apart from any questions of our existence, objectively existing notions of statement, argument, and so on and things which answer to them. If this be the case, our nihilistic reasonings will not have the undermining effect just mentioned. But, then, the direct arguments would appear to be quite strictly sound, and the indirect ones as good as any reductions to absurdity, though both leave the paradoxical situation that there are none of us to understand them. But then, we may say that, in *any* case, on *whatever* criterion is appropriate, our offered sorites arguments would not seem to fail of their purpose. And, more to the present point, who *now knows for certain* that, with respect to the appropriate criterion, whatever it is, all relevant sorites reasonings are inadequate? There is not a one of us, I submit, who has such certain knowledge.

As concerns us alleged human beings up until now, at least, this nihilistic adaptation works where its original, an evil demon argument, does not work so well. For in the original, there was a deception of me into my false belief, and so I was required to exist. Hence, no strong challenge was made to my putative knowledge of my own existence. But, with our adaptation, no such deception or error is required on my part, only the existence of some arguments, perhaps even some putative arguments. If I do not exist, and so I am not there to understand those arguments, or even putative arguments, that is paradoxical, but it does not affect the relevant matters. For there may still be adequate arguments there anyway and, *a fortiori*, putative arguments. More directly to the point, there is not a one of us now who *knows for certain* that there are no adequate nihilistic sorites arguments; much less does any one *know for certain* that there are no putative arguments adequate to their undermining purpose.

Our premise speaks of *all* sorites arguments against the alleged existence of the person. That person must know for certain that *they all fail*. But which arguments are these, the failure of all of which must be certainly known? We should not confine the arguments to the two or three humble formulations exhibited in our first section. For if someone spots a formulational flaw, it will mean little, unless of course it gets him to know for certain that no better formulation will fare any better. But how should such a spotting do that? To know for certain that all are failures, it appears, one would have to know that there is some "essential ingredient" of them, which feature is logically defective. Let us allow that some day this might conceivably be known for certain by somebody. But none of us could now come to know it for certain by simple reasoning. For the simple reasoning has been done, and we don't know for certain yet.

Against this apparently impeccable thinking, it might be held by someone that he simply *does know for certain* that he himself exists. Perhaps he might liken our sorites arguments to tricky little fallacies he had encountered in school, where mathematical impossibilities were allegedly proven. In the case of those mathematical arguments, he knew for certain that the conclusions were false, and, so, that *something* was wrong with the reasonings, even if he had no idea what it was. And, things are just the same here, he could maintain. But supposing that the objector did know for certain in the tricky cases he cites, mightn't things be different with sorites arguments? Mightn't the latter not be tricky little fallacies, but profound philosophical arguments, which undermine our whole alleged way of thinking, including our putative existence, which is alleged in its terms. It seems that no one now knows for certain that there is not such a difference here. And, so, it appears, no one knows for certain that our sorites arguments are fallacious failures, or that he himself exists.

Now, let us take pains to allow that, to this point anyhow, someone may be quite reasonable in believing, and even in being very confident indeed, that he himself exists. And, he may be very reasonable, too, in holding our sorites arguments to fail of their purpose. Indeed, to this point at least, we may allow that such a person may be *much more* reasonable in believing these things, and even in being *very* confident of them, than would be anyone who felt the least inclined to believe that the sorites arguments were adequate reasonings. (We allow, at present, that all of this may be, while of course also allowing that further reasonings may upset all of these matters.) But what does *not* seem allowable at this point, or at least not correct, is that any of us *knows for certain* that something is amiss with all relevant sorites reasonings. So there is, I submit, nothing for us now but to conclude that our adaptation of the evil demon argument is philosophically adequate. This adaptation, it appears, compels us to accept its own skeptical conclusion: there is no human person, at least, who knows for certain that he himself exists.

With this conclusion in mind, there directly arises the question: without knowing for certain that one exists, is there anything else which one may yet know for certain? With some matters of pure mathematics, we might seem to have our best hope of knowing some things for certain. But even this hope is dim. If we don't know for certain that we exist, then we don't know for sure that there is any language which is understood by us at all properly. When we rehearse in our heads, then, some such supposed sentence as "one and one are two", and take this to represent certain knowledge on our part, for all we know for sure, nothing at all might be expressed. Considerations of this sort lead me to think it impossible to separate relevantly our alleged mathematical knowledge from the already undermined knowledge of there being a person who understands appropriate symbols or terms. In way of something more specifically argumentative, we may offer these complementary thoughts: if I know for certain that one and one are two, then I will easily know for certain, what is if anything more cautious, that *it seems* that one and one are two. So, then, I will easily know for certain, what's less ambitious still, that *it seems to me now* that one and one are two. But, if I don't know for certain that *I exist*, then I won't know that *anything* seems to *me* to be so. So, without our knowing for certain of our own existence, we won't thus know either anything of an apparently "purer" variety ([4]: 131–4). Hence, it seems wrong to suppose that any human person knows for certain that one and one are two, and that one ever has. I submit, then, that as of now, at least, there is no human person who knows anything for certain.

## 3. The Third Step: The Deduction of Radical Skepticism

The skepticism we have just reached, while covering all *matters* for us now, looks rather mild in *manner*: saying that there is nothing we now *know for certain* does not appear to deny us very much. For without knowing things for certain, we might suppose, we may yet be quite well off epistemologically: we might know things in some lesser sense or way, or at least we might be reasonable in believing various things. But in fact such a pleasant appearance is illusory. If we don't know anything for certain, then it follows that we won't be even the slightest bit reasonable in believing anything. That is, the skepticism we have already reached leads deductively to radical skepticism. The course of this deduction may proceed in either of two mutually supporting ways. Both find their basis in argument given at length in my cited book. I sketch the basic argument first; then I will extend it in the appropriate new direction.

For anyone to be even the least bit reasonable in believing anything, there must be something which is his reason for believing it, or else some things which are his reasons. And, second, if something is someone's reason for believing something, then it is "propositionally specific", and likewise for his reasons. That is, for some suitable value of '$p$' his reason for believing it is that $p$, or for some of '$p$' and '$q$' and..., his reasons for that are that $p$ and that $q$ and... And, third and finally, if someone's reason for believing something is that $p$, it follows that he knows that $p$, while if his reasons there are that $p$ and that $q$ and ..., it follows that he knows that $p$ and he knows that $q$ and ... From these three premises, we deduce that if anyone is even the least bit reasonable in believing anything, then there is at least one thing which he knows to be so ([4]: 199–211, 214–26).

While various people might take issue with various of these premises, most, I imagine, will be most concerned with the third, for it is there that the family of terms whose central member is 'reason' becomes explicitly linked with the apparently stronger term 'know'. But the linguistic evidence indicates that any supposedly greater strength on the part of 'know' is only apparent. The most direct evidence comes with inconsistent sentences like "His *reason* (for believing it) was that there were footprints there, but he *didn't know* that there were." Related sentences conspire to confirm: "His *evidence* was that there were, but he *didn't know* that there were." And the more widely we look to examine the phenomena, the more broadly based our confirmation becomes. Hence, there seems little reason to deny this premise and so, it appears, little to deny the deduction of which it is a part ([4]: 206–11, 153–188, 214–26).

This rehearsed deduction concerned knowing; the skepticism we have so far reached concerns knowing for certain. The first way to get the deduction we seek from the one just rehearsed is to argue that someone's knowing that something is so actually entails that he knows it for certain. The direct evidence concerns this inconsistency: "He actually *knows* that it snowed, but he *doesn't know* it for certain." Further, we may develop suitable evidence for entailment chains: from the inconsistency of "He *knows* it, but it *isn't* perfectly *clear* to him," we see that if someone knows that something is so, then it is perfectly clear to him it is. And from the inconsistency of "It's perfectly *clear* to him, but he doesn't know it for *certain*," we understand that if it is thus clear, then he knows it for certain. Putting these two implications together, we deduce the one we seek. Indeed, the more we look at the language here, the more help it gives us ([4]: 24–36, 47–147, 183–89, 209–10, 231–39). It appears, then, that we may add another premise to our rehearsed deduction: if someone knows something to be so, then he knows it for certain. Hence, we may now deduce the crucial conditional: if someone is even the least bit reasonable in believing anything, then there is at least one thing which he knows for certain.

Our second adaptive procedure is to replace our third premise, in our rehearsed deduction, with a parallel proposition which makes explicit mention of knowing for certain: if someone's reason for believing something is that $p$, then he knows for certain that $p$, while if his reasons there are that *p* and *q* and..., then he knows for certain that *p* and he knows for certain that *q* and...We may focus our discussion, again, on the first and singular part, and obtain our direct evidence in the form of a contradiction: "Her *reason* (for it) was that there were foot prints there, but she *didn't know* for certain that there were." Further examination of the language, as indicated, further confirms our alternative third premise (see the just previous list of references).

The points just made apply to all matters whatsoever, for any values of *p* and other variables. In particular, then, they apply to alleged reasons of the form: it seems (to me now) that such-and-such. If such a thing is anyone's reason for anything, then he must know for certain *that it seems (to him now) that such-and-such*. If he *doesn't know that for certain*, then it won't be his reason and, in the absence of any others, he won't be reasonable in believing anything.

We may deduce twice over, then, in mutually supporting ways, our sought-after conditional: if anyone is even the least bit reasonable in believing anything, then there is at least one thing which he knows for certain to be so. This, of course, may be logically turned around: if nobody knows anything for certain, then no one is even the least bit reasonable in believing anything. But, then, we have already reached the conclusion that as of now no human person knows anything for certain. Thus we may conclude a thesis of radical skepticism: as of now, there is no human person who is even the least bit reasonable in believing anything.

## 4. From Skepticism Back to Nihilism: The Final Step of This First Cycle

In brief, let's review our progress. We first adapted the sorites so as to undermine any statement as to one's own alleged existence. A thesis of radical nihilism was thus motivated. But this thesis still seemed dubious, chiefly because of our general belief in common sense thinking.

We then turned to epistemological argumentation. Even if they wouldn't move us directly toward their objective, our sorites arguments appeared to compel at least this much: there is no human person who now *knows for certain* that he or she exists. This seemed mild enough at first, but from it we deduced a thesis of radical skepticism: there is none of us who now is even the least bit reasonable in believing anything.

We have thus exposed a most serious defect in our common sense thinking. At this point, then, there appears no great general presumption in favor of common sense. In this new light, we may consider our sorites arguments yet again, now for a third time, while being less disposed to judge them unfavorably. In the light of *all* of our arguments, we may now more strongly suspect that such terms as "swizzle stick", "human person" and even "I" are devoid of proper application. Not only skepticism, then, but even nihilism might now be appreciated as a valuable philosophical position, one which we might take on the way toward a thoroughgoing abandonment of our ordinary thinking. At the least, we should give it our serious consideration.

This completes my first cycle of argument. Before I begin my second cycle, I should like to make a few points regarding the logical character of the reasonings already encountered. As a first point, it would be something of a mistake to view our arguments as yielding conclusions which, because they conflict with common sense, are simply in opposition to common sense thinking. Rather we should notice that the premises of our arguments were themselves each part of common sense, although sometimes of the more highly educated or reflective areas of common sense. So too, then, our radical theses, which these premises entail, are themselves a part of common sense, though of course they are an implicit, unobvious part of it. Thus our arguments may be best taken, I suggest, as showing that common sense is inconsistent.

In the second place, our present arguments for epistemological skepticism do *not require* an internal incoherence on the part of our peculiarly epistemic locutions. At the same time, of course, they *allow* that this is so. In my cited book, I argued that such expressions were indeed incoherent ([4]: ch. III). With regard to these present skeptical arguments, based upon the sorites, those of the book are *a fortiori*.

In the third place, our present arguments for nihilism do *not require* an internal incoherence on the part of such putative referring expressions as "swizzle stick", "human person" and "I". They do, of course, *allow* that these expressions, granting they exist, are internally inconsistent and so, for that reason, will fail to provide adequate conditions for anything's existence. Interesting questions about the logic of these vague expressions are, then, left open by our present sorites arguments. But while *these exhibited* arguments leave this question entirely open, *other* reasonings may tend to close it, even in the radical direction of having our expressions be internally inconsistent. Indeed, it is just such an argument, related to but distinct from our sorites reasonings, with which I intend to begin my second cycle of argumentation.

## 5. Beginning a Second Cycle of Argument: The Argument from Invented Expressions

One hypothesis about our sorites arguments is that they are effective because key terms, upon which they turn, are logically inconsistent, and their stepwise reasoning is suitable to expose the inconsistency. This hypothesis suggests a strategic argument for nihilism: Invent a new expression which is *so devised that* it is inconsistent in the manner hypothesized. Then look to see if there is any significant difference, as regards the logic or semantics of the matter, between the invented term and familiar, inherited, ordinary expressions, including "person". If it seems that there is no such difference, but rather only parity, then we have a case for our hypothesis.

I shall, accordingly, and with your help, invent a new expression, "nacknick". This expression is meant to apply to objects of a certain shape, or shapes, and not to anything else. Now, I want you to think of some objects, say, two, which are quite similar to each other in shape, though not thus identical, and neither of which has a shape which could be described or categorized by any convenient available expression. Thus, you are not to think, for example, of a cylindrical object, for such an object may be so described in two convenient words.

You have your two shaped objects in mind. Now, I shall instruct you: objects of *just those* shapes are nacknicks. But an object *need not* be precisely of one of those two shapes to be a nacknick. Rather, if an object is a nacknick, then so too is any other which differs in shape from it only slightly. But, of course, there are to be shaped objects which are not nacknicks. So, we shall constrain things: if an object differs in shape from a nacknick by quite a lot, then it is not a nacknick. These objects, it is to be understood, include merely possible ones as well as actual.

In light of our previous reasonings, it is not hard to see that our new expression is logically on a par with "perfectly square triangle", that is, it is an inconsistent expression. Consider any alleged nacknick, even one of your two imagined exemplars, and another object which differs in shape from it quite enormously. By our instructions, the latter is not a nacknick. But, we may construct a series of shaped objects beginning with the first and ending with the second, with each differing only slightly in shape from each object directly next to it. One vivid way in which a suitable series may be imagined is this: A tiny bit is removed from the alleged nacknick, producing a new object. Such a bit is removed each time until only a speck remains. Then bits are added one at a time until the shape of the considered non-nacknick is realized. Now, if our starting object is indeed a nacknick, our instructions concerning slight differences have us say of each object in the series that it too is a nacknick, including the last. But we have said that this last object is not a nacknick. Thus, a contradiction.

Because our invented expression, "nacknick", is an inconsistent one, it can apply to no entities at all, there are no nacknicks. Indeed, what it is for an expression to be inconsistent is just this: the supposition that it applies to anything yields an inconsistency, a contradiction. With normal suppositions in force, including, for example, the assumption that there are people, we may agree, of course, that people can *use* inconsistent expressions to refer to certain entities. Thus, for a simple example, you and I might agree to use the expression "perfectly square triangle" to refer to such tomatoes as are both yellow and sweet. But while there might be such tomatoes, we now normally suppose, and while we might thus refer to them, there will not be any perfectly square triangles. There will be entities to refer to which we use the expression "perfectly square triangle", but there will not be any entity to which that expression actually applies.

With the meaning with which I have endowed it, our word, "nacknick", will apply to nothing whatever. Whatever the explanation, we ourselves will use the word to speak only of cases within a certain range, or ranges. This tendency on our part is only remotely related to the actual meaning of the term, which is inconsistent, but it means that the invented expression will be as useful to us as many ordinary ones. Now, many to whom we could teach the term would never notice the inconsistency. But even we, who now do notice it, are hardly hampered. Aren't you quite able to use the term, without hesitation, for a fair variety of possible objects? So, perhaps "nacknick" is logically on a par with "person", another word which we are all quite ready to employ and would be too even if an inconsistency in it were pointed out. Let me try to do just that with this much more familiar and important expression.

Entities differ in various ways or respects. In many cases, we may think of these respects as admitting of *dimensions of difference*, so that *how much* entities differ from each other in the respect in question might be considered with regard to such a dimension. Thus we may speak of a dimension of color in this way: a red thing differs *more from* a blue one, in respect of color, *than from* a purple thing. The dimension goes *from* red *through* purple *to* blue, as well as back in the other direction. Now, I shall not endeavor to state the dimensions of difference with regard to which "person" is meant to discriminate, which would be extremely difficult to do in any illuminating way. But, we may say, in these terms, that *there are some* such dimensions with regard to which "person" purports to discriminate. Perhaps, a dimension of intelligence, or power of thought, will be important; perhaps one of a capacity for varied feeling and experience. But, of course, these speculations are only illustrative, the point being that there must be at least one dimension with respect to which the term is to discriminate.

As our sorites arguments have helped to indicate, however, the discriminations purported by "person" fail for inconsistency, just as "nacknick" fails to discriminate any shaped objects from any others. With "person" there are implicit conditions parallel to those with which I endowed "nacknick": With regard to the relevant dimensions, if a given possible entity is a person, then so too is any other that differs from it only quite minutely. But, also, if an entity is a person, then there are *some* dimensions of difference (with regard to which discriminations are purported) which are such that, with respect to them, there are *some* (possible) entities which differ so much from the first that they are *not* persons.

If such conditions govern "person", then sorites arguments against people are readily explained. Take, for example, a sorites of decomposition against people. Consider a world in which matters are in fact as we believe them here to be. Well, then, the removal of one of our cells, in a suitable manner, will never mean more than a slight difference on any relevant dimension. By the first condition, there will, after any single removal, be a person in the situation. But by the time we are down to one living cell, we have gone too far with regard to at least one of the dimensions with respect to which "person" purports to discriminate. By our second condition, we shall have no person then; thus, the contradiction. It appears that "person" is indeed an inconsistent expression, and that sorites arguments against persons do not at base, despite some superficial looks to the contrary, ever rely upon matters of contingent fact. Even the gradual nature of our actual world looks to be helpful only as an aid to thinking up arguments: in the terminology of section 1, miracles of metaphysical illusion, even if they should occur, will not help matters at all. And, with inconsistency ruling here, no needed miracle of conceptual comprehension will ever be possible.[6]

I have been arguing that my existence is on a par with that of nacknicks. I shall now map out this Argument. We begin with this point about our invented expression:

(1) The expression "nacknick" is logically inconsistent.

---

6. I pursue these matters at some length in [7].

Then, we advance our idea of parity:

(2) The expression "person" is logically on a par with "nacknick"; if the latter is inconsistent, then so is the former.

To these two statements, we add what should be a rather uncontroversial proposition, also previously discussed by us:

(3) If "person" is a logically inconsistent expression, then there are no people.

These three premises, by simple logic, yield nihilism with regard to any putative people:

(4) There are no people.

To this sub-conclusion, there may be added a rather unproblematic conditional premise:

(5) If I exist, then there is at least one person, and so it is not the case that there are none;

from which it may now be concluded, paradoxically enough:

(6) I do not exist.

Can anyone now *know for certain* that such a result does not apply in his case?

## 6. Completing This Second Cycle of Argument

We shall now give the traditional evil demon's place, lately occupied by sorites arguments, to our Argument from Invented Expressions:

(I) In respect of any suitable thing, say that $p$, if someone knows for certain that $p$, then, either he already knows for certain that an Argument from Invented Expressions to opposite effect fails of its purpose, or should he engage in suitable simple reasoning, he could come to know for certain that this is so.
(II) There is no human person who now knows for certain that an Argument from Invented Expressions against his own alleged

existence fails of its purpose, nor is there any who could now, by simple reasoning, come to know for certain that this is so.

Therefore,

(III) There is no human person who now knows for certain that he himself exists.

The reasoning behind the first premise here is precisely the same as that supporting the first premise before, in section 2, and thus calls for no further comment. The relation of the premises to the conclusion is also as before, in any case not much of a matter for discussion. So, whatever we have to discuss now will concern (II), our new second premise.

As with the parallel premise before, whatever simple reasoning might be helpful can be quickly performed. Suppose it has. That leaves us to discuss only the first disjunct of (II), in effect, the question "Is there any human person who now knows for certain that an Argument from Invented Expressions fails to undermine his own putative existence?" With a proper perspective thus put on matters, it is futile to quarrel over the relations of our premises to their conclusion(s). Now, (4) is a sub-conclusion, and thus may now be ignored, while (3) and (5), though genuinely serving as premises, hardly leave much room for question or even discussion. Thus, to *know for certain* that our Argument is a failure, we must be in a pretty devastating situation as regards at least one of our first two premises.

Our first premise says that our newly invented expression, "nacknick", is a logically inconsistent term. I have introduced it by means of instructions chosen so that things quite certainly do look that way. Now, it is very strange to think that an internally inconsistent expression could seem so natural, or be so obviously well suited for our use. So there is a *feeling*, I admit, even on my part, that "nacknick" *really can't* be inconsistent, for it is so very natural and useful for us. But the more I have thought on the matter, the more this feeling has seemed like a baseless prejudice: we'd like for our thinking to be quite logical, at least for the most part, but, at bottom, this just doesn't seem to be so. Now, I *may* be wrong in denying this feeling, but which of us now *knows for certain* that I am? No one, I submit; nor is anyone even close to being in that position.

What about the second premise, then, the only remaining statement to consider? Is "person" logically quite disparate from "nacknick" or are they, rather, on a par? So far, things have looked to favor the latter alternative. Now, in the future, contrary thoughts might change the look of things. At the same time, more might be said to favor parity, and in another context I would go on to do just that.[7] But in the present context, either sort of additional remarks are quite beside the point. For the point now is whether any of us *now know for certain* that there is no parity here. And, such certain knowledge, if it is in fact already ours, cannot derive in any way from reasonings on these matters that are not already at hand. As there is nothing now available which quite decisively rules out parity, there is none of us who now knows for certain that "person" or "nacknick" are other than on a logically equal footing. And, so, I submit, our second premise, apparently our last chance to know certainly that our new Argument is an essential failure, gives us no good chance at all. Thus we are driven to accept the idea that there is no human person who now knows for certain that he himself exists. From considerations familiar from section 2, this leads to the relevantly more general idea: There is none of us now who knows anything for certain.

Thus we have performed the second step of our new cycle of argument. The remaining two steps are now little more for us than child's play, for no variation at all is required from the way previously taken.

## 7. An Entirely Comprehensive Cycle of Argument

I have presented two somewhat specific cycles of argument. The specificity of each consisted in the nihilistic argumentation provided in its first step. In our first cycle, we first put forward our sorites arguments against our own putative existence, in our second, the Argument from Invented Expressions, to the same effect. We could, as remarked, put forward further parallel cycles, each with its own specific, distinctive nihilistic arguments, comprising its first step. But we may now do more as well. We may generalize upon our specific nihilistic arguments, as they are all to the same effect or conclusion, so as to produce an entirely comprehensive first step and, based upon it, an entirely comprehensive cycle of argument.

In our first step now, we exhibit various arguments, each against our own alleged existence, including relevant sorites reasonings, the

---

7. In [7], I make further points in support of the logical parity between "nacknick" and "person".

Argument from Invented Expressions, and various others which may seem to us sufficiently compelling to be worthy of inclusion. I can assure you that there are indeed other distinctive nihilistic reasonings which are well worth our consideration, but actually to exhibit them here now is not much to the present point. For the point now is to reflect that given the nihilistic reasonings already exhibited, there may well be more, and amongst these, several which are each deeper and more compelling than those we have actually formulated and discussed. It is with this reflection in mind, based in specific reasonings while rather naturally going beyond them, that we may proceed to our second step in our entirely comprehensive cycle.

This time we put forward an entirely general version of our evil demon adaptation, giving the key place to *all* arguments (which there may be) against one's own alleged existence. The first premise now can read as our adapted first premise, (I), in section 2, with the single difference that the word "sorites" is deleted. In short, we may write this premise as:

(I) If someone knows something for certain, he knows any (putative) argument against it to fail, or can easily do so.

And our own second premise can read as our adapted (II) there, with the sole difference again being the deletion. In short:

(II) There is no human person who now knows for certain that all (putative) arguments against his own putative existence are failures, nor any who can easily do so.

As twice before in this paper, we get our conclusion:

(III) There is no human person who now knows for certain that he himself exists,[8]

and with it, by ways by now familiar, the rest of our cycle.

But, with such a general, entirely comprehensive formulation, where is the reference to our first step, or to any of the nihilistic reasonings we may have exhibited therein? The reference, if we want to

---

8. In chapter III of [4], especially in section 9 of the chapter, I advance an argument for this conclusion (as well as for a somewhat stronger one), That argument is rather different from those offered in the present paper. But, I am pleased to say, the arguments are all mutually supporting.

say there is one, is in the phrase "all arguments against his own existence", and the previous "any argument against it". But if this is any genuine reference at all, it is so general that it becomes puzzling whether our specific nihilistic reasonings are playing any part at all. By the same token, they seem to be the most novel and forceful sort of arguments, which give the rest of the cycle force and direction. How are we to resolve this puzzle?

There are two main things to be said. In the first place, it is our awareness of these nihilistic reasonings, only recently acquired, which get us to accept the second premise: (II) There is no human person who now knows for certain that all arguments against his own existence are failures, nor any who can easily do so. For without these arguments in mind, this premise would *seem* unmotivated, pointless and even quite plainly false. In this way, the nihilistic reasonings play the same role as was played before by a vividly described evil demon, or an evil scientist whose electrodes are hooked up to our helpless nerve endings. *Without such detailed hypotheses in mind*, who would think twice about any such premise as: There is nobody who knows for certain that there is nothing involving him in a false belief as to whether or not there are rocks? But, *with them*, how many philosophical ideas have been more thought about?

In the second place, we should remark on the difference between the evil agent and our nihilistic arguments. Part of the difference, which we have already remarked, is that our nihilistic reasonings do so much better than a demon against one's own present existence, and against any attempted *cogito* on its behalf. Thus, we now leave little temptation to found an egocentric epistemology, complete with the basic propositions and egocentric predicaments in which to become embroiled. We leave instead only radical skepticism and the motivation for an entirely new beginning in the formulation of epistemological ideas.

A bigger part of the difference, I think, lies in this: nobody ever gets to the point where he actually believes there is any such evil demon deceiving him into false belief in the relevant matters, nor even that there is any significant chance of that, so to say. We continue to believe just as firmly as ever that there are rocks, and tables, and so on, for all the effect the arguments may have on questions of our alleged knowledge or reasonableness. With the nihilistic arguments, however, it does seem that there is actually a threat *there*, and not just a hypothetical "possibility". For my own part, I often now believe that there really are no tables or rocks, and never so firmly belive that there are such things as I once did. So, the detailed reflections that now threaten claims to knowledge, and thus to reasonable belief, threaten even our mere beliefs themselves.

But I think that the biggest difference between these present reflections and the traditional Cartesian hypothesis is as regards future intellectual effort. For, what can one do with a hypothetical evil demon, but hope he is not there, and fashion one's thinking on the assumption that none is bothering one very much. In contrast, our nihilistic reasonings leave us with a lot to think about, and to try to do in consequence. Now, it must of course be admitted that these arguments undermine the possibility of any endeavor I should try to propose, or even the putative thought that I should propose anything, just as all of my putative essay is undermined. But even so, I shall (incoherently) propose that what we have now to do is invent new expressions which are not inconsistent ones, and by means of which we may, to some significant extent, think coherently about concrete reality. To continue in this somewhat heady (and incoherent) vein, I suggest that only when this much has been accomplished will there be no great need to advocate skepticism and nihilism, the point of radical philosophy having then been largely exploited.[9]

## References

[1] Cargile, James, "The Sorites Paradox," *British Journal for the Philosophy of Science, 20* (1969).
[2] Kneale, William and Martha, *The Development of Logic* (Oxford: Oxford University Press, 1962).
[3] Moline, Jon, "Aristotle, Eubulides and the Sorites," *Mind*, Vol. LXXVIII, N.S., No. 311(July, 1969).
[4] Unger, Peter, *Ignorance* (Oxford: Oxford University Press, 1975).
[5] ———. "I Do Not Exist," in *Perception and Identity*: Essays Presented to A. J. Ayer with his Replies to them, G. F. MacDonald (ed.), (London: The Macmillan Press, 1979).
[6] ———. "There Are No Ordinary Things," *Synthese*, Vol. 41, No. 2(June, 1979).
[7] ———. "Why There Are No People," *Midwest Studies in Philosophy*, Vol. IV: Studies in Metaphysics (1979).
[8] Wheeler, Samuel C., III, "On That Which Is Not," *Synthese*, Vol. 41 No. 2 (June, 1979).

---

9. In connection with this paper, I have had helpful discussions with many people. In particular, however, I should like to thank Terence Leichti and Samuel Wheeler, who were both helpful on numerous matters.

# 5

# TWO TYPES OF SCEPTICISM

Scepticism about knowledge is a thesis that, even in a very strong form, many people find forceful and appealing. In my paper, 'A Defense of Scepticism', I have argued for this thesis.[1] And, I suspect that even the universal form of it—the view that nobody ever knows anything to be so—may well be correct. While one may first find it shocking to have this thesis thrust upon one, the blow may be softened by accepting the idea that even if one never *knows* anything, one may at least be *reasonable* and *justified* in various things. For if this idea is correct, then in particular one may be justified and reasonable in believing certain things to be so. One of these things might even be the thesis of scepticism about knowledge.

One who takes this course of retreat will distinguish between two types of scepticism. Scepticism about knowledge, whether in a universal form or in some weaker one, is only a first type of scepticism. A second type of scepticism, which may also be advanced universally or in a weaker form, is scepticism about being reasonable and justified. The latter view may be conveniently distinguished by the expression 'scepticism about rationality'. At least on the face of it, scepticism about rationality seems logically independent of scepticism about knowledge.

---

1. Unger, P., 'A Defense of Skepticism', *The Philosophical Review* 80, No. 2 (April, 1971).

It seems that universal scepticism about knowledge will not entail any scepticism about rationality.

On becoming more convinced of the truth of scepticism about knowledge, I have tried the retreat to the position that at least one is reasonable and justified in all sorts of things. But in this paper, I will argue that this retreat is impossible. I will argue that universal scepticism of the first type logically entails universal scepticism of the second: If it is true that nobody ever knows anything to be so, then it follows that it is also true that nobody is ever (even the least bit) reasonable or justified in anything, in particular, in believing anything to be so.[2] I shall also argue, toward the end, that a partial but strong form of scepticism about knowledge entails a form of scepticism about rationality which is almost as strong. Somewhat roughly put, this is the idea that if in the case of every person there is at most hardly anything that he knows to be so, then in every case there is not much more than hardly anything in which the person is (even the least bit) reasonable and justified. In particular, there will be not much more than hardly anything which the person is reasonable or justified in believing to be so.

As I have previously argued that there is so little, if anything, which anybody knows, I must end by taking this present argument as motivating more than just the conditional proposition which links the two types of scepticism. I might respond by giving up scepticism about knowledge. But, I do not think that this is the only possible response,

---

2. I think that this agrees with one of Descartes' leading ideas. But, many contemporary philosophers take a line which is against this one. In contemporary writings, philosophers usually talk about things being certain or only being probable rather than of people knowing those things or only being reasonable in believing them. If the issue fundamentally concerns people, as I think it does, then such statements as these directly conflict with our Cartesian line: "Thus, if my reasoning is sound, it is at least misleading to say that unless something is certain nothing can even be probable" (A. J. Ayer, 'Basic Propositions', in *Philosophical Analysis* (ed. by M. Black), Englewood Cliffs, N. J., 1963, p. 70). "Whether any degree of doubtfulness attaches to the least dubitable of our beliefs is a question with which we need not at present concern ourselves; it is enough that any proposition concerning which we have rational grounds for some degree of belief can, in theory, be placed in a scale between certain truth and certain falsehood. Whether these limits are themselves to be included we may leave an open question" (Bertrand Russell, *Human Knowledge*, New York 1964, p. 381). On the Cartesian side, we find few contemporary figures, but here is a statement which does favor our position: "It is true that in order that the difficulties posed by scepticism be met, it is essential that there be *some* knowledge which is more than probable, and that such knowledge be pertinent to nature and experience" (C. I. Lewis, *Mind and the World Order*, New York 1956, p. 311). (The italics here are Lewis'.) While the wording differs from case to case, it seems that almost every philosopher of any ambition has expressed an opinion on these crucial issues.

nor even the one which all the arguments together most strongly motivate. There may seem to be a paradox in accepting all these arguments. For they have it that there is at most very little in which one will be at all justified or reasonable, and they strongly suggest that, in particular, one will never be at all justified or reasonable in accepting those arguments themselves. But there really is no paradox here. The arguments may be sound and effectively forceful—one who considers them may be brought to believe what is *true*. If he cannot be *reasonable* or *justified* in believing what is true, that may be only because the ideas of *being reasonable* and *being justified* are so impossibly demanding. This will not reflect badly on my arguments; rather, that is their whole point. To stress what's relevant, we may say that it's misleading to remark, 'One will not be reasonable or justified in accepting *those arguments*'. One puts the pressure where the culprits lie by remarking, 'One will not be *reasonable* or *justified* in accepting those arguments'.

## 1. The Main Argument

In the case of almost any argument, one can then go on to argue for or against its premises. I will begin by putting forth the premises of what I I call my Main Argument, so that I may draw my conclusion from them. To separate matters a bit, this will be an argument for the conclusion that if nobody ever knows anything to be so, then nobody is ever (at all) *reasonable* in anything. Later on, I will consider a parallel argument for the parallel conclusion about the necessity of knowing for anyone to be (at all) *justified* in anything. Here are the three premises of my Main Argument.

The first premise of this argument is the proposition:

(1) If someone S is (at all) *reasonable* in something X, then there is something which is *S's reason* for X or there are some things which are *S's reasons* for X.

For example, if Ralph is reasonable in thinking that it was raining, then there is something which is Ralph's reason for thinking that it was or else there are somethings which are his reasons for thinking it was raining. If he is reasonable in running to the store, then something must be his reason for that or else some things must be Ralph's reasons for running there. If nothing is his reason for it and no things are his reasons, then Ralph is not reasonable in running to the store.

My second premise is the proposition:

(2) If there is something which is *S's reason* for something X, then there is some propositional value of '*p*' such that S's reason *is that p* and if there are some things which are *S's reasons* for X, then there are some propositional values of '*p*' and '*q*' and so on such that S's reasons *are that p and that q* and so on.

For example, if there is something which is Ralph's reason for thinking it was raining, then there is some propositional value of '*p*' such that Ralph's reason is that *p*, e.g., that *Fred's hat was wet*. And, if there are some things which are Ralph's reasons for running to the store, then they must be that *p* and that *q* and so on, e.g., that *he needs milk* and that *the store will close at six*.

The third and final premise of this argument is the proposition:

(3) If S's reason (for something X) *is that p*, then S *knows* that *p*; and if S's reasons (for X) *are that p and that q* and so on, then S *knows* that *p* and S *knows* that *q* and so on.

For example, if Ralph's reason (for running to the store) is that the store will close in twenty minutes, then Ralph *knows* that it will close in twenty minutes. If, on the other hand, his reasons are this first and also that he needs milk, then he knows that the store will close then and he *also knows* that he needs milk. And, if Ralph's reason (for thinking that it was raining) is that Fred's hat was wet, then Ralph *knows* that Fred's hat was wet.

These three premises let us deduce the proposition:

(4) If someone S is (at all) *reasonable* in something X, then there is some propositional value of '*p*' such that S *knows* that *p* or else there are some propositional values of '*p*' and '*q*' and so on such that S *knows* that *p* and S *knows* that *q* and so on.

It is quite clear that our argument will not depend on which people or things we choose and that, in any case, it proceeds in a way which may be generalized. This allows us to frame in English the universal conditional: If anybody is (at all) *reasonable* in anything, then he or she *knows* something to be so. This is the conditional which, when contraposed, states the connection between the universal forms of the two types of scepticism: If nobody knows anything to be so, then nobody is (at all) reasonable in anything. And, of course, from this the more particular connection, aimed epistemologically, trivially follows: If nobody knows anything to be so, then nobody is (at all) reasonable in believing anything to be so. This is my Main Argument. What is philosophically interesting, and thus controversial, is what we need to get our conclusion (4); that is, what I call the three premises of the argument. I shall try to defend these premises, each in turn, so that the import of each is not misunderstood.

## 2. The First Premise: The Step from One's Being Reasonable to One's Reason or Reasons

To begin my argument, I claim that (1) if someone S is (at all) reasonable in something X, then there must be something which is S's reason for X or else there must be some things which are S's reasons for X. The consequent of this conditional is a disjunction between S's reason and S's reasons. One might think this a needless complication, but I think that we must make room for both the singular and the plural alternatives. The possessive form indicates uniqueness, at least relative to the context at hand and perhaps even universally. Thus, if S has more than one house, there is nothing which is S's house. Rather, there are things which are S's houses, and each of them is *one of S's* houses. The point is of course quite general. In the present case, we must consider the fact that we often say that a number of things were someone's reasons for something. If what we say is correct, then there is nothing which is the person's reason for the thing. One might think that his reasons might be viewed as conjoining to form one big reason. But this can't be. For if there is *one* big reason, then those others can't be the person's *reasons*. Thus, to allow truth in our talk of people's reasons, we must advance the disjunction of both the singular and the plural alternatives. A small fact of our language brings about a small complication in stating our first premise. But, what of the substance of this premise?

Our premise asserts only that whenever one is reasonable there is *something* which is one's reason, or *some* things which are one's reasons. It does not say anything about what these might be. And, of course, it allows that this or these might be different for different people and different situations. Now, someone's reason for something might be quite different from what anyone might suppose, including the subject himself; or at least this premise allows for this to be so. Suppose that a foreigner wanted to know what word we use for referring to toothbrushes. He holds up one and asks 'What is this?'. You say, 'It is a toothbrush'. What is your reason for saying this, or your reasons for it? Perhaps you thought that he wanted to know what toothbrushes were called, and you wanted to be helpful to the foreigner. If the foreigner only wanted you to explain why your dirty toothbrush was on his dresser, it might still be that your reason for saying the thing was that you thought he wanted to know what toothbrushes were called. Or, perhaps, your reasons were this first and also that you wanted to be helpful to him. Now, if you were right about what he wanted, that is, he did want to know what they are called, then your reasons might be these: that he wanted to know what we call toothbrushes, that you thought he wanted to know that, and that you wanted to be helpful. Or, they might be only the first and third of these. Any of these suggestions is pretty plausible, I think, for this case of the foreigner. But so far as our premise goes, your reason for saying the thing *might* be that you liked tuna fish, or it even *might* be that China is the most populous country. Still, the *plausibility* of the premise depends on our being able to pick out plausible reasons for any cases where someone is reasonable in something. But, of course, typical cases present no problem here.

It might be thought, however, that in certain cases matters are so simple or basic or whatever that nothing can be found to answer as the subject's reason or as one of his reasons. For example, when one said that something was a toothbrush, it may very well be that one believed, correctly, that it was a toothbrush. One may then think that one was reasonable, not only in saying that it was a toothbrush, but also in *believing* that it was. But what could plausibly count as one's reason or reasons for believing such a simple thing? I think that one's reason or reasons might plausibly be any or all of these: that one had learned to recognize toothbrushes, that one had seen many toothbrushes, that one was a native speaker of the language, that one wanted to believe what was true, that it looked to one as though there was a toothbrush there, and so on. Now, though I think these candidates quite plausible, others may not think so. But, if they do not think that *some* things are plausible as one's *reasons for believing* the thing, they should not think either that one is *reasonable in believing* the thing. Perhaps, one is 'beyond' being merely reasonable in believing the thing. It might be that, without being reasonable in it, one did nothing wrong in believing the thing, and it was perfectly all right for one to believe it. Or, it might even be that one was 'beyond' merely believing the thing; one might just *know* that that thing was a toothbrush. The point of our premise is this: that *if* someone is *reasonable* in something, *then* there is *something* which is his *reason* for it or *some* things which are his *reasons*. And, this comes out quite plausibly indeed for all sorts of cases.

Let us consider the most trying cases for the idea that there are things which are one's reasons. We have cases of exceedingly obvious things, or things which are quite obviously all right: being confident that one now exists, believing that one and one are two, preferring pleasure to pain, and so on. I agree with those who find a temptation to say that these cases are too simple or whatever to count as cases where one has a reason or any reasons. But it is precisely when such a temptation is encountered that there is also the temptation to say that the cases are too simple or whatever to count as cases where someone is *reasonable* in the thing. These are just the intuitions that one can't be *reasonable* in preferring pleasure to pain if one has *no reason whatsoever* for preferring the one to the other, and that one can't be *reasonable* in being confident that one now exists or in believing that one and one are two if one has *no reason at all* for these things. We have strong intuitions, then, that 'reasonable' and 'reason' connect in the way our premise dictates.

These intuitions and the truth of our premise may both be lost if one wavers from the locution with 'reasonable' that our premise in fact employs. It is crucial to our premise that it gives a condition for *someone's* being reasonable in something. It is the person himself that the premise focuses on. Thus the premise allows that *what someone says* may be reasonable even if nothing is his reason for saying the thing, and no things are his reasons for it. And, the premise also allows that it may be that *what someone does* in saying a certain thing may be reasonable even if the person has no reason at all for saying the thing. All sorts of *things* might be reasonable; but *the person himself will* not be reasonable *in anything* unless there is something which is his reason or some things which are his reasons for whatever is at hand. This is the reason that such sentences as '*What he believes* is *reasonable*, but *he* has *no reason at all* for believing it', sound and actually are quite consistent. It is also why it sounds and actually is *inconsistent* to say, '*He* is *reasonable* in believing that, but *he* has *no reason at all* for believing it'.

Finally, though it is a rather simple and obvious matter, one should not confuse being reasonable with *not* being *unreasonable*. The former implies the latter, but the converse doesn't hold. Thus, if *it is perfectly all right for* someone to run to the store, that may imply that *it is not unreasonable for* him to run to the store and that, *if* he does run there, *he is not unreasonable* in running to the store. All of this might be if, say, the matter is so indifferent or unproblematic that no reason is needed on the person's part for it to be perfectly all right for him to run to the store. In such a case, though, the person will *not* be *reasonable* in running to the store. There are many locutions which do *not* imply that there is anything that is the subject's reason or any things that are his reasons. None of them imply that the subject is (at all) reasonable in anything. Because one may be confused by or about these locutions, one may object to our first premise. But, it seems that there is no valid objection to it. If the Main Argument is to be stopped, it must be further along the line.

## 3. The Second Premise: The Step from One's Reason or Reasons to the Propositional Specificity of These Things

I want to end this argument in the idea that if someone is reasonable in anything, he must know *that something is so*. To this end, we employ the premise: (2) If something is S's reason for something X, then there is some propositional value of '*p*' such that S's reason is that *p*, and if some things are S's reasons for X, then there are propositional values of '*p*' and '*q*' and so on such that S's reasons are that *p* and that *q* and so on. What this premise does is to line up one's reason or reasons in a way where they are propositionally specific. In this way, they can line up with what is known when one knows that something is so. Now, one's reasons may or may not actually be the same things as certain things which one knows to be so. For example, what is known might be true *propositions* and one's reasons might be parallel *facts*. But, that they be the same things is not the point. The point is this: as long as at least a parallel may be established between any of one's reasons and things which one might know to be so, that will be enough to set the stage for the next step of this Main Argument.

In saying that reasons are propositionally specific, we are recognizing them to be on a par with beliefs at least in this one respect. But they are equally on a par with less familiarly occurring things: arguments, excuses, objections, and so on. In parallel with what we said about reasons, we may say about arguments: If there is something which is S's argument (for something X), then there is some propositional value of '*p*' such that S's argument is that *p*. For example, if something is Arthur's argument (for not building the Dinobomber), then his argument is that *p*, say, that the Dinobomber will soon be obsolete. Similarly, if there is something which is Oscar's objection (to Arthur's argument), then Oscar's objection is that *q*, say, that that argument does not consider the jobs of the bomber builders.

In certain cases, language may not be rich enough to specify reasons— or for that matter anything else—in any interesting way. But, we can generally indicate the way in which things are propositionally specific anyhow.

Thus, there may be little to be said about this, that and the other which we can rightly say. We may then, in order to indicate how they are propositionally specific, only be able to say such things as this about someone's beliefs: His belief is that this is more like that than the other is. Similarly, if something is the person's reason for preferring this to the other it will also be propositionally specific even if we can only indicate that in such bare terms as before: His reason is that he believes that this is more like that than the other is. The extreme case in regard to our inability to indicate things with words might be the one where all we can say is that someone's reason is that things are the way they are, where these words are used not as a banal tautology but as the poor expression of the all but wholly inexpressible idea that here things are a certain, particular way. If someone's reason is that things are the way they are, that will fulfill the demands of this premise as well as anything. Accordingly, I can't see how any significant controversy could arise over this second premise. Indeed, this is probably the least promising place to try to stop the Main Argument.

## 4. The Third Premise: The Step from One's Propositionally Specific Reason or Reasons to One's Knowing

What is perhaps the least obvious and most controversial step of this argument is the one expressed in the third and final premise. In this premise, it is claimed that (3) If S's reason (for something X) is that $p$, then S *knows* that $p$, and if S's reasons (for X) are that $p$ and that $q$ and so on, then S *knows* that $p$ and S *knows* that $q$ and so on. In standard English, the premise says that if someone's reason (for something) is that something is so, then he or she *knows* that it is so, and if his or her reasons (for the thing) are that this is so and that that is so and so on, then he or she *knows* that this is so and *knows* that that is so and so on. Even if one does not at all misunderstand this premise, it may take some doing to convince one of its truth. But if one does misunderstand it, then one will never be convinced. I begin to advance this premise, then, by trying to avoid any misunderstanding.

Perhaps the most common source of misunderstanding is the idea that this premise makes it out that one is always aware of one's reasons. If one thinks that this is what the premise says, then one will reject the premise quite out of hand. But this way of thinking confuses our premise with the following quite different proposition: If someone's reason for something is that thus-and-so, then the person must know what his or her reasons are, i.e., he or she must know *that his or her reason is that thus-and-so*. But this is clearly not what our premise is saying. This proposition entails what the premise says, but it says much more. The premise says only that if someone's reason is that thus-and-so, the person must know *that thus-and-so*; it does *not* say that he or she must know *that his or her reason is that* thus-and-so. This misinterpretation has the premise saying that a lot more must be known by the subject. If the premise did say this, then one might well reject it as false. But as it doesn't say so much, it is not clear that the premise is not true.

A second source of misunderstanding is the idea that this premise will have it that there are many more unconscious reasons than common sense dictates is really the case. This may occur as a reaction away from the first misunderstanding. But this premise says nothing at all to this effect either. It only articulates a logical requirement for what may be one's reasons: If something is one's reason, then there must be something which one knows to be so which at least parallels one's reason in the indicated manner. The premise allows that one may know all sorts of things to be so. It also allows that none, or few, or many, or most or all of these things may lie dormant, as it were, so far as providing the material for one's reasons.

A third source of misunderstanding is the conflation of *S's* reason *for* X with *the* reason *that* S X-es. S's reason for something will be the reason, or one of the reasons, that he does, prefers, believes, etc. as he does. But the converse generally does not hold. *The* reason *that* someone eats many sweets may well be that he needs lots of sugar for his health; but if he is ignorant of his biological condition, then that will not be *his* reason *for* eating many sweets. In such a case, it might be that nothing is his reason for eating many sweets even though something is the reason that he does precisely that. Somewhat similarly, it might be that *the* reason *that* someone washes his hands all the time is that he is afraid of being impure. We may suppose that he does not know that he is afraid of this. But, then, that will *not* be *his* reason *for* washing his hands all the time.

In clearing up these misunderstandings, we have, I think, cleared the way for accepting our third premise. Now, I must argue for the premise itself. In giving the argument, we are off to a good start in noticing that if someone's reason for something is that $p$, then it follows that it is true that $p$. In this respect, our locution, 'S's reason is that $p$', is like other important locutions with 'reason'. If *the* reason someone does something is that $p$, it also follows that $p$. It is inconsistent to say 'His *reason* was that the store was going to close, but it *wasn't* going to close' just as it's inconsistent to say 'The *reason* is that it was going to close, but it *wasn't*'. If the store wasn't going to close, then *that* can't possibly be

Ralph's reason for running there. If anything is his reason here, it will have to be something else, perhaps, that *he thought it was going to close*. But, then, if that is his reason, then he will have to know *that* thing: It is inconsistent also to say 'His *reason* was that he thought the store was going to close, but he *didn't* think that'.

Another necessary condition of knowing which is entailed by our key locution is that the subject *at least believe* that the thing is so. If Ralph *doesn't even* believe that the store is going to close, then that can't be his reason for running there. It is inconsistent to say, 'His *reason* was that Fred's hat was wet, but he *didn't even* believe that it was'. One might consistently say, for example, that Ralph's fear was that Fred's hat was wet though he didn't even believe that it was wet. But that is another matter.

We have noticed two quite independent necessary conditions of knowing to be entailed by someone's reason. This is ground at least for suspicion. But neither of these conditions is either a very severe or very unusual one. Each is entailed by things which do not entail knowing, e.g., by someone's *correctly believing* something. But a very demanding condition of knowing is also entailed by someone's reason. If someone's reason is that *p*, then he must be absolutely *certain* that *p*. That someone be absolutely certain is something which is entailed by little which does not also entail knowing. But it is entailed by someone's reason. It is inconsistent to say 'Ralph's *reason* was that Fred's hat was wet, but he *wasn't* absolutely *certain* that it was'. If Ralph is not absolutely and perfectly certain and sure that the hat was wet, then that can't be his reason for anything. Perhaps something else is; perhaps, that he thought it was wet. But, then, *that* must be something of which Ralph is absolutely certain.

Now we have gotten pretty fair evidence for our premise by checking out necessary conditions of knowing. Let's approach the problem from the other side to see how all the evidence looks. Accordingly, I will now look to describe a situation where many necessary conditions of knowledge *are* satisfied, but where the person still does *not* know that *p*. Suppose, then, that John believes that the crops will grow now and he says that his reason for believing it is that it was raining. But John does *not know* that it was raining, even though he meets many necessary conditions of knowing it. The following situation makes this quite clear. Does it also make it clear that it is *false* that John's reason is that it was raining, despite what he says? We must expect that it does.

In this situation, it is true that it was raining. And, John is perfectly certain that it was. Moreover, John's certainty is based on grounds which are quite good. But here is how all of this happened. John was indoors but then he came outside and looked around. The ground and objects outside were all wet just as if wetted recently by falling rain. And, other indications all pointed to its having rained. Indeed, this is why John is certain that it was raining. But, unbeknownst to John, while it did in fact rain, the rain was rapidly evaporated due to some extraordinary events: the temperature outside went up to 130°F for an hour. Right after the evaporation, some huge spray-and-sprinkle trucks swept by and covered the area with water again, and they did it in just the way that rain does. So, it all looked just as if nothing had evaporated. Because he sees the water, John is certain that it was raining. And, because he is certain of this, John thinks that the crops will grow now. Now, it is of course true that it was raining. But is it true that John's reason for thinking this about the crops is *that it was raining*? He says that it is. But it seems to me quite clear that that can't be his reason. Perhaps, his reason is that he thinks it rained; perhaps it's that there's water on the ground, and perhaps, even, there is nothing here which is his reason. It may not be clear what, if anything, is best to say about such a case in a more positive direction. But what is pretty clear is that it must be false that John's reason is that it was raining. And, the reason for this is also pretty clear: It must be false because John doesn't *know* that it was raining.

Our tests converge to suggest strongly that if someone's reason is that $p$, then that person must know that $p$. Any necessary condition of knowing must be satisfied for something to be someone's reason and, on the other side, no matter how many conditions are satisfied the thing will not be the person's reason unless the person knows. The more closely we examine our third and final premise, the more acceptable we find it. The only way to reject the Main Argument, then, seems to be to misunderstand what it says.

## 5. A Parallel Argument about Being Justified

The Main Argument concerned the idea of someone's being reasonable in something. It showed that a logical part of this idea is that the subject knows something to be so. To put this linguistically, it follows from the meaning of 'S is reasonable in X' that there must be a truth of the form 'S knows that $p$'. Now, in some different language, say, Martian or Indonesian, there may be a word which means something rather like our word 'reasonable'. But, this word may never require any knowledge on the part of the subject for the truth of its key sentences. What would this show? I think it shows that their word, say, 'queasonable', means something crucially different from 'reasonable', and, so that being reasonable in something is crucially different from being queasonable in it. If nobody knows anything to be so, then we all might still be queasonable in many things, but that doesn't mean that anyone will be reasonable in anything at all. So even if our argument may rest, in some sense, on points of our own language, that is nothing against either the soundness or the importance of the argument.

The Main Argument does not rely on any isolated feature of our language and thought. We have other locutions which have much the same meaning as 'S is reasonable in X'. They convey what is essentially the same idea as that conveyed by our key locution. They convey, that is, what is essentially the same idea as the idea of someone's being reasonable in something. One notable locution with much the same meaning is, of course, 'S is justified in X', and the idea of one's being justified in something differs little from the idea of one's being reasonable in it. As might be expected, then, we can provide a parallel argument about being justified.

The three premises of the parallel argument are:

(1′) If someone S is (at all) *justified* in something X, then there is something which is *S's justification* for X.
(2′) If there is something which is *S's justification* for something X, then there is some propositional value of '*p*' such that S's justification *is that p*.
(3′) If S's justification (for something X) *is that p*, then S *knows* that *p*.

These three premises jointly entail the parallel conclusion:

(4′) If someone S is (at all) *justified* in something X, then there is some propositional value of '*p*' such that S *knows* that *p*.

Generalizing on (4′), we get the parallel result that if anybody is justified in anything, then he or she must know something to be so. And, we get the conditional to link the universal forms of our two types of scepticism: If nobody knows anything to be so, then nobody is (at all) justified in anything. In particular, if nobody knows anything to be so, then no one is (at all) justified in believing anyting to be so.

The only difference in wording between the two arguments, other than the use of different key terms, is that now we don't make room for a plural alternative. So far as I can tell, when we take 'justification' seriously, so that it has something to do with someone's being justified, then *a* justification will always be what one appropriately has here. When someone is justified, we don't say that his *justifications are* that *p* and that *q*. Rather, we say that his *justification is* that *p* and *q*. If I am wrong about this, the argument may of course easily be rewritten with room for the plural alternative.

The points to be made on behalf of this argument are so similar to those for the Main Argument that I won't bother to defend these premises independently. But, I should say something, I think, to make sure that the third premise, (3′), is taken correctly. Some people seem to think that as long as someone *offers* something *as* a justification (for something X), then that can be counted properly as *his justification* (for it). They seem to think that 'justification' can be understood on a quite complete parallel with, say, 'excuse' and 'argument'. Now, we can speak of someone's excuse or argument (for something) even if the person *has* no (real) excuse or argument (for it), so long as he or she *offers* something *as* an excuse or argument. We need not raise our eyebrows, so to speak, when we hear these words used like this; there is a literal interpretation of the forms 'S's argument is that *p*' and 'S's excuse is that *p*' with such a more lenient meaning. But 'justification' works differently. If we say 'John's *justification* was that it was raining, but he *didn't* really *have* any justification', we have to put scare quotes on the first occurrence of 'justification' to get anything consistent. With 'John's *excuse* was that it was raining, but he didn't really have any excuse', no such device is needed for consistency. So it seems that, contrary to these lenient thoughts, there's always more to something's being one's justification than one's offering something as such. What more there is is at least this: One must *know* something to be so.

Even if I am wrong on this matter of meaning and there is such a lenient sense of 'justification', it won't be any sense which figures in our argument. Our argument will go through as long as there is at least one sense of the term where 'S's justification is that *p*' entails 'S knows that *p*'. This is clearly available. We hear it as inconsistent to say 'His *justification* was that it was raining, but he *didn't know* that it was'. For our argument, at least, justification has much to do with being justified. And, we can specify quite clearly what the relation is: Whenever one is justified in something, something or some things *justify* one in it. These things are facts. Thus, if S is justified in X, the fact that *p* justifies S in X or else the facts that *p* and that *q* and so on justify him in it. If what justifies S is *the fact that p*, then S's justification, in the only relevant sense for us, is *that p* and S *knows* that *p*. If the things which justify S are the fact that *p* and the fact that *q* and so on, then S's justification is that *p* and *q* and so on, and S *knows* that *p* and also that *q* and so on. Our parallel argument, then, rests on no equivocation of 'justification'. If such an equivocation is possible at all, which we may well doubt, that will only allow one to seem to avoid our conclusion. Any relevant sense of the term ties one's justification to facts which justify one, and the correct application of the term in that case clearly requires that the subject know the relevant things to be so.

In that we have parallel arguments to conclusions which are essentially the same idea, we are not trading on any fine features of our language or thought in our linking of the two types of scepticism. We find no precious claim in our conclusion that universal scepticism about knowledge entails universal scepticism about rationality.

We have defined the second type of scepticism in terms of being reasonable and being justified. But it may well be that conditionals like the following also will prove true: If nobody is ever reasonable or justified in anything, then nobody is ever rational, or sensible, or wise, or intelligent, or prudent, etc. in anything. If these conditionals are also true, then scepticism about knowledge will entail scepticism about rationality in an extremely comprehensive sense. It may even be that if nobody knows anything, then the language we actually have will be quite completely inadequate for us truthfully to assess ourselves or each other. But the full extent and implications of scepticism about rationality is a subject we must leave for some future occasion.

## 6. The Connection between Partial Scepticisms of the Two Types

If our main points have so far been correct, we have shown that *universal* scepticism about knowledge entails *universal* scepticism about rationality. This in itself is, I think, quite an interesting result. But it is most interesting only if universal scepticism about knowledge is in fact correct. If a man even knows so little as only that he now exists, the argument so far given leaves it very unclear how much philosophical interest our reflections will have. For so far as this argument is concerned, the man's reason for any number of very different things may in each case be that he now exists. And, so far as our actual argument can tell us, that reason may in each case be enough for the man to be reasonable in the thing. The man may be reasonable in thinking it was raining and reasonable in running to the store, in each case his reason being that he now exists. This is of course most implausible, but our actual argument does not rule it out. I will now remedy this situation.

While something's being known by someone is a requirement of something being that person's reason, or one of his reasons, it is quite clearly not the only requirement. There must be some relation of relevance between his reason—and so what he knows—and that for which it is his reason. This relation may depend on surrounding circumstances. But at least in almost any circumstances, comparatively few things will be related so that they might count as someone's reason. Even without having a defining criterion of this relation, we can still be pretty sure that in no circumstance of the actual lives we have lived would one's reason for running to a store be, say, that one existed at the time or, say, that one and one are two. The same point applies of course to what justification one might plausibly have in any actual situation. Thinking along these lines may not get us any airtight proof of an implication from a partial but strong form of scepticism about knowledge to a similar form of scepticism about rationality. But it may well allow us to make such a conclusion far more plausible than its opposite. This is what I will now try to do.

The partial but strong form of scepticism I have in mind will allow that one *knows* only of one's own present moment existence, of the present contents of one's consciousness, that is, certain relatively simple thoughts, feelings, sensations, etc., of the simplest necessary truths of logic, mathematics, etc., and very little if anything else. This is of course a very familiar form of scepticism. It is a position we come to when we think—perhaps only at odd moments—that one *can't be sure* that one wasn't created only a brief moment ago, and that one *can't be sure* that one wasn't created as, say, a brain in a vat with one's present, realistic experience artificially induced. If this scepticism about knowledge is correct, as is not utterly implausible, then what is there in which one might be at all reasonable or justified?

Might one be reasonable in believing that China is more populous than India? What would one's reason or reasons be? If I were asked about my reasons here, I would say that at least one of my reasons was that I had often heard China referred to as being the most populous country on earth. But do I *know* that I have heard this? Since I don't even know that I have a past, I can't possibly know this particular past thing. Perhaps, then, my reason is that *I believe* that I heard China referred to in this way, or that *it seems to me now* that I have. But, if believing or seeming to me now are treated as relatively simple aspects of my present consciousness, so that I might *know* about them, then at any particular time there are exceedingly few things, if any at all, which in this sense one believes or which seem to one to be so. At a particular time, it *might* be that this thing about what one heard is something which one believes or which seems to one to be so. But, if so, then, at any *such* time, it is most doubtful indeed that *another* thing which will seem to one to be so, or which one will believe, will be, say, that one heard Abraham Lincoln referred to as having been a President of the United States. Indeed, it is most doubtful that anything pertaining to Lincoln will then be present to one's consciousness. So, a time that one might be reasonable in believing that China is more populous than India will, almost invariably, not be a time when one is reasonable in believing that Abraham Lincoln was a President of the United States. Accordingly, there will be no time when one is reasonable in believing much more than hardly anything. More generally, there will be no time at which one will be reasonable or justified in much more than hardly anything.

Now it may be replied that neither believing nor even seeming to one now involve such strict conceptions. Rather, one believes many things at any time, and at any time there are many things which seem to be so. This is because the ordinary sense of 'seems' and 'believes' does not require anything to be occurring to one's present moment consciousness nor anything of the like, for one to believe something or for something to seem to one to be so. If one appreciates what these terms mean, one will admit that they are 'dispositional' terms, or something of the like. One will admit, then, that all the time almost everyone believes ever so many things, including that one has heard China referred to as being the most populous country and that one has heard Lincoln referred to as having been a President. One will admit that these things and ever so many more seem to one to be so, not just occasionally, but all the time.[3] But this sensible line will only alter the location of the sceptical problem; it won't remove it. If we interpret these things 'dispositionally', then we can't also hold that we can be perfectly *sure* or *know* that we believe what we in fact do believe or that, in this sense, all these things seem to be so right now. We have made ourselves a dilemma: If one takes a strict sense of 'believes' and 'seems', it won't even be true, let alone known, that many things now seem to be

---

3. This seems to be the motivation for taking some such line toward reasonable believing as that adopted by Roderick M. Chisholm. In his *Theory of Knowledge*, Englewood Cliffs, N. J., 1966, he advocates such principles as this (on p. 50):

(E)  If there is a certain sensible characteristic F, such that S believes he remembers having perceived something to be F, then the proposition that he does remember having perceived something to be F, as well as the proposition that he perceived something to be F and the proposition that something was F, is *reasonable* for S. (The italics are Chisholm's.)

so or that one now believes many things. If one opts for a more ordinary sense, while it might be true, it won't be known anyway. Mixing about with words won't alter the basic situation: If a partial but strong scepticism about knowledge is correct, it will be a rare occasion, if ever, when one is reasonable or justified in believing that Abraham Lincoln was a President.

When one dispairs about ever knowing much and retreats to the hope of being reasonable or justified in believing many things, one shortly constructs a more pragmatic view about what the latter involves. This pragmatic view tends to be rather easy on being reasonable and justified: So long as one's beliefs are consistent, or at least not quite obviously inconsistent, and so long as one is prepared to alter one's beliefs (in what ways?) in the light of experience (what experience?), one might be reasonable and justified in believing what one does. Now, I think that there is much that is important and right in some such pragmatic view as this, but it is not a correct view of being *reasonable* or *justified*. Our ideas of being reasonable and justified demand much more: They demand that the relevant things be *known*. The things which such a more pragmatic view picks out to be favored will, then, not be things in which we are reasonable or justified. Perhaps, we might coin new words and say that they will be things in which one is 'preasonable' and 'mustified' and that being preasonable and mustified in things is what we must focus on and often strive for. I am very sympathetic with such a move, though I am somewhat dubious about how easily one can really make even such an apparently isolated change in our language and thinking. On the other hand, the practical value of making such changes is not likely to be very great.[4]

Whether or not we should say that people are preasonable and mustified, we may plausibly accept that if nobody ever knows more than hardly anything to be so, then nobody will ever be reasonable or

---

4. I give a brief discussion of the general issue of the practical importance, or the lack of it, of words that don't correctly apply in Section I of 'A Defense of Skepticism'. The reason that our words work all right in the present case is something like this: Your statement that you are reasonable in certain things and I am not may, though false, be much closer to the truth than my statement to the opposite effect. In that case, my statement, but not yours, will be *badly* false and in some sense misleading. That sense is roughly this: One who accepts your statement and rejects mine will be in a rather good position to assess the two of us as regards these things, and one who does the opposite will be in a rather bad position. It may well be that, so far as any practical purposes go, one who accepts your statement will not have his position improved by accepting instead some similar statement, resulting from linguistic innovation, which lacks the implication to knowledge which both our statements here have.

justified in much more than hardly anything. Now, our arguments have not been precisely what we should call self-evident, even if they do make this conclusion more plausible than its opposite. So, we shall be obliged to accept the idea that, in particular, no one will ever be *reasonable* or *justified* in believing that no one will ever be reasonable or justified in much more than hardly anything. This may sound paradoxical. But to think that this devastates scepticism is to miss the point of both scepticism and paradox.

The sceptic proposes that serious inquiry into the idea of knowing will end in the result of at least a partial but strong scepticism about knowledge. And, he proposes that such an inquiry pursued also into the ideas of being reasonable and being justified, will end in the result of at least a partial but strong scepticism about rationality. If this should prove the result of these inquiries—and who can be certain that it won't—then this will be the situation: Due to the nature of our ideas of *knowing*, of being *reasonable* and of being *justified*, nobody will ever *know*, or be *reasonable* or *justified* in believing much more than hardly anything, including this thing. But, if people pursue these inquiries in an unbiased way and come to the sceptical results, then they may be *right* in believing, not only most of what they previously believed about most subjects, but also that nobody ever *knows*, or is *reasonable* or *justified* in believing much more than hardly anything, including this very thing. Perhaps one would rather be reasonable than right, but paradox only concerns the latter. And, if even a partial but strong scepticism about knowledge is right, one hasn't any choice.[5]

5. Ancestors of this paper were discussed at colloquia at Drew University, Livingston College of Rutgers University, Temple University and The University of Western Ontario. One was also discussed as an invited lecture to The Summer Institute in The Theory of Knowledge, held at Amherst College (in the summer of 1972) and sponsored by the Council for Philosophical Studies. I thank those who participated in the discussions and also give particular thanks to Gilbert Harman, Norman Malcolm, James Rachels and Michael Slote.

# PART II

# Comprehending and Transcending Stultifying Common Sense

# 6

# THE CAUSAL THEORY OF REFERENCE

There are two primary aims of this paper, both negative: a wider aim and a narrower one. My narrower aim is to argue against the causal theory of reference. My wider aim is to argue against the approach to philosophic examples that is characteristic of contemporary analytic philosophy. As will become clear, these aims are closely related.

In the course of my argument, I will sketch an alternative approach to examples, one that is broadly psychological. Vague and incomplete as the methodological sketch is, it represents the main positive point of this primarily critical paper.

At all events, if the paper is successful in its negative aims, some problems of philosophy arise. In addition to a problematic situation in philosophical semantics, there will be a general problem of philosophical evidence, of how to assess philosophical claims. Near the end of the paper, I'll outline these problems, and indicate some prospects for coping with them.

## 1. An Overview of the Causal Theory

By *the causal theory of reference*, I mean a certain view concerning the semantic conditions of many ordinary expressions of our language, and of relevantly similar terms of other human natural languages. Largely due to Saul Kripke[1] and Hilary Putnam,[2] but also deriving from the work of others,[3] the view addresses the semantics of expressions of at least two main classes: (a) ordinary proper names, whether "simple", as with 'Aristotle' and 'Greece', or whether "compound", as with 'John Locke' and 'Great Britain', and (b) certain ordinary single words which are true of one or more objects, as with 'horse' (but with an eye to some words that are true of none, for example, 'unicorn'). On this view, there is a unified treatment for terms of these two types: the semantics of the favored single words is *modeled on* the treatment of the proper names. As the proper names receive a causal, or a quasi-causal, treatment, so the favored words receive a similar causal account.

In this paper, I will not be much concerned with proper names. But I will be concerned to argue that what the theory says about words, about expressions more central to our language, is dubious. This is the narrower of the two main aims of the paper.

What does the causal theory say about the semantics of certain words? Even though it is fairly sketchy, the following passage from Kripke, presents the leading points of the theory clearly enough for profitable reflection:

> For species, as for proper names, the way the reference of a term is fixed should not be regarded as a synonym for the term. In the case of proper names, the reference can be fixed in various ways. In an initial baptism it is typically fixed by an ostension or a description. Otherwise, the reference is usually determined by a chain, passing the name from link to link. The same observations hold for such a general

---

1. Kripke's main work on the subject is his 'Naming and Necessity', first published in: D. Davidson and G. Harman (eds.): 1972, *Semantics of Natural Language* (D. Reidel, Dordrecht), and now available as a book: 1980, *Naming and Necessity* (Harvard University Press, Cambridge, Mass.). My references will be to the book.

2. Putnam's main contribution to the theory is 'The meaning of "meaning"', first published in: K. Gunderson (ed.): 1975, *Language, Mind and Knowledge* (University of Minnesota Press, Minneapolis). The paper, along with other writings of Putnam's on the subject, is reprinted in his 1975, 1979 *Mind, Language and Reality* (The University Press, Cambridge). My references will be to the 1979 reprinting.

3. The other most prominent contributor to this theory is Keith Donnelan as in his 1970, 'Proper names and identifying descriptions', Synthese 21 and in his 1974, 'Speaking of nothing', *The Philosophical Review* LXXXII. As Donnellan's work is mainly concerned with proper names, whereas I am mainly with common words, I will not refer to his writings in what follows.

term as 'gold'. If we imagine a hypothetical (admittedly somewhat artificial) baptism of the substance, we must imagine it picked out as by some such 'definition' as, 'Gold is the substance instantiated by the items over there, or at any rate, by almost all of them'... I believe that in general, terms for natural kinds (e.g., animal, vegetable and chemical kinds) get their reference fixed in this way; the substance is defined as the kind instantiated by (almost all of) a given sample.[4]

The idea that favored single words should be treated in parallel with proper names is clear enough here. So is the more specific idea that it is the names that are to have pride of place, their treatment serving as the model for the other. With the talk of "a chain", and of "passing the name from link to link", it is reasonably clear that this model is a causal one.

On the causal theory, the paradigm of how a name has a bearer is this causal, or quasi-causal, model: in some initial acts, some people attach the name to an (intended) bearer. They do this by being, along with the bearer, involved in an appropriate network of causal, or quasi-causal, relations. Then the name, as a name of that object, may be passed from these folks to others, all relevant parties being involved in an appropriate network of relations. These processes of passage can involve many people over much space and time. Finally, one of us now may use that name with a certain intention and, almost willy nilly, our use involves reference to that bearer. The current user needs no special knowledge of the bearer, but need only be appropriately involved in the network of relations with it, appropriate aspects of the network then being productive of that use of the name. Of course, this is a very crude statement of this view about names. Even so, it should be clear enough that this account of proper names is at least a pretty plausible one.[5] When we consider words, not proper names, the question of a bearer does not arise. But, as the quotation from Kripke suggests, the theory locates a sample of objects, or of stuff, in the place which the bearer had before. Then something like baptismal acts are performed by certain

---

4. Kripke, *Naming and Necessity*, pp. 135–136.

5. To say that the causal theory for proper names is plausible is not, of course, to say that it is free of difficulties, or that it is correct, or even that it is pretty nearly correct, issues on which I wish to remain neutral. For some interesting criticisms of this theory of proper names, see Paul Ziff: 1977, 'About proper names', *Mind* 86. Quite a few other philosophers have also presented difficulties for the theory. But my impression of the criticisms leveled so far is that they point to restrictions on this theory of names, or to modifications required in the theory, rather than to some fundamental error in the view; this, whether or not the view does have fundamental errors.

people with regard to a favored word, say, 'gold' or 'cat', and to so many sample items which share some common nature, or essence. This involves having those items in an appropriate causal, or quasi-causal, network along with the baptizers. For example, the people might be so many ancient Greeks who, through appropriate causal processes, are perceiving so much gold, or so many cats, and are coining the original cognate of our 'gold', or of our 'cat'. Then, by way of causal processes involved in communication, those Greeks pass the word along to other people, of later generations, who are involved with them in an appropriate network. Finally, I may receive the word or, more likely, an English equivalent. So, what my 'cat' is true of will be just those objects that are instances of the (salient) kind, the kind for the relevant essence, which was predominantly instanced in the sample for those crucially placed in the causal network reaching to me now. Presumably, as it happens, in the case of my 'cat' those objects were (a certain sort of) feline animals. But, from this theory's viewpoint, that is quite a secondary matter: historical happenstance aside, the accepted semantic conditions on 'cat' may have the word be true of just some vegetables, or else some robots, not animals at all.

What may we say about the *initial* plausibility of this theory, about how plausible it is quite apart from its ability to deal with examples? Even as the causal theory is initially rather *plausible* as regards *names*, so it is initially rather *implausible* as regards ordinary single *words*. Apart from its ability to treat examples, *on the whole*, this theory of words does not appear a very appealing one. Now, this is not to say that, before such treatment, nothing at all can be said on behalf of the causal theory. Rather, the point is one of overall balance: initially, whatever seems in favor of this theory for words is more than offset by what seems to go against it.

To be fair to the causal theory, we may distinguish two versions of that account of words. Kripke, as we have noticed, presents a version that is highly historical in orientation. Except for subsequent semantic shifts, not to be invoked lightly, the reference of our terms is long ago fixed beyond flexible change. In the case of proper names, this inflexibility seems no serious drawback. But with words, it is very implausible. What our words are true of should not be so rigidly bound to what ancients encountered in their environment, perhaps objects quite unlike any you and I ever have faced. To lessen the initial implausibility of a causal theory of words, then, we should opt for a version of the theory that is less resolutely historical, which gives more weight to recently encountered objects. At times Putnam advocates such a more current version.[6] This version decreases the similarity in treatment for words and for names. That makes it less implausible.

But as there is still a lot of similarity of treatment left, while the two sorts of expressions themselves seem so different semantically, this only lessens the implausibility of the theory for words; it does not remove it. As a matter of course, in what follows I will present arguments which go against both versions of the causal theory. Indeed, except for the discussion in Section 8, it won't matter at all what version one has in mind.

Even the most plausible version of the causal theory for words is implausible at least intitially. The statement that this is so is, I believe, uncontroversial. But why is it so? Part of the initial implausibility comes, I imagine, from the theory's suggestion that the semantics of words is to be modeled on that of proper names. Now, such names are at best very marginal elements of our language; perhaps they aren't even in the language itself at all. Shakespeare may be the greatest master of our language, but even his name is at best a part of English only marginally. The names of most folks don't even enjoy that status. In contrast, the common single words, 'cat' and 'gold', as much as 'king' and 'bachelor', are central elements of English; if one fails to translate these words, as they occur in a typical passage, one fails to translate from English. It strikes us as implausible that the semantics of such marginal elements should serve as the model for the semantics of so much of our basic vocabulary, that, semantically, 'Peter Putz' should be a model for, should have pride of place with regard to, 'gold' and 'pumpkin' and 'cat'.

Let me speculate on factors which may underlie our impression that words and names are semantically so unlike, and also our idea that words are central to the language, names at best marginal. Now, whatever we may also believe to the contrary, we all have an implicit common sense belief which may be expressed something like this: that the (main) *meaning* of a *word*, or the (most central) *sense* of the term, is a very important *determinant* of which (actual or merely possible) object(s), *if any*, that word is *true of*. In contrast, even insofar as we are disposed to think some (few) proper names each have a meaning, we do *not* similarly believe that the meaning of a *proper name* is an important

---

6. In 'The meaning of "meaning"', Putnam sometimes advocates such a more 'current' version of the theory. (But at other times in the paper, he endorses Kripke's historical version, which is incompatible with the current version. In his cited criticism of Putnam, Zemach notices this ambivalence.)

determinant of which objects, if any, *bear* that name. So, on the one hand, which are the entities that 'cat' is true of will largely depend on the meaning of this word, much as which entities 'bachelor' is true of will depend on the sense of that one. On the other hand, our implicit beliefs run, which entities bear the name 'Cat' will not importantly depend on any meaning that name may have; only the appropriateness of such a name will depend importantly on meaning here, which is not a semantic matter. (Just so, a collie dog may have the name 'Cat', the inappropriateness of that name for such a bearer promoting some humor, even if not humor of high quality.) Further, we believe unreflectively that, with central elements of our language, there is an important relation between meaning and other semantic matters: with favored words, between meaning and semantic application. Accordingly, it unreflectively seems to all of us, the causal theory of reference underestimates the rôle of meaning, as that is ordinarily conceived, in matters of which are the objects, if any, to which a given word (truly) applies.[7]

Whatever the reasons for it, as a semantic account of common words the causal theory is initially implausible. According to the theory's proponents, and on the methodology customary for analytic philosophers, this initial implausibility is to be *overcome* by support the theory will receive from examples. Let us see whether such powerful support is available.

## 2. The Customary Methodology for Treating Examples

As indicated, my wider aim is to question *the customary methodology for treating examples*, an adherence to which, among other things, gets philosophers to favor, or to reject, one or another theory of our language.

With this customary approach, our dominant responses to philosophic examples, to relevant questions regarding these cases, are our *intuitions*. When an example (quite directly) concerns some terms of our language, then the response is one of our *semantic* intuitions. Using this approach, a semantic theory of our language is to explain these

---

7. In one way or another, the idea that the causal theory of words underestimates the rôle of meaning has been advanced by other critics of this view. See Jerrold J. Katz: 1977, 'A proper theory of names', *Philosophical Studies* 31 and Eddy M. Zemach: 1976, 'Putnam's theory on the reference of substance terms', *The Journal of Philosophy* LXXXIII.

responses of ours, while not failing in predictions of response for other relevant examples. Now, just as nobody is very clear about this approach, people treating many matters of application as matters of art, so my characterization of the methodology is rather vague. But vague as this is, we may, I think, see the approach to be badly inadequate.

How does my wider aim connect with my narrower? The causal theory of reference is, as I shall explain, a logical result of accepting this customary methodology even in the face of certain surprising examples. Perhaps more than any other philosopher, Hilary Putnam has been a fertile source of these examples. I refer, of course, to his example on feline robots, and to his newer Twin Earth cases.[8] Our responses to these examples cannot be well explained by a classical semantic theory.[9] So, what is to be done? An acceptance of customary methodology will have two related consequences. First, we are to reject the classical theories. And, second, we are to accept in their stead a new semantic theory that will better explain these unexpected responses. The causal theory of reference is the accepted new theory, thus motivated.

While I will not endorse a more traditional semantic theory, I want to argue that Putnam's examples do not force the abandonment of any semantic account. On the contrary, they may suggest a quite different alternative: the customary methodology, requiring theories to be so closely tied to examples, might itself be abandoned. Of course, one can reject, or question, *both* the classical theories *and also* the customary methodology (which is the course I tend to favor). But the point here is that, at the very least, the methodology might well be doubted.

At least as it concerns common words, to be plausible the causal theory requires a good deal of support from the domain of examples. In the course of this paper, I will present examples which, if any examples support the theory, quite directly disconfirm the theory. If my

---

8. Putnam's feline robot case is presented as early as his 1962, 'It ain't necessarily so', *The Journal of Philosophy* LIX, and is variously discussed in several of his later papers. The Twin Earth cases are discussed in 'The meaning of "meaning"' and in several other papers which are also reprinted in *Mind, Language and Reality*.

9. On page 17 of 'A proper theory of names', Katz attempts an explanation of the dominant response to Putnam's feline robot example in terms of a classical semantic theory of words. In a long unpublished essay, 'A Study of Common Sense', I criticize Katz's explanation. But even without much scrutiny, his account seems very weak. Why does Katz offer it? Because, like those he opposes, he accepts the customary methodology for treating examples. In response to Putnam's examples, a classical semanticist should question this methodology, not continue to go along with it. This point follows directly from my discussion below in the text.

examples can do this, then that view is immediately in trouble. But I believe that my cases actually have a rather different impact, one which is both wider and more indirect.

These cases are intended collectively to undermine the customary methodology for treating examples. But, if the customary methodology is undermined, then whither the causal theory? Now, this view of words requires this methodology for it to receive support from examples; without that support, the causal theory, not an initially plausible view, will be a rather dubious semantic account. Accordingly, the argument I raise against the causal theory is well regarded as a dilemma: either my examples speak directly against the theory, in which case the theory is undermined, or the cases speak directly only against the customary methodology for treating examples. But then the cases (indirectly) speak against the theory anyhow, in which case that theory is also undermined. So, either way, there will be trouble for the causal theory of reference.

I believe there are many examples that appear, at least, to work against the causal theory for words. Here I will present a selection of cases that advance both of my stated aims. Now, even as regards my more limited aim, I have an uphill battle. Why is this? Well, at the time of writing this paper, the causal theory of reference is widely accepted by philosophers. (They have been impressed with how well the view seems to treat examples in the literature, while they accept the customary methodology.) Now, as is a psychological commonplace, people are forced to see 'data', thus to respond to examples, in conformity with what they take their accepted theories to require. So, with many people, responses to (at least) some of my examples will be governed more by acceptance of my target theory than by anything less theoretically involved. That is an obstacle. But a strategy of numbers and variety may nevertheless eventually prevail: different examples might work differentially in persuading different adherents to doubt the influential theory.

Another factor influencing my choice of examples relates to my wider aim: I want to present cases that elicit responses which, *taken together*, are most difficult for *any* semantic theory to explain. Now rarely, if ever, will a single example cause very much difficulty for a theory. But with a suitable variety of cases, it may be that no explanation of responses will be forthcoming from any semantic theory that is even the least bit probable. Of course, using the customary methodology, a preferred semantic account is to give these explanations. So, if I choose my examples effectively, that methodology will be undermined.

It is unfortuante, I believe, that we are so determined to believe in an accepted methodology unless an alternative approach is available. No matter how many problems may appear in the only approach we use, and no matter how severe those problems, we will be loathe to question the method unless we have something at hand to adopt instead. Accordingly, to persuade as many as I can that the accepted approach is inadequate, I will present, starting in Section 5, an alternative: *the psychological approach to examples*. As this is primarily a critical paper, I present only the barest outlines of this new approach now, reserving the detailed development for another occasion.[10]

Now, the methodology customary for philosophy of language has close analogues in the other areas of philosophy. In (virtually) every area, the idea that our responses to examples will test our theories for us, that our 'intuitions' will guide us toward philosophic truths, is accepted without question by the great majority of authors. Why is this the case?

The question is an interesting one. I have no confident answer to it, but only some speculative considerations. Though now somewhat less than was once the case, the idea is still prevalent that in philosophy we don't judge facts, but that, given the facts, we judge their most appropriate description, merely a matter of language. With this dichotomous picture in place, what is taken as right for philosophy of language will be taken as right for (almost all of) philosophy.

This strict distinction, between matters of fact and those of language, is not the only thought underlying the customary method for treating examples. What might be the most persuasive idea is this further, complementary, thought: in contemplating a philosophic example, we have in mind a *complete* (idea of the) world, with *every* fact fully in place.

Perhaps this complex of ideas, about philosophy, examples, facts, completeness and language, is the main motivation underlying our customary methodology. Suppose that it is. Then, I suggest, that motivation is psychologically unrealistic, perhaps even downright incoherent. But even if all of this is true, it still won't do much to undermine the methodology itself. Though it is unlikely, one may, for the worst of reasons, nonetheless employ a method that is itself quite excellent. To argue that the customary approach for treating examples is

---

10. I present some of the main details in 'Toward a psychology of common sense', *American Philosophical Quaterly* 19 (No. 2, April, 1982). More details are in *A Study of Common Sense*.

no such excellent method, but is an inadquate one, is my task now. Toward that end, I provide a selection of examples.

## 3. Examples of Illusion Producing Specimens

Let's consider *cases of illusion producing specimens*. Causal theorists rely upon some examples of this general type to argue against more traditional theories, which their view is meant to replace. Kripke gives an example of all the alleged gold turning out to have been blue, not anything like yellow, while having produced in us all along an illusion of having a 'yellow' color. As our response to the examples is that these encountered specimens were pieces of gold anyhow, this is to count against a definition of 'gold' proceeding in terms of the characteristic *yellow color*.[11] (As is evident, the argument here against such a definition relies on accepting the customary methodology. If that methodology is inadequate, then this might be a weak argument towards a true conclusion.) Similarly, another case of illusions is used against the idea that 'tiger' can be defined, in part, by reference to the property of four-leggedness as being typical to the species. Here, the example has all alleged tigers with three legs, so many having produced the illusion of the forth limb, an illusion now broken through for the first time. Our response is that all of these three-legged illusion producers will have been tigers anyhow.[12] Now, with each of these examples, the causal theory *at least appears* to give a good explanation of our response, which accounts I won't bother to detail. But, however that may be, this is only a small and narrow selection from the whole range of cases with long-term, widespread illusions. I'll try to broaden our perspective.

My own first example is a *two-sided case of illusion producing animals*. For this case, we suppose that entities of the sort that human beings have considered to be cats, for which our 'cat' and its cognates have so often been used, are actually quite different from how they have seemed. These creatures, modern radiation techniques now first reveal, have been secreting a substance which has hidden from us, and from many other organisms, their 'true natures'. Some of these hidden features are 'on the surface'; others are deeply physiological; still others concern behavior patterns. What are these hidden properties, beneath the natural disguise? Each alleged cat, we suppose, has just the relevant

---

11. Kripke, *Naming and Necessity*, pp. 117–119.
12. Kripke, *Naming and Necessity*, pp. 119–121.

objective properties that we have been attributing to those entities we have taken to be *dogs*!

That is one side of this example. The remainder may be put quite simply: entities of the sort that humans have regarded as dogs have been secreting another substance, which has also had an illusory impact on us. The illusion produced by the alleged dogs is opposite to that produced by the putative cats; that is, beneath the appearances affected by the alleged canines are just the objective properties we have so long been attributing to those entities regarded by us as *cats*!

What is the correct description of this case, as regards which of the things involved are cats, if any, and which are dogs? My dominant (unreflective) response is to think that the alleged cats are actually dogs, and the alleged dogs are cats. Short of much philosophic theorizing or complex skeptical argument, I'm rather content with this thought. Judging from my conversations on this matter, few would respond very differently.

But, given accepted methodology, the causal theory predicts the opposite response to be dominant: that the alleged cats are the only cats in the situation, and the alleged dogs are really the only dogs there. For it is just the alleged cats for which we have used 'cat' and cognates; it is just the alleged dogs for which we have used 'dog'.

I believe that this first case counts fairly heavily against the causal theory of reference. To deny that, a defender of the theory can avail himself of just two main options. On one option, which seems the more plausible, he can invoke some *confusion* on our part which is largely responsible for our response. But then he must invoke as well, to account for this confusion, some psychological mechanisms. When this is done, the defender departs from, and even confutes, the customary methodology, which gives no place to such psychological influence. So, albeit indirectly, such a defender serves to undermine the causal theory itself. While I won't bother to mention it much, as we observe other examples, this will be a recurrent theme.

Without recourse to such extraneous psychology, how might one attempt to defend the theory? For this second option, only *ad hoc* moves seem available. For example, one might attempt such a dodge as this: there is 'something about' this example which prevented any reference from being fixed, either for 'cat' or for 'dog'. The causal theory only applies to such cases as involve successful reference fixing. So, this case doesn't count against the theory.

This reply is very weak, and for at least two reasons. First, while 'reference fixing' may not have occurred, it does seem that, in such a case, we will have *developed adequate semantics* for both 'cat' and 'dog', in fact, the very semantics that those words now have with us. Indeed, it seems that 'cat' will be *true of* many objects, those many alleged dogs, and that 'dog' will also often apply semantically. These apparent semantic facts need an explanation. But if no reference fixing has occurred, the causal theory will be powerless to give any account.

Second, if one balks at reference fixing in this two-sided case, only some further *ad hoc* assumptions will allow there to be such fixing in other relevant cases, on which the causal theory depends heavily for such support as it might receive. To make my point here, and to introduce some related problems, I will present a *one-sided case of illusion producing animals*.

For this second case, we suppose that the situation with alleged cats is just as it was in the previous example: underneath the natural disguise are so many objective 'canine features'. But, now, there is *no* illusion effected by putative dogs: the creatures we have been regarding as dogs secrete no disguising substance, and have just the canine features we have been attributing to them. Without any protracted theoretical reflection, what is my thought as to the correct description of this one-sided case?

My *dominant* response this time begins, as before, with my thinking there are cats in such a situation, and also dogs. Well, then what is what? The alleged dogs are dogs. And, the alleged cats are dogs, too. But, further, as my dominant response goes, these alleged cats will be cats, as well as dogs. In this situation, cats will be just those dogs which affect the 'feline illusion', a bizarre sort of dogs. (In relation to this last matter, I sense a *dominated* conflicting response: those alleged cats won't really be cats at all; they will only be dogs with a certain power of disguise.) Finally, I have the thought that the inclusion does not run in the other direction: the alleged dogs are *not* cats.

Let's see how the causal theory might explain our dominant response to this one-sided case. To yield an explanation, the theory must assume that reference fixing has occurred in this situation, both for 'cat' and also for 'dog'. Consider, in particular, the question of reference fixing for 'cat'. Presumably, the word got fixed by way of encounters with so many illusion producing canines when giving semantic currency to the word. But, in what seem to be all of the relevant respects, the situation here with 'cat' is just the same as it was in the two-sided case. The only difference, after all, is what happens as regards experience concerning *another* word, 'dog'. But this difference won't mean successful reference fixing for *cat* in the one-sided case but failure in the related two-sided example. Realistically, in order to have reference fixing in the one-sided case, we must have it in both cases.

Now, as will be remembered, our defender of the theory tried to make light of our two-sided example by denying that reference fixing occurred there with 'cat' (or occurred with 'dog', for that matter). So, as the foregoing argues, that reply will undermine the theory's attempt to explain the related one-sided case. That reply, already seen to be a weak one, is again observed to be inadequate.

While the causal theory does very poorly with the two-sided case, it doesn't do so badly with the one-sided example. But even in this latter case, the theory is inadequate as it stands. Let me explain why this is so.

The problem arises as regards the last part of our response pattern to the example: that the alleged dogs are *not* cats. For on available versions of the theory, just as 'dog' will apply to the alleged cats, which is wanted, so 'cat' will apply to the alleged dogs, which is quite undesired. Why does the theory, in standard versions, dictate this problematic parallel?

The basis for semantic projection of a word, from old items to newly encountered ones, is in terms of the essences of the old items. As our responses go, it is clear that the production of illusions by the alleged cats is not part of the essence of those individuals. Hence, as regards their essences, the alleged cats and the alleged dogs are relevantly the same. On the theory, then, the semantics of 'cat' and 'dog' should not differ; each word should be true of just the objects of which the other is true. So, on the theory, cats and dogs are one and the same. In particular, dogs will be cats.

Taken by itself, this difficulty with the one-sided case might be accommodated by a more complex version of the causal theory. On such a complicated view, essential features would be given special weight in determining the natural kinds of things. But more superficial features would also be given their due. When the essential properties were not sufficient to determine enough kinds, nor to differentiate the semantic applications of the relevant different words, then certain superficial, accidental attirbutes would mean the difference. It is not entirely clear how all of this would actually proceed. But perhaps things could be worked out in detail in these matters, and perhaps the price of the attendant complexity won't strike many as exhorbitant.

The moderate prospect for success which the causal theory may enjoy with the one-sided case contrasts with, and thus highlights, the really troubling situation with the two-sided example. For the two-sided case of illusion producing animals, it is not just a matter of mapping out this or that complicated adjustment. Rather, to explain this case at all well, the causal theory should be altered so much that only a quite new and different theory would remain, and not any attractive new view either.

To keep the theory itself extant, the explanation of response must proceed, not in semantic terms, but by way of invoked psychological processes.

Suppose, as seems true, that things look bad for the causal theory of reference. Then how do things look as regards larger questions? Will *any* semantic theory do much to explain our dominant responses of belief to *both* of these examples? Among the few theories of which I am aware, those of a 'classical' stripe will seem to do fairly well in explaining responses to the two-sided case, but then they will fail to explain our dominant responses to the one-sided example. And the rest, which are of a 'causal' stripe, may look to do all right with the one-sided case, but will fail to predict our responses with the two-sided example. This makes for skepticism about available semantic theories; but not very much, I think, not just yet. Rather, going against the customary methodology used in these matters, perhaps we should *not expect* semantic theories to explain so many cognitive responses.

## 4. Examples with Disparate Pasts and Futures

According to the theory I criticize, as long as the causal network is in place, suitably linking us with enough sample items with a common nature or essence, the word used for, fixed to, those items will apply to further entities with that same nature, and not to objects with quite a disparate nature, not represented in the sample. So far as semantics goes, there is *no further importance in the specific* natures of any of the objects in question: if 'cat' was fixed to only some vegetables, then only such vegetables will be objects of which the word is true; if it was fixed to only some animals, then only such animals will be in the extension, and so on. Do our responses accord with this theoretical pronouncement? To some extent, of course, they do; otherwise the causal theory would never have been propounded. But to a considerable extent they do not, which goes heavily against the theory. Let us begin the discussion here with a case that seems favorable for the view.

What is perhaps the single most influential case in the literature on word semantics is this early example of Putnam's, which I will call a *case of unlimited robotry for putative cats*: a very long time ago, even before the advent of 'cat' or any cognate, Martian scientists placed on earth numerous feline robots which, in any ordinary conditions of observation, any normal human would take to be animals. So, until only just recently, humans have considered them just that. After all, both the entities themselves and their behaviors seemed so animate, so like what we see with mice and dogs and tigers. But, unlike mice, each of these specimens was wholly incapable of any self-governance—by way of a microminiature receiver in its 'head', electronic signals were constantly transmitted to each of these entities. In this way, every movement was controlled by a Martian duty officer, sitting at a master transmitting console. In due course, these entities, or 'descendants' of them, were considered to be cats by many humans, who then employed cognates of our 'cat' to refer to them. And, in the most common sense of 'cat', no other entities, not products of this Martian system, have been considered cats by human beings (discounting, of course, the occasional perceptual error and other such sources of variance from the norm). In particular, when you have used 'cat' of an object, the word has been used for such a feline robot, not an animal. Finally, we suppose that only yesterday the true nature of the whole business was discovered by us.

If this should be the situation, rather than what we now believe, will there have been cats or not? Most philosophers are apt to answer in the affirmative, including Putnam and me. That, at any rate, is our *dominant* response, our dominant thought as to the correct description. At the same time, many philosophers, including Putnam and me, sense a *dominated* response in the opposite direction: failing to be animals, those specimens will never have been cats.[13]

Both of these responses want an explanation. And there should also be an explanation, of course, of why it is that, for most people in most contexts, the affirmative response is the dominant one. As far as I can tell, the causal theory does nothing toward explaining the dominated response here. (Later on, I'll address this matter, with my own approach. Right now, I pass over the problem, being charitable towards the causal theory.)

On the brighter side, the causal theory does seem well equipped to explain our *dominant* responses to the example, that there will be cats anyhow. All of us humans have been using 'cat' and cognates of these robots, or of those many of them that we have encountered. By these uses and encounters, we have fixed the reference of 'cat' to items with

---

13. In his early paper, 'It ain't necessarily so', Putnam seems very much in conflict; he exhibits, I believe, considerable sensitivity. But in his later paper, 'The meaning of "meaning"', Putnam can see no conflict to be present, or so it appears: notice what seems to be the rather insensitive reply to Katz that Putnam makes on pp. 243–244 of the later work; he seems to deny that there is any conflict or even complexity in the response situation. So at the present time, I suggest, the existence of genuine dominated responses cannot be overemphasized.

just such a robotic nature. So, on the theory, 'cat' will be true of just such objects: they will be cats.

Now, ordinarily, we suppose the items we have been encountering to be animals, of a certain sort, to which sort of things the reference of 'cat' has been fixed by attendant usage. So then, quite in parallel with the robotic case, 'cat' will be true of just such animals. My response to contemplating the actual case is, of course, in accord with this: there are cats (and they are the things for which we have so often used that word). The causal theory thus gives a unified treatment both for dominant response to a bizarre example and for that to the actual case. But that is enough to say about apparently favorable developments.

Here is an example which, I think, goes quite heavily against the causal theory, a *case of feline robots in the past and feline animals in the future*. This example involves a change in the population of specimens which, in conjunction with uses of 'cat', we humans encounter over time. The moment of the change will be assumed to be the present time, right now. Until now this example is just like Putnam's classic case, with Martian robots as the objects of our uses of 'cat'. At the present time, the Martians are, in an undetected flash, replacing each robot with a similar appearing 'duplicate' animal. From here on out, we will be using 'cat' in encounters with such animals, there being no robots any longer on our planet.

Now, as this case will involve *one's own* thought and behavior from here on out, it will help if we explicitly assume that we all are to be ignorant of *any* of these presumed discrepancies from the actual situation. So we are to think of ourselves *as believing* all along that we have been encountering only such feline animals, and that we will continue to do so. In other words, our beliefs in the example are relevantly the same as those we now actually do have.

Where did the Martians get the animals to put in place of the most recent robots? We may assume what we like (for most subjects, it won't matter much in eliciting responses). So, for one, the Martians could have synthesized the animals, in a cell by cell manner, perhaps getting them to be 'enough alike', and 'enough different', from pumas and tigers they observed. Alternatively, the Martians could have captured some pumas many thousands of years ago and, by inducing and selecting appropriate mutations, could have bred them down to obtain the current generation of smallish tame creatures. With an eye to the impending replacement, the could have engineered the convergence in appearance of their animal breed and their robots.

In such a situation, what entities, if any, will be cats? Without undue theorizing, my dominant response, apparently not eccentric, is that *both* the past robots will be cats *and also* the future animals will be. (Moreover, I sense a dominated response with regard to the robots, that they are not really cats. But, I sense no such conflicting response with regard to the animals. For those not committed to the causal theory, this pattern of dominated response seems typical, a problem for the theory.)

My dominant response here is contrary to the prediction of the causal theory: given customary methodology, the theory would have my response be that the future animals are *not* cats. For no feline animals were in the sample faced by us human speakers. But, as noted, my response actually is that the future creatures *are* cats.

While that is my own response here, and it seems to be the most typical one, there is another dominant reaction which is also rather typical for theoretically uncommitted subjects: that only the future animals are cats, not the past robots. Given the accepted approach to examples, this response goes even more strongly against the causal theory. For with this second typical reaction, the theory disagrees not only with regard to the future animals, but as regards the past robots as well.

While there is a common aspect to them which means trouble for the causal theory, we have noticed *individual differences* of dominant response to our considered example. This matter of individual differences is, I think, a most severe problem for the customary methodology. On that approach, there is always some single correct sort of response, which is philosophically revealing. For any who do not make this response dominantly, some special psychological factor must be invoked, and one which is to the discredit of the respondents: they are confused in such-and-such a way; their intuitions are not sufficiently sensitive; or whatever. But I do not think that, in response to interesting examples, there must always be a right answer, other typical responses then being somehow wrong. On the contrary, each of several responses may be quite typical, each for a different group of normal, intelligent respondents, with no group being philosophically credited at the expense of any other.

In this more generous vein, we may recognize as well a third sort of response as one typical to our example: that only the past robots will have been cats, not the future feline animals. This is the only response which, on the accepted method, is favorable for the causal theory. Who makes it? As far as I can tell, it is made mainly by those who know of the causal theory. If that is so, then perhaps little can be learned from this sort of response here. But even that is not to say that this response is wrong, while one of the others is somehow the correct philosophical response. Rather, the relation of philosophical theories to examples, and to responses, is far more complex than such assessments allow.

This complex psychological matter of individual differences is a recurrent theme, to be observed with many examples. It always means trouble for the customary methodology; hence, some too for the causal theory. Having mentioned the generality now, I won't bother to make many particular references.

The difficulty for any semantic theory to explain much with *cases with disparate pasts and futures* is further highlighted when we consider, in conjunction with the case already before us, the *inverse* of that example: a *case of feline animals in the past and feline robots in the future*. In this inverse example, there have been many feline animals around right up until now; in relevant respects, the world up until now is just as we actually believe it to have been. Right now, the Martians replace each such animal with a 'duplicate' robot, in an undetected flash. In presumed suitable ignorance, we will be encountering henceforth only such feline robots. (What do the Martians do with the replaced animals? Well, they can destroy all of the beasts, cruel as that is.)

What is our dominant response to this situation? Mine is that the past *animals are* cats, but the future *robots* are *not*. This response seems quite typical. (Also typical, I notice no conflicting dominated responses here.) This contrasts interestingly with our responses to the just-mentioned case, itself the inverse of this present example.

With these two examples, we have a relevantly symmetric, or parallel, pair of cases. But our most typical responses to these examples are importantly divergent. What are we to make of this discrepancy? For one thing, it indicates that, for our cognitive responses, the specific assumed natures of the objects involved really does make a difference, not as the causal theory would have it. When it's certain mammalian animals in the future, then even when only unlike objects are encountered in the past, we are ready to reckon the future items cats. When it's robots, in contrast, we will not count the future items cats of any sort.

How will any semantic theory explain our divergent responses to these parallel examples? Short of unwanted gerrymandering, no answer appears available. Rather, a more broadly psychological approach seems indicated, the sort of approach best suited for explaining individual differences as well.

## 5. The Psychological Approach: An Alternative Approach to Response to Examples

In the customary methodology, when an understanding of a basic vocabulary word is highly relevant to describing a philosophical example, and we try to describe the case correctly in wanted respects, that understanding will govern our dominant response. As a case in point, consider our response to Putnam's standard example: we think there are cats there anyhow, the robots will be cats. So on the customary assumptions, this response is determined, in the main, by our semantic understanding of 'cat'. Using that methodology, we are to look for semantic conditions for that word the understanding of which led us to make the response just noted. The causal theory for 'cat' attempts to outline, however vaguely, the appreciated influential conditions.

It is my recommendation that, contrary to accepted methodology, we should not look for any semantic theory to explain our responses to Putnam's example, nor to many other examples. For, as I see it, what semantic understanding we have will often be a secondary influence upon our responses. Using a broadly *psychological approach*, which I recommend, our responses will often be determined by attitudes that, in their content, have no direct connection with semantic information nor, indeed, with any philosophically notable propositions.

On the psychological approach, we treat many examples as little *experiments* for determining the *relative strength* of our *powerful beliefs*, those which are so hard to confute by way of actual everyday experiences. A cleverly designed example can be used to stage a contest between two very strong beliefs, each of which saliently heads a competing group of related beliefs.

What beliefs are most saliently competing with regard to Putnam's example of feline robots? I suggest that one of the two prime contenders, in fact the winner, is a belief simply in the past existence of cats: that *there have been* acts. This *existence belief* as to cats need have no peculiarly semantic import; apparently, it hasn't any. (True enough, on the causal theory, the truth of this belief is a necessary presupposition for 'cat' to have definite semantic conditions. But even on that theory, the content of this belief would not itself be regarded as heavily semantic.)

What is the other most salient contender, the belief that most conspicuously loses the staged contest? It is the belief that (if there are cats, then) cats are animals, a *property belief* as to cats. Rightly or wrongly, many people have thought that this property belief is heavily semantic, that *animal* is a defining property for the word 'cat'. On our approach, this widespread opinion need not be refuted by the outcome of the contest the ingenious example stages.

Confronted by Putnam's example and a related question, we are induced to suppose there is a conflict in our strong beliefs. We regard the aforementioned salient beliefs as challenging each other. With regard to the example, the noted property belief urges a negative answer: that there won't have been cats. For we take the example's (salient) candidates for cathood to be mere robots, not animals at all. At the same time, my existence belief, that there have been cats, urges a positive answer. Relative to the example's course of experience, will the presence of no relevant feline animals be enough to do it in?

For most people, in most contexts, it is the positive answer that is dominant. What does this mean? On the psychological approach, it might mean nothing of any great semantic or philosophic import. All that is indicated is this: for so many people, that existence belief is stronger, more influential, than that property belief.

Just as this psychological approach allows for a simple and plausible explanation of dominant response, so it also lets us explain our *dominated* responses to such examples. Simply put, a person will have a dominated response to a certain effect when the belief urging that response, while weaker than its salient competitor, is *not very much* weaker. So it loses the contest, but it isn't totally shut out. In contrast, when there is a great discrepancy in belief strength, all that we sense will be the dominant response, urged by the vastly stronger belief, not any conflicting dominated response. In terms of examples, let's see how this works.

We believe that cats are *not green*. Like our belief that cats are not robots, while negative, this is a property belief of ours as to cats. Compared with many others, it is quite a strong belief. But just how strong is it? Suppose that, as we now first discover, all putative cats have been secreting a substance which made them look tan, or grey, or black, or whatever, but apparently never their true color. With new radiation techniques, we break through the natural illusion—the color of the alleged cats themselves, it seems, is always the same: *green*. We may ask, "If this should be the situation, will there have been cats anyway, or not?" Unsurprisingly, our dominant response is affirmative: there'll still have been cats, all right, they just won't have been green. That's only to be expected, and not so interesting. What's of a bit more interest is that, typically, there is *no dominated* response to this example. Why is that? Using our approach, we are ready with an explanation: the belief that there have been cats is *very much* stronger than the belief that (if there are cats, then) cats are not green. A corollary of these comparisons is, of course, that the belief that cats are animals, and that cats are not robots, is stronger than the belief that cats are not green. We obtain (much) the same results, as a matter of course, for our property beliefs that (if there are cats, then) cats are mammals, and that cats are four-legged.

After the assessing of the comparative strength of beliefs, there arises the further question of *why* one of a person's strong beliefs is stronger than another. To pursue this matter far will involve us in the details of the psychological approach, which I forego in this critical paper. For now, though, we may note one factor that will help explain the greater strength of some property beliefs as opposed to other, weaker ones. The belief that cats are animals, and that cats are not robots, derives *some* strength from a rather strong parallel *meaning belief*, even though the meaning belief is, I hasten to remark, weaker than it is: though I have 'sophisticated', skeptical beliefs to the contrary, even I strongly believe that part of the very meaning of the word 'cat' is that cats are animals, and also that cats are not robots. My strong meaning beliefs about 'cat' give extra support to my still stronger property beliefs as to cats which they parallel.

My belief that cats are not green, in contrast, has no parallel meaning belief to give it any such extra strength; nor does my belief that cats are four-legged. I do not (strongly) believe that part of the very meaning of 'cat' is that cats are not green, nor that part is that cats are four-legged. A lot more needs to be said about these explanatory matters, of course, but at least this seems a promising beginning.

Let's now consider our most typical responses to the examples of the previous section, cases with disparate pasts and futures. With the customary methodology, to explain these reactions would require us to import complex semantic conditions for 'cat', so that our understanding of such conditions will reflect the noted asymmetry of response. Using the psychological approach, in contrast, no such complex measures are required. Without going into details, let me note some aspects of an appropriately flexible, yet realistic, psychological explanation.

First, we'll consider the case of feline robots in the past and feline animals in the future. As you'll recall, the most typical dominant response is that both the past robots are cats and also the future feline animals are. And, also, there is our dominated response that those robots aren't really cats. The explanation of our responses regarding the past robots is, of course, the same as we gave before for Putnam's example. Well, what are we to say of the positive response for the future animals, a reaction that is apparently without conflict? In addition to the past-directed belief, we have the future-directed existence belief, too, that *there will be* cats. Now, this latter belief may not be so powerful but, relative to this example, it has no serious competitor; on the contrary, our strongest, most available property beliefs actually line up with it. So, for subjects not influenced by any semantic theory, typically there is, without conflict, the response that the future animals will be cats. (As will also be recalled, for other uncommited people, there is the response that *only* the animals are cats. For them a different psychological explanation is required, which I will not provide. But with this approach there is plenty of room to do so: individual differences do require explanatory effort and variety, but they cause no embarrassment.)

Let's consider the inverse case, with past animals and future robots. Here the (dominant) response is that only the past animals are cats. Why is this all that we get now? Well, we again have the very strong past-directed existence belief, that there have been cats, which prompts that response for the past animals. But, now, there is no very strong salient property belief to contest it, nothing like a conflicting belief that cats are animals. So we sense no dominated response this time, in relation to the past specimens. Finally, we think that the future robots are *not* cats. Why is that? I suggest that it has little to do with any interesting semantic conditions. Rather, the salient competitors here are my strong property belief that cats are animals and, on the other side, my much weaker future-oriented existence belief, that there will be cats. Because the former belief is stronger, we don't dominantly reckon those future robots to be cats. Because it is so very much stronger, we don't even have a dominated response to that generous effect.

Using the psychological approach, we are thus able to explain discrepant responses which would otherwise be puzzling. For the responses just considered, our explanation rests heavily on the proposition that our relevant past existence belief that there have been cats, is very much stronger than our correlative future-oriented belief. But, of course, this proposition is eminently plausible, something we're prepared to endorse anyway. By way of these symmetric examples and our asymmetric responses to them, the psychological approach allows us to confirm this plausible proposition.[14] We are in no way required to

---

14. For related examples, we focus on related beliefs of differing strengths. Suppose that, in the case of past robots and future animals, the animals to be placed on earth were not created suddenly, but were for a long time on Mars. Then if those distant animals are cats, as we take it, there will have been plenty of cats in the past anyway; we don't need past robots as cats to make true our past-directed existence belief. Still, we respond so that the past robots are cats. Why is that? We do need the past robots to make true this related belief: that, in much of the past, many people on earth have encountered many cats. That belief, too, is a very powerful past-directed attitude, and we respond so that it will seem true to us. In contrast, the correlative future-directed belief is not so powerful: that, in much of the future, many people on earth will encounter many cats. So, to an example where feline animals live only on Mars in the future, and feline robots are on earth, we do *not* respond by taking the robots to be cats. While there is a bit more complexity here, the basic structure of explanation is the same.

import some complicated semantic conditions to reflect the noted asymmetry.

## 6. Three Related Types of Examples: Epistemological, Metaphysical and Combined

In discussing the status of such statements as 'cats are animals', Kripke adduces two main types of examples. While interestingly related, the examples of the two types are quite different, as Kripke emphasizes.

In the first sort of example, which we may call *epistemological* we suppose that, all along, we have been *wrong* about the 'sort of thing' we have been encountering. It is examples of this type on which this paper has been focusing so far. So, in particular, Putnam's case of unlimited robotry for putative cats is a case of this epistemological type. In that case, we have been wrong about what general sort of thing putative cats are; we have taken them to have been animals when, all along, they have been robots and not animals.

In the second type of example, we have been *right*, not wrong, about the general sort of encountered things. What we do this time is to suppose that, *instead* of things of this sort, there *were* at the same places and times, and giving off the same appearances, things of *another* general sort. Let us call examples of this second type *metaphysical*. Then correlative with Putnam's epistemological example, we may contemplate this metaphysical case: suppose that, in all the places where the relevant feline animals are and have been, there were instead just so many feline robots. Then we have the question of describing that situation: would those robots be, and have been, cats or not?[15]

As Kripke pointed out, we have *different dominant responses*, or different 'intuitions', in trying to describe the two sorts of examples. For the epistemological case, when we ask the question, "*Will* there have been cats anyhow?", our dominant response is "Yes". For the metaphysical case, when we ask the parallel question, "*Would* there have been cats anyhow?", our dominant response is "No". This discrepancy in response came as a surprise to many philosophers, who must have assumed implicitly that our responses with regard to such related

---

15. The contrasting pair of cases just sketchily presented is more radical than those Kripke explicitly considers. Where I talk of robots versus animals, in relation to the topic of cats, Kripke talks of reptiles versus mammals. But, especially from the viewpoint of the causal theory, the main points will be the same, regardless of the degree of the imagined departures.

examples should be the same. Kripke's noted discrepancy raised a question for explanation: Why do we make different responses to the two sorts of case? The causal theory of reference offers an answer to this question. And it seems often thought that a main strength of this theory lies in its ability to give an adequate answer here.

On the causal theory, the semantics of 'cat' is determined by our appropriate encounters with actual specimens: the essential, underlying properties of enough of those actual specimens, whatever those properties may actually be, form the basis for projection of the word to further candidate items. Those further items may be still other actual entities in actual situations. Or, they may be actual entities in counterfactual situations. Or, they may be counterfactual entities. Where any such further entity has the requisite deep features, it is a cat; where it does not, it is not.

In the metaphysical example, the *actual* sample specimens are feline animals, of the familiar sort. And, for this example, we also contemplate *counterfactual entities*, which are not animals, only feline robots. Now, as regard the actual specimens, the feature of *being an animal* is an essential property. That is something of an assumption; but, in the context, reasonable enough. So according to the theory, it will be required of any further cats, beyond the actual items, that they have this feature. But the contemplated counterfactual entities lack this essential feature. So, according to the casual theory, they won't be cats. As noted, that is our response.

In the epistemological example, matters are quite different, a difference reflected in the causal theory. In this case, all the actual sample specimens share the deep feature of *being a robot*, and also share other requisite features. On the causal theory, 'cat' will be true of those sample items, and of any further specimens with those features. In the example, this favored group includes our putative cats. Consequently, on the theory, the putative cats, though robots and not animals, will be cats. As observed, that is our dominant response to this contrasting sort of case.

So it is that the causal theory of reference seems to provide a unified account of our divergent responses to these related thought experiments. But this appearance may have little reality behind it. For one thing, there is an alternative account of these responses which requires no implausible semantic suppositions. For another, when we consider *further examples*, only slightly more complex, our responses cannot be explained at all well by the causal theory. Let me take these points in reverse order.

Here is another example, a combination of the two just considered. Let us call cases of this third type *combined* examples. For this present combined example, we *begin* by supposing that we have things badly *wrong* about putative cats; the items have all been robots and not animals. That is the epistemological part. We want to combine a metaphysical part with it. So, *given* that surprising actuality, we are to contemplate the following doubly counterfactual state of affairs: in each place actually occupied by a feline robot, there was instead a look-alike feline animal, a mammal quite like a tiger or puma, and with a common ancestry, but smaller and tamer, and so on. Now we ask, "What *would have been* the case if, instead of so many 'deceptive' robots, this *were* the situation; *would there* then have been cats or not?"

To this combined thought experiment, my dominant response is distinctly affirmative: were there such feline animals, instead of robots, they would indeed have been cats. Moreover, I sense no dominated conflicting tendency. For those not already affected by the causal theory, this response pattern seems rather typical. For the causal theory, that is a very unfortunate result.

In relation to this combined example, the hypothetical feline animals lack the essential features of the actual paradigm specimens. For simplicity, suppose that the sample specimens are essentially robots. Then the hypothetical beings lack the essential robotry. At all events, on the causal theory, 'cat' can't be projected to the hypothetical animals. If the theory predicts our dominant response, then our response is that these animals are not cats. But, that is not the dominant response.

In combined cases, the causal view doesn't even appear to do at all well. This failure with our third type of case leads us to question whether the causal theory really does well with the simpler cases of our first two types. Perhaps such success as it seemed to have with them was only an illusory appearance? Perhaps a quite different approach will do better in explaining our responses to all of these cases, the simpler as well as the more complex? With an eye to a more comprehensive treatment, let's see how our psychological approach might serve to explain things.

With our approach, the epistemological examples pit strong existence beliefs against powerful property beliefs: for instance, 'there have been cats' against 'cats are animals'. By way of these examples, it seems, *we regard the existence belief as challenged.* Generally, we respond to this challenge by affirming the existence beliefs, by thinking along the lines they urge.

In the metaphysical cases, it does *not* strike us that there is a challenge to our salient existence beliefs. In such cases, we are *given* plenty of relevant objects *as actually existing*, say, plenty of existing cats, and we are asked to describe only some further items that are counterfactual, taken as not existing. In that the relevant existence is given, our strong property beliefs, say, that cats are animals, face no serious competitor. Accordingly, for the further items, they hold sway. If those counterfactual items aren't animals, then they aren't cats.

Finally, we may easily explain our response to the combined example. Because we will stave off threats to our existence belief as to cats, we judge the 'actual' robots to be cats anyway, our property belief that cats are animals thus being overridden. With the 'merely counterfactual' mammals, the existence belief has already been satisfied. So, for judgement on them, our property beliefs have no serious competitor. Thus they determine our response: those hypothetical entities, being the relevant sort of mammalian animals, are cats, too.

## 7. Twin Earth Revisited

With various related ends in view, Putnam has conjured up a series of examples regarding a supposed planet much like our own, Twin Earth. Our responses to these examples have been claimed, by Putnam, to refute certain traditional views of meaning and understanding which are incompatible with the causal theory. However things may be with these older views, it is more to the present point to see whether these examples afford positive support to the causal theory itself. Now, Putnam thinks that examples of the Twin Earth type do support this theory of our words' semantics.[16] But such a thought relies on only a quite limited sampling of such examples. As we have experienced with cases of other types, once we widen the canvass of Twin Earth examples, there appears little aid for the causal theory. But first let us look at some of the cases which, at first glance, appear to favor that view.

Following Putnam, we suppose that there is a planet, far, far away, which is just like our earth in all 'internal' regards save those to be further specified in the example. Of course, various of the 'external' astronomical relations of that planet will differ considerably from various of our own, but these factors of difference may be ignored. So, except for such few internal factors as may be further specified, this distant planet, Twin Earth, is 'qualitatively identical' to our earth. In particular, on Twin Earth there are people who are, in every respect consistent with the further specifications, just like you and me, one

---

16. In 'The meaning of "meaning"', Putnam begins his presentation of Twin Earth cases on page 223. His discussion of the import of these cases, both positive and negative import, runs throughout the paper.

apiece. Both of our counterparts speak English, or perhaps speak a very close counterpart of our English. Unless otherwise specified, Twin Earth is causally isolated from us, or as near to that as makes no important difference.

For one Twin Earth example, we suppose that wherever on earth we have $H_2O$, in that planet's correlative places they have a substance superficially similar but with a very different chemical composition, which we may abbreviate as *XYZ*. Just as it rains $H_2O$ here, it rains XYZ there. Just as $H_2O$ supports life here, so XYZ does that there. Just as we call $H_2O$ by our word 'water', so there our counterparts *call* XYZ *water*. On earth there is only $H_2O$, no XYZ; on Twin Earth there is only XYZ, no $H_2O$. But, otherwise the planets are as much alike as is possible.

What stuff *is water*? My dominant response, like Putnam's, is that only the $H_2O$ is water, not the XYZ. My word 'water', then, is true of only $H_2O$, not XYZ. What is the Twin Earthian's 'water' true of? My response is in parallel. His 'water' is true only of XYZ, not $H_2O$. As his word is true of different stuff than is mine, while both are common nouns, there are two different words, pronounced and spelled the same.

For a more telling variant on this example, Putnam rolls the time of consideration back to our 1750. On both planets, we now suppose, the people are ignorant of modern chemistry, thus are ignorant of the composition of the abundant liquid that rains down, flows in rivers, and so on. In all relevant regards, the heads of us earthlings are in the same state as those of the Twin Earthians. Each group associates the same 'ideas' or 'concepts' with their word 'water'. Yet even as to this early point, when our thoughts are relevantly the same, the dominant response is that our 'water' is true of only the $H_2O$, while their 'water' is true of, refers to, only the XYZ.

It is not hard to see how these responses, initially surprising, might be explained by the causal theory. Our civilization was encountering $H_2O$ when giving currency to our 'water' and cognates. Their society, in contrast, encountered just so much XYZ when giving currency to their 'water' and cognates. On the causal theory, the basis for projecting our 'water' is the essential property of the stuff our own society encountered, which is, we presume, the property of *being $H_2O$*. As the stuff the Twin Earthians *call water* lacks this property, our 'water' is *not* true of it; so, it is *not water*. Of course, conversely, water lacks the deep essential property of the stuff the Twin Earthians were encountering; it lacks the property of being XYZ. Just so, their word 'water' is not true of the stuff that flows in rivers here, is not true of $H_2O$.

In outline, this is how the causal theory might explain our responses to such Twin Earth examples. Similar explanations may be given for rather similar examples, several of which cases Putnam presents.[17] Now, there is certainly room for improvement here.[18] But, at least as an explanatory sketch, what the causal theory yields looks pretty good. Can this appearance of quality be maintained through a wide variety of Twin Earth examples? If it cannot, then, quite likely, there will be merely an appearance for any of these cases, no genuine explanatory power. And, in point of fact, the favorable look cannot be widely maintained.

Here is a Twin Earth example which is much more troublesome for the causal theory. In this case, the stuff they call 'water', like ours, is $H_2O$. But now what they call 'gold', unlike what we use our 'gold' for, is not even a metal: it is a rare and highly prized *wood*, with all of the superficial qualities of (our) gold. (Thus this substance, this wood, has many of the properties of other metals too, but all comparatively superficial ones.) As in the case just before, let the time be 1750. So, nobody yet knows anything of the true composition of what is anywhere called 'gold'.

As they are going by the appropriately suggestive appearances, the Twin Earthians (incorrectly) believe that the stuff they call 'gold' is a *metal*, just as is the stuff they call 'iron' and the stuff they call 'silver'. Because they (correctly) believe that *no* metal is a *wood*, they (incorrectly) believe that the stuff they call 'gold' is *not* any wood. After all, these people are as much like us as is possible, and that is just what we would think if we were in their place. So much for specification of the example.

To this example, we respond, first, that gold is the metal on our planet and is not that distant wood. But, for examining semantic theories, the more interesting question is this: relative to the example, what stuff, if any, is *their* word 'gold' *true of*? My dominant response to this question is that, first of all, it is *not* true of the stuff they use the word for. And, what is only a bit less pronounced is this: their 'gold' is true of *gold*. (So the dominant thought amounts to this: we all share the same word, true of the same stuff.)

This is quite bad for the causal theory, which loses out here on *both counts*. First, according to that theory, the Twin Earthian 'gold' should be true of that wood over there. For their society was encountering just

---

17. In particular, one should notice his Twin Earth aluminum—molybdenum example, presented on pages 225–226 of 'The meaning of "meaning"'.

18. Consider various difficulties pointed out by Zemach in 'Putnam's theory on the reference of substance terms'.

such wood when applying that word of theirs. As far as our responses go, the matter is otherwise. In the second place, on the causal view the Twin Earthian's 'gold' should *not* be true of *gold*. For nothing with the essential features of gold, say, nothing with atomic number 79, was present in the sample of the Twin Earthians: they faced only some *wood*. But our dominant response is that their word *is* true of our metal; apparently, this is a second, related failure for the causal theory.

Here is another Twin Earth example which means trouble for the causal theory. This is a combination of Putnam's two celebrated examples: Twin Earth *plus* alleged cats that are robots. We suppose, now, that everything is normal here on earth, and in our solar system. But things are more deceptive far away. On Twin Earth, there have never been any smallish, tame feline animals. Instead, a long time ago, scientists from Twin Mars put down on Twin Earth feline robots, of the sort now familiar to my readers. Thinking these entities to be animals, not robots, the Twin Earthians coined a cognate of Twin Earth 'cat' with respect to just those deceptive items. Even to this day, those benighted Twin Earthians are using their 'cat' and cognates to speak of just so many feline robots.

Naturally enough, we think that those robotic entities are *not* cats; in effect, we think that our 'cat' is not true of them. But, what about the Twin Earthian word 'cat'; is it true of those objects? My dominant response, not idiosyncratic, is that their word is *true of* those objects that *we* have been calling cats, that is, that it is true of *cats*.

As with responses to the previous example about 'gold' and the funny wood, the causal theory again loses out on *both counts*. For reasons that the reader can now easily work out, the theory says that the Twin Earthians' 'cat' *should* be true of their robots, and it also says that this word *should not* be true of our animals. A related point occurs: in these last two cases, we are disposed to think of the Twin Earthians and ourselves as sharing the *same* word, as having the same 'cat' and the same 'gold', not as having two different words each spelled and pronounced the same. This is quite the opposite to Putnam's Twin Earth cases.

Some Twin Earth cases do appear well explained by the causal theory; these seem badly explained, or not at all, by a classical theory of semantic reference for the words. Others appear to be explained by such a classical view; those examples baffle the causal theory. Given these discrepancies, it is doubtful whether any semantic theory is actually doing much to explain our responses to any of these cases.

Instead, what is wanted to explain our responses is a more broadly psychological approach. And now we can begin to see how broad this approach must be. It must include a study in *social psychology*. In such a study, as I understand it, we examine our attitudes toward, including our tendencies toward beliefs about, assumed other people. Some of these presumed persons will be taken as socially close to us, others as much further removed. How do these assumed differences influence our judgements? For us now, this standard question acquires poignancy. A few words can explain what I mean.

Consider, once again, Putnam's case about our putative cats and robots. And consider, in contrast, the recent case of a similar deception perpetrated on Twin Earthians. Where (our) Martians have gotten *us* to face only robots, as in Putnam's example, we respond by thinking that those specimens *are* cats, even if not animals. But where the Twin Martians have gotten *the Twin Earthians* to face only robots, as in my more recent example, we respond by thinking that the salient specimens are *not* cats. Nonetheless, our response also is that both we and they share the same word 'cat'. This seems quite bizarre, a very puzzling asymmetry. What is going on here?

It is my suggestion that these puzzling responses are to be explained by certain of our social attitudes, and by a certain egocentric tendency in these attitudes. The explanation begins like this. As a person typically perceives these matters, the falsity of certain of his beliefs will threaten a greater challenge to his or her total view that will the presumed failure of certain others. For convenience, let's call beliefs of the first sort those concerning that person's *main matters*. Then among our own main matters will be whether or not there have been plenty of cats around us for a goodly while, but not (so much) whether or not cats are animals. Our attitudes, then, operate so that we (seem to) come out *right* about our main matters, even if that means that so many robots be reckoned cats. For what is our alternative? If 'cat' is true of nothing, or nothing we encountered, will 'dog' be far behind, or 'tree', or 'table' or 'man'? We've got to put a finger in the dike, lest it appear that all our common words, and our concepts, fail of contact with (experienced) reality.

But we are *not* so ready to make *them* (seem to) come out right in their main matters, those distant Twin Earthians. After all, who are they to us? If their 'cat' should fail of reference to their encountered entities, if their 'gold' should likewise fail, that's just too bad. For them, we won't go against our implicit belief that like people have words with the same semantics, and have beliefs with the same content. For them, we won't go against our beliefs, either, about the meaning of common words, like 'cat' and 'gold'. In particular, we continue in the belief that, according to the very meaning of the word 'cat', a word shared by them and us, cats are animals. If their view seems about to crumble upon such an insistence, well, that's just too bad for them.

With these as our attitudes, we're not all that charitable in matters of who's been right or wrong. Nevertheless, when we've little enough to lose or risk, we lend a hand: in the 'water case', as will be noted, we needn't go against the strongly believed meaning of a common word to be charitable to the aliens, needn't admit anything like cats that are not animals. For we have no strong relevant belief as to the meaning of 'water'.

## 8. Troubles from the Past

In Section 3, we considered some examples where our society was first faced with one sort of thing, say, feline animals of the familiar domestic sort, and then later faced with another sort of thing, say, Martian feline robots, productive of the same appearances to us. In those examples, the earlier items were in our immediate pasts and on back, and the later items were from now on into our futures. Suppose, now, that we keep the idea of such a temporal shift in the population of target objects, say, in the putative cats, but *move the time of the shift backwards* a good way. Then we will have examples where at different past times in our civilization's history we and our ancestors encountered different sorts of objects. In this section, I'd like to examine a pair of examples that are both of this general sort, but which, I think, contrast with one another interestingly. Taken together these examples do at least two things. First, they help to undermine the causal theory of reference, working differently against the two (main) versions of the theory. And, second, they provide further motivation for the idea that a social psychological approach is our best bet for explaining responses to so many philosophic examples.

Consider a *case of five hundred years of recent robotry*. In this example, things are as ordinarily believed up until five hundred years ago. Plenty of relevant feline animals around, no feline robots. Then, five hundred years ago, in an undetected flash, the Martians replace each such animal with a 'duplicate' robot, taking the animals to Mars, say, where they were not subsequently encountered by any human being. For the past five hundred years, humans have been encountering just such robots, which 'inhabit' our planet in the by now familiar fashion.

Without protracted reflection upon the case, my dominant response is to think that, relative to this example, both the older feline animals are cats *and also* the more recent robots are. With regard to the recent robots, but not with regard to the animals, I have a dominated conflicting response as well. But my *dominant* reaction is 'generous' to the recent robots; I accord them the status of cats.

Now, consider a *case of five hundred years of ancient robotry*. This time, we suppose that the period of feline robots is of the same duration, five centuries, but is much further back in our past. Let us say that it ended five thousand years ago; then we can call that five hundred year period 'the time of the baptizers'. So, at the end of this baptizer time, each robot was replaced by a 'duplicate' feline animal, perhaps bred on Mars from some pumas abducted eons ago. And it is just such animals which we have been encountering, and have been considering cats, for the past five thousand years.

My dominant response here, to relevant questions of characterization, is that *only the feline animals* are cats, *not* those feline robots. And, I sense no dominated, conflicting response in the matter. Notice how different this is from my response to the just prior case. And, to both cases, my own responses are rather typical.

How do these responses bear on the causal theory? Even assuming the customary methodology for examples, the matter is rather complex. That is because there are two different versions of the theory (as well as 'compromises' between them), and the responses bear differently on the two versions. First, there is the resolutely *historical* version advocated by Kripke, and also endorsed by Putnam. Second, and in contradiction to the first version, there is the (more) *current* version, which Putnam has advanced. Let us consider each version in turn.

As I said in Section 1, the historical is the more implausible of the two versions (though the other has its own peculiar disadvantages as well). In line with this, it is notable that *both* of the cases just considered elicit responses which go against this implausible version.

Consider the case of five hundred years of ancient robotry. What does the historical version predict for this example? Well, as the linguistic originators were all encountering (almost) only robots in connection with uses of their (cognate of our) 'cat', *such robots should be the only cats*, the only objects of the sort for which 'cat' and cognates project. After all, this isn't just a few old cases gone awry, or even a bad week for ostending usage; it's five full centuries of nothing but these contraptions all over the earth. So, the causal theory will urge the aforementioned directive, which naturally may be divided thus: (a) such robots as the baptizers encountered *are* cats and (b) such animals as we later encounter, not being such robots, are *not* cats. In fact, our dominant responses, as noted, are directly opposite *both* as concerns (a) *and also* as concerns (b). As far as predicting response goes, the causal theory fails on both counts here.

Now, let's look at how this version deals with the example concerning *recent* robotry for five hundred years past. Here, the original specimens are all feline animals of the relevant sort; it's just those animals that the baptizers encountered. So, on the historical version, *only such animals should be cats*. This also naturally divides in two: (a) such animals will be cats and (b) the 'duplicate' robots, not being animals, won't be cats. As noted, our dominant response conforms with (a); but it goes *opposite* to (b). As far as predicting responses for this example goes, the historical versions scores on one count and fails on the other.

Taking the pair of examples together, as appears natural, the historical causal theory succeeds on one count while failing on three. That's very bad for any theory that would treat of philosophical cases, even for one, unlike the causal theory, that might do quite well with so many other examples. Nor is this failure an artifact of chosen specifics, e.g., the artificial character of the robotic specimens. Though a bit less marked, very much the same results are obtained with more natural examples. Substitute Martian reptiles for robots; compare metal specimens for 'gold' with wooden ones. Moreover, a natural interstellar wind can do the shifting; no intelligent agency is required, whether from Mars or elsewhere. As far as its historical version goes, the causal theory for words receives very little support indeed from our actual responses to examples.

Now, let's turn to the current version of the causal theory, the version where our current semantics is not (much) determined by encounters with objects deep in the past. On the whole, this version is less implausible. In line with that, the case of ancient robotry *doesn't* work against this version (while it is effective twice over against the historical version). But the case of *recent* robotry *is* effective against the current view.

On this version of the causal theory, the basis for projection of 'cat' will be the sampled items of our own (recent) social group. So, in both of our examples, the items encountered by humans in the past five centuries will be the basis for projection. In the case of recent robotry, only robots are such crucially sampled items. So, on this version, only robots will be cats; feline animals won't be. But as our dominant responses go, while the recent robots are taken as cats, so are the ancient animals. Indeed, there is a conflicting dominated response with the robots but there is no such conflict for the animals. So, as far as examples go, little will be achieved by adverting to this more current sort of causal view, abandoning the highly historical version. This remark presupposes, of course, that such a more current view does no better than did the historical version with respect to the examples already discussed in previous sections. But that supposition is correct. As the reader can easily verify, the current version does just as poorly with all those cases.

In defense of either version, some will object that these two cases can be handled by declaring that a change occurred in the semantics of 'cat', to mirror the change in the population of encountered objects.[19] But this defense is extremely weak. In the first place, our intuitive thoughts about the examples don't confirm the idea of any such semantic shift, and in fact actually go the other way. With respect to either of the cases, we may ask whether the older people and the newer had words for putative cats which meant the same or not, which were semantically of a piece or which were disparate. The dominant response, it is clear, is that there was no relevant change from their 'cat' to our 'cat'; rather, our 'cat' will give a (nearly) perfect translation, we respond, of the original cognate. Finally, in responding, we think of their word and ours as being true of just the same objects.

In the second place, the assumption of such a semantic shift goes against our more reflective thinking as well. The shift in sample objects, after all, was wholly undetected by any speaker of any relevant language. Each speaker was always under the impression that, in facing such an object, he was encountering an animal. Moreover, if such a semantic change occurred, *when* did it occur? As we think of each candidate time, none seems suitable. I suggest that, in these cases, no relevant semantic shifts occur.

In respect of our attitudes toward past people, their languages and their beliefs, as well as toward the objects they encountered, many interesting questions arise. The pair of examples considered in this section can give us some feeling for these questions. No semantic theory will help us to answer these questions, nor will do much to explain responses to the examples. That is because the questions are psychological, not semantic, and the responses are to be explained psychologically.

## 9. Egocentric Attitudes as Determinants of Response

In Section 7, we noticed that we respond quite differently to examples that are parallel in (virtually) all respects save this: in one case, say,

---

19. We must allow, of course, that a common word can sometimes change its meaning, just as we must allow that a proper name can change its denotation. In general, when a word changes its meaning there will occur a correlative shift in its reference as well. On these matters, see Gareth Evans: 1973, 'The causal theory of names', *Aristotelian Society Supplementary Volume* XLVII, pp. 195–196. Also see Kripke, *Naming and Necessity*, p. 163.

Putnam's standard robotic example, our own social group will be wrong about our main matters' if we admit that there haven't been cats, objects of the sort saliently in question. Then our total view will seem most seriously threatened. In the other case, say, our case of Twin Earth and Twin Mars, only some socially distant group will be so badly wrong on such a condition. Then their total view will seem thus threatened. We respond so that Martians will *not* have deceived *us* on the question of whether there have been cats around *here*; but we also respond so that the Twin Martians *will* have deceived our *counterparts* on the question of whether there have been cats around *there*. I suggested that this asymmetry of response was not based semantically, but was due to an *egocentric bias* in one's social attitudes.

There is a parallel asymmetry, I believe, in our responses to the pair of examples in focus in Section 9. In one case, the five hundred years of recent robotry, my own group will be wrong on such a matter of existence unless I think that many robots are cats; so I respond in that way. In the other case, with that much ancient robotry, only some rather distant group will be thus wrong, the old baptizers. Not caring so much about their having been right, I deny that their encountered robots were cats, letting them be wrong about whether there were cats around them. Perhaps, then, the asymmetry of response to this new pair of examples is also to be explained, not semantically, but by the same egocentric bias in our attitudes toward perceived others.

The egocentric bias that I am positing is far from obvious. Rather, it is sensed through the consideration of response patterns to groups of unobvious examples. But though not easy to see, the bias might nonetheless be real.

The tendency I posit will, under appropriate conditions, overcome more commonly observed tendencies that we have. What is such a more easily observed disposition? Well, we have a strong tendency toward taking smallish, feline, mammalian animals to be cats and, more to the point at present, we have a strong tendency *opposed* to treating as cats a group of things that are very different from them. The greater the perceived difference, the greater the opposing tendency. (So, I am more disposed to exclude robots from cathood than I am reptiles.) But, when countervailing psychological forces are at work, these opposing tendencies are sometimes overcome, even the stronger among them. On the psychological approach, we try to characterize these countervailing tendencies, and to watch their effective operation.

In generally outline, my relevant social attitudes, work like this: Some social groups I'll favor; some I won't. When I favor some folks, then I'll try to get their view of the world in touch with (what I take to be) reality. For a favored group, I'll treat their 'cat', for example, as being true of so many items encountered by so many members (subject, of course, to some qualifications). For a group that is not so favored, I'll be more of a stickler about what cats are supposed to be, even about what 'cat' is supposed to mean.

Which groups will I favor, and which groups not? There are several factors, often interacting, that determine my treatment. One factor is how *substantial* is the group perceived, itself a complex feature involving several simpler components. But, without analysis, the group of all mankind is more substantial than the group of all Africans; the group of all mankind for the past thousand years is more substantial than all of us humans for just the past ten. The more substantial I take a social group to be, the more I favor it.

I want to focus on another determinant, at the heart of my posited egocentric bias. This factor is *the social distance from the perceiver* of the social group in question. When I am the perceiver, the factor becomes the social distance *from me*, as I perceive that. When I am in the group, that distance is zero, the minimum. The group of all mankind for the past ten years, and also for the past thousand, is at this minimum social distance from me. The people at the time of the baptizers are at a much greater social distance. Those on Twin Earth, having no causal, and so no social, connection with my society, are at a much greater social distance still. The smaller the social distance from me that I perceive for a social group, the more I favor those people.

In terms of the relevant factors, notably the factor of perceived social distance from me, the earthlings get favored, but the Twin Earthians do not. And the earthlings for the past five hundred years are a favored group, but not those alive just during the time of the baptizers. Because of this, I treat the feline robots of the former groups as cats, but not the robots of the latter groups. My social attitudes, productive of this responsive treatment, are imbued with favoritism, bias or prejudice.

The explanation of our responses by such egocentric attitudes is hardly flattering. Consequently, many people will object. Let us see what they might say regarding cases of past times. As our own space and time here is limited, we consider just three types of objection. The first two can be treated quickly. But as the third places our posited bias in an interesting perspective, I shall deal with it at greater length.

First, the noted asymmetry of response to our two examples may be attributed to an asymmetry in the examples themselves, not to any interesting attitudes supposedly revealed by way of the cases. True enough, given our simple presentation of the cases, on the most natural understanding of them, they are not symmetric. In the recent robotry case, there was only *one* salient shift, from animals to robots. In the ancient case, on the other hand, *two* such shifts will be involved: first, from animals to robots, then from robots back to animals. Some may seize on this difference in the examples to explain the discrepancy in response. But that will not do. Either of the cases may easily be altered so that it becomes relevantly symmetric with the other, that other then held constant. Here is just one way: Hold constant the ancient robotry case. For recent robotry, suppose that only a few weeks ago, after five hundred years of machines, each of the feline robots was instantaneously replaced by a duplicate feline animal, perhaps from Mars. (During the past five centuries, we may suppose, the Martians kept breeding such animals on their planet, undetected by humans.) Accordingly, for the past few weeks, we humans have been encountering only these feline animals, no robots any more. With these suppositions in force, we think of each case as having two shifts in encountered population; the examples are relevantly symmetric now. But our dominant responses to the cases remain the same. There is still the discrepancy of response.

Another attempt to avoid the conclusion of egocentricity will proceed along these lines. The baptizers are a *much less substantial* social group than are the folks of the past five centuries. There are fewer of them, their culture amounts to less, and so on. With this objection, we have noted an important factor influencing our social judgements. But the factor does not seem telling in the case at hand. We may change the example so that the baptizers are numbered in the billions, and so that their culture is incredibly advanced: They took space trips to other planets (but did not discover the Martian shenanigans). Perhaps this does a *bit* toward moving me to accord their believed cats the status of cathood, but then not much. My dominant response remains the same, in the negative.

A third attempt to avoid the egocentric conclusion will involve the presentation of new, related examples where our responses do *not* seem governed by egocentric attitudes. For instance, suppose that there have been only feline animals everywhere but in New York State, where I was born and raised, where I now live and have spent most of my life, where most of my family is from, and so on. The Martians, we suppose, perpetrated their robotry, for however many centuries, just in New York. If this is the situation, will these entities have been cats anyhow? My dominant response is in the negative. As far as I can tell, I have no more tendency to think these robots cats than I would were the example shifted away from my region, so that, say, the robots were always just in Illinois, where my perceived social experience is very slight indeed. If I were egocentric, it might be claimed, there should be a discrepancy in these responses, which there is not.

This line may also be taken with examples where social proximity follows time, not space, as in our examples of recent and of ancient robotry. For one example of this sort, suppose that the Martian robots had the run of our planet, not for the past five hundred years, but for just the past *five*; otherwise it's always been the feline animals. To this example of recent robotry, my response is that the robots are *not* cats. I sense no tendency to think otherwise. If I were egocentric, it may be said, I should rule those robots to be cats, along with the animals. In that way, I would, after all, minimize the incorrect beliefs as to encounters with cats for me and my group, much as I seem to do in our original case of recent robotry, with the five hundred years. But, as noted, I don't seem so egocentric here.

In a rather similar vein, we may suppose a variant on the example of ancient robotry. In this version, there are only feline robots on earth from time immemorial until fifty years ago, which is well before I was born. Then a switch was made to smallish feline animals, to living 'duplicates', perhaps bred by Martians from abducted pumas. My dominant response this time is that *both* the older robots as well as the more recent animals are cats. If I were egocentric, it could be said, this would not be my response. Rather, I would reject cathood for the older items, according the status only to the recent animals, the specimens within my own lifetime.

Our third objection involved three examples. To each of these examples, my dominant response was not an egocentric one, not well explained by positing any such bias. But what does that show? Does it show that there really is no egocentric tendency in my system of attitudes? No; it does not. For there are other examples, we have observed, that do indicate such a tendency in me. Well, then, how can we reconcile the various indications of these two groups of examples? The reconciliation is easily affected: As some examples indicate, my social attitudes do have an egocentric bias. But, as other examples also indicate, this bias is *not* a *narrow* one; rather, it operates only in the large. While I am prejudiced to favor my own, my prejudice is a rather cosmopolitan one. The earlier of our examples indicate that there *is* a prejudice; the three later examples indicate *limits* of the prejudice.

Within cosmopolitan limits, the various psychological factors work together to produce my social judgements. By way of certain social judgements, I'll consider certain objects cats; by way of others, less favorable, I'll treat other candidates differently. In large measure, this is a matter of *degree*. So, along lines already laid down, we can produce an infinite spectrum of cases and notice increasing, and decreasing tendencies in responsive judgements. As a five hundred year period and its people gets closer to me now, I increasingly tend to judge its feline robots to be cats. As such a group moves further away from me, if only in my imaginative suppositions, so there is a decreasing tendency toward favorable judgement.

These variable tendencies are not importantly related to the semantics of 'cat', or of any other expression. To stick with accepted methodology and suppose otherwise is, I suggest, to become party to doubtful contentions about our language.

Suppose, contrary to my position, that our responses are to be accounted for by correct semantic understanding. Then our pattern of responses to these examples indicates that each person is, in an important way, the reference point for determining what's what, for example, for determining what is a cat and what is not. After all, as my responses go, what counts as a cat is *in relation to* the word uses and specimen encounters of *favored* substantial groups. And the large social groups thus favored are, as my responses go, those socially close enough to *me*. So, although indirectly, what 'cat' is true of; and thus *what things are cats*, is determined largely by the relation of many specimens to *me*, to Peter Unger. But, for two related reasons, this is doubtful.

In the first place, as even I can tell, I am *just not that important*. Which things are cats, which fish, which roses—none of these are matters that revolve around Peter Unger. Though I sometimes overestimate my own importance, on these matters not even I can think otherwise; I certainly don't expect you to do so.

Secondly, taking these responses as semantically informative promotes an *unwanted semantic relativism*. For just as my own responses will then indicate such supreme importance for me, so anyone else's will indicate the same exalted position for him or for her. For instance, if he bothered to examine such examples and his responses to them, David Hume should conclude as much for himself. As he lived so much earlier than I, the reference point he determines, or which he is, will be notably different from the one I am. Now, his 'cat', I submit, won't be true of so many different possible objects than mine is; rather, we share one word, true of just the same objects, or at least very nearly the same, no matter who employs it.

A cautious treatment of these matters suggests a broadly psychological approach, not a directly semantic one: whatever the positive features of our language, they are not conspiring to give each of us the impression that he, and he alone, is the measure of all things. Perhaps, as our responses to examples suggest, each of us has deep attitudes to such an egocentric effect. But that is a matter of our individual psychologies, including our socially oriented attitudes; and not of the language itself in which those attitudes, along with so much else, might find some expression.

## 10. Problems and Prospects

Given our experience with the foregoing examples, certain problems arise for philosophers to deal with, both in the area of philosophical semantics and, more generally, as concerns the appropriate methodology for philosophy as a whole.

As regards semantics, we now seem to lack an adequate theory of the conditions of many of our words. This remark implies that, at the present juncture, the causal theory for words does not seem adequate; but this implication itself seems correct. As we may recall, the causal theory was an initially implausible view, to be accepted only insofar as it did much to explain our responses to examples. And, as our experience has shown, this theory does not do much toward explaining many responses which are typical.[20] So, what are we to say now about the semantics of such words as 'cat' and 'gold'?

I do not think that a return to traditional definitions will be of much avail. Suppose that it is analytic, in the traditional sense, that cats are animals. Even if that is so, we would seem to have no adequate definitions. For we must then be able to *complete* the definition of 'cat', that we might then begin with *animal*. And it does not seem possible to do that. What sort of an animal is a cat? A *feline* animal, one may remark. But, in the ordinary sense of 'feline', this won't narrow things down much, since anything sufficiently like a cat will count as feline: not only the wanted cats, but lions and pumas, certain robots and toys, even certain human faces. Any animal that is sufficiently catlike will be

---

20. Recall that, as I signalled in Section 2, there are many difficult examples for the causal theory not presented here. So, I did not consider a wide variety of troubling examples where the sample objects are a heterogeneous bunch, e.g., a certain proportion are feline robots and the rest are feline animals. Nor did I consider troubling cases where the sampled objects do not match, or represent well, the surrounding population of objects. (While causal theorists have considered a few such cases, there is in fact a large and puzzling array of examples, many of which are hard for the theory to explain. On the psychological approach, I think I can explain the cases rather well.) Cases like these arise by assuming the failure of obvious presuppositions postulated by the theory. I thought it more illuminating to consider cases where, even while these presuppositions are fulfilled, troubles still appear.

a feline animal, not just our wanted cats, but lions, pumas, tigers and more. Suppose we have a special sense of 'feline' on which only the wanted cats will qualify, not lions or pumas. This seems unlikely to me; but let's suppose it's true. Then, most likely, that strict sense will require so much as to exclude the aforementioned toys and faces as well; most likely, it will imply *animal*. But then, in that sense, 'feline' will just be an adjectival form of the noun 'cat'; cats will just be *feline entities*. So, we will have so much given us now by 'feline' that, in this sense, the word will be useless for giving the wanted definition. Though in a modest and tentative manner, I suggest that the traditional method of definition will not be very helpful for our salient semantic problem.

Here is the bare outline of a suggestion which might prove more helpful: We should develop a semantic theory of our primary language along with a psychological theory of our attitudes and mental states. (Perhaps we might even best consider the semantic theory to be a part of the psychology we attribute to ourselves, a very central part of the developing psychology?) This psychology, including its semantic aspect, is to explain our cognitive responses to examples, along with a good deal else of our behavior, covert as well as overt. The psychology to be developed must, of course, allow for many individual differences (and should even help to explain many of them). But the leading idea is that, along with the differences, there will be some common lines of mental operation. I regard the task of developing this common psychology as a problem for both philosophers and psychologists.

If this suggestion is on the right track, then it is too soon to say much about the semantics of our language, in particular, much about the conditions for such words as 'cat' and 'gold'. For we have as yet done very little toward developing the psychology of ourselves along with which such conditions might find their place. So, at present, a great number of possible theories of our words each has some chance of being right, or of being nearly right. What, then, of the causal theory for words; won't it have some chance? Well, some chance, I suppose; but perhaps not much. For the rather simple character of that theory, the way it assimilates words to proper names, would seem to make it unsuited to playing a central rôle in the desired psychology. More likely, I suggest, the appropriate semantic account will contain some important elements of the causal theory, but not so much that it will be just a version of this available theory of words. But perhaps not even that much from the theory will find a suitable place; it is far too soon for us to say.

That is all I will say now directly about problems of philosophical semantics. Let me turn to consider a related problem, which I will call *the problem of philosophic evidence.* This methodological problem arises as soon as we are sensitive to the inadequacies of, or the limitations of, the customary approach.

As long as the customary method seemed adequate, there seemed available a rather reliable way to test philosophic claims. Try to conjure up examples the responses to which go against a proposed claim; if one finds examples which do prompt such a negative response, then the claim in question is untrue, to be rejected or at least modified; if no such examples are forthcoming, then, in light of the attempts to refute it, the claim is somewhat confirmed. Quite obviously, this artful procedure is limited, its effectiveness being mainly on the negative side. Still and all, within its limitations, this has seemed a very reliable method for testing philosophic assertions. But in the light of our recent experience, this presumed reliability is thrown in question.

In our responses to examples, we often are governed by powerful beliefs of ours whose content is not interestingly *philosophic*, not in any accepted sense of the term. So I will be guided by my belief that there have been cats, in response to certain examples, and by my belief that many people in my own social group have encountered many cats. Such powerful worldly beliefs as these might be expected to override others whose content is more directly philosophic, even if some of those others should happen to be true. So, examples which tap such strong beliefs as these might well divert us from some philosophic truths, and then cause us to accept philosophic falsehoods with which we would replace the rejected propositions. For this reason, responses to examples are not always to be trusted as a test of our philosophic claims, not by a long shot, But, then, faced with a proposed claim, whether banal, intriguing or outrageous, what is a philosopher to do? This is our problem of philosophic evidence.

In the case of at least some of our philosophic claims, there might be a restricted domain of examples useful for testing them. Whether positively or negatively, these examples will bear (directly enough) on these claims. The evidential problem will then take the form of spotting the examples relevant to a claim, of suitably characterizing these 'good' examples, and of justifying or rationalizing this somewhat exclusive characterization. Only insofar as we can solve this complex problem may we rationally ignore the 'bad' psychological cases that, having only extraneous import, will likely lead us astray. But only in such an event, I suggest, can we properly rely on the 'good' cases, whichever they be, to discredit a suspected assertion.

To obtain anything like an adequate solution to this problem is exceedingly difficult, but also, I think, very important. Now, even without an articulated solution, we might, I suppose, often employ the method of examples with what in fact may be a fair measure of success. But, even if that should be so, our success will largely be blind, philosophically unsatisfying. Nor is the problem just a theoretical challenge of epistemological skepticism, as the widespread acceptance of the causal theory itself amply testifies. And this methodological problem is as comprehensive as it is difficult and consequential.

Consider the domain of ethical theory. This is an area of philosophy that, as it seems, is quite distant from philosophical semantics (even if there is a continuum of connecting studies). But our problem of discriminating among examples arises just as much for the ethical area. To test an ethical principle, philosophers would rely on our dominant responses to 'morally relevant' examples, on what they *call* our 'moral intuitions'. But to examples which may at first appear crucial, a response may well be questioned: perhaps the reaction is due more to self-serving attitudes inculcated by a rather prejudiced, bourgeois culture than to beliefs that embody some genuine moral insight. This problem has been noted, of course, by writers in the ethical field.[21] I want to generalize on their complaint: this methodological problem for ethics is part of a comprehensive problem for philosophy.

Our problem is as persistent as it is comprehensive. Suppose that we view philosophy as continuous with other studies, in particular, with psychology. Then there may be no very sharp separation of philosophic claims from psychological ones. In this vein, we might say that philosophers should give at least *some* weight to our responses to *any* example which is even apparently relevant to any given claim. And on the other side, we should always be *somewhat* suspicious of our responses, too, so that we never let any examples serve as anything like a conclusive test. The idea is, then, that we should view these issues as *matters of degree*. Sensible as this idea is, will it resolve our methodological problem? I think not.

Our problem merely assumes another form: relative to certain claims in which philosophers take an interest, *which* examples should be weighted to a *greater degree*, and which to a lesser degree? Some examples tap attitudes, it seems, that have relatively little bearing on the claims in focus; others invoke beliefs whose content has more relevance.

---

21. For a recent example, see James Rachels: 1979, 'Killing and starving to death', *Philosophy* 74. In particular, notice the psychological explanation of 'moral intuitions' given on page 171. Whether his account proves correct or not, Rachel's readiness to wax psychological is, I think, quite appropriate.

But, presuming that there are the wanted differences between cases, *how* are we to affect the needed discriminations of the *various* degrees of bearing and weight? As I said, our methodological problem doesn't readily resolve; it just assumes one form and then another.

There is no guarantee that there is any solution to our problem of evidence, waiting there for us to find. But, for the sake of their subject, it is well for philosophers to proceed on the assumption that there is some success to be enjoyed. In what direction, then, do our best prospects lie? My suggestion is a direction already marked: toward the development of a psychology of our attitudes, both weaker and stronger. Now, I am mindful of many problems to be dealt with in this matter, and even of some limitations which any such study is likely to face.[22] Even so, at the present juncture, and at least for the meanwhile, I can see no better alternative.

Why is a psychology of beliefs and other attitudes important for us now to pursue? To solve our problem of evidence, in a suitably general and articulate way, we want principles to exclude examples that dominantly produce responses that are largely due to certain strong attitudes we actually do have. Only by noticing the influence of properly attributed strong beliefs will we have any basis for saying which attitudes are relevantly distorting, thus which examples are to be excluded as unsuited to testing given claims. With the inadequacies of the customary methodology before us, the need is clear, I suggest, for philosophers to engage in some substantive psychological investigation, however informal, modest and tentative our efforts are likely to be.[23]

---

22. In some recent papers, Stephen P. Stich questions the usefulness for psychological theory of our ordinary notions of propositional attitudes, of *belief, desire*, and the like. As he often relies on examples and on the customary methodology for treating them, to so some extent Stich's doubts may themselves be questioned. But I do not think that all of his worries can be dispelled in this manner. So, on the whole, I find his skepticism convincing. See his 'On the ascription of content', in: A. Woodfield (ed.), *Thought and Object* (Oxford University Press, Oxford, forthcoming) and also his 'Cognitive science and folk psychology', unpublished but circulated.

If this skepticism is well taken, then what of the psychology that I am advocating as a needed enterprise? At least in its first formulations, this psychology will be conducted in these limiting ordinary terms, for example, in terms of beliefs. So the psychology will itself be limited. But it might be an early step toward some more comprehensive, and less ordinary, psychological science which may ultimately be of greatest value for philosophy.

23. Many people have been helpful in the preparation of this paper, too many for all to be mentioned. But special thanks are due to Allen Hazen, Thomas Nagel and David Rosenthal.

# 7

# TOWARD A PSYCHOLOGY OF COMMON SENSE

Though the Eleatics tried to do so, it is extremely hard to speak effectively against our beliefs, or apparent beliefs, that there are stones, that there are chairs and tables, that there is wood and water, and that there are cats and dogs. Let's say that beliefs in such things as these, in their existence, are *existence beliefs as to ordinary entities*. Then, like Parmenides and Zeno well before me, I too have endeavored to argue against existence beliefs as to ordinary entities.[1] But, in almost any context, it is hard even for me to find such arguments convincing. Why is this? While it is not very illuminating to say so, the cause of my resistance to these negative efforts may be summed up like this: Supposing that there are people with beliefs, these existence beliefs as to ordinary entities are among my most *basic* beliefs. They are, it appears, extremely *powerful* beliefs; they are quite *firm, persistent, confidently held*, and *influential* upon the ebb and flow of our other beliefs and attitudes.

Intrigued by the power of these beliefs, for the past couple of years I have been developing a psychological study of them. Perforce, the

---

1. See the author's "There Are No Ordinary Things," *Synthese*, Vol. 41 (1979), pp. 117–54, and "The Problem of The Many," *Midwest Studies in Philosophy*, V (1980), pp. 411–67. Along with these nihilistic ideas, some still more radical suggestions are to be found in these three other papers of mine: "I Do Not Exist," in G. F. Macdonald (ed.), *Perception and Identity*, (London, 1979), pp. 235–51; "Why There Are No People," *Midwest Studies in Philosophy*, IV (1979), pp. 177–222; and "Skepticism and Nihilism," *Nous*, Vol. 14 (1980), pp. 517–45.

study concerns the whole of common sense thinking, for these existence beliefs are part of that everyday attitudinal system. Though the study is only impressionistic, it has already become lengthy and complex, containing many claims and hypotheses that are bound to prove quite controversial. It occurs to me, then, that it would be useful to present, in relatively brief compass, some of the simplest and least controversial aspects of the investigative project. That is the aim of this paper.[2]

## 1. On the Interpretation of Philosophic Examples

A belief that is powerful is not apt to be confuted by experiences of everyday life, or by beliefs in or responses to such mundane experiences. For it has long since survived, and in a state of current power, any such trials or tribulations. What we shall do, then, is to consider various philosophical examples, often of a quite wildly hypothetical nature, wherein "possible courses of experience" are offered or described. This is stock in trade, of course, for contemporary philosophers. What is not so usual, it seems, is much careful reflection on the best *use* for such examples, or on how they might best be *interpreted*. It is generally assumed by philosophers, nowadays, that many interesting examples elicit *correct intuitions* of ours, which can help us to get away from false philosophic claims and move toward true ones. My own suggestion, on the contrary, is that, at least in the beginning, we treat such examples as psychological experiments, and try to notice our *cognitive responses* to them, which we may then attempt to explain. If after all of this there seem some responses which look to be the wanted intuitions, we may move toward philosophic pronouncements from there. But to reckon there is philosophic insight right from the start is hasty and, perhaps, quite unrealistic.

Here is an important example of Hilary Putnam's, a case which has proven enormously influential during the past couple of decades.[3] Suppose that, as far as any experience can suggest it, the following

---

2. The entire controversial project will be presented in a book which is now in preparation under the working title, *A Study of Common Sense*. Certain aspects of the project are presented here in a paper, "The Causal Theory of Reference," *Philosophical Studies*, forthcoming.

3. See Putnam's "It Ain't Necessarily So," *The Journal of Philosophy*, LIX, 22, (1962), pp. 658–71. The paper is reprinted in *Mathematics, Matter and Method*, Volume 1 of Putnam's *Philosophical Papers* (Cambridge, 1975; second edition, 1979), pp. 237–49. I will refer to the reprinting.

discovery has recently been made concerning such entities as we have called cats, or considered to be cats, and concerning such others as are most relevantly similar: Since time immemorial, anything giving a suitable appearance as of a cat, even as to its apparent innards, has been wholly incapable of any self-governance or genuine activity. In this salient matter, these entities have, it turns out, differed from other specimens that have been regarded by us as animals; from those we have regarded as dogs, as mice, as tigers, and so on. With the putative cats alone, in the common household sense of that term, there is a tiny radio receiver in the "head" of each, constantly receiving signals from an intelligent controlling alien, a Martian who sits at his console dutifully maneuvering these robots. Indeed, long ago, before the invention of human languages, it now appears, the Martians put down such spying devices here on earth, perhaps to monitor the development of human culture. Ever since then, every flick of an eyelid, so to say, every apparent ingestion, excretion, fornication, birth and death, has been produced by some such Martian duty officer. So, all of these entities are mere robots, in marked contrast to those we have considered dogs, or mice.

With minor changes of wording, that is Putnam's influential example. The story is rather intriguing. But with no question posed regarding it, the example itself is likely to produce any response or none in almost any typical reader or hearer: For example, someone might just think "That sounds like science fiction." What we now want, and what Putnam's writing suggests to us, is a relevantly provocative *question*, which may be put like this: "If things should develop as the foregoing example describes, will there ever be, or will there ever have been, any cats?" In most contexts containing the foregoing material, and in the most ordinary of such contexts, my *dominant response* is to believe that the correct answer to this question is in the *affirmative*: "Yes; there will still be, or will still have been, many cats." Putnam himself appears to make a similar dominant response, as do various other philosophers. What are we to make of these responses?

As will become apparent enough, these matters are not very neat and clean. Even with something of a mess, though, it is important to have *some* clarity as regards the sort of test, or thought experiment, just conducted. We have noted my dominant response, *made here and now*, as to the *correct answer* to a certain *conditional question*. We have *not*, in contrast, made any prediction as to how we *would* respond to any question, including the categorical "Are there cats?", *under* the hypothetical conditions of experience to which the conditional question, in its antecedent, alludes. This latter issue concerns, perhaps more than anything else, the stability or fragility of one's mind as a whole; even whether one should go haywire in certain bizarre situations. This issue of prediciton of response under stress, it seems quite plain, will have little direct bearing as to the comparative strength of any of a person's present actual beliefs, involving so heavily, as it does, all sorts of complex further psychological factors. But our actual present responses, to actually posed questions, however conditional in content those queries themselves may be, appears a useful guide in assessing the strength of those beliefs that we now do have.

Along related lines, it is important to note that these experiments are to be performed on a subject in isolation, not in a group, and to concern that subject's own belief about the matter, not about how some group might think or speak of it. The question posed is meant to reflect this single-minded interest, not an interest in what *we* would say, or even think, to be so. Our concern here is not with the social dynamics of patterns of speech or of belief, interesting as those matters are. The strengths of the beliefs of individuals will, no doubt, be a factor in these social processes; but as discussions of coordination indicate, so will so many other things.[4] Thus, I make no predictions about society's behavior.[5] So this study does not address the question of why, say, so many people stopped believing in witches, and of why, in contrast, so many people continued to believe in (complex) atoms.

Irrelevant stresses and predictions put aside, then, in most contexts the response is an affirmative belief. This suggests that our *existence belief*, that there are or have been cats, is *stronger* than our *property* belief, that cats are animals. For the existence belief wants an affirmative answer, lest it be denied in the "light of such experience" as the example envisions. And the property belief, in contrast, urges a negative answer: The example's salient candidates for cathood, in the relevant, household sense of "cat," are different from its dogs and mice and tigers in just such a way that, according to our system of beliefs, only the latter are its animals. So, if our property belief had its way,

---

4. An interesting discussion of various of these further factors is provided by David Lewis in his *Convention* (Cambridge, Mass.: Harvard, 1969).

5. The present approach may be compared with that of David Lewis in *Convention*, especially pp. 60–68. In a useful paper, which has not, unfortunately, been sufficiently well heeded, Jerry Fodor warns against having any great confidence in wildly hypothetical examples as sources for genuine semantic data: "On Knowing What We Would Say," *The Philosophical Review*, Vol. 73 (1964), pp. 198–212. Nonetheless, there does seem to be *something* of philosophic interest in ever so many of these examples, notably in Putnam's example of feline robots. With the present psychological approach, we may, at once, both heed Fodor's warning and also do justice to these feelings of interest.

those salient candidates would thus fail to be cats and, as nothing else there fares enough better, the example would present no cats at all. The property belief does not have its way; the existence belief wins this suitably staged contest.

None of this is to suggest, much less does it require, that any belief works in isolation from other beliefs or, indeed, from others of our attitudes. On the contrary, we do well to suppose that each belief is part of an entire attitudinal system. Nevertheless, certain contexts of response are mostly *directly* trying on certain of that system's components. In the example just considered, with the question posed to elicit response, the two beliefs just noted are components which are most directly involved. In most such contexts, the rest of one's system will not *peculiarly* favor either belief over the other. So, in that the existence belief is favored *anyhow*, the fact of its triumph indicates that it is a *stronger* belief than one's belief that cats are animals.

Notice that we do *not* make *just one* response to the question asked. Even while our *dominant* response is to believe that the correct answer is "Yes," we make a *dominated* response, of believing oppositely, that the correct answer is "No." Or, at the very least, we have a felt tendency to believe in that negative direction. It is important to emphasize this. For while there surely does appear to be this messy result, philosophers, perhaps in a quest for the elusive "correct intuition," have not focused much on this complexity.[6]

These conflicts of response do not occur all that frequently. So the belief that cats are animals really is an unusually strong property belief as to cats, worthy of some notice. In contrast, we may compare a similar test for the property beliefs, say, that cats are mammals, that cats are (typically) four legged, and, as I now shall do, that cats are not green. Now, this last belief, it should be clear, is itself no weakling. But, in

---

6. An examination of pp. 237–39 of "It Ain't Necessarily So" indicates such a conflict on Putnam's part: Apparently using himself as a basis for inference, he says that different people may feel differently about what is the correct description of his main example, and that there is nothing for him to say that will settle the differences. Here, Putnam exhibits considerable sensitivity. Unfortunately, by the time of his later paper, "The Meaning of 'Meaning,'" Putnam seems to see no conflict. This later paper, a stimulating and important work, appeared in K. Gunderson (ed.), *Language, Mind and Knowledge*, Minnesota Studies in the Philosophy of Science, Vol. 7 (Minneapolis, Minn., 1975). The paper is reprinted in *Mind, Language and Reality*, Volume 2 of Putnam's *Philosophical Papers*, (Cambridge, 1975), pp. 215–71, and this reprinting is cited here. With Putnam's earlier sensitivity in these matters compare his rather insensitive reply to Jerrold Katz, on pp. 243–44 of the later paper, where any conflict or even complexity in the situation is vigorously denied. So, as I just suggested in the text, at the present time, this fact of conflict needs emphasis; indeed, it can hardly be overemphasized.

relevant contexts of questioning, no relevant example will have the belief produce a conflict. For instance, suppose that all the entities we have called cats, and those saliently similar, turn out to secrete a substance which, in any normal situation, gave them the appearance to humans of being tan, or grey, or black, as the case may be, but not green. With new radiation techniques, we "get behind" the substance and its effects. For the first time now, it is supposed, we discover that all these entitles are green. We ask, "If this should be the case, will there have been cats?" Our response, unsurprisingly, is to think "Yes" to be the correct answer here. Of more interest, in contrast to Putnam's case, *I have no conflict, no tendency at all to think the opposite*, to think that the entities we have called cats are not cats.

While noticing the somewhat unusual power of the property belief that cats are animals, we need not doubt our explanation of response to Putnam's example. On the contrary, that account does not require this existence belief to be all-powerful, always an easy winner. Given the felt conflict, we can suggest that while that belief is the stronger of the two, it is *not all that much* stronger than the property belief there most saliently involved.

## 2. Beliefs, Contexts and Desires

In comparing the power, or "relative basicness," of two beliefs, various standards or measures might be used. We will not try to define or employ any refined or scientific test. Rather, we shall be concerned only with some rather informal, impressionistic considerations. Even with our concern so limited, one consideration, say, influence on the formation of numerous other beliefs, might indicate one of two given beliefs as more basic, while another, say, resistance to abandonment, might indicate the opposite. While always open to such complexities in our beliefs, on the whole we shall not bother much about them. Unless some reason presents itself to suppose otherwise, we may assume a given comparison to come out the same no matter which of the more significant considerations is employed.

Generally speaking, even with a given measure employed throughout, say, power to produce other beliefs, one belief may look stronger in some *contexts* while the other looks stronger than the first in others. Likewise, one group of beliefs and other attitudes may dominate another in some contexts, the other group dominating in others.

Let's consider questions of *social* context, to see how such contexts may variously affect our responses to philosophic examples. What we shall do is to enlarge, in a relevantly social manner, the context in which Putnam's example is first offered to a person, not in reality, of course, but in suppositions. Suppose, then, that one *first* hears the example while with an avid cat lover, perhaps a lonely old soul who depended on (putative) cats for company. This cat lover, we assume, has *no* great liking for machines of any kind, thus none for anything he or she should consider a robot. Now suppose that this person responds to the example's question, as seems likely, by saying something like this. "Oh my goodness, in *that* case, there won't really be any cats at all, and I should be living all alone, with just a bunch of contraptions around the house." Being a sympathetic person, as you are, in the presence of such a remark as that, you might believe that the negative answer was quite the correct one; in this context, that might be your dominant response.

Heavily social contexts are not the only ones for us to avoid, to ignore or, perhaps best, to discount. Generally, a philosophic example is presented in a context of other examples; there is an ongoing essay or discussion in which several are presented. Unless the example in question is presented first, one's responses to related examples are apt to influence one's response to it. In this way, the subject's *general tendency* of response to the given example is likely to be masked. Other examples, and a subject's remembered responses to them, can form a distorting context for the beliefs which, by means of a given pointed example, we want to compare as to strength. So, as best we can, such presentational contexts should be discounted. In providing my examples here, I shall try for a most revealing *order of presentation*. The reader, however, is urged to try for himself various orderings for the examples presented.

Suppose, contrary to fact, that I had presented, as the first philosophic example here considered, not Putnam's, but this other related one: *As of tomorrow*, for however long you like, all of this will transpire. Everything which, without the deepest investigation, we should be disposed to call a cat, will be in fact a Martian robot, just put down on Earth by the aliens. The aliens will control these robots in such-and-such ways; so it appears that they behave appropriately, and they multiply, for however many generations. Suppose the question was asked, "In such a situation, will there, in the future, be cats or not?" My dominant response *this* time is to believe that the correct answer is in the *negative*; and, indeed, there appears no conflict here, no tendency toward the opposite response.

Now, suppose that you were first presented with Putnam's example, explicitly concerning the past, *only after* we had discussed the future oriented case just above, where no mention of the past is made at all. In this *context of ordering*, one's response to Putnam's example, to its question, can easily go either way. In some "moods," so to say, one is inclined to go with what seems the *general* tendency anyhow. In others, one is inclined to go with the response just made to the future oriented example. To be sure, the existence belief is powerful, which explains the first of these inclinations. But, there is also a strong *desire* to be *consistent*, along with the belief, of course, that a negative answer here is one's best and only chance for a consistent total pattern. That explains the second of these inclinations. It would be interesting to explain these "moods," why one inclination sometimes dominates, why sometimes the other does. But that will take us far afield from our present main topics. The lesson for us now is simple enough: We shall try to discount, as best we can, the influence that presentational order itself generates in us, thus focusing on other, more relevant influences.

The presentation of a philosophic example to a person itself creates a context for him, in which beliefs, or tendencies toward belief, compete for dominance. Unlike the contexts just considered, however, the best philosophic contexts serve to reveal, not mask, our common sense beliefs and the relations among them. There should be no surprise in these statements; nevertheless, their importance for us now cannot be overemphasized.

So long as masking contextual factors are avoided, or discounted, in many cases suitably decisive examples can be found for indicating which of two powerful beliefs is the stronger, for a given person at a given time. But recall our avid, dependent cat lover, who cares little for contraptions and machines. For such a one, in virtually any context, Putnam's example will not prove revealing of any interesting general psychologic tendencies, or so we may plausibly assume. Why this should be so is, I think, quite plain: Both Putnam and I don't care so much about cats, don't desire so very strongly for there to be *cats* around. So, given what we care more about, in comparison to our cat lover, lots of times we will let almost any sort of thing, so to say, do well enough as a cat for us. Our cat lover, in contrast, has *such a different ordering of concerns or desires* that, in virtually any surrounding context, Putnam's example, and the question posed, will call forth as dominant a belief in the *negative* answer. For such a person, though not for most, the *property* belief that (if there are cats, then) cats are animals will be *stronger* than the belief that there are cats. Quite beyond mere questions of context, then, the strength of one's beliefs appears to depend on various of one's other psychological attitudes. This is hardly surprising, I should think; but especially in the current philosophical climate, it is, I suggest, well worthy of our notice.

What one *desires* most, what one *cares* most about, may often determine, in conjunction with other factors, what one believes. And, most important for our present study, it may determine, as well, which of one's beliefs are stronger than which others. To get at the relevant attitudes of the cat lover, that is, those which he or she shares with the rest of society, we *change the original example*, not just the context for it. Thus, presuming the person doesn't care so much about roses, we might show that his or her belief that there are roses is stronger than the belief that roses are flowers. Presuming that he or she doesn't care so much for iron, a suitable example may indicate that the person's belief in iron is stronger than his or her belief that iron is a metal. For virtually any normal person, then, a general tendency may be thus perceived: a tendency toward very powerful existence beliefs as to ordinary entities.

## 3. Existence Beliefs and Property Beliefs

It is our concern to compare as to strength various *existence* beliefs with such *property* beliefs as appear interestingly related to them. So, we don't want the content of a noticed property belief (obviously) to entail that of the correlative existence belief. But we also want convenient locutions to discuss the interesting comparisons. Accordingly, we shall understand 'our belief that cats are animals' to express, or to denote, our property belief that, *if* there are cats, *then* cats are animals. With this conditional understanding, there is no (obvious) implication to the existence of cats.

Let me say a few more things about the beliefs we are comparing. So that the comparisons will be interesting, we want to test beliefs that we hold quite strongly indeed. Regarding cats, what sort of existence belief is that, however we may conveniently express it? When we speak of our belief that there are cats, or of any other such existence belief, we will understand it as something of a shorthand. The belief in which we have much interest may be better represented, in ordinary discourse, by a verb in the past tense, as well as in the present, and perhaps should even emphasize the former: the belief that there are, *or at least have been*, cats. Even for one to answer negatively as to whether there now are cats, it would take, to be sure, a conditional question involving a rather *bizarre* scenario: If it appeared that one had been sleeping for a long while, and upon awakening discovered that a worldwide disease had annihilated all the entities we had considered cats, and all those relevantly similar, will there, or would there, still *be cats* around? The dominant response, to this example and question, is a spontaneous belief that a negative answer is correct: "No." But to yield such a belief as to the question of whether there *have ever been cats*, a far *more* bizarre scenario would be required, perhaps even involving items on the order of Cartesian demons, that all along had been producing in one experiences "as of cats." So this latter belief, involving the *past*, seems quite the stronger of these two existence beliefs. And, while we will generally use the convenient device of just a present tense of 'to be,' it will be to a disjunction, including such a basic claim about the past, that we will be alluding.

Along with logicians, we may understand our belief that there are cats to be made true even by just one cat. So, it might better be represented, in ordinary discourse, as this belief: our belief that there is (or at least has been) at least one cat. While this understanding has my belief to be logically safer, there seems no significant difference in strength between our belief in a large number of cats and our belief in at least one. This is just an impression, I suppose: If there haven't been *many* cats, then probably the whole business as to cats is some sort of weird illusion, or whatever. Still and all, while we will use the plural form without qualification, if only for convenience and style, the strong belief thus represented may be understood so that even a single entity of the kind at hand renders the belief a true one.

We understand that our property beliefs, as to stones and cats and other ordinary entities, are conditional in their content, though rarely expressed here with the conditional nature made explicit. But more should be said as to the nature and range of these beliefs. What is a *property*, then, as we shall understand the term? To make matters interesting, I propose a fairly broad or liberal usage, more so than seems sanctioned in ordinary discourse. So, we may say that it is a property of stones that (if there are stones, then), stones do *not* think, and speak of other such *negative* properties. Also, we may say that it is a property of cats that (if there are cats, then) cats are *larger than* mice, and talk of other such *relational* properties. Now, relational properties, thus understood, imply the *existence* of other, *related entities*. But, generally, *these* matters of existence, and of our beliefs concerning them, need *not* interfere with our testing of the existence beliefs as to *the entities we have in focus*. Still further, we shall allow that it is a property of cats that each cat *either* has been seen by someone or *else* resembles closely, as to appearance, cats that have been seen (or both), and thus permit *logically compound* properties. This is somewhat bizarre, to be sure, but such an extension of 'property of' will prove convenient, and will not interfere, I think, with making fair comparisons. Also, some of the bizarreness may be removed by reflecting on the following somewhat *abstract* property of cats: cats *belong to a kind* each member of which either has been seen by someone or else closely resembles, as to appearance, members that have been seen (or both). Finally, and in contrast, we will *not* regard it as a property of cats that cats are identical with cats, or that cats are such that either there are stones or not, or anything of that ilk. Ordinary usage most certainly does not regard those as properties of things, and the enormous extension would not prove interesting for us here.

Our focus on these property beliefs, as we call them, brings to the fore some matters of belief that concern their *quantificational* aspect, to borrow a term from the logicians. For us now, the problems arise with the consequent of a conditional belief. But, if we believe anything, then we do believe many such conditional things, even if they are not often singled out for attention. And these same quantificational problems arise anyway, with normally reported beliefs: When we believe that cats are four-legged, *what* do we believe—that *all* cats have four legs, that *almost all* do, or *what?* Let us grant that, at least generally, in such a case we will have, along with a belief simply as to concrete entities, a corresponding more abstract belief. Perhaps here it will be this: that (all) cats *belong to a kind typical members of which* (all) have four legs. But that can't be the *only* belief we have here; so, what are we to make of the simpler belief, not so abstract? If we take it as universal, then it may be doubted that we really do believe that (all) cats have four legs: a moment's reflection, revealing freaks and amputees, would be enough for a sincere denial. If we take the second option, with 'almost all,' then we seem to have *substituted* a much more articulate, hedged sophisticated thought for the one more simply related, *that cats* have four legs. Perhaps, even with such a quantificational aspect, there is a *vagueness* in what we believe.

The considerations of this section, while not unlimited in scope, apply over a wide range of belief phenomena. While 'animals' has so far figured only in expressing a property belief, our belief that cats are animals, we may notice our existence belief associated with that familiar word: the belief that there are (or have been) animals. This belief is, I suggest, stronger than almost any property belief *as to animals* which we have. For example, it is stronger than our powerful beliefs that (if there are animals, then) animals are animate beings, that animals are *not* inanimate objects, and that animals are *not* robots. To see this, we just alter our example appropriately, pose a question and note the pattern of response. So we suppose, this time, that *all* of the entities we have called *animals* "turn out" to be wholly governed Martian robots, not just those called cats, but also those called mice, and dogs, and tigers. Will there have been animals, anyhow? Our dominant response is to believe in the affirmative. (At the same time, we may note a dominated conflicting tendency.) So, as is thus indicated, our existence belief as to animals is stronger than the powerful property beliefs, just mentioned, as to those putative entities.

## 4. On Existence Beliefs as to Ordinary Entities: Familiar Words as a Guide

In the conduct of these reflections on our beliefs, a leading hypothesis is that our existence beliefs as to ordinary entities are very powerful. We have, now, a fair idea as to which beliefs, regarding certain entities, are the existence beliefs. But, we must still ask, to see the content of this hypothesis, which entities are *ordinary* ones. Thinking it impossible to find one, I seek no rigorous criterion, but only a modestly helpful guide. Thinking language and belief intertwined, I look to our vocabulary for this help.

Among the words in *our basic vocabulary* are "hand" and "foot," "table" and "chair," "mother" and "father," "pain" and "feeling," "wood" and "water," "eat" and "drink," "red" and "round," "in" and "out," and so on, and so forth. This is, of course, a matter of degree: "harmony" and "salivate" are not so basic for us as the words just listed, but they are more so than words we occasionally look up in the dictionary.

Among our words, and so among our basic ones, certain *common nouns* are words *for things*, for entities, in a way that other words are not: in a *more direct* way, so to put it. In the sentence, "The man hit the tree," "man" and "tree" are words *for things* in a way that "hit," being a verb, is not. In "The shortstop got a hit," "hit" is a word for a thing, more so, or more directly so, then "got."

Among our common nouns, some are *concrete*; we regard them as *words for concrete things*: for concrete individuals and whatever concrete stuff or substances may constitute them. So, "blood" and "flesh," like "hand" and "foot," are concrete nouns; in the relevant senses, so are "pain" and "feeling." In contrast "nation" and "number" are more abstract. Abstractness seems to be a matter of degree; but below all the degrees, we believe, are the putative referents of words for concrete things.

Among our common nouns for concrete things are those we have learned as *words for real things*, and have not had subsequent events direct us otherwise. We focus on just these concrete nouns. For most people, in most contexts, many words already listed thus contrast with "witch" and "unicorn," with "ghost" and "elf." (For some philosophers, like Parmenides and Zeno, and me, too, subsequent events can include deep involvement in disconcerting argument. But, even for me, in most contexts, such reasoning is inoperative. And for most people, nothing *ever* puts "hand," "table" or "mother" in such a doubtful light.)

Our guide, rough and ready though it be, is oriented toward our language and our learning of it, rather than toward a perceptual criterion, or one in terms of some standard sources of knowledge about things. So I am not calling on a distinction between *observational* terms and (more) theoretical ones, not even as a distinction of degree. This is *not* because such a distinction is laden with problems; true enough, it is so laden, but so are many other common distinctions, some of which we are employing here. No, our reason is more pertinent: Where such a distinction would mark an entity as ordinary, and we want to do so for our study, our more linguistic criterion already has it marked. For in fact, though not as a matter of logic, our *basic* vocabulary does not include such words as "electron," "gene," and, perhaps, even "magnetism." And, if we rule out terms that are not observational, we rule out some, like "air," that we had best leave in: our belief that there is or has been air is a very powerful belief, more so, I suggest, than our strong belief that (if there is air, then) air is a mixture of gases, or than the belief that air includes nitrogen. While not so ready to be observed by us, air is, by our lights, an ordinary entity.

Our beliefs in ordinary entities, then, at least the central cases, are our beliefs in what are the (putative) referents of the concrete nouns of our basic vocabulary which we take as words for real things. Within this group, there are differences, of course: Perhaps for logical reasons, the belief in people is more basic than the belief in men, and the latter more basic than the belief in fathers, or in bachelors. Perhaps for experiential reasons, our belief in wood is more basic than our belief in air. But we are not so interested now in these comparisons. Rather, our interest is in distinguishing our beliefs in the existence of ordinary entities from all of our other existence beliefs, and then in comparing each of the former with various property beliefs we have concerning the same (putative) entities.

To proceed with our wanted distinction: We may say that each of our noted nouns *stands for* an ordinary *kind* of thing or things. Then our ordinary existence beliefs will be beliefs in the existence of those things which are, in fact, of those ordinary kinds. This is not very difficult.

To get our kinds straight, however, there is still a bit more to say. This will involve noticing certain *beliefs in meaning* that we have. We believe that the word "rock" has several meanings, or senses. Perhaps we do not have any belief as to the detailed nature of them each but we do believe these senses to be there; we could hardly have grown up in our culture and be otherwise. Perhaps our beliefs in meaning are not very basic ones, but then they are weaker beliefs that we do have. Perhaps we have conflicting beliefs, to opposite effect, possibly arrived at through skeptical argumentation. If so, then we may at various times think poorly of our beliefs in meaning, regarding the conflicting beliefs more highly. But even then, we do have those beliefs in meaning, thus poorly regarded.

We believe, then, that the word "rock" has several different senses. In some senses it is a verb, as with cradles and, again, with jazzy music. We are now most interested in those senses in which it is a noun. Now, we believe that the noun "rock" has several senses, even as it may figure in the belief sentence, "We believe that there are rocks." In one sense we believe the word to have, "rock" means *something* like what "stone" means, in one meaning we believe "stone" to have; but I'm *not* sure *how* like. Still, it is in *this* sense, that such a belief sentence reports one of our basic beliefs.

We believe that "rock" has another sense, where it means much the same as "tough guy," suitable for it to occur in such a standard belief sentence. But, in that second sense, the sentence *won't* report one of *our basic beliefs*. For we are not so very confident that there are tough guys; perhaps there are only dangerous, belligerent men and youths. Perhaps we are more confident in certain property beliefs here—if there are rocks, then rocks are tough guys—than we are in the belief in these rocks. But, it is only *in the former sense of the word* that the noun "rock" is an item of *our basic vocabulary*. At all events, we must distinguish, for our inquiry, between these two beliefs of ours *each* of which may be reported with the standard belief sentence, "We believe that there are rocks." In that we *believe* that "rock" has two senses appropriate to just that distinction, we believe that the required distinction is available to us. In our system of beliefs, we associate the first sense of the noun "rock" with a certain kind of things, which we take the word thus to stand for; we associate the second sense with a very different kind, for which in that quite different sense that word stands. Our basic belief here is in the existence of those entities which are, it is assumed, things of that first kind. So, our beliefs in ordinary entities, thus glimpsed through suitable senses and matching kinds, will be our beliefs in what are the purported referents of the concrete nouns of our basic vocabulary which we take to be words for real things, but only in those senses of those nouns in which they are just such basic vocabulary items of ours.

Let's try to get a good example for "bachelor," in the most common meaning of that favorite of philosophers. We may follow Putnam's paradigm of Martian robots. But now the application of it will be far more difficult, far more complex and much more bizarre than with "cat." That's partly because this time *I* will have to make very peculiar assumptions about *myself*, as well as about various other entities. But these peculiarities do not relevantly change matters.

How strong is the belief that bachelors are men? Well, let's see. On a common enough reckoning, anyone who is under twenty, and in contemporary America, is too young to be a bachelor. But you can pick your own safe dividing line for age. Now, suppose that, before someone approaches this line, one of two things happen: Either he gets married, quite young, and thus gets saved. Or, alternately, he gets killed by a Martian, who then replaces him by a "duplicate" well-controlled robot. Well, what about *me*, what am *I* to be? As far as I can tell, I did not get married in my teens. Am I to be a robot, and not a man? Now, the example could be developed adequately along those lines, bringing in psuedo-memories and the like. But that is so depressing that we shall take a different line of development.

Let us suppose, what is only now to be revealed to me, that I was secretly married when seventeen years old. The young bridegroom was under some drugs at the time, we may suppose, and thus unaware of the proceedings; but apparently it was perfectly legal. Or, rather the same, he was wide awake, but while on a lengthy honeymoon got selective amnesia, forgot his wife, who disappeared, and the matter has never been mentioned until just recently. Suppose that plenty of fellows, like myself, went through such an early marital experience with no lasting memory of it.

Suppose as well that many others did not. Then they got killed, and replaced by "duplicate" robots from Mars. Right now, this disjunctive fate is first revealed: For all male humans, there is either early marriage or early death. We ask: "If this crazy scene is indeed the situation, will there still have been bachelors or not?" My dominant response is to believe there *will* have been bachelors. This is, of course, the response in line with the strong existence belief. My strong property belief, that bachelors are men, urges the opposite response here: For the only salient candidates are these Martian robots who, unlike myself and other fortunate early marriers, are not men at all. True enough, I am in *conflict* on the matter. But the *dominant* response is to believe affirmatively; only the *dominated* one is a belief, or a tendency to belief, in the other direction. Our domain of results is indeed a wide one.

## 5. Property Beliefs That Are Stronger than Related Existence Beliefs

Our existence beliefs in ordinary entities are quite powerful, it appears; but they are *not more* powerful than *every property* belief with which they may properly be compared. For example, our belief that cats are not the square roots of natural numbers, unlike our belief that cats are not green, does appear stronger than our belief that there are cats. Perhaps there is no example, or any other experimental test, to show that; but it does seem to be so. If the comparison does indeed run this way, why should these beliefs be so ordered? I postpone an attempt to answer this intriguing question.

The belief just considered, about square roots, does not have much opportunity to explain responses of ours. But another strong property belief, also negative in character, is more fortunate in this regard: our belief that (if there are cats, then) cats are not wholly illusory entities. It is this enormously strong belief, or one much like it, that explains responses to Descartes' passages in the *Meditations* where he introduces an arch-deceiver. It also explains responses to similarly radical scenarios: a brain in a vat. Such arch-deceivers, stimulated brains in vats and the like are especially bizarre examples, where one's supposed experiences are so wildly at variance with reality. Properly introduced, and with appropriate questions concerning them, these examples are suitable for experimenting with response.

Suppose, then, that all of your experiences were, it turns out, entirely produced by some arch-deceiver, who only now reveals that this is so. Once the deception is lifted, we suppose, and his explanations given you, there seems nothing to suggest that your experiences of a cat were produced in any orderly correlation with any real, objective entity. Nor does it seem, at such a juncture, that your idea of a cat even comes close to being satisfied by any non-illusory thing, beyond the contents of your own mind. When the deceiver allows you to perceive the world around, perhaps you see mice and dogs, perhaps not even such "familiar" things as those, but certainly no better candidates for cathood. Now, we ask: "If *this* is the situation, will there still have been cats around or not?"

Here one's dominant response is, quite markedly, to believe that "No" is the correct answer. This is quite the reverse of our example with the Martian robots. While the existence belief still urges an affirmative answer, in this present, Cartesian case, the dominant response is opposite. The property belief that cats are not hallucinations urges an answer in the negative. That is indeed the dominant response. So, as our Cartesian example indicates, *this* property belief is stronger than our powerful existence belief in cats.

The result here is quite striking indeed, more so than in Putnam's example. Nevertheless, the dominance is not total. Weak as it may be, there is some slight tendency toward belief in the affirmative direction, toward a dominated conflicting response. What further tendencies go along with this one? There is the tendency to believe that, perhaps unlike mice and dogs, cats are (merely) an aspect of one's own experience or a certain sort of hallucinatory phenomena. True enough, this way of responding to the example appears desperately heroic; it has only a *very weak* appeal. While this conflict should be noted, the main point now is this: even as responses to examples suggest, our belief in the existence of cats is *not* all-powerful; some comparable property beliefs are stronger than it is. And, of course, the situation here is hardly peculiar to the topic of felines.

Our belief that cats are not wholly hallucinatory, as well as the one that cats are not square roots, is stronger than our belief that there are cats. At the same time, that existence belief is more powerful than the belief that cats are animals, and the belief that cats are not robots (let alone the belief that cats are not green). Why is there, on our part, this ordering of belief strength? We leave this important question for discussion elsewhere.

## 6. The Problem of Discriminative Beliefs

When we take a psychological approach to both belief and language, things can often seem quite free of difficulties. But that is only at first blush. Upon reflection, there are plenty of problems; indeed, there are skeptical dilemmas at almost every turn. I will close this essay by presenting, for your reflection, just one case in point, which I call *the problem of discriminative beliefs*. Not only does this problem have some interest of its own, but it serves to illuminate a skeptical strand in the philosophy of W. V. Quine.

Recall our enormously strong property beliefs as to ordinary entities. Let us think about them, for a problematic pattern seems to emerge: Our terribly strong property beliefs as to cats each appear to be *matched* by a similarly strong belief we have as to a property of dogs, or even as to stones. For example, the belief that cats are not wholly illusory is matched by the belief that dogs aren't, and by the parallel belief about stones. Now, if this really should be the case with *all* of one's strongest property beliefs as to cats, all those stronger than one's belief in the existence of cats, then there will be, it does appear, something of a problem. In such an event, it seems, one will have *no* property belief as to cats which will, in his or her system of beliefs, serve to *discriminate* cats from many other ordinary entities. In such an event, then, the belief that there are cats will amount, it seems, to a *blind insistence* on one's part, with no genuine content at all.

This matter appears to be a quite serious one. We may appreciate it anew by focusing on the words directly involved. Let us suppose, as we do, that the semantics of "cat," whatever it is, is suitably distinct from that of "dog," and that of "stone." Then there should be *some* property belief as to cats which is both terribly strong, stronger than the existence belief in cats, and also which is *not* matched by a parallel, enormously strong property belief as to dogs. Otherwise, it would appear, whatever meaning one's words possess will have little or nothing to do with one's attitudes. And this would seem to be an intolerable result. It will perhaps even undermine the idea that one's words, here "cat" and "dog," have any genuine meaning or semantics. And that, in turn, just might undermine the supposition that there really are these words, and that one has any attitudes involving them. In such a dismal light, the apparent objects of our present study, such as our (putative) belief that there are cats, will themselves appear to have been wholly illusory.

Let us call any such belief as to cats, which is both stronger than a person's existence belief as to cats and is also unmatched by a parallel, similarly strong belief of that agent as to other ordinary entities, a *discriminative belief* (of that person as to cats). Then for each of our ordinary words, we may formulate a problem: Either locate a discriminative belief for that term (in a person's system of attitudes) or else show how the term is semantically adequate, and figures in genuine, contentful attitudes (of that person) even in the absence of any such discriminative belief. Naturally enough, we may call this *the problem of discriminative beliefs*.

Now, I have canvassed our beliefs as to cats, as well as to various other ordinary entities, with the aim of locating just such a discriminative belief. Even when looking at various *social* beliefs, I have failed to find even one such characterizing belief to be suitably strong: For example, the (relational property) belief that cats are things to which many people have often (correctly) applied the word "cat" (but dogs and stones are not), strong though it be, is weaker than the belief that there are, or have been, cats. (Adequate support for this statement requires far more space than we have here.) So, what I have been able to find is, in these regards, only a rather depressing absence. At the same time, there seems no way of showing that some such discriminative belief is not required, for one to have genuine attitudes as to cats, which are not shams or blind insistences. So it appears that this problem of discriminative beliefs, whether or not it is a new puzzle, will be an outstanding, or unsolved, problem.

As is familiar, in his justly celebrated paper, "Two Dogmas of Empiricism," W. V. Quine offers a challenge to the view, commensensical as well as championed by many philosophers, that there are *relations of meaning* among various of the terms of our language.[7] Now, ordinarily, we think we understand how we have a language largely in terms of such meaning relations. If they are not available, then the path begins to open for the idea that we really have no language. To block such a path, Quine suggests that it is our *system of beliefs* which can underlie, and can account for, a language on our part: Whatever structure there is in our language, and it seems that there must be *some* such, will arise from a *suitable structure in* our beliefs. This is one of the important benefits to be derived from Quine's distinction between (more) *central beliefs* and those which are (more) peripheral.

Perhaps we may view the problem of discriminative beliefs as an extension of Quine's challenge.[8] Much the same, in the light of this problem, perhaps his challenge is more extensive than is generally realized: For more central beliefs should be, it seems, with enough appropriate speakers of the language, *stronger* beliefs of theirs. And, it seems, for these speakers these stronger beliefs should be some *property* beliefs, by way of which they think what's what, not just existence beliefs. If we are to have a system of beliefs with structure adequate to yield a language on our part, then we should have some such ordering of attitudinal strength. But, it seems that in fact, with all too few exceptions, we have no such ordering. So, *how do* we have a language? An Eleatic might invite us (*sic*) to consider the possibility of never having any. But perhaps we may demur.[9]

---

7. This famous paper appears in Quine's *From A Logical Point of View* (Cambridge, Mass.: Harvard, 1953).

8. For this suggestion, I am indebted to Allen Hazen.

9. At various stages in my thinking on these matters, I have been helped by discussion with others, too many to mention them all. But thanks are due to Tamara Horowitz, Jerrold Katz, David Lewis and Stephen Schiffer. I owe an especially large debt to Allen Hazen.

# 8

# MINIMIZING ARBITRARINESS: TOWARD A METAPHYSICS OF INFINITELY MANY ISOLATED CONCRETE WORLDS

A particular fact or event often appears arbitrary and puzzling, until it is exhibited as the outcome of certain causal processes. Usually, though not always, such a causal explanation helps to relieve the feeling of arbitrariness, at least for a while. But it is easy and natural for our feeling to reassert itself: We are moved to ask why just *those* causal processes governed the situation of that fact or event, rather than some others. To deal with this further, larger question, often we can exhibit those causal processes as being, themselves, the results of, or certain specific instances of, prior or more general causalities. Or, much the same, we can redescribe the initial particular fact, and perhaps the cited cause as well, and display the items thus described as an instance of some very general, fundamental law or phenomenon.[1] But any of this will only push the question back one step more. For we can always press on and ask: Why is it that just *that* very general phenomenon, or law, should be so fundamental, or indeed obtain at all, in the world in which we have our being? Within the usual framework of explanation, law and causation,

---

1. See Donald Davidson, "Causal Relations," *Journal of Philosophy* 64 (1967).

there seems no place for such curiosity to come to rest. There seems no way for us to deal adequately with the brute and ultimate *specificity* of the ways in which almost everything appears to happen. And what seems worse, the specific character of certain of these laws or ways, even of quite fundamental ones, often seems so quirky, the very height of arbitrariness.

For an example of what I mean, why is it that, as science says, there is a certain particular upper limit on velocities for all (ordinary) forms of physical objects (which is, in familiar conventional units, very nearly 186,000 miles per second)? Why does just *this* limit obtain and not some other one, or better, some *range of variation* of uppermost speeds? Why must causal processes involving motion all conform to *this particular* restriction, rather than to some other, or to no such restriction at all?

For another example, why is it that almost all of the matter that there is comes in just *three* (rather small) sorts of "parcels" (protons, electrons, and neutrons)? Why not so much matter coming in just *two* sorts of parcels, at the level now in question, or better, just *one* sort?

For a third example, we may consider what current science takes to be the basic (types of) physical forces of nature: As of this writing, scientists recognize exactly four of these forces. At the same time, physicists are hard at work seeking to unify matters at least somewhat, so that there will be recognized no more than three such basic forces, possibly fewer.[2] Certain deep intellectual feelings, feelings that are, I believe, shared by many scientists, philosophers, and others, motivate this reduction. Along such reductionist, unifying lines, these *rationalist feelings* will not be much satisfied until we think of our world as having, at base, only one sort of basic physical force (or, alternatively, having none at all, forces then giving way to some more elegant principle of operation).

## 1. Two Forms of Rationalism

How far can these rationalist feelings be followed? Unless his world is so chaotic as to be beyond any apparent cooperation, for a scientist it will almost always be rational to follow them as far as he can: Reduce the specificities of one's world to a very few principles, maybe one, operating with respect to a very few (kinds of) substances, maybe one;

---

2. I usually get my science from the popular press. For example, see Timothy Ferris, "Physics' Newest Frontier," *New York Times Magazine*, 26 September 1982.

further, have the ultimate quantitative values occurring in the principles be as simple and unquirky as possible.

If scientists are *extremely* successful in satisfying these feelings, a philosopher (who may of course also be a scientist) might rest content with just those findings. Such a philosopher will hold a unique and beautifully simple principle to hold sway over *all* of (concrete) reality. Let me call this philosopher a *moderate rationalist*.

Another sort of philosopher will press on with these feelings, even in the face of the enormous scientific success just imaginatively envisioned. He is an *extreme rationalist*, and even in that happy situation, he will say this: Though the working of *our world* is as elegant as might be, why should *everything* there is behave in accord with just *this* specific principle? Why should *any* specific way, even a most metaphysically elegant, be preferred to any *other* specific way for a world to be? Why shouldn't there be *somewhere*, indeed be *many domains*, where things are less beautifully behaved? If so, then, *over all*, everything there is will be metaphysically most elegant, the *universe as a whole* preferring *no specific* way to any other, but, rather, giving each and every way its place and due. With a suitably enormous infinite variety of independent domains, of mutually isolated concrete worlds, we will have, over all, *the least arbitrary universe entire*; otherwise we will not, over all, have so little arbitrariness.

Both of these forms of rationalism are appealing to our deep rationalistic feelings (even while we have other feelings that go against them both). In this paper, I will not substantially favor either form over the other. Nor will I argue that it is most rational for us to adopt either of the rationalisms. My aim will be avowedly rationalist, but it will also be modest: I will be arguing that, at least in the evidential situation in which we do find ourselves, the metaphysics proposed by an extreme rationalist (for any evidential situation) should be taken very seriously. In other words, at least in our actual evidential situation, we should take very seriously a metaphysics of infinitely many mutually isolated concrete worlds.

Now, though it is not quite so dominant as it was some years ago, a heavily empiricist approach to concrete reality is, still, much more fashionable than a more rationalist approach. Accordingly, many philosophers will tell us not to worry about any apparent brute and fundamental arbitrariness in nature, which we seem to see and are, in fact, at least somewhat troubled by. Taken altogether, they will say, things just are the specific way that they are or, if one insists in putting it so, the specific way they happen to be.

Perhaps this basic empiricist attitude is unobjectionable; I do not know. Although I find it somewhat unappealing, perhaps there is no way it can be faulted. At the same time, there seems nothing that requires us to prefer this fashionable approach and to reject a more rationalist approach to all of concrete reality.

## 2. A Rationalist Motivation for Concrete Possible Worlds

In our physical science, I am told, certain magnitudes are taken as fundamental and universal. For instance, an example already cited, there is a fundamental upper limit on the velocity of any (normal) particle or signal. But, why just *that* upper limit, for *all* such speeds, everywhere and always? Why not just a bit more speed allowed or, alternatively, not even that much, if not around here and now, then many, many galaxies away, or many, many eons from now?

Consider a physical theory according to which there was a limit on speeds, but one that varied with the place of the mover in question. This might be due to, as the theory says, the mover's place being under an influence that varies with respect to place—for example, the influence of vast structures of intergallactic structures of matter, which surround any given place in all, or many, directions. On such a theory there would be no universality to, and thus no universal preference for, just the limit in our (only pretty big) neighborhood. Far away enough over there, the limit would be higher; and far enough away over *there*, it would be lower. Because it would not be universal, our neighborhood speed limit would not seem, or be, so arbitrary. By localizing our specificity, we minimize the arbitrariness that is associated with it.

A strategy of localization, it seems to me, does have its merits. But the present attempt at applying the strategy has at least two difficulties. First of all, according to what science seems to tell us, there is little or no evidence for thinking that our world conforms to the sort of theory just considered. Rather, available evidence seems to indicate the opposite: (Even if given infinite space) we'll get the same speed limit for *every* (big) neighborhood, no matter how remote from ours it may be.[3] (Morever, there seems to be a lot of evidence that we don't have infinite space, or infinite time.) So an attempt at spatial localization does not in fact seem feasible.

Second, and perhaps more important, any imagined law of variation of speeds would *itself* have some numbers constant for it. And

---

3. There may be some special exceptions to this that science recognizes. But my point does not depend on whether or not that is so.

then we might ask: Why should velocities vary with surrounding spaces in just *that* way, with just *those* constants constraining variation? Why shouldn't the regularities of varying speeds be otherwise, other than they happen to be in our whole physical world?

To remove or to minimize this remaining arbitrariness, we might try to "localize" the mode of spatial variation, too, staying with our general strategy. But how are we to do so? We might stretch things out over time: Different variation factors for different vast epochs. But the same problems arise here, too. First, what evidence there is about physical time is not so congenial. And, more fundamentally, there will be left as universal (and unexplained) some factors for variation over time of the space-variation constant(s). Why should just *those* temporal factors hold, and hold universally? Why not some others? Either we must admit defeat or we must reach out further, in order to achieve a *new form of localizing*.

Having used up all of space and time, even assuming both are infinite in all their directions, where do we go? We must expand our idea of the "entire universe," of all that there is. But in what way? A certain philosophical conception of *possible worlds* might provide the best route for our rationalistic localizing strategy. Indeed, it might provide the only route. It is my rationalist suggestion, then, to try to make more sense of concrete reality by adopting a metaphysics of many concrete worlds.

## 3. Two Approaches to a Metaphysics of Isolated Concrete Worlds: The Rationalist and the Analytic

It will be in a tentative and an exploratory spirit that I will advocate a metaphysics of many concrete words. The view I will favor is at least very similar to, and is perhaps the very same as, the view of such worlds developed by David Lewis.[4] My present motivation for taking such a view seriously, however, is quite different from his (main) motivation. The differences are such, it will emerge, that my approach is aptly called *rationalist*, or rationalistic, whereas his approach might better be called *analytic*, or analytical. It seems true however that, at least in their main elements, the rationalist approach and the analytic approach are entirely compatible with each other.

---

4. Lewis has published a very large body of work developing this view. One good place to look for a statement of this metaphysics is in his book *Counterfactuals* (Oxford, 1973), especially on pp. 84–91.

Let us suppose the two approaches are indeed compatible. Then whatever motivation each yields can add to that from the other, so as to make more acceptable their shared metaphysical position. It is my hope that this is so.

At the same time, there are those philosophers unfriendly to this metaphysics for whom, I suppose, Lewis's analyses themselves are entirely unhelpful and implausible. Now, insofar as my rationalistic approach can be made appealing, such thinkers will have, perhaps for the first time, at least some motivation for accepting a metaphysics of many concrete worlds.

## 4. Possible Worlds as Concrete Entities

It is fashionable for philosophers to talk of possible worlds. But much of this talk seems metaphorical, or heuristic, at best. This observation has moved several philosophers, J. L. Mackie being notable among them, to question the (significance of) this fashion. In his *Truth, Probability and Paradox*, Mackie writes "... talk of possible worlds ... cries out for further analysis. There are no possible worlds except the actual one; so what are we up to when we talk about them?"[5] In my opinion, these words express a dilemma felt by many philosophers, though Mackie expresses it in a somewhat oblique and indirect way.

More directly put, the dilemma is this: Philosophical accounts of possible worlds fall into either of just two baskets. In the first basket are accounts where 'possible world' is to denote some "abstract entity," such as a set of mutually consistent propositions that, together, purport to describe comprehensively the world in which we live. Presumably, just one of these sets yields a completely successful description, all the others than failing.

Whatever their philosophical value, such accounts use the expression 'possible world', and even the word 'world', in a way that is bound to mislead. For such accounts, the world in which we live is *not* a possible world at all, let alone the most vivid and accessible example of one. For we live in a world consisting, directly and in the main, of stones, animals, people, and suchlike, not of sentences or propositions (however numerous and well behaved). We live in a world that is, at least in the main, *concrete*. So it is most unclear how any other candidate

---

5. J. L. Mackie, *Truth, Probability and Paradox* (Oxford, 1973), 90. This passage is quoted by Robert Stalnaker in his paper "Possible Worlds," *Nous* 10 (1976).

worlds, on the one hand, and the world we live in, on the other, might be suitably related so that *all* of them are *worlds*. Such accounts, then, tend to collapse into mere heuristic devices, even if some may be very helpful heuristically.

In the second basket, we find the story told by David Lewis and variants upon it. On such accounts, possible worlds are concrete entities, generally constituted of smaller concrete things that are at them, or in them. In this central respect, all of the (other) possible worlds are just like the actual world, the world in which *we* live. On this sort of account, the relations between worlds are just those of qualitative similarity and difference, as regards the various respects in which these concrete entities may be compared. These relations are of the same sort as some of those that obtain between "lesser" objects, e.g., between individual inhabitants, whether of the same world or of different ones.

On Lewis's treatment of worlds and their parts, no object can be at, or be a part of, more than one world, while every concrete object is at, or is a part of, at least one world. So each concrete entity that is itself not a world, but is only a world-part, is a part of exactly one of the infinity of concrete worlds.[6] I shall assume this treatment in what follows. I will advocate a many worlds metaphysics where each chair and each person, for examples, are at one and only one concrete possible world: A given chair, or a given person, is just at its own world and, thus, is *not identical* with *any* chair, or *any* person, that is at *any other* world. At most, the others are (mere) *counterparts of* the concrete objects first considered.

How does such a story go as regards relations of space, time and causality? First, there are some tiny worlds; the whole world here is, say, a single space-time point. Beyond those, the concrete inhabitants of a given world are related spatially and/or temporally and/or causally to at least some other inhabitants of that same world, so the world forms a spatial and/or temporal and/or causal system. But inhabitants of *different* worlds do *not* bear any of these relations to each other, nor does any complete world bear any to any other complete world. Causally,

---

6. This idea of "world-bound individuals" wants convincing argument. In a recent paper, "Individuation by Acquaintance and by Stipulation," *Philosophical Review* 92 (1983), Lewis offers an argument for the idea from his analytical approach. The argument is on pp. 21–24. Now, even discounting the small gap in the reasoning that Lewis points out in his footnote 15, I find the argument less than fully convincing, only somewhat persuasive. In conversation, Dana Delibovi has suggested an argument for this idea from the rationalist approach. But that argument, too, leaves something to be desired. For now, I will adopt this idea as a working assumption. It makes for a more elegant system, and I know of nothing wrong with it.

spatially, and temporally *isolated* from each other are the infinity of worlds.

In this second sort of account, it seems to me, it is clear enough, and not misleading, how the others, like the actual world, should *all* be *worlds*. But there is another sort of trouble with this account: It seems incredible, crazy, way beyond the reach of any even halfway reasonable belief.

So this is, in brief, our dilemma of possible worlds. On any account where matters are not incredible, things seem badly obscure or misleading. On any where things seem much less misleading, we face a "universe" that seems utterly incredible. What are we to do?

Formally, at least, there are three alternatives: First, we just don't take talk of possible worlds to be literal or serious; we treat it as *at best* a helpful heuristic. Second, we work out some way in which it's clear how both some abstract structures, on the one hand, and our actual concrete selves and surroundings, on the other, can all be worlds. Finally, we try to make a story of isolated concrete realms somewhat more credible, or less incredible.

Largely by way of a rationalist strategy of "localizing" specificity so as to minimize arbitrariness, we will be attempting the third alternative. So, we are at once involved in two tasks: One, making our own world seem more intelligible by incorporation of it into a relevantly vaster universe; two, making sense of other worlds by showing how they can form a system, a vast universe, by reference to which our actual world can be seen as being less disturbingly peculiar.

## 5. The Analytical Motivation for Concrete Possible Worlds

At least for the most part, the analytical motivation for the metaphysics of many concrete worlds is best provided by Lewis. He does this in, among other writings, his early paper "Counterpart Theory and Quantified Modal Logic" and, later on, in his book *Counterfactuals*.[7] For present purposes, I might assume a familiarity with that motivation, especially as there is little of it that I can express as well as Lewis already has done. Still, as some may want reminding of the relevant aspects of the works in question, I will attempt a sketch of the analytical motivation here, a sketch that must be as crude as it is brief.

---

7. The mentioned paper originally appeared in *Journal of Philosophy* 65 (1968); the book is that cited in note 4.

Now, some of the things believed by us are clear enough as regards their content. For example, it is relatively clear what is believed when I believe that the chairs in my living room are arranged in a rectangular pattern. In contrast, other things we believe seem to be quite obscure and even mysterious: that the chairs in my living room *might have been* arranged in a circular pattern (instead of in a rectangular pattern). Now, either we construct some theory, some analysis, of the content of the latter beliefs that renders the obscurity and mystery superficial, thus removing or at least lessening it, or else we leave things alone, our opinions then continuing to be fraught with mystery. The latter alternative is philosophically unappealing. Hence, there is motivation to construct a clarifying analysis.

On Lewis's analysis, we quantify over, or refer to, concrete objects that are other than our actual world or any part thereof. So the believed proposition that the chairs in my living room *might have been* arranged in a circular pattern is understood, *roughly*, as the proposition that there are worlds with chairs very similar to my living room chairs in rooms very similar to my living room, all in a very similar set of relations (mainly of "possession") to people very similar to me, and in at least some of those worlds the relevant chairs *are* arranged in a circular pattern. The subtlety of Lewis's analysis lies, of course, in the details that make such a rough treatment as the one above into a very much smoother treatment. But the general point is clear enough even now: the more mysterious "might have been" is understood in terms of the quite straightforward "are." By acknowledging many *more* chairs, rooms, and people than we ordinarily envision, we can understand everything here believed in terms of rather unmysterious relations—similarity and also circular arrangement—obtaining among suitably "full-blooded," unmysterious objects—chairs, rooms, and people.

Of particular interest to Lewis and to many other philosophers are our beliefs in counterfactual conditional propositions. An example is (my belief that) if the chairs in my living room were arranged in a circular pattern (instead of their actual rectangular one), then I would have been displeased at their arrangement. When reflected upon, such propositions appear to involve very mysterious nonexistent situations. But we believe many of these propositions to be true. So, again, a clarifying analysis is wanted.

Lewis offers an analysis that is of a piece with that offered for the simpler modal beliefs just considered. For our example, the analysis proceeds at least roughly as follows: There are the many worlds; among them are some where there is someone much like me who has his living room chairs arranged circularly; among these worlds some differ more than others from our world; in the ones that differ least—scarcely at all, except for the arrangement of such chairs—the chair owner, or any chair owner most like me, is displeased at the circular arrangement of his living room chairs.

As before, so again: By admitting lots more chairs, rooms, and people than are usually entertained, and by admitting lots more worlds for all those things to be in, we can understand accepted propositions in a manner that renders them relatively straightforward. We can understand them in a way that dispels much of the air of mystery that initially seems to surround them.

Sometimes we are in a mood when philosophical analyses seem of substantial value. When I am in such a mood, Lewis's analyses of the noted propositions often, though not always, strike me as accurate enough to be of value. Sometimes we are in a very different mood: How can any proposition apparently so fraught with obscurity, mystery, and problems be equivalent to one that is so very much more straightforward and, apparently, problem free? The mood this question signals is hardly peculiar to our thought about modals and counterfactuals, much less to Lewis's analyses thereof. The same doubts concern, for example, analyses of propositions about knowing, where the statement doing the analyzing seems so very much more free of all sorts of skeptical problems and paradoxes than does the knowledge claim itself. Further examples abound; the philosophical situation is quite a general one.

When we doubt the value of philosophical analysis, two things can be tried. First, we can try to show ourselves, via subtle psychological explanations, that two propositions can indeed be equivalent, in as serious a sense of "equivalent" as we might wish, and yet *strike us* as being so different in those respects just noted. With enough ingenuity, perhaps this can be done for a substantial range of interesting proposed analyses; perhaps it can be done, in particular, for Lewis's analyses of modal and counterfactual propositions. But maybe that won't really work well, either generally or for the particular cases currently in focus.

A second thing we might try is to construe a proposed analysis as an *explication*. Now, we take what we begin with as inherently problematic, not just of a form that, typically, engenders illusions of real problems in beings with minds like ours. In a sense, what we begin with is beyond full redemption. Then, explicating, we do this, or something of the like: We put forth something that preserves a relatively unproblematic core, but then only such a core, of that which we find so problematic. Generally, an explication will add something to the core that it preserves. When something is added, the addition will dovetail well with what is preserved from the original; it will yield something very much "along the lines" of the original problematic thought, but, at the same time, it will be relatively clear and problem free. We can, then, have a variety of explications of any given problematic thought, none of which is equivalent to that thought or to each other, but none of which differs very greatly in content from the original thought. Each of these, if there is more than one, will be a *good* explication of that troublesome original.

I do not think that Lewis ever offers his system as (part of) a program for such explications, not analysis proper. Yet I feel free to take it either way and, depending on how I feel about analysis itself, sometimes I take it in one way, sometimes in the other. Whether taken as analysis proper or as explication, Lewis's proposals can give us some analytic motivation for the metaphysics of many worlds.

Somewhat conservatively, I'd like to say this: Either Lewis's proposals provide accurate analyses, as he intends, or, if not that, then at least they provide good explications of those troublesome thoughts to which he turns his attention. That is something I'd like to say. Is it true? I am uncertain.[8] Fortunately, we need not decide this issue here.

As will be remembered, our own project is to present appealingly the *rationalist* approach to many worlds, not the analytical one. Even so, we will continue to refer to Lewis's motivation. This is understandable. By noting its contrasts with the analytical approach, we can help make clearer the rationalist approach we are proposing.

## 6. The Mutual Isolation of the Many Concrete Worlds

To minimize arbitrariness, and make the world more intelligible, we need to employ our strategy of localization. Then any particular way things happen will be less than universal and will be offset by, and thus not preferred to, other ways things happen elsewhere. This gives an argument for the causal isolation of concrete worlds and their respective inhabitants.

Suppose there is a concrete world A and another one B with, say, an individual rock, *a*, an inhabitant of A and not of B and an individual

---

[8]. The philosophical literature contains ever so many criticisms of Lewis's analyses. A couple of prominent examples, fairly representative of the lot, are Alvin Plantinga's "Transworld Identity or World-bound Individuals?" in Milton Munitz, ed., *Logic and Ontology* (New York, 1973) and Robert Adams's "Theories of Actuality" in *Noûs* 8 (1974). I believe, but am not certain, that Lewis defends his analyses adequately against such objections, especially in various of the postscripts in his *Philosophical Papers*, vol. 1 (Oxford, 1983), and that his treatment is also well defended by others, such as Allen Hazen in his "Counterpart-theoretic Semantics for Modal Logic," *Journal of Philosophy* 76 (1979).

window, $b$, a part of B and not of A. Can rock $a$ have any effect upon window $b$, perhaps if accelerated to some enormous velocity and at once being exceedingly massive?

Suppose that $a$ interacted with $b$ so that it broke $b$ or, perhaps, so that it turned $b$ into a translucently colored, purple window. Then there would be certain laws, or regularities, or whatever, that governed or described the way that at least some objects of A interacted with at least some objects of B. However interesting or uninteresting to us in their formulation, any such law would have *some particular character*. We can then ask: Why do the interacting objects of A and those of B interact in *just that* way, or in *just those* ways, and not in some other manner? Why is the character of their interaction just the way it in fact happens to be? We face the threat of arbitrariness.

Our strategy is to localize any such threatening arbitrariness. We implement it, in this case, by having A and B as two (only *somewhat* isolated) *realms* of just one *world*. (We can talk of these realms, of course, as worlds, but then we use 'world' in a new sense. To avoid needless ambiguity, let's not now talk in that way.) Then the way in which realms, or objects in realms, interact in this world, $W_1$, will be just one way things happen in the universe entire. There will also be (infinitely) many other worlds, $W_2, W_3, \ldots, W_n, \ldots$, in each of which there are two realms that interact in *other* ways. And there will be infinitely many *other* worlds with *no* interacting realms. And there will be infinitely more *still* other worlds with *three* interacting realms, and so on. Now, all of these worlds together allow us to see as local any specific manner of the interacting of any objects. But they can do that only if they themselves are all mutually isolated and present no higher-order interactions of any particular character or manner whatsoever. Thus, from the point of view of our strategy, there must be largest *isolated* concrete parts of the universe entire. It is these concrete items that we have been calling *worlds* and that, quite understandably, we will continue to speak of with that appellation.

Perhaps the argument just given is, even in its own rationalist terms, somewhat incomplete. Suppose that for any given world, $W_1$, there is interaction between it and *every other* world of an enormous infinity of worlds. Then there might be no arbitrariness for a given interaction law and each of the, say, two worlds it relates. For a world with just the character of either one of the two will interact in each of an infinity of other lawful ways with (at least) one world with just the character of the other. And perhaps we can generalize from two worlds, and pairwise interaction, to any number whatever. Then there will be, even across worlds, objects interacting in every imaginable way and then some; no way of interacting will be preferred to any other.

Is so *very* much *interaction* for a world a coherent possibility? Can there really be *laws* operating in *such* multiplicity at all, or any such *infinitely various causality*? I think not.

Suppose, as may be, that this negative thought is misplaced. Then there still remains one rationalist line of argument for causal isolation: It is at least somewhat arbitrary that a given world, any world, interacts *at all* with any other world, whether the world interacts with only one other world or whether with an enormous infinity. Interaction is one specific way of relation, and noninteraction is another; so neither happens universally. For any candidate world of any character, at least one such candidate interacts with other candidates and also, elsewhere in the universe entire a duplicate candidate doesn't interact. The candidate that does interact is but a realm of a larger world, the world itself containing such interaction but not interacting. Only the duplicate candidate that fails to interact is a proper world and not a realm, or inhabitant, of a world. Whatever interacts, then, is not a world; so there are infinitely many concrete worlds, none of them interacting.

The rationalist approach argues for causal isolation among real concrete worlds. The analytical approach moves us in the same direction: It often seems puzzling what is claimed where we say one event *caused* another. So we want a clarifying analysis of what it is for one particular thing or event to cause another. Now, following a suggestion of Hume, Lewis and others have attempted to analyze such singular causal judgments in terms of counterfactual conditional statements involving the (alleged) cause and the (alleged) effect.[9] Very *roughly*, "c caused e" is analyzed as: if c had not occurred, then c would not have occurred. (To make matters smoother, the analyzing counterfactual must be made more complex and must also be understood in a suitably context-sensitive manner.) Hard as the work is to smooth things out adequately, the underlying idea is intuitive and appealing.

Now, as a formal possibility, one may adopt some such counterfactual analysis of causality and, at the same time, have no theory of counterfactuals themselves. But, at best, that would be displaying two apparent mysteries as being at base one. So we are moved to adopt a clarifying analysis of counterfactuals as well.

As indicated previously, Lewis's analysis of counterfactuals is a promising view. Wedding this analysis to a counterfactual analysis of causation gives one an analysis of causation in terms of relatively

---

9. See David Lewis, "Causation," *Journal of Philosophy* 70 (1973), for an early statement of such an analysis.

straightforward (noncausal) relations among concrete worlds and inhabitants thereof.

With this background well enough in view, we ask: What does the analytical approach indicate, or perhaps even require, as regards causal relations between concrete worlds? There occur two sorts of argument: a "cautionary" one and a more substantive one.

The cautionary argument: Propositions about causal relations in a given world are, as remarked, analyzed in terms of (less mysterious) noncausal relations between the relevant parts of that world and certain parts of other worlds. Now, providing that these worlds do not themselves enter into causal relations, there will not lurk somewhere in the relations analytically employed a circularizing causal feature. But if there are causal relations between worlds, as well as within worlds, there is at least a threat of circularity.

The substantive argument: Any propositions as to transworld causation will be unanalyzable in terms of the theory. Then they will be without any noncircular analysis and, requiring one as they do, these propositions will have a content at least as mysterious-seeming as our more ordinary causal judgments. So there will be an insoluble problem just in case some such positive propositions are true. Given this approach, we conclude that there are no true propositions stating transworld causal relations.

If the inhabitants of any given world never interact with those of any other, then the items from the different worlds will not be *connected* in any realistic way. So they won't form very much of a unified system. Still, if the inhabitants from different worlds were spatially related, they would be in a system of spatial relations, and that would satisfy our idea of unity to some considerable degree. Likewise, if the events of one world were related temporally to those of others, then that would be an inclusive temporal system that could play some unifying role. But, it can be argued, these relations do not obtain, nor do any other "dimensional" relations.

We have just supposed a separation between causal relations, on the one hand, and relations of space and time on the other. But perhaps there really is no such separation. Rather, space, time, matter, energy, and causality, in a suitably general sense of this last term, must all be understood in terms of each other. So a real space has causal properties that influence the course of matter and energy in it over time. The causal features of a space are inherent to, inseparable from, its real geometry. Now, some (whole) spaces will bend light rays a certain amount in a certain direction, others more so and others less. Still others will leave the light's path unbent. As the former spaces will be understood as influencing the light's path in (what are to us) more striking ways, so the latter may be understood as influencing it, too, but in what are (regarded by us as) less striking ways. Well beyond this example, the considerations can be generalized. So causality cannot be removed from realistic spatial and temporal relations between concrete items, that is, from any spatiotemporal relations that might suitably serve to connect them into a unity. If this is right, then the arguments just preceding, as they undermine *all* alleged transworld causal relations, will, in particular, undermine any arguments relevant to any alleged transworld spatial and temporal relations. In conclusion, any (inhabitant of any) concrete world will be spatially and temporally unconnected with any other (inhabitant of any other) concrete world.

Suppose one has no belief in what I've just said. Suppose one thinks, instead, that space and time really are independent, in every important sense or way, from questions of causal relation. Even so, our rationalist approach will lead one to think that the concrete worlds are isolated spatially and temporally.

Recall our discussion of section 2. We saw there that, in order to implement our strategy of localization satisfactorily, we need a universe entire that comprises much more as to space and as to time than all of the time and space of our world (even if our space and time are infinite in all their directions). We need, that is, a universe comprising infinitely many spaces and times and infinitely many worlds of which those are (some of) the dimensions. These worlds will not themselves be spatially or temporally related, for that would fuse into one the various spaces, and the various times, needed as distinct for a full implementation of our localizing strategy. From our rationalist perspective, therefore, we are motivated to accept the idea of many concrete worlds that are each totally isolated from all of the others.

## 7. On the Resistance to the Idea of Infinitely Many Isolated Concrete Worlds

Let us confront the great resistance people feel toward the view of many mutually isolated concrete worlds. For unless we unearth implicit factors of resistance and promise to do something to disarm them, any more positive steps toward greater credibility are likely to fall on deaf ears. Why, then, are so very many philosophers, as indeed they are, so terribly resistant to such a view? Why do people think it so crazy to consider such a view a serious candidate for acceptability?

The metaphysics we propose to take seriously posits a group of concrete worlds with two salient features. First, *infinite diversity*: every way for anything to be, or behave, is a way that (some) things are, or do behave, if not in a particular given world (say, the actual world), then in some other one. Second, *total isolation*: each world is totally isolated from every other world. Each of these two features does, as a matter of psychological fact, promote much resistance to our metaphysical view.

The matter of infinite diversity has been rather extensively discussed in the literature. For example, this diversity has been thought to undermine the rationality of predictions about the actual world, and it has been thought to foster an attitude of indifference toward our own future actions and their consequences.[10] Does the infinite diversity implicit in our metaphysics have such dire implications, otherwise avoidable? If so, then that would be reason, even if not conclusive reason, to reject the metaphysics.

Especially in his most recent writings, Lewis has argued, convincingly to my mind, that there are no such problems stemming from a metaphysics of infinitely many concrete worlds, but only various confusions to such a threatening effect.[11] Although it would be useful for still more to be said to counter this source of resistance, there is not now an acute need to do so.

I turn, then, to spend some energy meeting resistance stemming from the other main feature of our metaphysics, total isolation. The total isolation of each world promotes two main sorts of worry. One of them is more blatant and obvious; the other, I think, is more profound. Both merit some discussion in the present essay.

The more obvious worry is this: in that there is total isolation of worlds, there is, in particular, complete causal isolation among them. So nothing in our world, ourselves included, will ever interact with any other world, or anything in any other world. Accordingly, the metaphysics in question posits all sorts of things that none of us ever will, or ever can, connect with any experience or observation. Worlds there are with cows that fly, and with particles generally like our electrons but a hundred times as massive. As we are causally isolated from these worlds, cows, and heavy electrons, we can never perceive them, nor any of their causes or effects. So it seems that we can never have any experiential reason for thinking there to be such things. But if no experiential reason for such a thought as to such contingent existents,

---

10. For a prominent example, see the paper by Robert Adams cited in note 8.

11. See the postscripts in his *Philosophical Papers*, vol. 1, especially the postscripts to "Anselm and Actuality."

then no reason is possible for us at all. Such a rarified metaphysics is difficult even to tolerate, let alone to find at all acceptable.

This worry can be met in either of two main ways. As I understand him, Lewis would meet it by arguing that we need not have *experiential* reason to believe in such otherworldly things to accept them with reason. Rather, adequately searching ratiocination about contingency and necessity, conducted (largely) a priori, will give us reason enough for our metaphysical view.[12] This is, or is very close to, a position of extreme rationalism. Now, whatever the strengths and the weaknesses of this sort of answer, there is another way to meet the worry in question.

From a position of moderate rationalism, we can argue that there can be some *very indirect experiential* evidence for the idea of such outlandish, isolated entities. Near this paper's end, in sections 10 and 11, I will attempt such an argument. Moreover, I will there argue that we *now do have* some such indirect experiential reason, or evidence. But, as indicated, this argument will have to wait.

For there is another worry stemming from causal isolation that is, though less obvious, philosophically deeper and more important. That deep worry is this: According to so much of our commonsense thinking, all of concrete reality forms a single, unified system of concrete objects. We are among the objects of the system, as are our parts and the particular experiences and thoughts we produce, or enjoy, or suffer. So are the many things around us. Each of these objects is, somehow or other, temporally related to every other one. Each of those that are in space at all (and *maybe* all of them are in space) is spatially related to all the other spatially located objects. Finally, there is at least a presumption regarding any two concrete objects that they are both embedded in (at least) one causal, or quasi-causal, network or system.

However well or badly conceived it may be, this aspect of common sense is very important to us. For it would serve to satisfy our belief, perhaps even our desire, too, that all of reality be sufficiently *unified*, at least all of concrete reality. Or so we are given to think. For, as we usually reckon matters, without causal, spatial, and temporal relations among them, the concrete entities that exist will not be sufficiently *connected* for all of them to be parts of a universe that is an intelligible unity or whole.

The view of isolated concrete worlds, with their mutually isolated different inhabitants, does not allow for these wanted connections.

---

12. For example, see Lewis's *Counterfactuals*, especially pp. 88–91.

Thus it does *not* present all of the concreta there are as forming, or as belonging to, what is an encompassing *unity*.

Let us now turn to deal with this negative thinking, proceeding by stages through the next two sections.

## 8. The Universe Entire, the Objects in It, and Conditions of Unity

In the face of this negative conclusion, how might we make less incredible a metaphysics of infinitely many concrete worlds? They, and their respective inhabitants or parts, will be utterly isolated from, and unconnected with, each other. Yet we do believe that they all belong, somehow, to one universe entire. How can they be so unconnected and yet participate in an appropriate *unity*, so as to achieve this belonging?

We want a credible answer. But it is important not to expect too much from a candidate answer. For we might well be confused, at least much of the time, in our conception of what the *whole* universe *is*. We might often be prone to take it to be very much like one of its mere parts or constituents, whereas it may in fact be very unlike any constituent, however great, that it ever might have. If we are prone to such a confusion, then we might be prone to think like this: The conditions of unity for the universe entire must be very like those for certain of its objects, in particular like those for some grand and complex possible world. Now, the unity conditions for individual worlds are rather stringent; perhaps each part of any such world must be at least temporally related to (at least some) other parts. Hence, we might conclude, the universe itself must have all its part in such a connected system. From this perspective, perhaps a badly confused one, the metaphysics of possible worlds will seem to yield a universe so many of whose parts are so very, very inappropriately related.

It is my suspicion that, at bottom, this line of thinking, or at least one rather like it, is the main cause of resistance to the metaphysics we are trying to advocate. So I will argue for the inappropriateness of any such line of thinking.

The universe or, as we may say somewhat artfully, the *universe entire* is very different indeed from anything else there is, or ever may be. For the universe entire is, of necessity, more *inclusive* than anything else and, indeed, is absolutely all-encompassing. As it is distinguished from all else by this feature, there is nothing else required to guarantee its existence. In particular, we do not need any distinctness, or boundary conditions, required for at least many lesser objects, perhaps for all.[13]

In the case of such lesser objects as require some such broadly construed boundary conditions, and perhaps all of them do, how are the conditions to be fulfilled positively? Suppose that the object is concrete and not infinitesimal. So it has concrete parts that are so related as to constitute it, but not any other object. So each such object has, for a plausible suggestion, a special *cohesive* unity that holds between all of its parts, in virtue of which they are *all* of *its* parts and in virtue of which *it* is *just that object*, none other. An example: The stars in our galaxy are united, via mutual spatial and (other) causal relations; these unifying relations distinguish the galaxy they thus form from the rest of the actual world. So, deriving from these relations of unity, there is the distinctness required for our galaxy to be a genuine object.[14]

Because the universe entire is guaranteed unique in any case, there need not be any unity imposed on, or found in, its parts to generate the distinctness for it that, perhaps, every object must have. Even if the universe is wholly concrete, as many nominalists believe, this will be so. Accordingly, when the object of our consideration is the universe entire, we may relax our usual requirements for unity.

## 9. A Sort of Unity for a Universe of Many Isolated Concrete Worlds

On a metaphysics of many concrete worlds, the universe entire will not be unified through connecting relations among its main concrete parts. But this does not mean that the universe will not be a unity. For it, or the concrete aspect of it, might be unified in some other way, where connections and dimensional relations are not the unifying factors. But, then, *how* might such a universe still qualify as a unity?

Being sympathetic with my rationalist project, though not going so far as to believe in it, David Lewis has offered me in conversation

---

13. As I must do for the remark to stand, I use the terms of difference in a very lenient manner. So, I regard as distinct two overlapping objects. Indeed, if a certain bronze statue is one thing and a piece of bronze in exactly the same space at the same time is another, then, in my sense of 'distinct', each of those objects is distinct from the other.

14. I take seriously the view that what counts as an object is relative to the context in which it is claimed that a candidate is an object, and that part of the context is the perhaps temporary interests of the speaker or of some assumed audience. So what is an object might be interest-relative. Even if that is indeed the case, the present points remain unaffected.

a highly appealing answer. Let me try to recount it, develop it a little, and then notice its implications (as Lewis has done) for a metaphysics of (infinitely) many unconnected concrete worlds.

Consider a circle dance with boys and girls partnered one to one. After going through a certain sequence of steps, a dance unit, the boys and girls change partners; perhaps each girl goes one boy in the clockwise direction, each boy then going one girl in the counterclockwise direction. With new partners, the boys and girls go through the dance unit sequence again. And, then, they change partners again in the aforesaid manner, and so on.

Consider three variations of this dance. In the first, each girl dances with all the boys except for two; no girl gets all the way around the circle nor, then, does any boy. On this variation, the dance is, with respect to major elements, *incomplete*. In the second variation, each girl dances with each boy exactly one time; so everyone goes right around the whole circle and then stops. This variation has the dance being relatively *complete*. A third variation has each girl dance with each boy once and, then, dance a second time with each of her first two partners. So everyone goes right around the circle and then some. On this variation, the dance will be *redundant*, in a salient and relevant way. The second variation is, I suggest, more of a unity than either the first or the third: For, unlike the first, it is complete and, unlike the second, it is not redundant.

The unity of just the middle (second) dance will be clear enough, I think, whether the dance is taken as a particular occurrent event (concrete) or whether as an (abstract) choreographic structure. Of course, all three variations must be treated the same with respect to such a further consideration. But that is easily enough accomplished. In such a case, connecting relations—causal, spatial, and temporal—will be alike for the three variations; either they will be present in all or else absent in all. As far as such relations go, then, the question of unity should receive the same answer in each of the three cases. But, whether such relations are all absent or whether all present, that question receives a different answer for the second variation, a positive answer, than it does for the first and the third. So, for the question of unity, whether related items be concrete or whether abstract, connecting relations are not always crucial. On the contrary, at least for a certain range of cases, the combination of relevant completeness and nonredundancy can make for unity.

Let's consider another example, one that seems more directly concerned with nature itself, indeed with fundamental features of nature. Consider, first, a concrete world with exactly three types of fundamental particles: one type has mass and positive electric charge, one type has mass and negative electric charge, and, finally, one type has no mass and positive electric charge. Consider, next, a world that has each of these three types of basic particles and, also, just one more type: a sort of particle that has no mass and negative electric charge. The second world is, I suggest, more of a unity than is the first, even though there is no relevant difference in connecting relations between the two cases. For the second world, though not the first, is relevantly complete.

Explicitly suppose that each type of particle is instanced an equal number of times, in both of the aforesaid worlds and, thus, in particular in the second, more complete one. Now consider a third world that has, as regards fundamental particles, just the same four *types* as in the second world. But, unlike in the second world, in this third there are many more particles of the fourth type, with negative electric charge and no mass, than there are of the other types, the numbers for the three others being, again, exactly the same. This world is, it seems to me, less of a unity than is the second world, again despite no relevant difference in any connecting relations. And the reason for this is, it appears, that there are *extra*, or *redundant*, particles of the fourth type in this world. Of these three worlds, just the second one has both a relevant completeness along with a relevant lack of redundancy. Because of that, just this second world is (much of) a unity, whereas the first and third worlds are not. Connecting relations for the small concrete items have nothing to say in the matter; but, apparently, a good deal gets said anyway. So, by themselves, the combination of relevant completeness and nonredundancy can make for unity and can do it in what would appear to be quite an extensive range of cases.

Contemplating our main subject, the suggestion is that the universe entire, as a universe (whose concrete aspect is one) of many isolated concrete worlds, is a case in this extensive range. The main relevant elements are the concrete worlds. When will there be a universe that is a unity? When the worlds altogether exhibit completeness, but do not exhibit redundancy. Well, when will *that* be?

The universe will be complete providing that every way that a world could possibly be is a way that some world is.[15] What are the

---

15. On Lewis's analytic approach, a way for a thing to be just is a thing that is that way. So a way for a world to be just is a world that is that way. *For the analytical approach*, the sentence "Every way that a world could possibly be is a way that some world is" will express a tautology, a proposition that will hold true even if there is only one (concrete) world or even none at all. *Relative to that approach*, such an apparently useful sentence will not, in fact, allow us to express what we want to express, namely, the relevantly *plenitudinous* character of the group of concrete worlds.

possibilities here? As far as the details go, I have no way of knowing. But we need not say what they are. To help ensure the wanted completeness, though, we should have a *very liberal* conception of possibility at work. We need not, I think, allow "situations that are to make true statements that are contradictory." But our range of possibilities, our range of various worlds, must be enormously abundant; in an old-fashioned word, we need a *plenitude*. So our range of metaphysical possibilities must include, I imagine, many that are quite beyond our own abilities to conceive of in any illuminating way or detail, as well as many that may at times seem mere fabrications of mind-spinning: As a (self-styled) rationalist, I need unity for the universe entire. For this unity, I need an *extremely great infinite variety* of worlds; without so very many qualitatively different worlds, we'll lack completeness and, thus, lack unity.

For unity we need nonredundancy as well, not just completeness. What does this mean for the ultimate case, presently being considered, of the universe entire, with its infinitely many varied worlds? In particular, does it mean that no world has any qualitative duplicate? It would be nice and neat if it did mean that. However, nonredundancy will not yield as much as that, I am afraid, but rather will yield this slightly weaker proposition: Either each world is without qualitative duplicate or else if any world does have at least one duplicate, then each world has as many duplicates as does every other world.

With completeness and nonredundancy thus available, we have a universe entire that is at least something of a unity. Indeed, as suggested in the section just preceding, it might be a unity of the only sort one should ever expect for the universe entire. At any rate, the

---

Both the analytic approach and also the rationalist approach require a plenitude of concrete worlds, an enormous infinity of various concrete worlds. It is also important to an advocate of either approach that he be able to express this required plenitude. This *problem of expressing the plenitude* was raised by Peter Van Inwagen and sharpened to this present form by Lewis.

A tautology will not express the required plenitude properly, nor will it express anything of much metaphysical interest. So, what are we to do. As rationalists, our problem is not acute because we can give up our partnership with the analytic approach. Then we can express our plenitude by taking possibilities, including "designs for possible worlds," as appropriate abstract structures. Then we can say: Every possibility for a world, or every design for a possible world, is *realized by* at least one concrete world. But, as advocates of a metaphysics of many concrete worlds, we rationalists hope that we do not have to give up this partnership.

For the analytical approach, the problem is an acute one. The matter may not be one of do or die; after all, at least in philosophy, no problems for views have an absolutely crucial bearing. But this is a very serious problem for the analytical approach.

foregoing considerations do a fair amount, I think, to motivate serious consideration for a metaphysics of infinitely many isolated concrete worlds. But, especially from our rationalistic perspective, some new problems seem to arise.

Suppose that each concrete world had exactly seven duplicates. Then there would be exactly eight worlds of each character. There would be *unity* enough, for there would be completeness along with no relevant redundancy. Still, the universe imagined seems highly *arbitrary*: Why should there be just *eight* worlds of each character, rather than some other number? Our rationalist feelings are repelled by the suggestion of such an eightfold way.

Well, how many worlds are there of each character? The rationalist aspects of my mind find two answers that seem at least somewhat more appealing than any others: one and, at the other extreme, an *infinite* number of each character.[16] The latter answer, infinity, itself raises questions as to what *size* of infinity we have at hand. As this further question appears to find no motivated answer, there seems to be a preference, generated thereby, for the former. In addition, the former answer—no duplicate for any world—might find some adequate indiscernibility argument in its favor, though really good indiscernibility arguments are, I think, very hard to come by. At any rate, all things considered, I hesitantly advocate the answer, *one*. So, I thus advocate a metaphysics of an *extremely* great infinity of mutually isolated concrete worlds, not even one of which is duplicated even once in the universe entire.[17]

## 10. Empirical Science and Metaphysics

The arguments so far presented for our many worlds metaphysics, both rationalist and also analytical, are a priori, either entirely or at least to a very high degree. Except for purposes of illustration and exposition, (virtually) no appeal is made to our sensory experience.

---

16. At the very outset, the answer *none* also seems appealing. But given the existence of the actual world, that answer is soon excluded. As we are given that, we ignore this appeal.

17. Inconclusive as this argument is, it is something. In contrast, the analytical approach seems to give no way at all for motivating any answer to this question of qualitatively identical worlds. Perhaps that is why Lewis does not advocate any position on this question. Though it is not wanted without some supporting argument, some position on this question is wanted.

Now, perhaps the matters here treated are, indeed, always best treated by way of some such a priori approach. Given the nature of these matters, that is not implausible. On the other hand, it may be that, instead, certain of these matters should receive a more empirical treatment, a treatment that contains both elements of experience and those of pure reason, and each to a significant degree. Let me try to explain and motivate this mixed, more empirical treatment, and then examine some of its consequences.

Near the beginning of this paper, it will be remembered, I said that any given universal limit on velocities, as it gave absolute universality to some special, particular feature of things, would be arbitrary; it would, indeed, be highly arbitrary, too much so to be tolerated by a rationalist approach to the universe entire. In the spirit of this enquiry, I will stand by this statement, which seems correct from any rationalist approach that is even moderately vigorous or pure. But, then, I went on to say, or at least to imply, that it would be *just* as arbitrary to have *no* velocity limit as universal. This is, or is very close to, the position of extreme rationalism. Although this further contention can be made appealing from a rationalist perspective, it does not seem to be required by such a perspective, as was the previous statement. In other words, from a general rationalist point of view, it does not seem, or does not always seem, so *highly arbitrary* to have *no* such *universal* limit as it does to have any *given* universal limit.

Suppose that this is indeed the case. Then a world where there is no such limit will, other things equal, be a less arbitrary world than a world where there is such a limit, whatever the limit's particular value. The following question then arises: Which is a less arbitrary *universe entire*, a universe that contains only a world (or worlds) of the first, less arbitrary sort or a universe that contains that and, besides, all those worlds that are more arbitrary ones? From a purely a priori stance, there is something to be said for each of the two alternatives.

On the one hand, a universe entire that contains even the more arbitrary worlds does not prefer any world to any other one. So on the vastest scale we can (yet) conceive, the universe will not then show any preference. That makes such a universe, with infinitely many concrete worlds, seem less arbitrary than a more restrictive universe entire.

On the other hand, a universe with such arbitrary worlds seems to have all sorts of quirky, mutually isolated brute facts: There's this world with just this upper limit, and there's that world with just that one, and there's nothing grander in the world that displays these two isolated brute facts as various *instances* of, or *outcomes* of, some *deeper, less quirky* reality.

Suppose that the second sort of universe entire contains, as does the first, (infinitely) many concrete worlds but all with no universal velocity limits. Suppose, further, that it contains worlds that have, even as quite fundamental features of them, arbitrary features. For example, suppose that some form of quantum theory governs many of these worlds, as it seems to govern the actual world, so that only *certain* configurations of "small particles" ever obtain. *Other* configurations are never found anyplace in these worlds. Now, a universe entire that contained certain sorts of more arbitrary worlds, say, quantum worlds, but failed to contain other sorts, say, worlds with universal speed limits, would, it seems from a rationalist perspective, clearly be more arbitrary than a universe that excluded no world at all. If this is right, then the dilemmatic question we are facing reduces to another one.

Suppose that there is at least one world that is as free of natural arbitrariness as can be. Vague as my formulation of it is, we will entertain this supposition. Now we may ask: Which is the less arbitrary, a universe entire that contains only such a least arbitrary world, or a universe that has every sort of world there might be, however quirky and peculiar? From a purely rationalist perspective, this question seems impossible to decide.

Now, the case for a universe entire with just a metaphysically best world is *helped* if it can be shown, a priori, that there is only *one* world that is least arbitrary. The case for having all worlds is *helped* if it can be shown, a priori, that there is *no uniquely* least arbitrary world. But, whether or not either of these alternatives can be argued a priori, such considerations are less than decisive. So it is that, from our rationalist perspective, a priori arguments can take us only so far in the matter of whether there are, in the universe entire, many concrete worlds or only one, the actual world. At least, this is how the question often does appear.

With this appearance before us, the suggestion arises that we import some empirical evidence into our discussion. Conjoined with some appropriate a priori reasoning, perhaps such evidence can point the way toward a rational stance for us in the matter, at least rational from our general rationalist perspective. For this to happen successfully, we must import the evidence quite indirectly. This is, or is very close to, the position of moderate rationalism.

Suppose the world we live in, our actual world, provided us with sensory evidence that did much to support a conception of it as highly unarbitrary. Somewhat specifically, what do I mean by this supposition? I am uncertain. Nonetheless, these may be some illustrative examples: Evidence indicated that the real geometry of our world was Euclidean, so that there was zero curvature to space everywhere; the world seemed to be spatially and temporally infinite in all directions, rather than of some specific finite size and age; matter did not mainly come in three main types of "elementary particles," but only in one type or, perhaps better still, in different numbers of types in different very large regions and eras. I think that you may be getting the idea.

Further suppose that, as more experiments were performed and observations made, they tended to support a conception of our world where it appeared increasingly less arbitrary. According to available evidence, our world seemed, more and more, to be very nearly the metaphysically best, most elegant world. There was, in a phrase, epistemological convergence toward the metaphysically best world.

In such epistemic circumstances, it would be rational, at least from a rationalist perspective, to give credence to the following propositions. First, that our world was the least arbitrary world. And, second, that our world was the only world there was at all.

The rationality of the first of these propositions is, I presume, acceptable enough for such a context. But how do we move from it to get the second as well? Here is an argument that is, I think, suggestive and even appealing, though quite far from being conclusive.

There is an enormous infinity of candidate worlds, or "designs for worlds." There is even a very great infinity of such candidate worlds with a place for intelligent, philosophical beings. In this latter great infinity, the number of least arbitrary candidates, only one, is very small in comparison to the number of those more arbitrary than the minimum. Now, if all of these candidates were successful, it would be *highly* unlikely that we should find ourselves in the least arbitrary one. But, we are assuming, that is just the sort of world in which we are. So it is highly unlikely that they are all successful. We accept the very likely idea that is the negation.

Furthermore, it would be more arbitrary for some and not all of such (more arbitrary) candidates to be successful than it would be for none of them to be. So, on our perspective, and given that evidence, it would be rational to accept the idea that our world, the (minimally arbitrary) actual world, is the only world in the universe entire.

We may perhaps agree that in the face of certain "favorably convergent" evidence, and given our rationalist perspective, it would be rational to accept a metaphysics where the actual world is the only world and to reject our metaphysics of many concrete worlds. On the other side of the coin, we may then also agree that in the face of very different evidence, which supported a conception of our actual world as a very quirky, highly arbitrary world, the reverse would be rational: At least from our rationalist perspective, we may then accept our metaphysics of infinitely many concrete worlds and reject a metaphysics of the actual world as the only concrete world. Or, at the least, in such an evidential situation, it would be rational for our rationalist to take many worlds metaphysics very seriously and to be somewhat doubtful about the more ordinary view. This is (a modest form of) moderate rationalism.

As in the previous sections, the material so far presented in this one is purely (or almost purely) a priori argument. What we have newly done so far is to add some *a priori epistemological arguments*, concerning how a rationalist might best interpret various sorts of evidence, to an a priori metaphysics already in place. Let's now inject some empirical evidence itself into the mix of our available considerations.

Well, then, what *is* the available empirical evidence, and what *does* it indicate about the actual world? As empirical science presents it to us, is the world we live in, the world of which we are a part, is this a world notable for its lack of natural arbitrariness? Far from it, the actual world, our evidence seems to indicate, is full of all sorts of fundamental arbitrary features, quirks that seem both universal for the world and absolutely brute. The particular universal limit on velocities in our world is just one conspicuous example. Another is the apparent ultimate, universal validity of quantum physics. A third is the tripartite division of most matter. And so on, and so forth.

According to available evidence, and to such a theory of our actual world as the evidence encourages, the actual world has nowhere near the lack of arbitrariness that rationalist intuitions find most tolerable. To satisfy the rationalist approach, our evidence tells us, we must look beyond the reaches of our actual space and time, beyond our actual causal network. For there to be a minimum of arbitrariness in the universe entire, indeed anything anywhere near a minimum, we might best understand the universe as including, not only the actual world, but infinitely many other concrete worlds as well.

There are other options, of course. Perhaps most conspicuously, there is this: Our available evidence is, at this time, badly misleading. Almost as conspicuous is this: Our scientists are insufficiently imaginative to articulate an intellectually satisfying cosmology, one much more elegant than any now available, that even our present evidence supports. Such options as these are not highly irrational. And they do hold out the hope for a universe entire whose concrete parts are all part of one vast causal, dimensional network, all satisfyingly interconnected. (The question arises: When, even if perhaps not now, *would* we have enough evidence about the world around us, and about our ability at theory formation, to make these options appear as dogmas, and rightly so?) But, just as these options are now worth at least our serious consideration, so, too, is our hypothesized metaphysics of many concrete worlds.

## 11. The Two Forms of Rationalism and the Analytical Approach

We have just explored a form of rationalism that is rather open to empirical evidence, even while it constrains interpretation of such evidence. This moderate rationalism strikes a nice balance, I think, between respect for intuitions of reason and respect for sensory experience. For that balance, we must pay a price.

Extreme rationalism, unlike moderate rationalism, will *always* work hand in hand with the analytic motivation for many concrete worlds. No matter what the empirical evidence, such an extreme view runs, it can have no bearing on the question of the structure of the universe entire. Rather, it can only inform the inhabitants of any given world, one of infinitely many, as to the features of their world; empirical evidence just helps them learn which of all the worlds is their world.

On this more rigid view, it is supposed that, no matter what the empirical evidence, the least arbitrary *universe* is (the) one where every world that can possibly be is a world that does exist. So, with extreme rationalism, all the worlds are there in any case. So a real model is always available for a Lewis-type treatment of our (superficially) mysterious beliefs. Extreme rationalism, then, is guaranteed to work hand in hand with the analytical approach to many concrete worlds.

With a moderate rationalism, the analytically wanted worlds won't always be available: In certain evidential situations, we do well to suppose that they are not. For moderate rationalism, there is no guarantee of partnership with the analytical motivation. That is the price of this more flexible form of rationalism.

Is this price exorbitant; or is the empirically open form of rationalism at least the equal of, and maybe superior to, the form that is guaranteed to coincide with our analytical motivation? This question is, I believe, a difficult one to answer, even in a mildly satisfactory way. But, fortunately for present purposes, we need not address this difficult question.

The reason for this happy state of affairs is, of course, pretty obvious: For us, such evidence as would threaten a partnership between moderate rationalism and the analytical motivation is utterly hypothetical. Our actual evidence poses no such threat at all. For there is precious little in our available experience to indicate that our world is the metaphysically best world that there is, and there is much to indicate that, on the contrary, it is highly arbitrary in various fundamental respects.

Perhaps in any case whatsoever, but certainly given our actual experience, a metaphysics of infinitely many isolated concrete worlds is a view to be taken very seriously. To be sure, such a view has its unattractive aspects. But so, too, does any serious alternative position of which we are aware.[18]

18. For very many of the thoughts that help to shape this paper, I am greatly indebted to David Lewis. Anyone who has read from the paper's beginning to this point would be apt to think my debt to him is a very large one; it is even larger than one would be apt to think.

For useful ideas and suggestions, I am also indebted to Dana Delibovi, Allen Hazen, Thomas Nagel, John Richardson, and, especially, Peter Van Inwagen.

# PART III

# Knowledge, Ethics, Contexts: Shades of *Philosophical Relativity*

# 9

# THE CONE MODEL OF KNOWLEDGE

Over the last twenty years and more, there have been offered an increasing variety of analyses of knowledge, roughly, of what it is for someone to know that something is so. Generally, these have taken the form of a list of conditions: Each condition in the list must hold true if the person is to know the thing, so each condition is logically necessary. And at least some of the conditions in the list are logically independent of some of the others. But unless all in the list hold true together the person won't know the thing, so there are at least some conditions that are not logically sufficient. When all the conditions together hold true the person will know, so jointly the conditions in the list are logically sufficient for his knowledge.

Naturally enough, we may call any such analysis an *essentially conjunctive* analysis of knowledge or, for short, a conjunctive analysis of knowledge. Because we can place to the side trivial logical maneuvers that serve to generate conjunctions in a wholly unmotivated way, we have a good appreciation as to when an offered analysis is, as is so often the case, appropriately referred to with such a label. For one example, Ayer's old analysis in *The Problem of Knowledge* is meant to exemplify this form.[1] Twenty-five years later, so is Nozick's new analysis in *Philosophical Explanations*.[2] Attempts of this sort have been the norm for the field for

---

1. A. J. Ayer, *The Problem of Knowledge* (Baltimore, 1956).
2. Robert Nozick, *Philosophical Explanations* (Cambridge, Mass., 1981).

quite some time, and the indications are that this norm of conjunctive analysis may well continue to hold sway for quite a while longer. For a number of reasons, I think that no such attempt will offer us much that is both interesting and right about what it is for someone to know something to be so—none will much illuminate what this is.

For one thing, such analyses at least ignore, and perhaps even deny, the *unity* that we feel must obtain in our knowing the truth. There may be little unity in, say, someone's being a bachelor—the person's being male hasn't very much to do with the person's being unmarried—but then things seem different with someone's knowing—the person's "attitude toward" the thing that is so should have a lot to do with its being so, and all of this should have a lot to do with the person's being justified in having this attitude, and all of that should have a lot to do with the person's being in a position to rule out relevant competing "possibilities," and all of the foregoing should have a lot to do with the person's not being right by accident, and all of the foregoing should have a lot to do with the person's attitude being a preferred guide to action, and so on. In an illuminating account of knowledge, all of the *aspects of knowledge* should be seen as fitting together intimately, more intimately than is involved in any mere causal or quasi-causal relationship; in an essentially conjunctive analysis that is not going on at all, or not going on to nearly a great enough degree.

Though this is a severe failing of conjunctive analyses, the ideas that lead to this point suggest at least a mild virtue that such analyses may have. Each of the foregoing conditions seems important to knowledge—at least *something* like a necessary condition for someone to know—but none seems much more significant than every last one of the others. By making each of these conditions, and more, individually necessary, and making them all—indefinitely many of them to be filled in—jointly sufficient, a conjunctive analysis can find a place for all of these aspects. Moreover, it may do so in a way that does not make any one aspect, or any few, much more important than all of the others. This virtue is not present in accounts that, for example, stress non-accidentality while giving a subordinate place to, say, justified personal certainty or, for another example, give the latter condition a place superior to the former. An account that, for example, says that it is non-accidental that all of the conditions of a certain conjunction hold will, in so favoring non-accidentality, lack this mild virtue of giving parity to what seem to be so many equally important aspects of knowing.[3] (This is not to say that *all* of the above conditions are equally important.)

---

3. This point is in response to helpful correspondence with Peter Klein.

As I see it, the available analyses of knowledge that are not essentially conjunctive ones, while an improvement over conjunctive analyses, lack this virtue of parity. So they give us only a somewhat modest improvement, not a large enough improvement. We want an account that, though it highlights the unity in our conception of knowledge, does this in a way that yields *parity* for at least quite a few of (what at least seem to be) the important conditions of, or aspects of, knowing. While they do not give us unity, conjunctive analyses at least do give us parity. So much for any positive remarks about essentially conjunctive analyses.

As a second main point, we want an account that is sensitive to the dialogues that ensue, and that might well ensue, between advocates of skepticism, who deny that our claims to knowledge are true, and those many anti-skeptics who defend the (presumed) truth of these statements. The account should show how a wide variety of skeptical arguments, and less formal moves, are very appealing; it should also show how an equally wide variety of positive replies can be just as appealing and, to all of us most of the time, even more appealing. At least judging from the material available, conjunctive analyses will not do justice to the richness, scope and fluidity of this "web of dialectic." There are other reasons that we might cite for looking to develop an account of knowledge that is about as far away from a conjunctive analysis as can be. But these two, which are not entirely independent of each other, are perhaps the most important.

The failure to illuminate the feature of unity, and especially the failure to illuminate the feature of *dialectical fertility*, is not confined to conjunctive analyses. It is to be found, to a very considerable degree, in (virtually) all contemporary accounts of knowledge of which I am aware.[4] But it is most blatant in, and most clearly inherent to, essentially conjunctive analyses. For that reason, in trying for a better account now, it is a good strategy to develop something that looks, as it is, very different indeed from any mere list of conditions. That is one thing that I will aim for in trying to develop a *model of knowledge*, a model of what it is for someone to know that something is so.

Now, on a broad and perfectly ordinary use of "analysis," my model will be an analysis of knowledge; on a broad enough use, so too will be the work of certain psychologists, or even sociologists. At all

---

4. As regards illuminating the feature of unity, a possible exception is Peter Klein's "Real Knowledge," *Synthese* 55 (1983), but I suspect that even Klein does not go far enough in this direction.

events, I intend nothing to depend on any difference in the senses of the ordinary terms "analysis" and "model": whatever virtues my account possesses will neither be significantly added to, nor subtracted from, by my calling the account a model rather than an analysis. At the same time, it does seem to me fitting to call the account I will offer a *model*; this label seems more appropriate for my account than for (virtually) any of the offerings that philosophers have made in the way of analyses of knowledge. Part of why this is so is simple: as with so many models in so many fields, my model of knowledge will involve much in the way of geometrical representation; in contrast, the available analyses of knowledge typically involve little or nothing in this direction. But there seems to be more to the differences between the two types of accounts than just that. As an interesting side-issue, I leave to the reader to discern what features are peculiar to my account that make it seem so fitting to call it a *model* of knowledge, not just an analysis.

Now the topic of knowing is so complex and difficult that it is most unlikely that my model, or any account, will do it anything like full justice. But I will be content with a lot less than that. What I would like is that my model do more to illuminate our two—or, counting parity, three—crucial features than what is now available, and that the advance here not be a very small one. More than that, I would like to provide the sort of model, and the sort of advance, that incorporates much of what is good in previous offerings—even in quite a few conjunctive offerings—and that may naturally stimulate (still) better accounts from others.

There are interesting connections, I believe, between the model of knowledge to be proposed and some main ideas of my recent book, *Philosophical Relativity*.[5] These will be discussed, somewhat briefly, in the final section of this paper. But the material of the first five sections is quite independent of the book, as is much of the interest that the cone model may have for theorists of knowledge, in particular, and even for philosophers quite generally.

## 1. A Sketch of the Model

Imagine a cone with its apex oriented upward. Think of what we may call *the ideal case of knowledge* as the point, or as at the point, that is the apex of this cone. Perhaps nobody, no (logically) possible being, can ever be involved in this ideal case. Perhaps an enormously infinite

---

5. Peter Unger, *Philosophical Relativity*, (Minneapolis, Minn., 1984).

intelligence, like the omniscient God of traditional theism, can be in this case. It will simplify matters considerably, and not be overly dogmatic, if we suppose the second alternative. So we do that. Can we finite human beings ever be in this case? Let us now leave this question open, supposing neither that we can nor that we cannot. In any case, we often are not in the ideal case even with regards to propositions, or truths or whatever, to which we are cognitively very well related by any ordinary standard. When someone is not in the ideal case but his cognitive relation is rather good, then his situation may be represented by a certain sort of curve, or profile, somewhat down from the apex at all or most of its points, and going around the surface of the cone. In a little while, I'll sketch how we might suitably think of, even visualize, such representations. Let's first try to get some feeling for what some of these curves might represent: we will look for curves (at least most of whose points) are progressively further down from the apex and, as a consequence, usually are progressively longer.

Even on the supposition that we cannot be in the ideal case, it is suitable to suppose that we human beings can come quite close to being in the ideal case. Perhaps most of us do about as well as we ever can with regard to the proposition (or tiny part of the whole truth) *something exists*. Our situation with respect to that will, for most of us, be represented by a quite tiny curve all of whose points are at least quite close to the apex. We may do just a bit less well with regard to *some thinking is going on*, a bit less than that with both *I exist* and *I am now thinking*. So our situation with respect to those propositions, or "things," will be represented by somewhat longer curves whose points are, for the most part, somewhat further down on the surface from the apex. We do worse still with *I seem to be in pain*, perhaps worse yet, perhaps not, with *I am in pain*. Generally, someone will be further down on the cone still with respect to *there is another person who is now in my presence*. Typically, we are yet further from involvement in the ideal with regard to *there is a person speaking to me who is thinking about having dinner*. But if there is such a person and he is suggesting we both go to an Italian restaurant, I will still be at least pretty near the apex, by any standard of nearness that we should then typically employ. Even with this last, my situation may be represented by a curve many of whose points are not very far down from the top of the cone.

We have at least a moderately clear idea of what is represented by the point that is the apex of the cone: the ideal case of knowing. What about points at the other extreme of our model, points on the base of (the external curved surface of the) cone? What is represented by the points on (the largest circle of) the base of the cone? Perhaps we may say that at least some of these points will represent the satisfaction to a minimal degree of certain conditions that must be satisfied at least to such a degree for us ever to recognize an ascription of knowledge to someone as appropriate, let alone as true or strictly correct. Other points may then just help to constitute a connecting curve for these representational points. Perhaps it is better to think of the representational base points as marking bottom *limits* for satisfaction of these degree-like requirements, or as we may say, for these *aspects of knowledge*. Or perhaps some aspects have a least degree while others have such limits. Let us not try to decide among these three mutually exclusive, and jointly exhaustive, options for interpreting representational points on the base of our cone.

In just a while, I will say something about what I mean by such aspects. Then we may get clearer about what the representational points may be doing on this conception, not just those at the base and at the apex, but those very many such points that, on the cone's curved surface, lie between the two.

With regard to *the car that I parked on a New York City street last night is still where I left it*, we will typically be what we may consider a significant distance from the apex. Then my position will, typically, be represented by a curve many of whose points are rather closer to the cone's base than to its apex. If the matter concerns a car left there a month ago, not just ten hours, our distance down the cone from the ideal case at the top is rather large, by any ordinary standard. Even a person who is quite confident that a car he has parked on a New York street a month ago is still there, even one who in fact happens to be right about the matter, will have his cognitive situation represented by a curve almost all of whose points are rather near the base of the cone. By now you should have some feeling for what I might be getting at with all of this talk about a cone and curves on its surface. Then you might want to hear more about the model of knowledge, the *cone model of knowledge*, that we might develop with the aid of such geometric descriptions. I hope that you do.

Can we know something to be so even if we are not involved in the ideal case of knowing with regard to that thing? It is instructive to think of (universal) skepticism about knowledge as deriving from, and as requiring, a negative answer to this question. Let us think of it that way now. It is instructive to think of ourselves ordinarily as confidently giving a positive answer. I will now suppose, as I usually do believe, that a positive answer is correct. But our model of knowledge itself will provide no answer to this question. This is one way that our model is neutral in dialogues between skeptics and those who actively advocate our strong beliefs to the effect that we so often know things to be so. I regard this neutrality as a virtue of this model, though I am aware that it is a virtue that it may share with more than a few rather standard analyses of knowledge.

In the ideal case, any even plausible condition for knowledge is satisfied. The knower will satisfy, amongst others, all of the following descriptions, and on their strictest possible interpretations. He will be absolutely certain, that the thing is so; he will be completely justified in being as certain and sure of it as he is; there will be no possibility, chance, or room for his being in error about the thing; the perhaps uniquely best way that he may have attained, and in which he may maintain, his certainty about it is absolutely, completely and perfectly reliable; he can rule out absolutely as untrue any proposition whatsoever whose truth is, or would be, incompatible with the thing; it is wholly rational for the person to disregard as entirely irrelevant any putative new evidence that may seem to bear negatively on that of which he is so certain; it is wholly rational of him to act on the basis of (the truth of) the thing no matter what might be "the consequences of his failing to act on the truth" (in what he knew to be a fair situation, it would be rational for him to bet his life on it, so to say, even for the sake of a desired noodle); if the thing were not true, then he would not be certain of it (nor even believe it) no matter *what* else may then also be true; there is no real difference between the state of his mind with regard to the thing, his certainty, and the thing's being so. Each of these descriptions may be said to apply to the highest point of an *aspect* of knowledge.

I will not try to be very precise about this rather technical notion of an aspect of knowledge. But perhaps I should say just a bit more about what I here have in mind. An aspect is something that may be satisfied more or less completely. Every aspect must be satisfied to at least a minimal degree for a subject appropriately (whether or not truly) to be considered as knowing a particular thing in question, even by the most lenient standards we may ever properly employ for such consideration. An aspect must be satisfied to the very highest degree for the subject appropriately to be considered as being in the ideal case of knowing the thing, to be appropriately considered as knowing the thing even according to the most stringent standards we may ever properly employ for such consideration. An aspect of knowledge is different from, but related to, a logically necessary condition for knowledge. If *a* is an aspect of knowledge, then for someone S to know something, say, that p, it is logically necessary that *a* hold to a least a minimal degree. It is a substantive, and often controversial, matter whether *a* must hold to a higher degree than that. Now certain logically necessary conditions of someone's knowing something to be so do not admit of degrees at all, or else the degrees there involved are not relevant to how appropriate it is to consider the subject as knowing the thing to be so. Thus it is with the truth condition, that the thing be so, and thus it is also with the condition that the subject actually exist. The first of these, as I see it, is not a condition that can be satisfied more or less fully; if the thing is not so, then the condition just fails to be satisfied at all. The second of these seems to be like that as well. And whatever sense we may attach to "someone's existing to only such-and-such a degree," this would have little to do, it seems, with whether or not that subject knew certain things to be so or not. So much for trying to give you some idea, in advance, of what I mean by an "aspect of knowledge." Insofar as this phrase will have more meaning for us, that will be owing to such constraints upon it as emerge from our employment of it in what follows.

Before I said that I would leave it an open question whether we humans, who are less than omniscient, are ever involved in an ideal case of knowing. When reflecting upon the above aspects, however, we seem to have a pretty good case for concluding, in an appropriately tentative spirit, that we never are in the ideal case. That is because we can argue, plausibly enough, that to be in the ideal case, a knower must know *everything* that is the case: The general idea, suggested to me by Jonathan Adler, is that anything, or just about anything, might seem to count against the truth of anything (else) that is presumably known, if not very directly, then at least indirectly. So it will be *extremely* hard for a being to properly reject as irrelevant any putative evidence against that of which he is certain (or toward which he has some lesser positive attitude.)

The following seems to be a rather telling case in point. By way of making many "amazing" but correct predictions, and retrodictions, a being might establish credentials of enormous believability, or of great epistemic authority. This being then might say to you, the would be knower, "You may never understand how it could be so, but take my word for this, too. All of the experience that you ever have is part of a vivid, rather unrealistic dream. In fact you have no arms or legs, nor any correct ideas about numbers, nor even any sanity or rationality." How could you properly regard such a knowledgeable being's remarks as completely irrelevant to the matter of, say, whether (you should be certain that) you have arms and legs, or even, say, the matter of whether (you should be certain that) two and three are five? How could you properly rule out the apparently relevant "possibility" that what this being said was indeed true? Perhaps only by knowing how it is that he functions as well as he does in making all of the correct predictions and retrodictions that he makes and why he nonetheless said what he said to you; in other words, by knowing how everything about him undercuts the idea that in the end he spoke correctly. You must be able to do this for *any being no matter how knowledgeable*. But to properly reject such a challenge from such a knowledgeable being, you must be at least as knowledgeable as he. (If the challenging being is omniscient, just as you must be, then you will know that at least part of his challenge is insincere, and so that the being is not omnibenevolent.) Thus, in order for you to be in a position properly to disregard as irrelevant any such challenge at all, you must be absolutely omniscient, you must know everything that is the case. And to be in the ideal case of knowing, you must, among other things, be in that position. So, I tentatively conclude, to be in the ideal case of knowing *anything* one must know *everything* that is the case. Not being omniscient, we humans are never in the ideal case.

It may well appear that, though this argument holds for almost all propositions, it will fail for some. In particular, it may fail for *something exists*. The idea here is, of course, a modified Cartesian one: In the foregoing scenarios, both you exist and also that challenger exists, so there are at least two things that exist, so, surely, in the relevantly liberal sense of the sentence, something exists. But this apparent counter-instance is not as forceful as first appears.

Suppose that the challenger, after establishing his authoritative credentials in ever so many matters, says to you something like this: "You have a tendency to confuse your words and, with that, what they mean. For one thing, you often confuse "exits" with "exists," wrongly thinking the first to mean much the same as "goes out" and wrongly thinking the latter to mean much the same as "is." In fact, the meanings are quite the reverse. Moreover, though few realize it, Zeno was actually correct in his arguments against motion. Accordingly, nothing really goes out at all, that is, nothing really exists. Now a number of things each *exits*, it is true; the world is not so very empty. But contrary to what you are thinking, nothing exists." It is not so easy to know for certain that what such a being advances cannot be so. It is not so easy, therefore, to be in the ideal case with respect to *something exists*. To do that you must know at least as much as the generally authoritative being, so as to know how and why what he says gets said by him, but nonetheless cannot undermine your idea that you know, and know ideally, that something exists. To do this, you must be more than a moderately sophisticated philosopher; you must be an omniscient being.[6] To be in the ideal case of

---

6. The foregoing is a mild variant of an argument that I present in my book, *Ignorance* (Oxford, 1975), especially at pages 132–34.

knowing with respect to *any* matter, then, requires one to know absolutely everything that is the case. We are not complacent or dogmatic about this universal result, but we do accept it, however tentatively and modestly.

Because being in the ideal case requires omniscience, in particular it implies that, for anything that one knows, one knows that one knows it. But there might be no such implication for any case of knowing, if such cases there be, that is less than an ideal case of knowing.

Is there anything about approximating to omniscience that may properly be regarded as an aspect of knowledge? Is there anything relating to knowing that one knows that may be so regarded? I suspect that in each case the answer is *yes*, though I am unsure in these matters. At all events, we will not try to be precise about what are, and what are not, the various aspects of knowledge.

A person's being in the ideal case of knowing with respect to a certain proposition will, I have said, entail that all of the aspects are satisfied in the highest degree. But at least some aspects may be satisfied in the highest degree, I suppose, and the person involved may yet fail to be in the ideal case of knowing. I suppose, though am not wholly sure, that this occurs with the aspect of personal, or psychological, certainty, that is, the aspect of a *person's* being absolutely certain that the thing is so: Suppose that someone is so certain of something that, as a matter of logic, nobody could ever be any more certain of anything than he then is of that thing; on the strongest interpretation of the expression, the person is absolutely sure of the thing. Even so, it seems that the thing might fail to be so. If, as it seems, such absolute psychological certainty fails to imply truth, then it will fail to imply knowledge and, a *fortiori*, fail to imply being in the ideal case of knowing. Let us call any aspect that even when satisfied to the highest possible degree fails to imply the ideal case of knowing, an *independent* aspect of knowledge. Then, as far as I can tell, the aspect of personal certainty will be one such independent aspect.

What we may regard as the most interesting aspects of knowledge, however, will not be independent aspects. Or so it seems to me. Suppose that I am *completely justified* in being absolutely certain, that is, absolutely sure, of something, on the strongest interpretation of those words. What sort of thing might I there be so certain of? For me to be so justified in being all that certain the thing had better be something with respect to which I am about as well off as I am to *something exists*. But if I even believe anything at all, it must be true that something exists. So the truth condition of knowledge is here satisfied. It is plausible to suppose that any other necessary condition of knowledge will also be met. Moreover, it is plausible to suppose that each of the other aspects will be satisfied to the highest degree, and so that I will then be in the ideal case of knowing.

We may reasonably suppose that all of the aspects of knowledge that are not independent ones fit the general description just given. Then we might well call all of these more interesting aspects of knowledge *interdependent* aspects. The idea that an interdependent aspect is at its limit, holds to the highest possible degree, entails that *all* of the other aspects, both independent and interdependent, are at their limits. And when an interdependent aspect is at its limit that implies, also, that all of the nonaspectual necessary conditions of knowledge are satisfied. In particular, it is implied that the thing (known) is indeed the case: truth is implied. When an interdependent aspect is below that, when it holds only to some lesser degree, the situation is variable: the aspect that it not be an accident that the person is right will still imply truth, because it implies that the person is right and that implies truth; but with many (even) interdependent aspects, truth will not be implied. For example, a person may be completely justified in being *pretty* (near to being absolutely) certain of something even while that thing is in fact not so.

Let me suggest, then, that the following condition not only distinguishes independent aspects from interdependent ones, but does so in a heuristically helpful way: When an interdependent aspect is satisfied to the highest degree, that logically implies that the truth condition is met. But when an independent aspect is satisfied, and that aspect is described in barest terms, it is not logically implied that the truth condition is met. This doesn't really add anything to what we've already said, of course, but it will help us keep in mind, for any given aspect, whether it is an independent aspect or an interdependent one.

Because we do not attempt a conjunctive analysis with our model, nor any standard sort of analysis at all, it is not crucial that we specify all, or even nearly all, of the aspects of knowledge. Rather our model provides a general schema by means of which aspects of knowledge are related to each other. We may specify more and more aspects in terms of the schema that this model provides, learning more and more about the concept of knowledge with the further aspects we may specify. Certain further specifications will be more interesting than others; from them we will learn more. Certain interesting aspects may at first seem unrelated to aspects already specified, but reflection upon them may reveal logical relations with some of those specified aspects. From the consideration of such further aspects, we may learn much about our conception of what it is for someone to know that something is so.

In terms of our conical model, how are we to represent the aspects of knowledge, both those that are quite illuminating and even those that are not? It is convenient to think of each aspect, whether independent or interdependent, as a line running from the cone's apex down to its base. But that most convenient picture may be distortingly simple beyond what we can tolerate. For in addition to the condition that, in the ideal case, all aspects hold together at the apex, there may be other logical relationships, involving the aspects, where things are further down the cone. Probably it is impossible to represent all of this logical complexity adequately via a geometric solid, at least one as simple as our three-dimensional Euclidean cone. But even using such a cone, we might come pretty close to an adequate treatment with only a moderate increase of complexity.

Instead of representing them by lines, we may represent each aspect by a triangle on the cone, perhaps by an isosceles triangle with a curved base that is part of the cone's base. At the upper limit of an aspect is a vertex of its triangle. For any *interdependent* aspect, this vertex will be at the apex of the cone. Now think of the line running from the apex down to midpoint of the triangle's base, and call it the triangle's *center line*. The degree to which an aspect of knowledge is satisfied will be represented by a point on the center line of the triangle that represents that aspect: the greater the degree of satisfaction, the nearer the apex will be that point.

Some triangles may overlap with some other triangles. That will represent this: Where one of the aspects holds to a certain high, but not highest degree, the other represented aspect must hold to at least a certain degree. The greater the overlap, the greater the extent to which the two go together. (But one aspect may be the controlling one of the pair; perhaps its triangle will be a lighter color, or brighter, than the other's.) A triangle may overlap with any number of other triangles. Which overlaps are in order, and which not, will take detailed conceptual inquiry to discover. For the most part, I will not attempt such inquiry.

At least apart from the cone's apex, some triangles may overlap with no other triangles. These non-overlapping triangles might be replaced by their center lines: there is no need to represent the aspects thus represented by triangles rather than lines, but perhaps there is no harm in doing that, either.

How can we represent the difference between the independent aspects and the interdependent aspects? Let there be a large isosceles triangular zone on the cone with its vertex at the cone's apex; we may call this the *independence zone*. Independent aspects will be represented by triangles both of whose equal sides lie within the equal sides that are the limits of this zone, and whose uppermost vertices lie, not on, but just below, the vertex of the triangle that is the enclosing independence zone. Why will an independent aspect have its highest point below, not on, the cone's apex?

The cone's apex represents the ideal case of knowing. If the highest degree of satisfaction of an aspect were represented by a point at the apex, that is, by the apex, then that would imply the highest satisfaction of all the other aspects. Hence any such aspect must be interdependent, not independent. For an independent aspect, then, its highest representational point must lie below the apex, in the independence zone.

We have a problem of representation. How may we represent the merely one-way entailments between the ideal case of knowing and the highest satisfaction of independent aspects such as psychological certainty? We need a suitable convention of representation. We may draw short lines from the vertex of any triangle for an independent aspect to the cone's apex. These little line segments may be treated as on-off switches. When there is an ideal case of knowing, the relevant point relating to any such aspect is in the on position, at the higher end of the little line segment, at the apex of the cone. When there is not an ideal case of knowing, the relevant representational point will be at the lower end of the line segment, below the cone's apex.

How can we represent such logical relationships as may hold between certain independent aspects and certain interdependent aspects? For example, if someone really is very fully justified in being almost absolutely sure that something is so, that may imply that the person must be at least moderately high up along the aspect of psychological certainty; otherwise he will not have perceived the implications of such evidence as he has, and have been appropriately affected by his intellectual perception, thus not really being all that well justified. We want to be able to represent some such relationships as these. Well, we may say that an interdependent aspect may have one of its (triangle's) sides cross over into this zone, to represent a logical relationship with certain independent aspects. (Perhaps it may have both sides cross over to represent yet more relationships.) We may say this because we may also say that interdependent aspects cannot have their triangles confined to the independence zone.

Consider triangles not confined to that zone; we are considering aspects of knowledge that are interdependent. When any is satisfied to the highest degree so are all of the others, and so are all of the independent aspects. There is then an ideal case of knowing. But when there is a situation that is less than ideal the aspects may be satisfied to varying degrees. In certain contexts, the satisfaction of some to high degrees will be enough for us to allow that there is a (less than ideal) case of knowledge, providing only that the non-aspectual conditions of knowledge, such as the truth condition, are met in the first place. Because we may do this adaptively and usefully, the model we have just sketched may help to explain our ordinary thinking about when people know and when they do not.

## 2. How We Adaptively Think in Terms of Knowing

At different times we think differently about who knows what. That is because we are in different contexts, with different interests dominant, as much as because we think about different people (and other creatures) in different cognitive positions. We want an account of knowledge that can help explain this variable and adaptive thinking that we do. Our model can help.

When we make or hear a claim as to knowledge, we implicitly appreciate quite a lot about the context in which the statement is made, including what are then the dominant interests of the party, or parties, most involved with the making or the understanding of the statement. Someone says that John knows that Sam's car broke down yesterday. Is what he says true? What will we think about this? Among other things, that depends upon our interests in the context.

Suppose that the speaker and we listeners are mainly concerned about John as a source of truths. Then we will be interested a lot in this: How strongly does John's belief in, or even very weak favoritism for, a "proposition" correlate with the truth of that proposition? We would like a strong non-accidental correlation, the stronger the better across as wide a variety of matters as we can get.

Of course, as regards many matters we may care little about having a reliable source of truths. We may be interested in John not so much as a source of truths in general, but more as a source about breakdowns. Alternatively, we may be mainly interested in a source of truths about Sam. This variability in our interests may well affect our evaluation of a knowledge claim made in a certain context, where one rather than another of these interests is dominant. For expository purposes, however, we may bracket these more detailed considerations within the general aspect of reliability.

Given an interest in (John as) a source of truths, we are likely to be much concerned with how reliable was the way, perhaps the causally dominant way, that John arrived at or maintained his belief (or other favorable attitude for the thought) that Sam's car broke down. We will be little concerned with how certain John may or may not have been. And, typically, we won't be much concerned with his justification: we might not care much whether he is as nutty as a fruitcake when it comes to Sam, or car breakdowns, or any other matters. So long as John is right—that car did break down then—and the relevant way of his coming to be so (and staying so) is reliable enough, we will allow as true the statement that he knows. Sam's car broke down then. How can our model help us to understand this appropriate judgement of ours?

We focus on certain aspects of knowledge and neglect others. For the ones in focus, we require that at least a moderately high standard be satisfied, how high determined by the context, as we also appreciate well enough. Aspects in focus get assigned minimum standards represented by points at least fairly high up (on the center lines) in the triangles that represent those aspects; the greater the minimum for an aspect, the higher the point in its triangle. In most contexts, most aspects are largely neglected. Where an aspect is neglected, we have low standards for satisfaction; we assign it a point at or near the base of its triangle. We may call the appreciated group of points, group of assignments, the *profile of the context* for the statement that attributes the bit of (presumed) knowledge in focus. This profile is to represent all that we then care about as regards conditions, or approximations to conditions, for the truth of the statement that John knows Sam's car broke down yesterday.

Whatever else I'm doing here, I'm engaging in a lot of picture thinking. Such thinking can persuade one of much that is untrue; no doubt, at least something of that is going on here. But I am much more concerned to provide a fruitful beginning for new approaches in epistemology than to provide accurate detail (that, most likely, won't lead us much beyond itself). So I'm going to engage in even more picture thinking now.

When there is a profile in the sense (somewhat loosely) specified above, we will connect the points of the profile with a line. Then we will have a line curving around the outside surface of the cone. Where on the cone we have the aspect of reliability, and where we have closely related aspects, then for the example we've chosen our profile curve will be fairly high up. For all of the other aspects, which together we may suppose to occupy most of the cone's surface, the curve will be closer to the cone's base.

Given context, our understanding of the knowledge claim imposes a particular profile on the cone. The situation of the putative knower in the world, including his state of mind and all sorts of supervenient facts about him, gives another total assignment. That assignment will also be given a profile curve on the cone. We may call this second profile the *profile of the facts* that relate to the statement that attributes that bit of knowledge to that creature.

Of course, we may be wrong about these facts and, right or wrong, we always make our assessments more directly in terms of our beliefs (or other attitudes) as to the facts, not very directly in terms of the facts themselves. But for present purposes this point may best be discounted: we will suppose that what we take to be the facts of a situation indeed are the facts of that situation. Especially as we are specifying our own examples, this simplifying assumption will do no harm.

One thing that our cone model does is to give us a sense of the relationship between the profiles of the facts for any two epistemic situations. Suppose that one such situation has a given such profile. Another may be an improvement on this first by way of the subject being higher up with respect some interdependent aspect. Then, since the aspect is interdependent, he will be higher up as well with respect to at least certain other aspects of knowing. What may this imply for our aspects? With respect to those aspects most closely related to the given one, whose representing triangles have most overlap, the degrees of improvement will be greatest. Perhaps this upward ripple effect may even extend to *all* other aspects of knowing. We leave this conjecture open.

With certain interdependent aspects, it *may* be that the upward ripple effect holds only with certain provisos, or only through a somewhat limited range.[7] Even if this should be so, the main point will remain. For any interdependent aspect, there is at least a presumptive tendency for the upward ripple effect, and there is at least a certain range, presumably near the top of the cone, where the ripple effect will hold without qualification. Now, it is my suspicion that only some confusions lead to the idea that some such restrictions on, or qualifications of, the indicated upward ripple effect are required, and that the simple unqualified relationship posited will be seen as adequate to the phenomena once they are properly understood. But if this suspicion is wrong, that will only mean that we must conduct our discussion in

---

7. What I have in mind here are certain puzzles discussed in, for example, Carl Ginet's, "Knowing Less by Knowing More," *Midwest Studies in Philosophy* V (1980). Ginet's discussion is prompted, in part, by some ideas in Gilbert Harman's *Thought* (Princeton, 1973). In turn, Harman's ideas are stimulated in part by a "paradox about knowledge" orally offered by Saul Kripke.

a somewhat more complex and qualified way, as indicated, not that we must alter the direction of the discussion.

In contrast, when two epistemic situations differ in that one has the subject be higher up with regard to an *independent* aspect, it does *not* follow that, at least relative to some qualifications, he must be higher up with regard to other aspects. Even after any needed qualifications have been satisfied, and throughout any range whatsoever, two profiles of the facts may differ, then, *only* in that in the one the subject is situated higher up, or lower down, than in the other as regards any given independent aspect of knowledge. With independent aspects, unlike interdependent aspects, profiles of the facts exhibit no upward ripple effect at all, as far as I can tell, not even a qualified or restricted one.

In contrast with profiles of fact, profiles of context show no such difference between independent and interdependent aspects. That is because these profiles, unlike profiles of fact, have so much to do with our own interests. And we may sometimes be more interested in the increased satisfaction of a certain interdependent aspect even while we have no such increased interest in other aspects to which it is logically related. Perhaps that is not highly rational. But if so, then we are not always so highly rational.

On the basis of these considerations, we may say that contexts of fact have a certain *rigidity*, owing to the logical relations flowing from interdependent aspects. In contrast, we may say that profiles of context lack this rigidity, and may be completely *elastic*, or completely *fluid*. These terms may help to give us some intuitive feeling for the content of our cone model of knowledge.[8]

In any case, when the profile of the facts relating to a knowledge claim lies on or above the profile of the context of the claim, it is appropriate for us to allow that the claim is true. But should the profile of the facts ever dip below the profile of the context, then in that context it is only proper for us to disallow this and to consider the knowledge claim untrue. Now the way I've just put things may make it seem hard for a claim properly to be considered true by us; one slip and it's done for. But that's not right. Reasonable folks that we are, in many contexts we generate profiles of context that are quite easy for facts to satisfy.

On our assumption that our beliefs as to the facts are correct, and on other most plausible assumptions here implicit, we often properly allow a claim to knowledge to be a true statement. Does this mean that

---

8. This way of looking at these matters was suggested to me by Tak Yagisawa.

these statements about knowledge will actually be true statements? No; it does not. For our model of knowledge is not put forth as a model of the semantics of the terms of knowledge. Now, it is quite plausible to think that, insofar as it offers much truth of any sort, our model is indeed a model for the semantics of statements of the form 'S knows that p' and for kindred expressions. Indeed, this *contextualist* view, as I have called it, is the most plausible more detailed view of the role our model plays in the adaptive thinking about knowing in which we so often engage.[9] For those who like things more definite or detailed, and only like to think much about what is most plausible, this is the view to take. But if we commit ourselves to this much detail, as we have not done, we may miss out on thought about some philosophically interesting alternatives. So we will not do that now. For a broader perspective on these matters, we may then discuss some of these alternatives, as we shall do somewhat later in the present study.

Let's consider a rather different sort of context now. Suppose that we are not so much interested in John as a source of truths, but are more interested in explaining some action that he has recently performed and, as often happens with such explanation, in making what he did seem reasonable and proper. Suppose that although Sam is John's best friend, John just lent his car to Bill, his next best friend, instead of Sam. Paul, a mutual friend of all, asked John for the car on Sam's behalf, but John lent it to Bill instead. Why is that?

Suppose that further facts of the matter are these. John heard of Sam's breakdown only at a noisy party last night, and barely remembers anything first heard there. If asked about whether Sam's car broke down, for example, he'd reply with some such words as, "I suppose it did, now that you mention it, but I can't imagine why that seems right." He has no strong conviction about any such breakdown. However, he is very sure that Bill is without the use of a car, needs one, and will remain carless during the time of need unless he, John, loans him the car. Paul should have taken the time to convince John of Sam's real trouble, but as it happens he did not.

The loan of the car to Bill instead of Sam is now no mystery at all. What is one ordinary way for us to explain John's action? We might well say that John knew that Bill needed his car, but he did not really know that Sam needed it; for he did not know that Sam's car broke

---

9. See my *Philosophical Relativity*, where contextualism is (loosely) defined and (extensively) discussed.

down yesterday. Suppose that someone said this to us in such a context. We would allow that what he said was true.

In this second context, we are interested in the aspect of personal certainty. We are also interested in the related aspect of preferring to act on what one knows over what one does not. We are also interested in the aspects of justification that relate to these conditions. We are not much interested in reliability or those aspects of knowledge closely related to that aspect.

The profile of this context goes high up on the cone where we have the center lines for those aspects of most interest. It is much closer to the base for aspects relating to reliability now. A quite different profile is assigned than was appropriate to the earlier context. The profile of the facts is always above the profile of that earlier context, so there we allow that John knows. But this same profile of facts is not always above the profile of this second context; it dips below it significantly. So here we do not allow that John knows that Sam's car broke down yesterday.

In the different contexts where attributions of knowledge, or denials of knowledge, are made and accepted, we may have a wide variety of interests. In any given context, the interests most dominant for us there will help to determine a profile according to which such attribution, or such denial, will be deemed in place or not. But there are limits on how much our interests can do. Bertrand Russell's case of the stopped watch is a case in point[10] and, with the same ordinary background suppositions inforce, so are the much discussed, much more recent cases of Edmund Gettier.[11] Consider Russell's example, the wording slightly changed.

John looks at his watch. It reads, say, two o'clock. As a consequence of seeing this, John strongly, and quite justifiably, believes that it is about two o'clock. Suppose that the time is in fact two, or very close to it, so that what John believes is true. With no further ado, we would ordinarily allow that he knows that it is two. But in this case there is further ado. While John's watch is a very reliable one, as he knows from much experience, in fact it happened to break down—for the first time— precisely twelve hours ago, when John looked at it last. So the only reason that it reads the right time now is this lucky coincidence between the time of its breaking and the time of its recent use. We suppose that there are no further exotic details that push things around the other way, so as to improve John's cognitive relation to *it is two o'clock*.

---

10. Bertrand Russell, *The Problems of Philosophy* (New York: Oxford, 1912).
11. Edmund Gettier, "Is Justified True Belief Knowledge?" *Analysis* 23 (1963).

To such an example, we will respond that John did not know that it was two o'clock. It does not matter what our interests are; that is what we are disposed sincerely to think. Why is that? We may explain the matter well enough in terms of our cone model. The example itself highlights so well the aspect of non-accidentality that anyone who understands the example at all well cannot but focus upon it, whatever else he may also have in focus. And there are certain minimum standards for this aspect of knowledge that must be met if we are properly to reckon an example a case of knowledge.

We may be rather lax in these standards at times, depending upon our interests. But in Russell's case John is specified to have pure luck, so any such minimum will be undercut. If we understand the example at all well, we see this. So we react to it as we do. In geometric terms: any profile of context must be more than marginally above the cone's base on the center line (of the triangle for) the aspect of non-accidentality. But in Russell's case, the profile of the facts is at the base, or so near to it as makes no difference. So we do not allow that, in such a case, the person knows.

We should notice a point of logic here. We demand, for knowing, that it not be entirely accidental, or coincidental, or lucky that the subject is right that the thing is so. This demanded condition entails that the subject is right, and thus that the thing is so. Because we demand that this aspect be satisfied at least to some degree—the point on its triangle's center line must be at least somewhat above the cone's base— we demand that the thing be so. This alone is enough to ensure that the truth condition of knowledge is satisfied. So we don't need any additional statement to the effect that truth is satisfied, independent of minimal satisfaction of other conditions. This must be a positive feature of our approach, for it allows us to understand our strong reactions to examples like those of Gettier and of Russell. In turn, this emphasizes the difference between our cone model and many, though perhaps not all, of the traditional attempts at analyzing knowledge.

For a final sort of illustrative example, let us consider some cases that bear an obvious similarity to those just discussed, but which may be importantly different as well. I have in mind examples of lotteries, another sort of example much discussed by epistemologists in recent years. Suppose that you hold a single ticket in a lottery with ten million tickets, and that it is a fair lottery with only one winner, as you know. It may be that the winning ticket has already been chosen, but the winner not yet announced. Then the odds are one in ten million that you have won the lottery. Let us stipulate that your ticket is not the single ticket that was chosen, or drawn. Thus even though no announcement has yet been made, you have, along with so many others, in fact lost the lottery. Can you know, in such a circumstance, what is true, namely, that you have lost that lottery?

It is common for philosophers of knowledge to say that you cannot, and that it is always proper only to disallow any claim to the effect that you know you have already lost. But suppose that you are indulging yourself and spending money that, unless you won, you can ill afford to squander. A friend may advise you to stop immediately, for otherwise you will surely worsen your situation. Being superstitious, however, you think that a certain "omen" you saw yesterday means there is a very good chance that you will be announced as the winner, that you have not lost but have won. To press his point upon you, the friend may well say, "Be reasonable, for heaven's sakes, you know you've lost that lottery, you only held one ticket in it out of the ten million." In such a context, and on the assumption that you have indeed lost, we may well allow as true what your friend said in way of claiming knowledge here for you.[12]

In making his knowledge claim, what your friend is emphasizing is knowledge as a guide for rational action. In this context; the aspects of knowledge that will be most relevant to consider will be those most directly related to this action-guiding role that the concept has in our lives: Between something known and something believed but not known, you should, other things equal, choose or act on the basis of what is known. In the case at hand, your friend counsels, you should act on the basis of the proposition that you have lost, no matter how strongly you may feel about the omen. In terms of our model, the profile of this context is a curve that is pretty high up on the cone when it comes to such aspects of knowledge as have to do with it as a basis for rational action, and is rather low when it comes to such aspects as have little to do with that. Given the assumed facts of our example, the profile of the facts is everywhere above such a profile of the context. For your situation is one, we presume, where your rationally maintained belief that you lost provides you with a very good basis for acting on that idea, despite your conflicting feeling about the omen. So the facts have things higher up even at the comparatively few center lines where the context places anything much in the way of demands and, we may presume, is also higher up at all those other, lower points where the context is very undemanding.

In other contexts, it would only be appropriate to treat knowledge claims in an opposite way. Suppose, in contrast to what we assumed just

---

12. Here I am indebted to discussion with Stephen Schiffer.

before, that you hold, not just one ticket in such a lottery as that just mentioned, but hold every ticket but one. Now, the odds are enormously in your favor, you are quite (near to being absolutely) certain that you have won, you are quite justified in being so certain, you are quite rational in acting on the proposition that you have won, and so on. With respect to many aspects of knowledge you are quite well placed. But suppose that one wants to focus, as so many epistemologists quite understandably do want to focus, on the ideal that the acquisition of knowledge is a systematic enterprise, one where our beliefs are not correct as a matter of any luck or coincidence, but rather because they were arrived at by reliable methods and, like other of our beliefs so obtained, form a more or less coherent system or body of beliefs, various of whose parts or members help to explain the truth of various others. Then one may appropriately say, of any such lottery situation, that nobody will ever know whether he has won or lost until an announcement to that effect has been properly made and accepted.

The epistemologists who discuss lotteries are typically concerned to emphasize some such ideas about knowledge as a well-grounded, coherent, explanatory system.[13] In the contexts of their discussions, a profile of context is generated where the points are quite near the apex for those aspects of knowledge of the sort they mean to emphasize. And in those contexts, the profile of the (assumed) facts is, with respect to those relevant center lines, at or near the base of the cone, even though the facts relating to so many other aspects are rather near to the apex of the cone. Hence, when and where those philosophers make their remarks about these people who await announcements of lotteries, we allow that their remarks are true: These ticket holders cannot then know whether they have won or not.

We could go on and on examining more and more examples and more and more contexts in which discussion of them may be variously embedded. I hypothesize that the more one would do this, the more one would be able to see applications of our cone model of knowledge. I leave to the future, and perhaps to other writers, the search for more and more revealing examples and surrounding contexts for them. It is my hope, of course, that such a search will confirm the hypothesis that this model is a reasonably accurate and fruitful one. In the meantime, I would like to explore how this model might help to illuminate the

---

13. An interesting treatment of these interests may be found in two papers by Jonathan Adler: "Knowing, Betting and Cohering," this volume and, especially, "Knowing: Would You Bet on It?" (unpublished).

perennial dialogue between the skeptic about knowledge and the philosophers who affirm the truth of our many positive claims to know about things. Why are there so many ways that skepticism about knowledge can be brought forward as an intriguing challenge? Why are we intrigued by this challenge only intermittently, and so easily and often brought back to agreement with the positive knowledge claims made in the discourse of everyday life? And why are we never completely satisfied for long with this adherence to the idea that so many of these knowledge claims actually and literally are true? In the next couple of sections, we turn to consider these questions.

## 3. Routes to Skepticism

Each aspect of knowledge provides a place for a skeptic to challenge a typical claim to knowledge. When such a challenge is severe and unrelenting, it leads to a skeptical position about the knowledge claim. Accordingly, there are many ways, perhaps indefinitely many ways, in which a skeptical position about a typical knowledge claim can be promoted.

The ways of promoting skepticism, however diverse, are importantly interrelated. Suppose that a statement is made, in a context, to the effect that a certain being knows a certain thing to be so. The skeptic suggests that we expand the context, not stick to the comparatively narrow contextual limits that, for more or less practical purposes, we have temporarily accepted. Because we do not want to seem narrow-minded, the skeptical suggestion seems appropriate and is inviting. The skeptic's suggestion seems most inviting when he establishes a context where the chief interest is in uncovering what is logically required for a knowledge claim to be, not just useful for us to make and accept, but a genuine (expression of) the truth. Where such a spirit of exploration prevails, we feel that we should take seriously all of the aspects of knowledge that there may be. We also feel that we should be serious in exploring each aspect to its limit, to its highest level of satisfaction. Accordingly, by focusing on almost any aspect of knowledge, the skeptic can make inviting the suggestion that we not stick to such comparatively low standards as is customary for almost all knowledge claims made in the course of our everyday thought and talk.

Each aspect of knowledge provides an opening for the skeptic to begin such an inviting challenge. Any interdependent aspect will provide an opening that is quite interesting, and potentially quite compelling; for any challenge broached there will eventually involve all of the other aspects of knowledge.

One interdependent aspect, as we have noted, is the reliability of the way, suitably specified, in which the subject comes to have, or in which he maintains, his favorable attitude toward the thing that might, or might not, be known. Sometimes the context of a knowledge claim may signal that this aspect is almost wholly irrelevant: given that we are happy enough about how things are with other aspects, satisfaction of a very minimal standard for the indicated aspect is enough for us to allow that the person said to know does know.

One thing a skeptic can do is to bring this aspect into focus, perhaps by reminding us how often we do require of people that their ways of arriving at or maintaining beliefs must be at least pretty reliable if we are (correctly) to allow that they know. If a person's state of knowing concerns his own cognitive situation, as it seems to do, and has quite little, if anything, to do with our own momentary interests in him, then how can we be correct in neglecting this aspect (of reliability) at those times when it suits our convenience? This does not seem right. So we agree that at least a pretty reliable way must be operative for any genuinely knowing subject, and we retract the claim that the person in question knows the thing in question.

This sort of move can be generalized. So one thing the skeptic can do, and do very invitingly, is suggest that *all* of the aspects of knowledge be satisfied to at least a pretty high degree, if a subject is to know a particular thing in any particular situation. With some things, like *I am now in pain*, it may often be that all of the aspects are satisfied to a fairly impressive degree. But with many things, like *my car is in the garage downstairs* and *there is a desk right now in my office over at the university*, this will rarely be so. Accordingly, the skeptic can, in this way, rather readily get us to have second thoughts about how often, if ever, one knows things that, say, involve much beyond one's own present moment thought and experience.

There is a complementary way that the skeptic can promote his position. Even where we are agreed that a certain aspect is quite relevant, and happily attribute knowledge in the case anyway, the skeptic can get us to be less happy. In such cases we are, by hypothesis, in agreement that the aspect in question is satisfied to at least a fairly high degree. Because we've just been discussing it, we do well to make the point with the aspect of reliability, though any interdependent aspect will do. So the way the subject came to be as certain as he is may be quite highly reliable, that is, reliable even when judged by quite a high standard of reliability. But how high is high enough? The skeptic may compare our subject's reliable way with one that is more reliable. That more reliable way may have been enjoyed by someone else with regard to the same sort of proposition, or subject matter. Because the subject's present way compares unfavorably, we become less happy with the thought that he knows. That other person may have known, we might allow, but our subject seems less qualified and less fortunate as concerns his having any such knowledge.

In recent work, both published and unpublished, Jonathan Adler brings this sort of move out in a forceful way. Though perhaps not very closely, we may follow his lead here. A man may arrive at his belief in a way that is generally quite reliable and that happens to be effective on this occasion: he is in fact right about the matter now. But the skeptic can point to actual cases of other people who employed a way that was just as reliable, or even more reliable over even a broader domain, but were wrong about a relevantly similar matter then. Those people did not know. So how can our present subject know? With respect to an important aspect of knowledge, he is no better placed than they and, in fact, is even worse off. This is a powerful move.

Here is an example of what Adler has in mind, upon which we may amplify. Someone sees a cup before him and, on the evidence of his eyes, believes that a cup is before him. He is right. Ordinarily, we allow that he knows there is a cup before him. But some other people have been in circumstances that, as far as either they or he could tell at the time, were just the same as his. These others, however, were not looking at cups, as they believed themselves to be, but were confronted by holographic images of cups, produced so well that any ordinary human being would take a real cup, and no trickery, to be there. The others may have better eyesight than our subject; they may also be generally more circumspect than he; any relevant way that they employ is, if anything, more reliable than that which he uses. Because it cannot ferret out the cups from the holograms, these ways are not all that reliable; there are some lengthier, more exhaustive and more reliable procedures. So going by the evidence of his eyes, in a rather uncritical and ordinary manner, is not all that reliable a way for our subject to have correct beliefs about what objects are before him. If a very high standard of reliability is required for knowing, as it now seems to be, then our subject does not know that there is a cup before him.

The skeptic suggests ways in which our contexts should be expanded: all aspects of knowledge should be duly in focus, none neglected, and the standards for any aspect in focus should be high, not as low as may be convenient. In terms of our cone model, he suggests this. There should be no center line where a point near the cone's base is allowed to pass as contextually appropriate, for neglect of that aspect of knowing whose representative triangle is there positioned;

moreover, we should move up the triangles of our now non-neglected aspects to points much nearer the cone's apex than we ordinarily find it convenient and adaptive to require. When we expand our contexts, so as to learn more of the truth about knowledge itself, we find acceptable only such profiles of context that are everywhere at least quite close to the cone's apex, very much closer to that than to its base. When these are our appreciated profiles of context, then very rarely, if ever, will the profile of the facts be everywhere on or above the relevant curve on the cone. Because we will see that the profile of the facts does dip below a more revealing, if less practical, profile of context, we will see that we should deny knowledge for the subject of the proposition in question.

It is the relation between interdependent aspects, I think, that allows this cone model to be illuminating with regard to the dialectic the skeptic offers. All of the interdependent aspects are fully satisfied in the ideal case of knowing, at the cone's apex, and none will be fully satisfied in any case less than the ideal. As is represented by their overlapping triangles, a movement upward along the center line for any one of these aspects exerts some force for movement upward along the center line for any of the others. How strong the force, how great the relation between the upward movements, will depend on the interdependent aspects involved—those whose triangles overlap strongly will undergo upward movements that are quite strongly in parallel.

When the skeptic starts to demand that a way be highly reliable, then it follows from his demand that other aspects be satisfied to at least a fairly high degree. For example, we may consider the requirement, or aspect, that the knowing subject be in a position to rule out as untrue statements that logically conflict with what he is to know. When standards of reliability are allowed to be fairly low, as we so ordinarily do allow them to be, there may be only a very tenuous connection required between these two aspects. But as the standard for the one much increases, it brings in considerations of the other.

A more highly reliable way of arriving at beliefs about what is before one's eyes will involve one in ruling out as untrue the statement that only a holographic image is before one, and that it is this image and no real cup that is (causally) responsible for the evidence of one's eyes, for one's visual experience. As higher reliability is required, one thing that the way, or method, or whatever, must do is enable one to rule out competing alternatives. Which competing alternatives need it enable the knowing subject to rule out? Those that are relevant. Which are relevant? More and more are relevant as the standard for reliability goes up and up. What are the standards for ruling out; how high must they be? These standards get higher and higher, too, as the standard for reliability gets closer and closer to the maximum, to the limiting point at the apex of our cone.

A *perfectly* reliable method will serve one well, indeed, unerringly, in any logically possible circumstance in which there arises any question at all as to whether one knows a particular thing to be so. Such a method or way will *automatically involve one* in ruling out with absolute certainty all propositions that conflict with that one of whose truth one is absolutely certain (because of one's involvement in that totally, completely and perfectly reliable way.) When involved in such a way, one can rule out with certainty, for example, the statement that a powerful evil demon is getting one to have false belief, or misplaced certainty, in the matter. If one cannot do this, then one's way, of method, is less than perfectly reliable, on the very strongest interpretation that those words can bear.

By the same token, if one can absolutely rule out all possible competing alternatives, then the way in which one gets to be, or keeps being, certain is absolutely reliable. It is reliable with respect to the proposition at hand; it may be reliable with all strongly related propositions; perhaps it must even be a way that is reliable with respect to any proposition whatsoever. (If this last alternative is correct, then in the ideal case perhaps one will need to know everything that is so, every single part of the whole truth about the world. If that is so, then only an omniscient Being will ever be in the ideal case of knowing.)

At all events, the interrelatedness of the aspects of knowing is the key point for us now. It helps us to understand that there is no single route for the skeptic that he must prefer by much to any other route. Some routes begin in triangles that overlap more strongly with more other triangles; other routes begin in less well placed triangles. For a quick punch that will get upward movement off to a good start, the skeptic may prefer to focus on routes of the former sort. But there need not be any great preference for these. Eventually, any of the routes, in any of the triangles for any of the interdependent aspects, will take us to the very top of the cone. Eventually, any route will take us to the extraordinarily demanding ideal case of knowing in which every aspect, independent as well as interdependent, is satisfied completely, is satisfied in the very highest degree. No matter which of indefinitely many routes the skeptic starts us out on, we end up with a mere point for our profile of context, our context itself being progressively purified and expanded.

In correspondence, Francis Dauer has suggested what is a sort of reverse method that the skeptic may employ in trying to further his position. In terms of our model, instead of raising curves by pushing them upward at various points, the skeptic may seek to nibble away at the base of the cone. For example, the skeptic may produce an argument to the effect that we are never in the least bit justified in having even a weak belief to the effect, say, that we have arms and legs. He might advance the idea, toward such a radical end, that in order to have any justification for any such belief, we must have something *accessible* to us on which to base the belief. But all that anyone has that is both sufficiently accessible and relevant for even a modest basis is his very own present moment immediate experience. And given the quite sparse content of any of our present moment immediate experience, something which we certainly do seem to be given, there is then no adequate basis for any such belief. So the belief has no adequate justification; so, we are not in the least bit justified in having any such belief. Inasmuch as we cannot even be at all justified in believing that, say, we have arms and legs, we quite certainly will never so much as *know* any such thing to be so. Accordingly, a skeptic about knowledge may well argue from the bottom up, so to say, rather than first urging upon us any very high standards for anything. There is a lot that is right, I think, in Dauer's way of looking at the matter. What are we to say of this other perspective, in terms that relate to our model?

First, we may notice that the skeptic can begin his undermining nibbling almost equally well in any of a rather considerable number of different ways. We may say, then, that he may begin with any one of a number of different aspects of knowledge. The aspects that are most promising for him will be interdependent aspects, not independent ones. For example, the skeptic might begin another undermining challenge in some such more or less parallel way as this: Given that each of us has little or nothing more to go on than his own very limited present moment immediate experience, it is a *sheer* accident if any of us be right in the matter of whether he has arms and legs, and so on, and so forth. Such promising interdependent aspects have, no doubt, interesting logical relations. Both those aspects and even those relations can, I think, be well represented, and thus well characterized, in terms of our cone model. All of this allows us to say, as John Richardson has suggested, that when the skeptic operates in the way emphasized by Dauer, *what he is doing is trying to lower what we will agree on as the profile of the facts*. Ordinarily, we will often take this profile to be at least moderately high, especially as regards the representation of an aspect in focus. The skeptic may offer arguments that we are being too generous to ourselves in the matter.

Second, the two perspectives may best be viewed as complementary rather than as opposing. For the skeptic may then be viewed, and it is an accurate view, as working both sides of the street at once. He questions whether, for very many of the aspects of knowledge, the aspect can ever be satisfied even in the least degree, or satisfied to any significant degree. When he does this, the skeptic is trying to lower, perhaps as much as is (logically) possible, what we will accept as the true profile of the facts. At the same time, working from the other side, he may say that, even if such an aspect may be satisfied to a very low degree, the degree of satisfaction required for knowledge is considerably greater than that, and so the person, whoever he is, will fail to know anyway. He is then trying to raise what is, and what we will accept as, the profile of the context. It need not be important which of these complementary sorts of moves he chooses to make first, and which second, because he can repeat either sort of move any number of times. Sometimes the one sort of move, say, the urging of higher standards, will serve to create dialectical contexts where the other sort will be more effectively pursued than otherwise; sometimes the reverse will be true; most favorably of all for the skeptic, sometimes each sort of move will set the stage well for the other.

Third, the interrelatedness that we have seen in connection with the first perspective can also be seen from the second, or "fact-lowering," perspective. As the skeptic seeks to make our situation with regard to any interdependent aspect seem woefully inadequate, for failure to be satisfied to even a slight degree, he even quite directly threatens to make our situation with respect to many other interdependent aspects seem quite low, too, those whose representing triangles overlap with the triangle on the cone that represents the aspect he may first question: With only a few steps added, we feel, the sort of argument that might work well against the idea that our belief in our arms and legs is ever justified will work well too against the idea that such a belief of ours might be obtained and maintained in a manner that really may be relied upon, and against the idea that such a belief, if it is correct, is not just coincidentally correct. Further, such other interdependent aspects as are not forcefully challenged in a direct manner by some such argument, even as the reasoning may be somewhat amended, may well be indirectly challenged. As our situation with respect to those aspects that are rather directly undermined by the argument falls, it brings with it a lowering of our situation as regards related aspects, which in turn bring still further lowerings, until in the end our situation with regard to every last one of the interdependent aspects of knowledge seems threatened.

Fourth, a skeptic may work back and forth between these two perspectives in a way going far beyond anything contemplated under our second heading just above. For example, he may start by trying to raise the profile of the context, by concentrating on one or another of the interdependent aspects of knowledge. He may, for example, have us tentatively conclude that it is never possible for any of us, for any human or finite being, to know anything about the "external world." Having obtained something of a victory there, perhaps a rather inconclusive one, he may then offer some such principle as this, which I have elsewhere argued for at length, in what is already a quite rarefied and severe context: In order for someone to be in the least bit justified in believing anything, it must be at least *possible for* the person to know the thing to be so.[14] And as I have also argued at some length, there are other at least plausible principles expressing apparent logical requirements of knowing (that *certain* things are so) for having any reasonable or justified belief (that certain *other* things are so).[15] The skeptic may exploit these kindred principles, too, in a rather similar manner and with considerable persuasive force. We may then get the feeling that we very well might not ever be even the least bit reasonable in believing anything about, to follow this example out, the external world. This may get us yet more forlorn as regards our ever so much as knowing any such thing. Even as a skeptic may work back and forth with regard to any single (especially interdependent) aspect of knowledge, so he may sometimes more effectively work back and forth among (eventually) all of the indefinitely many interdependent aspects. Thus the skeptic about knowledge may well appear, as he often does appear, to have a fertile field in which to sow the seeds of his intriguing position.

We should now notice a very general point about skeptical argumentation in epistemology, one that is strongly suggested by the plausible principles indicated in the paragraph just above. We cannot best understand the force of skeptical reasoning for more radical conclusions, say, for the idea that we are never even the least bit reasonable in believing things, except insofar as we relate this to skeptical argumentation for less radical conclusions, for the idea that we never know things (with absolute certainty). For the concepts involved in the arguments, both in the conclusions themselves and earlier on, are logically related

---

14. In my book, *Ignorance*, I present, illustrate, argue for, and employ such a principle at pp. 231–42.

15. In *Ignorance* I similarly treat this other principle at pp. 199–214.

concepts. Many quite different, interesting and true things may be said about justification, to revert to that particularly conspicuous example. But central among all of these things is this: No understanding of justification will be anywhere near complete unless it includes some good idea about how justification is logically related to knowledge. Our cone model of knowledge, then, may contribute substantially to our understanding of justification, perhaps contributing nearly as much as with our understanding of knowledge itself.

Following the suggestions of Dauer and Richardson, we have considered two different, though complementary, perspectives on the skeptical challenge to our claims to knowledge. Whichever perspective it may emphasize, any adequate attempt to characterize skeptical argumentation must take account of the great interrelatedness among the many interdependent facets of knowledge. To be adequate, it must show how there are so many different starting points for the skeptic each of which is at least somewhat plausible. It must also show how the skeptic's argumentation is appropriately all-encompassing; no matter where he plausibly starts, eventually he may bring all of these facets into the discussion, and he may do so in a way in which they are apparently all on his side. Our cone model of knowledge allows us to provide such a characterization, as we may thus identify each of these facets with what we have been calling an *aspect* of knowledge.

## 4. Routes Away from Skepticism

Many can be impressed with the skeptic's challenges briefly, but few will agree with such tempting suggestions and severely negative assessments for long. One of the main reasons for this is obvious. We are only rarely interested in exploring the logical landscape of knowledge claims; we are much more often and urgently interested in assessing a subject's cognitive position relative to the lenient standards for such judgement needed for adaptive discriminations among the positions of various subjects. These more urgent everyday needs help create contexts, often and inevitably, in which the profiles of context are obligingly low. The profile of the facts, as we see the facts, will often be everywhere above the accepted profile of the context. So, in the inevitable return to the course of everyday life, we will abandon any temporary advocacy of skepticism about knowledge, and will often affirm that particular people know many particular things to be so. We remain friendly to skepticism, insofar as we do, only in our most theoretical philosophical contexts and, even for the most rarefied and least robust of us, these contexts or moods form small parts of our lives.

As regards our getting away from skepticism, and staying away for most of the time, in general outline that is most of the story. But for many philosophers it is, or will seem to be, an uninteresting part of the story. The reason is this. Most philosophers, even when they are involved in philosophical inquiry or discussion, are prone to judge that people know all sorts of things, and that the skeptic's inviting challenges are somehow misplaced and beside the point. When they were first introduced to the philosophy of knowledge, many of them found skepticism somewhat attractive. But now they are very far removed from those early days, and are well beyond feeling much temptation on that score. Why is this so?

A large part of the reason, no doubt, is that the current philosophic fashion is for philosophers to endorse as being true almost all of the sorts of statements regarded as true by common sense, that is, regarded as true by almost all of us so much of the time in everyday life. As I have argued elsewhere, this fashion has a powerful psychological basis in each of us to take root in and to exploit.[16] About the great majority of positive statements that we make, we are very strongly disposed to think that those statements are true. We will almost always think such a thing, almost no matter what we may then (at least seem to) have to think is the meaning, or the semantics, of the terms of the statements made and assessed. For example, we will believe to be true the great majority of statements we have made to the effect that there were *cats* in encountered situations, almost no matter what we may then seem driven to think is the semantics for 'cat'.[17] The current fashion in philosophy, then, is one that would have us happily go along with what is already a very powerful psychological force in each of us. Moreover, as the last fifty or sixty years have all too amply shown, this fashion is itself a terribly powerful social force; the internalization of the fashion having a strong additional psychological influence on the many philosophers under its sway. Indeed, the overwhelming majority

---

16. See my papers, "Toward a Psychology of Common Sense," *American Philosophical Quarterly* 19 (1982) and "The Causal Theory of Reference," *Philosophical Studies* 43 (1983). Also see chapters 4 and 5 of my *Philosophical Relativity*.

17. I am here alluding to Hilary Putnam's famous cat-robot example, first presented in his paper, "It Ain't Necessarily So," *The Journal of Philosophy* LIX (1962). In the works cited in the note just preceding, I argue that the best treatment of this example is one that makes little use of our semantic understanding but much use of our semantically mute common sense beliefs about the world.

of philosophers are no more inclined to go against the prevailing social forces of their culture circle than are most people in what might seem to be less intellectually adventurous and questioning walks of life, such as chemistry or haberdashery. This is true, I am sure, but perhaps it is not very illuminating. For we must ask, how did such a fashion take hold? And, even then, whence comes its great staying power? To the second question, the strong psychological disposition to regard our positive statements as true, no matter what their terms may then seem to mean, provides a good part of the answer. But it does not do much to answer the first question. So how did this fashion get going?

There is no simple answer to this question. But a good part of the answer can be gleaned, at least in general outline, by attention to the figure of G.E. Moore.[18] Before Moore, many philosophers, notably Bertrand Russell, found it easy to accept as theoretically sound the skeptical idea that we really didn't know, say, anything about the external world, anything about the character of things beyond the contents of one's own mind.[19] Thinkers such as Russell would consider our cognitive position with respect to a statement like *there is a table before me* and then would compare this unfavorably to our cognitive position with respect to a statement like *it now seems to me that there is a table before me*. Because of this unfavorable comparison, while the latter statement might possibly be known by us to be true, the former was at best the object of mere probable belief and was not something that we knew.

In contrast, our cognitive position with respect to, say, *there is pain that I now feel* would not compare so unfavorably with our position with respect to *it now seems to me that there is pain that I now feel*. So, while no one would know there was a table before him, perhaps someone might know that he was feeling pain. I do not mean this to be a very accurate rendition of Russell's views about knowledge claims as they were at that time, but only to convey something of their spirit. It was against this spirit, and not any mere details, that Moore made his influential stand.

---

18. In Moore's *Philosophical Papers* (New York, 1962), see "A Defense of Common Sense," "Proof of an External World," "Certainty," and especially "Four Forms of Scepticism."

19. In the American edition of Moore's book, cited in the note just above, he specifically focuses on Russell at pages 196-97, where he says: "All four of the sceptical views with which I shall be concerned have, I believe, been held in the past, and still are held, by a good many philosophers. But I am going to illustrate them exclusively by reference to two books of Russell's—his *Analysis of Matter* and the book which in the English edition was called *Outline of Philosophy*, and in the American edition *Philosophy*."

In philosophical discussion, Moore would say things like *I know that here is a hand* and things near enough to *I know with absolute certainty that there is a table before me*. Sooner or later, if not right away, these staunch knowledge claims were accepted as true by most of his audience, a group consisting mainly of seasoned professional philosophers. These people were prone, as prone as almost anyone, to accept as legitimate, at least in such discussions, the idea that the predominat interest should be into the conditions under which we could know. They were sincerely concerned with the question of when we could truly have knowledge of the world, and truly have well placed absolute certainty. Even so, they were much impressed with the apparent truth of what Moore claimed. Why was that so?

My conjecture is this: When someone makes a statement and no pressing context is very firmly established, his audience, who may be himself, implicitly conjures up an average, or typical, context for that statement, or for statements of that sort. If the statement implies the relevance of certain standards, as knowledge claims do, then we implicitly accept as enough for the statement to be true that a presumed typical contextual profile be exceeded or equaled everywhere, not a very demanding condition. Typically, when Moore made his claims the facts of the context were highly favorable: his hand was not numb or paralyzed; he could see his hand clearly in good light, and so on. The profile of the facts was, then, able easily to exceed the implicitly accepted typical context for the claim to knowledge, even for the claim to knowledge with absolute certainty.

For somewhat similar reasons, skeptical attempts to lower what we may properly take to be the profile of the facts can be made to seem inappropriate and, so, misplaced. In an average context for a statement concerning, say, justified belief, standards for it that are rather low will be found entirely proper, while arguments to the effect that not even low standards can be met will seem irrelevant intrusions. In getting us to think of such situations as generally involve, or generate, contexts that are average or typical ones, a forceful speaker gets us to focus on just such situations where intricate philosophical argumentation of *any* sort is out of place, and where *challenging* and rather *theoretical* philosophical argument is especially out of place. So we are then in no mood to take any such argumentation very seriously, much less are we in a frame of mind where we are at all open to finding it at all acceptable. We then take the profiles of the facts to be exactly what we ordinarily suppose them to be.

As Adler has pointed out in conversation, Moore's strategy here is what we may call *socially contagious*. When we accept low standards with regard to knowing for ourselves, we are disposed to assume as well that those low standards are the proper ones for others. For if we allowed others, such as Russell, to have higher standards than we ourselves find acceptable, we lay ourselves open, at least to a certain degree, to the objection that our standards should be as high as those of such other people. This challenge will make us uncomfortable. To avoid the discomfort, we preemptively suppose that one like Russell himself should, in most contexts, really accept just such more modest standards as we do.

In one fell swoop, then, a philosopher like Moore can get us to think ill both of attempts to raise profiles of context and of attempts to lower what we take to be profiles of the facts. Having noted this point, which I take to be an important one, we will pursue the epistemological dialogue almost entirely in terms of the perspective of attempts at raising, lowering or maintaining the contextual curves. Generally, complementary points concerning any attempts to lower what we may recognize as true profiles of fact can be supplied by the reader for himself.

In contrast, consider someone who claims right off the bat: I know with absolute certainty that *no evil demon is deceiving me about my having a hand by unremittingly inducing in me so much coherent lifelike experience as of there being a hand that I have*. This person is not likely to gain widespread agreement among people prone to a mood that Russell's doubts exemplified. Why is that? There is very little that can contribute to an average or typical context for a knowledge claim such as this. Such things are rarely claimed to be known. When questions of the knowledge of these matters is at issue, the most likely context would be, perhaps, a discussion of Descartes' skeptical passages.

Now the claim that I know that here is a hand is not all that different from the claim that I know that here is an index finger, or even from, I know that here is a blister. Those knowledge claims all go together in the mind fairly closely, so to say. But one's attention is on quite different sorts of matters, as matters appear to one, when thinking of the presence or absence of deceptive evil demons. So claiming knowledge of their absence would be an ineffective way to begin a route away from sympathy with epistemological skepticism.

For reasons such as these, Moore would have been silly to begin his reply to skepticism by claiming to know that demons and the like were not at work. So he did not. Rather he began by claiming to know that here was a hand, and such other less exotic looking things. Once that's done, the audience is in the business of accepting low standards for knowledge. By giving a few such humdrum examples in a row, momentum is quickly built up for according such lenient treatment. Once this is done, then the claim can be made that one knows that no evil demon is deceiving one into falsely believing one has a hand, by the continual induction of unremittingly lifelike experience. When we are already in something of a mood to accept standards for knowledge that are not very high ones anyway, we can get ourselves readily enough to accept them for such an exotic looking case as this as well. Moore's strategy is an effective one.

Indeed, Moore's strategy is more effective than one might think, even at this point in our discussion. That is because his strategy is much more widespread than one will be apt to suppose. We make knowledge claims often; but not so very often. Almost all the time we speak and even think verbally, however, we use straightforward declarative sentences to make statements, to make assertions, such as *there are four chairs in the dining room now*. As *I* discussed at length in *Ignorance*, when we make such assertions, even to ourselves, though we do not say or claim that we know the thing in question, we *represent it as being the case that* we know the thing in question.[20] When I make the statement that there are four chairs in the dining room, for example, I represent myself as knowing, not just as believing, that there are four chairs in the dining room. That is why there is a feeling of contradiction with "There are four chairs there, but I don't know for certain that there are," just as much as there is with the Moorean parallel, "There are four chairs there, but I don't believe that there are." (The contradiction offered is real enough; it is just that the contradiction is offered at the level of representation in general, not the level of explicit statement: In saying the first of those two funny sentences assertively, one thing I do is represent it as being the case that I know there are four chairs there and also [and more explicitly] that I do not know that.)

In getting us to find acceptable such straightforward assertions as *I have a hand*, then, Moore gets us to find acceptable the idea that each of us knows that he has a hand. It is surely hard for one to resist going along with such innocent-appearing straightforward assertions as Moore's *I have a hand*, or *Here is a hand*. But, in that we then accept that Moore is not falsely representing himself, or his situation, this is tantamount to accepting the idea that Moore *knows* that he has a hand and, by extension, that we (his intended audience) know that, too.[21] By the same reasoning, we can readily understand why it would *not* be an effective strategy, but would instead seem to help the skeptic, for a

---

20. This is a main theme of chapter VI of the book.

21. For reason to believe in the noted extension, see David Lewis, *Convention* (Cambridge, Mass., 1969).

philosopher to *begin* by straightforwardly asserting anything like *no evil demon is deceiving me about my having a hand by unremittingly inducing in me so much coherent lifelike experience as of there being a hand that I have.* For in so doing, one begins one's discussion by representing oneself as *knowing* that all of *that* is so. And, at the outset at least, such a representation as that is a lot for one's audience, and even a lot for oneself, to accept with equanimity. So, by proceeding in *just the favorable order* for his case, Moore employs an effective strategy. And, as we have seen in the last couple of paragraphs, he employs a strategy whose application is so exceedingly widespread as to be all that much more effective psychologically.

The resistance to skeptical temptations that this strategy exploits is a multi-faceted resistance. Our cone model of knowledge helps us to understand its multi-faceted character: On the whole, just as getting us to demand high standards for any one interdependent aspect of knowledge will get us in the mood for demanding high standards for any other one, so getting us to accept *low* standards for any one such aspect will get us in a *lenient* mood for the *other* aspects. When we are consciously convinced that we know we have hands, and are focused on what we thus take ourselves to know, we are apt to be quite accepting with regard to any of the aspects of knowledge. It may be pointed out to us that some well endowed people have been fooled by holograms in situations relevantly like ours, and so did not know that there were cups before them. But the context of those people was unusual. And the context of calling them to our attention is also unusual. With more typical contexts in mind, we tend to think, quite confidently, that we know there are cups before us: the cups are rather ordinary ones plainly in our view. We are under the influence of more typical contexts, an influence that can quickly gather much momentum. When under this influence, we do not demand that the way of one's coming to have, or of one's maintaining, correct belief be all that reliable, any more than we demand that one be able to rule out so very strongly all that great a range of logically incompatible propositions.

The cone model of knowledge, along with independently plausible suppositions, can help us account for the dialectical fertility of the concept of knowledge. It helps us understand the many related ways that a skeptic can make his position seem attractive, and understand something about how these ways are related to each other. Equally, it can help us understand how the defender of common sense epistemology can make the skeptic's position seem unattractive, and even seem plainly false. It helps us understand how this robust defender can, in one fell swoop, make all of the skeptic's apparent openings seem always to have been illusions as to points of vulnerability.

Actually, the dialectical situation is somewhat more complex than I have so far made out. That is mainly because we are all psychologically quite complex, and the more complex and insightful philosophical personalities among us can be bothered by previously untroubling complexities. So we also must notice Wittgenstein's contribution to the dialectic between the skeptic about knowledge and the defender of common sense.[22] For Wittgenstein, someone who, in any very mundane situation, says something such as "I know I have hands," will then fail to express anything true, or false, at all. Rather, in any such context, any idea to the effect that I have hands is part of the epistemological background for me. It is against such a background that I might both ordinarily and truly say, "I know that I hurt my left hand last night, for it was all right yesterday but hurt so much when I awakened this morning." While I will not argue the point here, like most philosophers, and almost anyone else who might (be brought to) bother to think about such a position, I find Wittgenstein's idea absurd, though intriguingly absurd. Why should anyone think anything like this, that I might be "too well and firmly placed" with respect to the matter of having hands for it to be true for me to say that I know that I have them?

Adler has proposed what I take to be most of the correct explanation. While there is much power in Moore's strategy, there is also a certain weakness or vulnerability. Moore brings to our attention knowledge claims that, except for people in certain very special situations or with certain very special interests, nobody would ever think of explicitly making, let alone questioning, but would instead simply take for granted. The making of such uncommon, and quite certainly true knowledge claims, as, e.g., "I know I have hands" may be effective where one's audience consists mainly of philosophers who were somewhat disposed to be convinced by such skeptically oriented thinkers as Russell. But for almost anyone else, including almost any later and rather differently inclined philosophers, the making of such a statement might as easily backfire as have the desired reassuring effect.

Outside of a vigorously contested dialogue with a skeptic in a climate where both sides had a significant appeal to third parties, why

---

22. The most directly relevant work is Ludwig Wittgenstein's *On Certainty* (New York, 1972). The body of the book begins: "1. If you do know that *here is one hand*,[1] we'll grant you all the rest."

The footnote cites Moore's "Proof of an External World" and "A Defense of Common Sense."

should anyone bother to mention that he knew he had hands?[23] Maybe he has a sneaking suspicion that he just may be wrong, and doesn't really know? In more recent philosophical discourse, then, the making of such a knowledge claim is too apt, even if not very apt, to upset the apple cart, to cause some to worry where, as Wittgenstein would believe, no cause for worry is present at all. To help us philosophers out of our tendency to worry needlessly about these matters, one may declare the serious uttering of such sentences as "I know I have hands" almost always to be out of place, almost always to fail to express any genuine truth *or any genuine falsehood*.

Wittgenstein's reaction is an overreaction. But it is a reaction to a situation whose complexity might otherwise be underestimated. Contexts can almost always be made to shift and change in all sorts of ways, *including in ways that would tend at least somewhat to favor a skeptic's remarks*. Anytime that this is done, the skeptic can then launch a multi-faceted attack on the idea that we know things to be so, and can do so in a manner that, at least for a brief while, does not seem all that wild or inappropriate. There is no way to prevent contexts favorable to the skeptic from *ever* arising; Wittgenstein was wrong in thinking that we already had a way and that it was always at work for us. However briefly they may dominate our thought and talk, such contexts can, and will, be generated again and again. When they are generated, the skeptic will be better placed to issue a challenge, and our cone model shows how it will be, eventually, a multi-faceted challenge. When these contexts are dispelled, and they will as soon as we return to the business of almost all of everyday life, then the skeptical challenge will seem easy to counter, in ever so many ways and in one fell swoop. Our cone model of knowledge also helps to describe how these many routes away from skepticism may all at once be taken, how they are related to each other in such a way that this may be so.

---

23. Of course, special situations *sometimes* do arise. In a lengthy discussion of Moore in his book, *The Significance of Philosophical Scepticism* (Oxford, 1984), Barry Stroud cites an example of Thompson Clarke's involving a physiologist who is lecturing on certain mental abnormalities. Following Stroud, I "quote Clarke's physiologist," who, near the beginning of his lecture says: "Each of us who is normal knows that he is now awake, not dreaming or hallucinating, that there is a real public world outside his mind which he is now perceiving,... In contrast, individuals suffering from certain mental abnormalities each believes that what we know to be the real world is his imaginative creation." These words are from Clarke's, "The Legacy of Skepticism," *The Journal of Philosophy* LXIX (1972).

But these situations arise so *rarely* as to have negligible effect on what we deem an ordinary or average context for consideration of our knowledge claims. The main line of our discussion, then, remains unaffected by such special situations.

## 5. Objective and Subjective, External and Internal

Our model of knowledge, though offered as suggestive, incomplete and even rudimentary, is already a somewhat complicated affair. Now such complexity as it has is, I believe, not idle, but helps to explain the judgments we make about who knows what, as well as the tensions that can be brought to bear upon these judgments. Even so it might be that, as presented so far, our model is nowhere near complicated enough to capture everything involved in the truth of, or in the correct making of, claims to knowledge and related epistemological statements. In certain moods, at least, I feel there is a very substantial incompleteness in our model, a feeling that, no doubt, others will have as well. What might be a constructive lesson to be learned from these feelings that we have?

Now, as I said early on, it is doubtful whether any modification of this cone model will enable it to capture absolutely everything that is involved in the truth of knowledge ascriptions, let alone in the truth of related epistemological ascriptions, such as a statement to the effect that a certain person has a justified belief in a certain thing. Nonetheless, it may be that there is something that we can do, and perhaps that we also must do, to get our model to come reasonably close to such an elevated goal. That may require us roughly to double the complexity of our model, a significant cost, but perhaps a price well worth paying.

The general idea here is that we may recognize a subjective as well as an objective side to knowledge, and we may do this by way of recognizing a subjective as well as an objective side to, if not absolutely all, at least each of very many aspects of knowledge. The objective sides may be considered as external and, in a quite literal way, may be represented externally in our cone model; the subjective sides may be represented internally. Both by way of quite general considerations and also by way of more particular and detailed ones, this would seem a strategy worth exploiting. We may begin by looking at the most general sorts of considerations.

In many areas of philosophy, it is at least fruitful, and perhaps even necessary, to distinguish between a subjective aspect of the phenomena under study as well as the perhaps more familiar objective aspect. In ethics, it has long been a common practice to distinguish between what is objectively the right thing for an agent to do in a situation and what is subjectively the right thing for him then to do. Often this amounts to little more than distinguishing between what are all of the objective facts of that situation, on the one hand, and what the agent knows, or justifiably believes, to be such facts, on the other, subjective rightness then being a relativization to that latter, more skimpy cognitive basis for the subject's action. But such a distinction may sometimes involve more than what is involved in such a relativization to relevant epistemological background.[24]

In the philosophy of mind in general, and in particular in the central topic of personal identity, it has also become common to make such a distinction. In these matters, this is often put by distinguishing between the first-person and the third-person points of view. Then the first-person viewpoint is said to relate to the subjective side of these matters, to how things seem from the inside, and the third-person viewpoint is said to relate to the objective side, perhaps to how things may appear to a suitably placed objective observer. It is unclear exactly what the ultimate value of making such distinctions will be in this area, but a reasonable assumption is that there will be some such value even if it may not be nearly as great as it sometimes seems to be.

In epistemology, too, some such distinctions have a role. There has long been a recognition of the distinction between the objective aspects of probability, on the one hand, and the subjective probabilities for a particular agent, on the other, who is typically in a situation of uncertainty and incomplete information. More recently, there has been something of a controversy between epistemologists who espouse an externalist view of knowledge, or of epistemological justification, and those who espouse an internalist viewpoint.[25] Perhaps much of this controversy is misplaced, each side focusing on different features of justification and of knowledge. Typically internalists may be focusing more on subjective features while externalists may be focusing more on objective ones. It is an appealing idea that justification, and even knowledge, might have such differing but complementary features, perhaps somewhat in the way that probability does. It might then be that much of the complexity in issues of knowledge and of justification is owing to their having both subjective features as well as objective ones. In regard to the issue of knowledge, in particular, we might do well to suppose that there is a complex objective side to the matter as well as a complex subjective side.

We will try to incorporate into our model the appealing idea that, as well as an objective or external side to knowledge, there is also

---

24. See Thomas Nagel's "Subjective and Objective," in his *Mortal Questions* (Cambridge, 1979) and, for a much more extensive treatment, his new book, *The View from Nowhere* (New York, 1986).

25. Some examples are Alvin Goldman's "The Internalist Conception of Justification," *Midwest Studies in Philosophy* V (1980), Lawrence Bonjour's "Externalist Theories of Empirical Knowledge," the same volume, and Robert Nozick's *Philosophical Explanations*, especially at pp. 280–83.

a subjective or internal side. The leading idea in effecting this incorporation is that there may be, as well, two such sides to very many, perhaps even to all, of the aspects of knowledge. Looking at the general matter in one way, it may be useful to say that it is because so many of its aspects have these two sides that knowledge itself has these two sides. But, then, at the same time we should also say that those things that are aspects of knowledge, especially those that are interdependent aspects, can be well understood only by understanding them all in relation to each other: Reliability of way, justification of "attitude," nonaccidentality of being right, and so on—each can be well understood only by understanding it as an interdependent aspect of something central of which each of the others are also interdependent aspects. That central something may be nothing but knowledge itself.

We may think of the subjective side of each of these aspects as the *internal* side of the aspect, and we may think of the more familiar objective side as the *external* side of that aspect of knowledge. Because a cone has an internal side to its surface as well as an external side, as does any standard geometric solid, the very terminology now chosen will help us to see how we may appropriately complicate our model of knowledge.

Consider the aspect that it not be (to such-and-such a degree) accidental that the person is right. The description of the aspect may be interpreted naturally in either of two ways. One interpretation characterizes the subjective, internal side. This aspect has to do with things like the following. The subject has available, or highly accessible, a batch of evidence, or data, or appearances or whatever, that psychologically suggest, and perhaps rationally support, his belief that, say, there is a cup before him with a blue handle. The situation is an ordinary one, and for him a very familiar one; the support from the appearances is close to overwhelming. And he is right; no surprises here. Is it accidental that he is right, subjectively speaking? Since by hypothesis the situation is a quite ordinary one, by any ordinary standard it is not. But his data do not entail such a cup's presence. Moreover, we may suppose that there are in fact hologram experts that can produce most of that same data, enough to deceive, and have done so to some others that are relevantly like him, similarly endowed with similar data. Now our subject has no data, one way or the other, about whether one of these experts is now, or has recently been in his neighborhood, though he has much data as to their existence and numerous successes under widespread conditions. In short, he is much like we are in fact. In most contexts and for most purposes, we would judge that his data was adequate; given his data, it was not accidental that he was right. In some contexts, we may demand high standards. Then we will say that (given his data) it was at least a bit of an accident that he was right; he did not have, but he needed to have, data as to the whereabouts of hologram experts. Also, in most contexts, we would say he knew there was such a cup there, and in a few contexts, we would say he did not. This is suggestive for our model of knowledge.

What may we say about the objective, or external, side of this aspect? A consideration of two quite different "world scenarios" will be useful to us now. First, suppose that some very strong form of determinism is true of the world; perhaps the world is quite nearly the way that Leibniz would have it. Then objectively speaking, even by very high standards, it is not at all accidental that the man is right about the cup. There was no real chance, we might well say, that anything but that cup would be there, none that he might fail to believe that it was there with its blue handle, none that any hologram expert would decide to work his wiles in that place at that time, none that our perceiver would not have been born, none that there would not have been plenty of cups made with blue handles, no real chance that he would not have bought some such cups, and so on. Everything tightly fits into place, including his being right about the cup. In contexts where we emphasize the external side of the aspect of non-accidental lightness, we may, even when we employ very high standards, insist that it is not at all accidental that this man is right about that cup's then being there. Also, we might notice, in almost any of those contexts where we most strongly emphasize such external considerations as these, we would be happy enough with the idea that his man knows about the cup.

Now suppose a very different sort of world is the one where we all live. All sorts of genuinely random things are going on almost all the time. At times cups cease to exist for no reason or cause. People hallucinate the appearances of cups quite spontaneously, even if rather infrequently. Hologram experts, and others, show up at the oddest places, despite often having made firm plans to the contrary. Occasionally, there will quite spontaneously occur, say, the complex event of a cup's going out of existence and someone's hallucinating just such a cup in just the same place. As with most folks most of the time, this is not happening with our subject who properly sees his cup right there. But emphasizing the objective side of the matter, and employing only moderately high standards for such judgments, we will say that it is at least somewhat accidental that this person is right about whether there is before him a cup with a blue handle. And in contexts where we are much concerned with this side of this aspect of knowledge, and where our standards for non-accidentality are at least moderately high, we will not be so happy with the idea that the man knows. Having discussed these two contrasting world scenarios, we may be content that we have a fairly good idea about the objective side of the aspect of non-accidentality.

What is, at least as a matter of fact, the relation between the subjective and the objective side of this aspect of knowledge? Unless we are much deceived about the character of our actual world and about our experiential relationship to it, which I do not for a minute believe, for almost any given subject or agent, the internal side of non-accidentality and the external side will run pretty closely together the great majority of the time. So there is rarely any need for us to notice, let alone to press, the distinction between the two sides. So it may also be with various other aspects of knowledge. And with each of these aspects, such a distinction may be, not only valid, but worth pressing on occasion. We do seem naturally to think in this way.

A very natural candidate for such a dual treatment is the interdependent aspect that the knower be *justified* in believing, or in having whatever positive attitude he does have, to the effect that the thing is so. The objective side of this aspect of justification may well have strong logical relations with the objective side of the aspect that the knower have arrived at his attitude, or maintained it, in a way that is reliable. Perhaps the subjective side of the justification aspect has a similarly strong relation to the subjective side of the reliability aspect; or perhaps on the subjective side the relation between the two is weaker. This is a question that would seem worth investigation, but I don't want now to become involved in such apparently more specific matters, however interesting and important they may prove to be. My aim now is to suggest a way of capturing whatever dual relationships there may be in terms of our cone model of knowledge.

Any cone may be properly regarded as having an outside (of its) surface and an inside (of its) surface. Let's represent the external, objective aspects of knowledge by triangles on the outside surface of our model cone, and the internal, subjective aspects will be represented by triangles on the inside. There may be a strong overlap, rather than an exact coincidence or congruence, between the inside and outside triangles of any given interdependent aspect of knowledge, or of almost any. But the inside triangles will have their vertices at the very same apex as do the outside triangles. At the (upper) limit of any such aspect, its subjective side and its objective side are as one.

Not having access to the apex, owing to our quite limited mental capacities if to nothing else, we cannot get full intuitive support for these last remarks. But we can do pretty well towards being at the apex when we consider our relation to *something exists*. By very high standards, in virtually any context, and *subjectively* speaking, it seems not at all accidental that you are right in thinking, or being certain, that something exists. By very high standards, in virtually any context, and *objectively* speaking, it seems not at all accidental that you are right in thinking *that* to be so. The two sides of non-accidentality appear to be, or to be on the verge of, melding perfectly and completely together.

Now I do not mean to suggest that every aspect of knowledge has a subjective as well as an objective side. For certain aspects this distinction may simply not apply. That may well be the case with the independent aspect of personal, or psychological, certainty. Should an aspect require no such dual treatment, it is pointless to insist that the aspect is really only objective, or is really only subjective, or that it is really neither because the distinction does not apply. But for any such aspect we must have some convention of representation anyway. Let us simply say that any such aspect will be represented by a triangle on the outside surface of the cone. As needed, we may help ourselves to other conventions of representation.

How are we to represent the duality of profiles of context, and of profiles of fact? In any given context, there will be generated a group of points both for the center lines of outside triangles and for the center lines of inside triangles, according to the dominant interests of the people of the context. The internal, interior points will represent, with respect to each aspect of knowledge, how much is required of the would be knower in way of that aspect's subjective or internal side. These representational points may be joined so that an internal curve is formed.

Just as a context generates an internal curve, so it generates an external curve on the cone. It does this of course, by generating a group of points, to be connected, each representing how much the context requires by way of the external side of each of the aspects of knowledge. In earlier sections, we have been thinking of this external curve as the entire profile of the context, an idea that we now regard as a heuristically useful oversimplification.

By convention, we may have the internal curve go through the cone at its lowest point, and then join up with the closest point to its exit of the external curve, on the outside (of the cone's) surface. Accordingly, we may understand there now to be a single long curve that goes around both the outside surface and also the inside surface of the cone: This long curve is, or represents, the full profile of the context. It is really this longer curve, and not the more limited curve we have been discussing in previous sections, that is the profile of the context.

As there are facts about the extent to which a given subject, in any given context or situation, satisfies the objective, external side of each of the aspects of knowledge, so there may be facts about the extent to which he satisfies the subjective, internal side of each of the aspects. In geometric terms, even if not in philosophical ones, previously we have been considering unambiguously only the external side. But now we may assign points as well to the center lines of the triangles on the inside of our cone, to represent the extent to which a subject, in a context, in fact satisfies each of the subjective, internal sides. We may connect these points as well to form a curve, and have the curve run through the cone, at some suitable conventionally determined point, so that it joins with the curve of the facts on the cone's outside. This total curve, going around both the outside and the inside of the cone, is the full profile of the facts for our subject in our context.

The procedures for appropriate evaluation are just as before, only now there are these greater curves to consider and compare. For us appropriately to say or think of a given subject, in a given context, that he knows a certain thing to be so, the profile of the facts for him there must everywhere be above the profile of the context, both on the inside as well as on the outside of the cone. In a sense, there is now twice as much for a would be knower to satisfy in order that an ascription of knowledge to him in a context be a correct one. This may make it seem that, when we consider both the internal and the external sides of knowledge, it is rather more difficult for people to know things than we may first have thought, at least rather more difficult for us correctly to ascribe knowledge to them. But, in parallel with a reply made earlier in connection with smaller curves, this need not be so. In many contexts, we may so strongly emphasize the external side, and even the external side of just one or a few aspects, that the internal part of the profile of context is everywhere *comparatively* low down on the cone, everywhere easily below the internal part of the curve of the facts. And, in many other contexts, exactly the opposite may be going on, making the other part, the external half of things, rather easy for a subject to satisfy. Thus it may be very rarely that both sides are focused on at once, rarely that there is a context with a profile having points high up on the cone both inside and outside, rarely a context that makes it as difficult for a subject to know things as we might first think is required by this duality of external and internal.

With our cone model complicated and enriched in this fashion, we may be able to give a better treatment to our judgments about the presence and absence of knowledge over a wider range of examples and of contexts of judgment. That would be of considerable interest to investigate, though I will not pursue the matter here, as any even moderately good treatment looks to be a very extensive and detailed one.

A matter of even greater interest, I imagine, would be how this enriched conical model might help us better to understand the perennial impulse toward advancing skepticism about knowledge, and toward the rejection or abandonment of these skeptical advances. Here, too, any decent treatment would be a quite extensive and detailed one; so I will forgo any such effort now. But a small suggestion might be of some use, even if left undeveloped: With two sides to each aspect, a skeptic has twice the places with which to advance his position, whether by urging that contextual curves be raised or whether in the undermining fashion concerning accepted profiles of fact. This may not make things any easier for the skeptic, as all of his advances might still just as effectively be beaten back at one fell swoop, whether by contextual argumentation to the contrary or whether only by time and the press of the many contexts of everyday life. But it will imply that the dialectic is a more complex one than we have previously recognized, conducted along both subjective and objective lines, sometimes along a complex, and perhaps even an unclear, combination of the two. This implication would, I think, be all to the good, reflecting well on this enriched and more complicated version of our cone model. For as history shows, the dialectic between skeptics about knowledge and their less adventurous opponents is about as complex as can be, and may be often infused with what appear to be deep unclarities and ambiguities.

## 6. The Cone Model and Philosophical Relativity

The most plausible way to take this cone model, whether in a simple version or whether in a more complex and, I think, enriched form, is as an outline for a contextual semantics for the ordinary terms of knowledge. We would then be adopting what I have called the semantic position of *contextualism*, and would be understanding our cone model as presenting the general outline of the interrelated contextual features that characterize the semantics of the terms of knowledge.[26] On this semantic view, these terms will have quite easily satisfiable semantic conditions. As the world is not a terribly uncooperative place, we would then very often know what we claim ourselves to know. Briefly and in passing, we said this much in section 2.

---

26. I discuss contextualism throughout most of my *Philosophical Relativity*. My discussion of this view in relation to epistemic terms is mainly at pp. 46–54.

At that point in our study we also said some related things. We said that if we insisted on taking our cone model in this most plausible way, we might well miss out on some quite interesting philosophical alternatives. One such alternative may be the view that the semantics of the terms of knowledge is, unlike our adaptive thought about knowledge, quite simple and highly demanding: For a statement of the form "S knows that p" to be true, the creature or being, S, must be in the ideal case of knowing; he must be at the point represented by the very apex of our cone. This is the semantic view of *invariantism*. This view, insofar as it might be correct, will be greatly helpful to skepticism about knowledge. Can it be part of a tenable, or at least remotely plausible, view of what goes on in our adaptive thinking about knowledge? Perhaps it can.

In my recent book, *Philosophical Relativity*, I offer sustained argumentation for the position that invariantism is at least a tenable semantic position. Very briefly, the general idea behind that argument is this: The invariantist requires only a quite simple semantics to be assigned to us, and a simple psychology of semantic understanding. He pays his price in assigning to us, as he then must, a very complex pragmatics, a complex psychology of, roughly, associated unconscious inference. The contextualist pays the same total price of complexity, just distributed differently: the contextualist pragmatics is quite sparse in comparison, but the semantics is correlatively complex. But either particular distribution lacks any objective factors on which to be the better based, and is only one acceptable option for theoretical description. Each theory's total view of our behavior is just as simple as the other's, and so has just as much truth to it, neither more nor less. So it is, too, with the semantic component of each of the two explanatory views. This crude statement is enough, I hope, to make invariantism seem modestly plausible. What is in the book, I think it fair to say, is enough to make it seem rather more plausible than that. What might an advocate of this at least somewhat plausible view say about the relation of our cone model of knowledge to the statements we make, and that we accept, about who knows what?

For an invariantist, what will be represented by a group of points on our cone (at least many of which) are below the apex? He may allow, just as anyone else may allow, that some of these groups will be profiles of contexts and that others will be correlative profiles of what are accepted as facts in those contexts. The profile of a context will then represent what the people of that context allow as *acceptable departures from the ideal case*. When the profile of the accepted facts is wholly above this contextual profile, the departures from genuine knowing are to be disregarded. In our example about John and Sam's broken car, the departures in which John is involved might properly be taken as irrelevant: Relative to the interests in the context, and the standards for departure thus imposed by the context, there is no difference between John's being in the ideal case and his being as he is. Though it is thus adaptive, and proper, for us to *treat* John's case as a case of knowing, it is *not true* that John knows that Sam's car broke down.

In my book I advocated the hypothesis, though not so much as the belief, that there is no fact of the matter as to which semantics is the correct semantics of 'know' and of other expressions, most having little to do with epistemological discourse. This is the *hypothesis of semantic relativity*. Applied to philosophically interesting expressions, like 'know', 'certain', 'free', 'power', 'cause', and 'explain', this semantic hypothesis generates, at what may be called the "object level," the *hypothesis of philosophical relativity*. We might say that, as directly applied only to those interesting terms that are most heavily epistemological, like 'know' and 'certain', and as indirectly applied to such terms as may logically connect with them—prime examples might be 'reasonable' and 'justified'—the semantic hypothesis generates the less ambitious, but still philosophically interesting, *hypothesis of epistemic relativity*.

While I do not so much as actually believe it, the idea that this should be the semantic and philosophical situation is not a wildly crazy one. It is an idea worth exploring with some seriousness. By now putting forward my model of knowledge as neutral with regard to semantic questions and approaches, I allow for, and perhaps even encourage, such open-minded exploration.

The hypothesis of philosophical relativity has it that, as regards those philosophical problems that are best expressed in terms to which semantic relativity applies, there is no objectively correct position, either one way or the other. Thus, on this hypothesis, there may be no objectively correct answer to the question of whether free action or free will is logically compatible with a strong form of metaphysical determinism. As well, there may be no objectively correct answer as to whether the skeptic about knowledge, or whether the defender of common sense knowledge claims, holds the true, or even the truer, position. By way of implication from this, there may be no fact of the matter, either, as to whether we are justified, or reasonable, in believing what we do, or whether skepticism upon this matter is in the right. The relativity hypothesis, if correct, may provide at least a partial explanation of why philosophical discussion in such areas goes on and on, without progress being made toward a solution that serious thinkers can agree upon for more than a relatively brief period. That is, or would be, a great advantage of these hypotheses. Still and all, I do not so much as believe the hypotheses to be true, or to be as (nearly) true as anything else in the area; rather I just seriously entertain the idea that they might be true, or as nearly true as any (apparently) competing statements.

Why do I not so much believe the hypotheses of semantic relativity, philosophical relativity and, now, epistemic relativity, but only take them to be worth serious exploration? It is for the same reason that contextualism is the most plausible semantics in the field, and provides the most plausible way for us to interpret our cone model. What reason is that? It is really just this: in allowing so much more of what we actually say and consciously think to be *true*, rather than false or indeterminate, contextualism *accords more fully with more of common sense belief* than does invariantism and, thus, more than do any of the relativity hypotheses. This much is quite obvious and is acknowledged at the outset by all interested parties. The question of interest that remains is this: Is there any significantly *independent* reason to suppose that contextualism, and with it common sense philosophical positions in the relevant areas, is the objectively correct position? Without some such independent reason produced in some detail, we might do well, at some late date, to conclude that the relativity hypotheses represent one of the few areas, perhaps, where common sense proves misleading.

Now it is easy to think that one has some such independent reason available, such as some "principle of charity" or "maxim of truth-saying." But it is very, very hard to find some objective basis for just such a principle or maxim as will extend fully into the area that the hypothesis of semantic relativity concerns. Even if there are *some* objectively true principles or maxims that objectively place *some* constraints on acceptable total theories of our behavior, it is very, very hard to see why more limited principles of this general sort will fail to be better than, or at least as good as, such a strong principle as would resolve what is, after all, the rather modest indeterminacy required by our hypothesis of semantic relativity. When one realizes how hard it is to supply a strong and significantly independent reason for rejecting the relativity hypotheses, one takes them all that much more seriously.

Beyond anything offered in the book, the cone model of knowledge offers additional reason for us to take a serious interest in these hypotheses. This additional reason is not very great, but it is, I think, at least moderately significant. Let me explain what I have in mind here in a somewhat roundabout fashion, as I attempt to make some points of independent philosophic interest along the way.

In my book, in arguing for the idea that such relativity hypotheses are at least somewhat plausible, I looked only for logically necessary conditions, not logically sufficient as well, for the truth of statements of philosophically interesting forms. I said that, for each term, and regarding the statements that appropriately contain it, the necessary condition in focus could as properly receive an invariantist interpretation, perhaps impossibly demanding, as well as a much more easily satisfiable contextualist interpretation, the one interpretation being no better and no worse than the other. For the purposes of that advocacy, perhaps that cautious or safe or unambitious line was the appropriate one to take. But here my main purposes are different.

In looking only for conditions that are logically necessary, we will never understand very much about the semantics of philosophically interesting terms. This is clearly true if these terms do not admit of any illuminating conjunctive analysis, as I believe to be their situation. For then no matter how many necessary conditions one finds, one cannot add them up to get a good account of the term wanting illumination. For this purpose we should try to do something else, something less cautious and more ambitious. For different interesting terms, quite different ambitious projects might be suitable.

Whatever the semantics of 'free', in order to understand what freedom is, or what it is for someone to be free to do something, it is important to understand how we adaptively think about various situations in terms of 'free' and kindred expressions. Of course, other things are also important to such understanding. Similarly, whatever the semantics of 'know', in order to understand what knowledge is, or what it is for someone to know that something is so, it is important, among other things, to understand how we adaptively think about various situations in terms of 'know' and kindred expressions. I offer no project now to help us with the first set of tasks, relating to freedom. But I hope that the model of knowledge now being offered will help with the second set of tasks, relating to knowledge. Perhaps this might most likely happen if the model is taken as neutral between various apparently conflicting semantic approaches, rather than as an account of our adaptive thinking that requires the adoption of just one approach to language and meaning.

Having just said some things of a sensible, and perhaps even of a conciliatory, nature, let me now try to be fruitfully provocative. When I tried to take a cautious line in arguing for philosophical relativity, I missed an opportunity to make the position seem as plausible as it might be. For it is not very plausible to think that central philosophical terms, like 'know' and 'free', have "dangling" logically necessary conditions that are among their philosophically most perplexing, or most intriguing, conditions. And for each of these terms, and others, I bid us consider just such most perplexing conditions for their correct semantic application. For example, I bid us consider that a statement of the form 'S knows that p' will be true only if S can rule out as untrue any proposition q, incompatible with p, that is a relevant competitor of p. For the invariantist, any incompatible proposition whatsoever is a competitor that is always relevant, and the standards for ruling out are always as high as can be. For the contextualist, neither of these things is so, the condition being properly interpreted only in a much more lenient way. The semantic relativity hypothesis, here applied, is to the effect that neither interpretation of the considered condition is correct at the expense of the other; there is no fact of the matter as to how such a condition is most properly interpreted or understood.

To be most plausible, the very perplexing and intriguing condition under discussion should not merely be a necessary condition, interpreted more strictly or more loosely. For then it would "dangle." Would it add up with other conditions to a conjunctive analysis of knowing? That is not very plausible, as we remarked near the outset. But, if not that, we want some account of how it is to *fit in* with other conditions of knowing that seem interesting. Otherwise we may well doubt that anything of interest is really going on with knowing here at all. Our cone model of knowledge gives us just such a wanted account. By relating our considered condition to other aspects of knowledge, and by allowing us to treat it as one of the interdependent aspects, the model erases the impression that this condition dangles mysteriously; rather, the model helps to reveal that our considered condition fits right in with the other aspects of knowledge in such a way that it does not dangle at all.

A related consideration immediately arises. As I said, insofar as our cone model is adequate to our thinking about knowledge, the most natural invariantist treatment of the model involves the idea that only someone in the ideal case, at the very apex of the cone, will ever know anything to be so. This allows for very strong arguments from invariantism to skepticism about human knowledge; it very strongly encourages the idea that that semantic theory will yield an enormous amount of direct support for that traditional philosophical position. For an extreme case in point, it can be argued, as in section 1 we did argue, that to be in this case, with respect to any proposition, the subject must be absolutely omniscient. As we humans are quite clearly not omniscient, there is, then, along with so many other skeptical arguments now available, even this intriguing piece of reasoning from invariantism through our cone model to skepticism about human knowledge.

Owing to these considerations, our cone model of knowledge lends some support to our hypothesis of philosophical relativity. But it does this just to the extent that it furthers the more restricted hypothesis of epistemic relativity. For more support for the more ambitious hypothesis, more conceptual understanding is wanted. We want models of freedom, of causation, of explanation, and of other philosophically central concepts that suggest how these ideas might be unities, in at least something like the way that our concept of knowledge is a unified concept. Indeed, quite apart from any interest in the hypothesis of philosophical relativity, we should like to have such models. Our cone model of knowledge is, of course, both quite imperfect and quite incomplete. Even so, looking from epistemology out toward the rest of philosophy, perhaps it is a first step in the right direction, the direction that should be pursued by any who would better understand our philosophically most central ideas and whatever in the world might answer to them.[27]

---

27. A number of people helped me with their comments on various versions of the present work, the last of which is before you now. John Richardson was enormously helpful from the start to the finish of the project, saving me from serious logical blunders, as well as making useful positive suggestions. Jonathan Adler also contributed useful ideas at several stages. In addition, I received substantial comments, at one stage or another, from Anthony Brueckner, Francis Dauer, Peter Klein, Steven Luper-Foy, John Tienson and Tak Yagisawa. I am thankful to them all.

# 10

# CONTEXTUAL ANALYSIS IN ETHICS

When assessed by an appropriate ethical standard, most of us usually behave quite acceptably. Or, so we generally judge. And, when assessed by an appropriate epistemological standard, most of us usually do quite well, too: First, we know many things about the world and, second, we're usually justified in holding those of our confident beliefs that aren't quite instances of knowledge. Or, again, so we generally judge. As we generally judge, then, both in our behaving and in our believing, things are usually quite acceptable.

As is familiar, philosophers have challenged these very common, and very comfortable, judgments. Without yet presenting the argument, here's an example from ethics: When we spend money on dinner in a fancy restaurant, instead of sending money to feed the starving, are we behaving in a way that, ethically, is *acceptable*? Even as we realize that making the donation is the *ethically better* thing to do, still, the ordinary supposition is, of course, that there is *nothing wrong* in our behavior. Not doing what is ethically better, we do what is, even so, ethically acceptable. But as Peter Singer and others have shown, it's possible *rationally to motivate* this: First, the common, comfortable thought may be *properly questioned*. And, second, *sometimes* it might be *correctly judged* that such costly pleasurable behavior *isn't ethically acceptable*.[1] Now, what's most

---

1. The original argument is in Singer's "Famine, Affluence and Morality," *Philosophy and Public Affairs*, 1972. A more recent argument is in chapter 8 of Singer's *Practical*

interesting about this is that, in motivating the harsh ethical judgment, the philosophers need employ, along with undisputed empirical facts, only some ethical ideas that, at least implicitly, are already widely accepted.

Again without yet presenting the argument, here's an example from epistemology: When you haven't been in your office for an hour, do you *know* that your desk is still there? The ordinary judgment, of course, is that you do. Even if you don't know this with the certainty that you know you yourself exist right now, still, you do know the thing. Not knowing them in a way that may be epistemically better, still, we do know ever so many things to be so. But as Peter Unger and others have shown, it's possible *rationally to motivate* this: First, the common, comfortable thought may be *properly questioned*. Second, *sometimes* it might be *correctly judged* that you *never know* any such thing[2]; indeed, *sometimes* we may *correctly judge* even that you *aren't ever justified in believing* any such thing.[3] Again, what's most interesting about this is what, in motivating the harsh epistemological judgments, the philosophers employ. These ideas, too, are part of *commonsense thinking*.

Along with important differences, there may be a deep commonalty holding between these two sorts of dialectic, the epistemological and the ethical. As is my hypothesis, a main common point is a *semantic* one concerning the *contexts* in which we make, or grasp, particular normative judgments. Now, elsewhere, I've argued for this hypothesis: In many cases, the truth-value of a judgment about whether a person knows a certain thing depends on the context in which the judgment is made, or is grasped.[4] Here, I'll argue for a parallel hypothesis: *In many cases, the truth-value (or the acceptability) of a judgment about whether*

---

*Ethics*, Cambridge University Press, 1979. Also see James Fishkin's, *The Limits of Obligation*, Yale University Press, 1982.

2. The mention of my name here is meant to provide a euphonious parallel, and I hope a humorous parallel, with my friend Peter Singer. As is obvious, many philosophers have done very well at establishing such skeptical contexts long before I ever existed. The most seminal of these is Rene Descartes, whose name, unlike mine, has little in common with Singer's. Most famously, Descartes does his job in his *Meditations*. Much less famously, I do mine in "A Defense of Skepticism," *The Philosophical Review*, 1971, and in *Ignorance: A Case for Scepticism*, Oxford University Press, 1975.

3. Among many places in the literature, arguments for this are in chapter 5 of *Ignorance*.

4. A fairly early discussion of knowledge and context is Fred Dretske's "The Pragmatic Dimension of Knowledge," *Philosophical Studies*, 1981. Although I was being too much of a radical about questions of knowledge and skepticism, still, as far as treating contexts is concerned, I go beyond my friend, Dretske, in my *Philosophical Relativity*, University of Minnesota Press, 1984. (See, most especially, Chapter 2, section 4.) To date,

*a person's behavior is morally permissible depends on the context in which the judgment is made, or is grasped.*[5]

As with the epistemological-semantic hypothesis proffered before, so with the ethical-semantic hypothesis offered now: My argument is far from conclusive. Indeed, it consists only of observations that, more than does any rival of which we're aware, the hypothesis helps explain the (largely linguistic) behavior, and the associated thoughts and feelings, found with a certain large class of judgments. It's in this modest spirit, but also ambitious spirit, that we proceed.

## 1. Commonsense Ethics and Harsh Ethical Judgments

Even in our rather materialistic society, a few work hard on behalf of the poorest and most wretched people of the earth. And a few give much of their money for the most worthwhile purposes, such as helping to prevent children from dying from easy-to-beat diseases. As most of us agree, these people are, certainly morally and perhaps overall, much better people than (almost all) the rest of us. As is no news, most of us aren't (morally) extremely good people.

What of our *conduct*, or our *behavior*? Because it's not wicked, and so on, most of the time, and to our credit, our behavior isn't extremely bad. But, and as the previous paragraph makes plain, most of the time our behavior isn't extremely good, either. So, we may agree on at least this: In terms of *better* behavior and *worse* conduct, pretty far from the great extremes, most of the time our own conduct lies somewhere in a vast middle ground: We could do a lot better and we could do a lot worse.

But, what of *right*, and *permissible*, and *wrong*? When confronted with any particular case of what a person might do, the main matter, it

---

perhaps the fullest discussion of the contextual approach to knowledge remains my quite *conservative* "The Cone Model of Knowledge," *Philosophical Topics*, 1986. In later notes, this last will be called "The Cone."

On the general matter of contextual semantics, the seminal work is David Lewis's "Scorekeeping in a Language Game," *Journal of Philosophical Logic*, 1979, reprinted in his *Philosophical Papers*, Vol. I, Oxford University Press, 1983. In later notes, this will be called "Scorekeeping," and I'll refer to the reprinting.

5. As the bracketed expression concerning acceptability indicates, the discussion of this paper does not assume that (positive) moral judgments are ever true, although I myself think that such judgments often are true, just as common sense has it. Whatever her metaethical view, the intelligent reader can readily cast my ideas in terms she finds most congenial.

appears, is to get things straight about what's right, or at least what's *all right*, and what's wrong. As things generally appear, we must go beyond the merely comparative judgments of better and worse behavior to arrive at a more decisive assessment.[6]

Judging our behavior in more decisive terms, how does it shape up? Singer and others, I said, have argued that commonsense ethics helps deliver the conclusion that, throughout most of our lives, we behave wrongly. At first glance, this idea seems to have no chance of being correct. But the question may be a rather complex issue: For one thing, our common ethics may include at least *pretty* demanding principles, even infinitely many of them, which we may rarely notice. Second, while in infinitely many possible worlds these precepts will make hardly any demands on us, in the *actual* world *some* of them might require us to extend ourselves, or to deprive ourselves, to *at least a moderate* degree.

In discussing these principles, we'll think about how they might apply to you, a pretty typical agent. As will be helpful, we'll *stipulate* this: *Apart from what's often (misleadingly?) called the ethics of benevolence*, throughout your life you'll be doing *everything* that commonsense ethics ever requires of you. So, you won't ever be harming anyone; and you'll be keeping all your promises; and you'll be taking good care of all your children; and so on.

With that in mind, consider:

*Cheaply Decreasing Limb Loss.* Other things being even nearly equal, if *at (nearly) insignificant cost to yourself* you can (help) prevent one or more other people from each loosing at least one arm or leg, and if *even so you'll still be at least reasonably well off*, then it's wrong for you not to (help) prevent such others from suffering such loss of *limb*.

Especially for the *first* stressed clause, concerning the *tiny* cost to the agent, *even on its face* this precept is just enormously appealing to moral common sense. And, owing to the *second* stressed clause, concerning continued good prospects for the agent, the precept's appeal is *retained*

---

6. In a fine recent book, *Common-sense Morality and Consequentialism*, Routledge & Kegan Paul, 1985, Michael Slote shows a keen awareness of this feeling. His fairly radical response to it is that, at least in our ethics of benevolence, we might best proceed no longer to pay much attention to right and wrong. Instead, we may just rank, as judged by their consequences, the actions open to an agent at a time. (Elsewhere in the book, Slote also offers some less radical responses.) Perhaps we may view this as a step toward the present treatment. So viewed, the idea seems less radical.

even for philosophical sophisticates: Not even sorites reasoning can yield that the agent's compliance with the maxim will *ever*, in *any possible* world, be extremely demanding on the agent. While its presentation may need changes, this precept's substance is part of *commonsense* ethics, which isn't, of course, an extreme libertarian morality.

Notice that, though the principle *allows* for their conspicuousness to you to endow certain people with a *bit* extra by way of their having a moral call on you, the maxim *doesn't find* a very *great* deal to favor just those who strike your attention. Rather, when it comes to losing an arm or two, if you can so very easily (help) stop the terrible occurrence, then it's wrong for you to pass by those strangers in the dark or far away, not just those well lit or nearby. But, of course, at least this *modicum* of impartiality is, if not an absolutely central part, at least *a* part of commonsense ethics.[7]

Now, in this actual world of ours, it's only very rarely, it seems, that the likes of you and me, who aren't surgeons, *even get a chance* to do much about people losing their limbs. As it happens, then, and with very little cost to ourselves, we laymen seem to do quite well by Cheaply Decreasing Limb Loss.

Closely allied with that maxim is a yet more compelling precept:

> *Cheaply Decreasing Deaths.* Other things being even nearly equal, if *at (nearly) insignificant cost to yourself*, you can (help) prevent one or more other people from each *dying soon*, while substantially raising the chances that they'll live healthily for years, and if *even so you'll still be at least reasonably well off*, then it's wrong for you not to (help) prevent such others from suffering such loss of *life*.

As does Cheaply Decreasing Limb Loss, this still more compelling maxim does not favor greatly just those who happen to be conspicuous to you. Perhaps even *partly because of* that, Cheaply Decreasing Deaths is just a stupendously compelling moral maxim.[8] But, of course, the main

---

7. How well does this precept stand up to our responses to examples? As hard work shows, it stands up very well indeed: In addition to what I've found in the literature, in the past couple of years I've devised several hundred relevant cases. As a study of response to the cases makes clear, *except insofar as a factor serves to make a needy stranger's dire needs salient, or her bad troubles dramatic*, a respondent is *not* much moved even by such factors as these: whether a poor stranger is in an *emergency*, by whether the stranger is in the respondent's *community*, by whether the respondent is *the only one who can* help the stranger, and so on. Indeed, except for contributions to such conspicuousness and excitement, we aren't much moved by such factors even when *many are presented together*! As I intend, the best of this big business will appear in my book-in-progress for the Oxford University Press, tentatively titled *Living High and Letting Die: The Illusion of Innocence*.

8. See the just previous note.

reasons for its extraordinary grip are the most obvious ones: First, this maxim, too, has that first emphatic clause concerning the *tiny* cost to you. And, second, here we're not just talking about innocents just losing a limb or two; it's people losing their very *lives*. Third and finally, as the present precept also has that second emphatic clause concerning continued good prospects for the agent, it gives an *absolute guarantee* that even *full* compliance with it won't *ever* be extremely demanding on you.

But, *unlike* what actually happens with regard to the prior precept, what actually happens with Cheaply Decreasing Deaths is this: Owing to the nature of the horrors facing so very many young folks in the actual world, and owing to the nature of the available means to decrease those horrors, we're *(almost) always facing* a chance to comply with, and *a chance to fail to comply with*, Cheaply Decreasing Deaths. So, as regards this yet more compelling precept, it's *not* obvious that our behavior usually measures up. As many of the details of this are worth confronting many times over, I'll quickly rehearse just a few of them now. First, a little bit about some of the horrors: During the next year, unless they're given Oral Rehydration Therapy, several million children, in the poorest areas of the world, will die from—I kid you not—diarrhea. Indeed, according to the United States Committee for UNICEF, "diarrhea kills more children worldwide than any other cause."[9]

Next, a medium bit about some of the means: By sending in a modest sum to the U.S. Committee for UNICEF (or to CARE) and by earmarking the money for ORT, you can help prevent some of these children from dying. For, in very many instances, the net cost of giving this life-saving therapy is less than one dollar.[10] (As almost all will agree, to the great majority of North Americans, and Western Europeans, and Japanese, and so on, this is a cost that's [nearly] insignificant.) But, how are you to get even a few dollars into the efficient

---

9. I take this quote from a letter of appeal from the Committee that I received in the fall of 1989.

10. In their Christmas mailing, a month or two later, UNICEF said "Your $40 Holiday Gift of Hope could help provide 400 doses of Oral Rehydration Salts to save children from dehydration caused by diarrhea—the number one killer of children worldwide." Well, that's ten cents a dose. Allowing for overhead costs, for possible exaggeration, and so on, let's quarter this claim. So, we figure that it takes 40 cents to save a child's life.

While there's been some significant inflation over the last four years, near the end of 1993, when I'm writing the most recent of these sentences, the price of this great bargain, at least, remains very much the same. So, year in and year out, it's a tremendous opportunity to help reduce serious suffering very substantially to which so very many of us so consistently give a pass.

hands? Saving you the trouble of doing even the least bit of research, I provide you with the address of a previously mentioned organization:

United States Committee for UNICEF
United Nations Children's Fund
333 East 38th Street
New York, N.Y. 10016

Now, you may send this effective group a modest sum, simply by mailing in, to that address, a check made out to:

United States Committee for UNICEF

And, you may earmark the funds for the purpose of fighting killer diarrhea, simply by enclosing a very short note. The note may simply read:

USE THE ENCLOSED FUNDS FOR ORAL REHYDRATION THERAPY.

So, even if you might not have known before, now you know how to do something, on any given day, that will help save the lives of other people. With both some sensible ethics and some empirical facts before us, we're well along a commonsense route to harsh ethical judgment of common behavior. Let's keep going: Well, as it's not in the past, *today* is one of the days in which you can act. Have you sent anyone any lifesaving money yet today? Perhaps. If so, that's fine. But, almost certainly, that's not the end of what, with regard to the desperately needy children, is morally required of you. For, of course, there's tomorrow to consider, and the day after that, and so on. With this thought firmly in mind, we're nearly ready for a nice application of Cheaply Decreasing Deaths.

Before we make the application, there's a partly practical and partly ethical question to consider. As each person's circumstances are different, this is a question that each of us must think through herself. Right now, I call on you to do that: On a typical day, how much money is the least amount that, ethically, *you* should send? Because we have a reasonable ethical understanding of our compelling ethical principle, the relevant answer will be a sum that's at least *pretty* high up in a certain vaguely indicated range. This is the range of all those precise-to-the-penny sums that each represent what is, for *you*, a (nearly) insignificant cost. So, among other things, *your* proper answer depends on many egocentric objective factors, such as *your* family responsibilities, *your* income, *your* assets, and so on, *much of which might have been much affected by significant sums you've already given to save lives*! Not knowing *your* particular situation, and trusting you to do your honest best, I leave the matter *up to you*.

To reduce uncertainty about all this, and to help you along, I'll present a simple, standard multiple choice format, with just four choices. Each member of Group 1 will send the short note and just $5, in the appropriate way and a bit later today, to the address displayed just above. A little higher up, Group 2's members will send $10 apiece; Group 3's will send $15 and Group 4's, including Leona Helmsley and even me, will each send a full $20. You are to place yourself, as honestly as you can, in the highest group that pertains to *your* particular case. As I suspect, you can place yourself at least in Group 1.

For the sake of the argument, let's suppose that you did choose just Group 1. So, a bit later today, you'll send $5, along with the indicated short note, to 38th Street, saving some lives. To be hard on our argument, let's grant that, if you do even just this, then, with regard to conduct open to you on this present day, you will be *fully* complying with Cheaply Decreasing Deaths. On the other hand, if even while you are easily able to save lives you *don't* do this, and if you do *nothing else* of at least *comparable* moral importance, then today you'll behave wrongly. With only sad confidence, I'll say, and you'll agree, that, on the day you read these words, you won't do anything else of comparable moral importance. So, unless you soon do send (at least) a $5 contribution to 38th Street, your behavior today really will be wrong.

Although I doubt it, perhaps inspired by my words, you will *soon* send at least $5. But, will do you the same tomorrow, and the day after? Although you won't stop brushing your teeth daily, it's all but certain that, eventually, you'll give up this other routine, forsaking the world's most sickly children. Then, *eventually, you'll behave wrongly at least almost every day for the rest of your life.*

All of that is quite a good commonsense argument, I submit, to a very harsh judgment of your (probable future) behavior. Some, however, will think the reasoning to be unrealistic: "Really," they'll say, "who can bother to do that every day?" But, as can be made plain, words like these can't ever point to any *serious* objection. We need only observe that commonsense ethics allows for certain *moral equivalences.* Picking a naturally convenient time and a nice round figure, you may, instead of sending $5 to 38th Street each and every day, send *30 times* the amount, or $150, once a month. Not even requiring much time or money for postage, there now won't be anything in what you're to do that's the least bit *unrealistic*, not on *any* reasonable interpretation of the term. Indeed, it's so very easy to make the practice completely routine. For example, you may send the $150 to 38th Street on the day that, by mail, you pay your (main) monthly telephone bill.

Will you send $150 to 38th Street this next month? If you do, then you'll save the lives of *very many* horribly diarrheic little children. Perhaps you will do that. Or, although it's unlikely, perhaps you'll do something this next month of comparable moral importance to the saving of these *very many* young lives. But, what about the following month, and the month after? Eventually, I'm afraid, and likely pretty soon, there will come a month when, *from that month on*, at least most months will *not* see you send a check to save so many children's lives. So, in all likelihood, *starting at least pretty soon, you'll behave wrongly at least most months for the rest of your life*. Shall we go on to get a parallel conclusion concerning your remaining *years*? Along with common sense, mercy suggests that we not.

Anyhow, by commonsense reasoning, we recently reached a second very harsh ethical conclusion. This was only to be expected. For if you will behave wrongly for *(at least) almost all the days* of the rest of your life, as we first concluded, then, from that and from such boringly familiar truths as that there are from 28 to 31 days in each month, it follows that you'll behave wrongly for *(at least) most of the months* of the rest of your life. But, now, an interesting question arises: Starting pretty much from scratch, is there any commonsense ethical *precept* that may provide a quite direct route to our second conclusion? If our arguments are to be trusted, then our common morality had best include some such precept.

But, of course, our shared ethics does include (infinitely) many such principles. As we may agree, just as is Greatly Decreasing Limb Loss, one of them is:

> *Greatly Decreasing Deaths*. Other things being even nearly equal, if *at quite moderate cost to yourself*, you can (help) prevent *very many* other people from *dying soon*, while substantially raising the chances that they will live healthily for years, and if *even so you'll still be at least reasonably well off*, then it's wrong for you not to (help) prevent such *very many* others from suffering such loss of *life*.

Because it speaks of *very many* folks losing their very *lives* and of a cost to you that's only *quite moderate*, the grip of this maxim is scarcely less firm than it's finer-grained cousin, Cheaply Decreasing Deaths. Just so, these two maxims, along with (infinitely) many other precepts, form a *family of maxims*. According to commonsense ethics, a most sensible idea runs, often it matters precious little *which* member of the family is the maxim to which one *most directly* complies. (Very often, but not always, compliance with *any maxim in the family* will mean good compliance with *all in the family*). But, if we don't at least *pretty directly* comply with *at least one* of the precepts in the family, then, as we've been noticing, *throughout most of our lives* our behavior will be wrong.[11]

## 2. Ethically Demanding Contexts

In the previous section, you ended up accepting a *harsh* judgment of your (probable future) behavior. But, unless you're very unusual, *before* reading this material, you *didn't* do that. Instead, at that earlier time, you accepted only a much more lenient judgment. Now, as things first appear, these judgments must contradict each other. On the contextual analysis to be developed, however, there really is no contradiction.

In the previous section, I established a context in which the standards for moral assessment were *not* ordinary standards, but were *uncommonly high* standards. While it's not clear exactly how I did this, in large measure it was by doing these eight effective things.

First, I articulated, and so brought to our attention, several behaviorally demanding, but intuitively appealing, ethical principles. Almost all the time, as I imagine, little that relates to precepts like these figures prominently in the contexts of our actual lives. Accordingly, almost always, our commitment to such principles is far from our attention. With the articulation of three of them, we changed that. This helped set a context ethically more demanding than most.

Second, I actually *said* that, if you contribute a rather modest amount of money to UNICEF, then *you will save people's lives*. Of course, sending in money to UNICEF is really very far indeed from being

---

11. Often, when I present the argument, people try to avoid the conclusion by coming up with alleged facts. But, even if they should obtain, such facts will be irrelevant. Representative of others, perhaps the most frequent response is this complaint: "If these children do not die now, then, later, they will produce yet more children. So, we will help create a situation where, in the future, there will be even more children painfully dying. So, if we do nothing to prevent the present children from dying, we will *not* behave wrongly." This is badly misguided: Suppose that, during one of the few years when there is *no* serious nutrition problem there, you are travelling in a very poor country and you come across a child on the verge of drowning in a wading pool. Even with the idea of "future overpopulation" in mind, is it morally permissible for you not to pull her out? Of course, not.

a paradigm case of saving people's lives. And, far beyond that, even this may well be true: Between the donors to UNICEF and the children saved by UNICEF's efforts, the causal relations may be far too "amorphous" for it to be true to say, of any of these donors, that *she saved* some children's lives. But, even if that is true, there's no detraction from the present point which, after all, is just this: Semantically proper or not, by my going ahead with that use of those terms, I made the UNICEF case look pretty much like *ordinary* cases of people actually saving people's lives. This also helped to set a demanding context.

Third, I actually *said to you that*, if you don't give a certain modest amount, $5, to UNICEF, then *you will behave wrongly*. By just saying this to you, I was able to raise the standards, slightly, from their more usual level. *How* was I able to do this? By trading on, what David Lewis has called *rules of accommodation*:[12] Going by our most common standards, with which we began, my harsh judgement *would not have been* acceptable. So, straightaway, and going by our rules of accommodation, the context changed, the standards rose, and what I said *became and was* acceptable. Well, that's fine; but now a further question arises: How was I able to *trade further* on these conversational semantic rules; how was I able to *keep you* being sufficiently accommodating?

Fourth, by not asking too much of you too soon, I pretty much ensured that there would not be, in you, much resistance to my effort: While I *began* by allowing that the $5 contribution might be a one-shot affair, later I *went on* to make moves that cancelled any such suggestion. Trading on the momentum of the initial small rise, I said further things that got our ethical standards to rise further. This could happen because, in my presentation, I did not ask for any jumps upward that might well have generated resistance from you. Rather, I proceeded in a way that, apparently, was natural and acceptable: As is obvious, we often think about our behavior in terms of days, e.g., "What did you do today?" and "She just wasted her time yesterday." So, it was easy for me to make the *day* an acceptable period for consideration. And, for a whole day, $5 did not seem like much at all. So, naturally enough, and in a manner designed to meet with little resistance, I then suggested that you do this every day. A bit later still, I said that, equivalently, you might send in $150 each month. Now, especially at this pretty late stage, that amount did not appear too daunting. Proceeding in this way, I found little resistance in you and, so, there was much accommodation.

---

12. See "Scorekeeping," 240 ff.

As I believe, this point is worth some emphasis: Consider what would have happened if I *began* by saying that, in order to avoid behaving wrongly this coming year, you must pledge, immediately and irrevocably, *at least $1800* of your liquid assets, or of your coming year's income, to some such life-saving group as UNICEF. Most likely, I would then have done precious little to establish an ethically demanding context. Rather than having been accorded much accommodation, I would have generated a lot of resistance. Notice, too, that if I began by suggesting that you should mail in $5 not each day, but each minute, or even each hour, then, for much the same reason, I would have done little to set a demanding context. So, I didn't make any of those impolitic suggestions.

Fifth, I focused our discussion on your possible, and your probable, future behavior. Hardly at all did I even allude to your *past* conduct, let alone to the great failing we might have found for all those years. By going out of my way not to do anything even *remotely like* insulting you, I took a path where, from these potential quarters, too, I'd find little resistance and lots of accommodation.

Sixth, as generally happens when you read, there was created, for you, a quasi-social context involving only two people, the writer and the reader. By saying that I should be in Group 4, the highest group, I professed that fully half of these two thinkers judged that he should, and would, try to conform to a *quite high* ethical standard. By saying that I would be content to think of you as being only in Group 1, the lowest group, I politely put you under some pretty significant quasi-social pressure: The least you could do, it then began to appear, was to live up to a much more modest ethical standard than the one deemed apt for me, your faithful author. So, especially for you, that also helped to set a demanding context.

Seventh, I presented you, in a reasonably politic way, with a fair amount of *very specific information*: I told you just what your few dollars really would do, namely, that they would help prevent several children from dying soon. And, very specifically, I told you how to get the money in place to help prevent horrible deaths. With this information provided, matters no longer seemed a vague question of what might, or might not, be done about desperately needy people. To the contrary, it was now a question of whether you yourself would do a certain specific thing, namely, send $5 to 38th Street, which would have a certain very specific effect, namely, several fewer children dying soon. The provision of this specific information helped to create a *highly focused* context, and a relevantly *very practical* context. This was a context in which, ethically, you were right there on the spot. So, this also helped set an ethically demanding context.

Eighth, even if it was in only moderately forceful terms, I kept referring to the awful plight of many poor little children. I didn't make such a reference just once; rather I made it several times over. Thus, their impending deaths, each so inexpensive to prevent, became the *vivid* focus of our discussion. That also helped.

Relating to this last point, there were certain things that I did *not* do, but that, had I done them, would have helped make the context demanding. Why didn't I do these other things? Well, in that I was just writing an essay, I was confined to using only words. But, of course, most of the time, contexts are not only, and are not even mainly, set by words. Rather, either entirely or mainly, contexts are usually set by non-linguistic factors.

If I'd shown you an hour-long movie focusing on the suffering children, and showing how some were saved from dying by the efforts of UNICEF, that would have been more effective than this mere writing. And, if I'd flown you to the worst parts of the world and you stayed there—right in the thick of things—for at least a week, then some of those children themselves would have greatly helped to set a *terribly* demanding context for you. (By the way, in this last sort of circumstance, in addition to helping *set* the context, those suffering children would actually have *become part of* your tough context.) So, being very limited in my means, I was only pretty successful, and not extremely successful, in attaining my goal.

As I trust, this section's remarks have told you plenty enough about why you might have recently been in an ethically demanding context. Anyhow, let's not get side-tracked by asking anything even much like: What, exactly, *is* a *context*? Nor even anything much like: What is it, exactly, that *determines* when a given person is in a *certain* context, rather than just being in *other* contexts? As regards the present essay, which makes not even a pretense toward being a study of the fundamental aspects of language, or of linguistic behavior, such perfectly general questions are perfectly irrelevant. For many, that's all quite plain. For many others, perhaps some help is needed. So, being an accommodating fellow, here's some help.

Although there are doubtless many moral matters about which you and I *disagree*, there are some, surely, where our *beliefs are the same*. For one thing, we both believe that, other things being even nearly equal, it's wrong to cause someone to lose even one of his limbs. For another, we even believe that, modulo verbal niceties, Cheaply Decreasing Limb Loss is correct. Now, in certain contexts of very general inquiry, regarding the fundamentals of the propositional attitudes and those of mental content, it may be useful to wonder widely about the truth I just propounded: What, exactly, *is* a *belief*? And, what is it, exactly, that *determines* when a given person has a *certain* belief, rather than just having *other* beliefs? But, in any even *somewhat* narrowly focused context, like that of the present essay, it's pretty silly to ponder these highly general questions. And, just as with these terribly general questions about beliefs, so it is, too, with those terribly general questions about contexts.

Rationally not bothering with *any* such awfully general questions, we may reasonably agree about some far more specific matters. Even if not quite certainly, most plausibly one of them is this: Because I actually did work in at least the eight indicated ways, in the previous section I set an *ethically demanding* context. So, at the present juncture, this idea suggests itself: In large measure, it was *because of this established demanding context* that, at least for the time being, we found acceptable the noted harsh judgments concerning your behavior. But, then, even if only roughly, how did *that* work?

## 3. Contextually Sensitive Semantics for Ethically Useful Terms

Central to any good account of this, there must be at least the sketch of a suitable semantic story. Happy to tackle central tasks, I'll now try to provide that.

As is my semantic hypothesis, many of the terms we use in our moral judgments have an *indexical aspect* to their semantics. Because these terms are thus indexical, they can be *sensitive to the contexts* in which they are used or understood. These morally useful terms include "right," "all right" and "wrong," "permissible" and "impermissible," "acceptable" and "unacceptable," as well as "ethical," "moral" and their antonyms. Of course, most of these terms, like "right" and "wrong," are very often used in utterances that have nothing to do with moral matters. But, as will emerge shortly, that doesn't affect my present points. For, at present, I'm concerned with the terms as they occur in sentences standardly used to assess, with respect to morality, people's conduct, or behavior.

As is common, in morally assessing your conduct, I may employ such widely useful words as these: *What you did was all right.* As is common, I may then have assessed your behavior in this contextually sensitive manner: *What you did was, in respect of the conditions for acceptability determined by this very context, at least close enough, in order to be properly judged acceptable, to being in complete conformity with (a) certain standard(s) for acceptability, namely, with just the standard(s) whose prevailing right now is (or are) determined by this very context (of use, or of understanding).*

In saying "What you did was all right," I may be assessing your behavior morally or I may be assessing it in another way. In a context where the judgment is *not* moral, then some standard other than morality is implicitly picked out; it might be the traffic laws of Idaho. When the assessment is moral, however, then it is morality that, implicitly, is indicated as the relevant standard. Now, although it wasn't done, this standard could have been indicated *more explicitly*. That would have happened if I had said, instead, something that, typically, is more pompous: *What you did was **morally** all right.* Preferring to be effective rather than pompous fools, generally we leave out such explicit qualifiers as this "morally" and let context determine the relevant standard.

A point of clarification: On this account, there is nothing in the semantics of "all right," or even of "morally all right," that identifies morality with our commonsense ethics. Rather, my idea is this: In our ordinary moral thinking, we take commonsense ethics to be at least very much like, and thus to be a very good guide to the substance of, morality itself. By contrast, ethical deviants, including some admirable reformers, will take other (systems of) precepts to be much better guides. As it should do, the semantics of the terms leaves all this open.

An expository point: In most of what follows, I will assume that our commonsense ethics is a good guide to morality itself. Because I'm trying to understand some of our ordinary moral thinking, and its potential for issuing in harsh ethical judgments, this assumption is entirely appropriate.

A second expository point: Because our essay so largely concerns ethics, I will just specify that, generally, it's ethics, or morality, that's the standard of behavior that our essay's contexts pick out as relevant. That will greatly simplify exposition. For example, we may then express the import of the noted moral assessment in this notably simpler manner: *What you did was, in respect of the conditions for acceptability determined by this very context, at least close enough, in order to be properly judged acceptable, to being in complete conformity with morality.*

Besides picking out the relevant standard, context does something that, for our present topic, is more important: Context also determines what, relative to the standard selected, is *close enough* to *complete* conformity in order to be properly judged acceptable. Now, especially when morality is the standard, what is close enough can *sometimes* involve the complexities of *competing* morally relevant factors: How much of your available time should you spend with your sick mother, how much with your healthy but quite rowdy young children and, perhaps, how much—just by yourself alone—ecstatically playing your slide trombone? In such conflict cases, I suppose, you may be close enough when your behavior gives morally appropriate weight to each of the factors. In certain cases, the weight given may be fairly close to, but may not be in perfect congruence with, the weight that ethics itself assigns. (Or, it may be fairly close to, but may not fall within, the *range* of weights that ethics assigns.) Now, when contexts are sufficiently lenient, as rather often happens, that may be close enough. In such a lenient context, the moral judge, who may or may not be the agent himself, can *correctly* say: What you did was all right.

As regards our main topic here, we need say little about cases where there are competing moral considerations. For, as will be remembered, we have even *stipulated* this much: Beyond any possible obligations you might have to aid the world's neediest people, you will always be doing very well morally. So, in effect, we are dealing with what may be fairly counted as just a single dimension. And, as has been agreed, quite beyond the point needed for you to be reasonably well off, the more you give, the *better* is your behavior. Our question, then, is this: How good is good enough for your behavior to be ethically all right?

Possibly, your *complete conformity* with ethics might require two related things: First, it might be required that, beyond that needed for reasonable comfort and security, you give *all the additional money you now have*. And, second, it might also be required that, as they continue honestly to come your way, you continue to contribute *any such additional money*. But, as we have been suggesting, in order properly to avoid a judgment of *wrongful* behavior, perhaps you *need not* behave in *complete* conformity with ethics. Rather, perhaps you need only be *close enough* to complete conformity with morality. That is, in order for you to thwart a judgment of behaving wrongly, you need only meet the level set by the context in which that very judgment is made, or is grasped.

## 4. Contextually Sensitive Terms and Ethically Lenient Contexts

In section 1, I set an ethically demanding context, which set a high level for the passing line. Since then, a fair amount was said that, as it happens, served to move us into *somewhat less* demanding contexts. Most of this happened in section 2, when I *explained to you how* I managed to create some very demanding contexts for us. And, a further downward slide was effected by the analytical points made just above in section 3.

Nonetheless, as I'm pretty sure, you're still in a context that, by most *usual* sorts of reckoning, is at least a *pretty* demanding context. Why is that?

First, a certain phenomenon holds for a wide variety of discourse: *Within a particular text or conversation*, it's easier to get high standards in force than to get back to lower standards.[13] For example, once there is in force a very high standard for being certain, or for being flat, or even for being rich—all easy to bring about, then, if one remains in the same discourse, it's hard to get much lower standards to be in force. So, what we find in the present instance is just a particular case of a very general phenomenon. (As yet, nobody understands much about *why* there's this general asymmetry.)

Second, and in close relation to the foregoing, there's this: Since you read the words that set our most demanding contexts, not much time has passed. Because there will have been little fading of relevant memory, my messages will still be pretty near the forefront of your mind. Now, when there occurs the passage of much more time, this will cease to be so. At that point, most will be in very much the same sort of *ethically lenient contexts* that, for them, prevailed before they started to read this essay. But that will be then and, by contrast, this is now. As a help toward getting a better grip on contextual analysis, it will be worth our discussing these two points.

To a certain extent, as I have indicated, movement toward leniency can be generated by various replies to the writing that produced the demanding contexts. To some extent, the explanations and analyses provided in the previous two sections constitute such replies. Further, when read in a reverse sort of way, the explanations yield recipes for making more forceful replies. Just do the *opposite* of what I did when setting the demanding context. For example, you may say that there is nothing *wrong* in someone sending UNICEF *a full $1000 a year*, rather than $1800, and using $800 for an interesting trip.

As I recently suggested, however, the most effective way to obtain downward movement is not by way of any active reply at all. Rather, the best way is, first, to leave the context and, then, to allow yourself to be in different sorts of context. Building on this suggestion, you might avoid, for a long time, contact with discussions that create, or that maintain, tough contexts. As time goes by, your prevailing contexts will be much more lenient, the prevailing standards then being much lower.

Right now you may still be in a pretty tough moral context. So, right now you may judge that, for most of your life, you have behaved

---

13. See "Scorekeeping," 245

wrongly and, likely, you'll continue to do so. But, as is also likely, a month from now you won't make such judgments. Rather, with the ravages of time, a month from now you'll judge that, throughout most of your life, your behavior has been, and it will be, morally all right.

On our contextualist account, in making that judgment a month from now, you will *not* be making any false judgment, or any unacceptable judgment. Rather, because you will be in an ethically lenient context, you will then be judging quite correctly.

Not just with ethical discourse, but quite generally, in order to understand the import of a contextualist account, it's crucial to avoid committing a certain fallacy, which we may call the *fallacy of conflating contexts*: Although it's tempting to think the opposite, it can *never* be correct for you to say anything that is even remotely like *this*: "Today, when I am in a demanding context, I do wrong if I spend much on myself and give hardly anything to the neediest; but, a month from now, when I will be in a lenient context, I will do nothing wrong even if I spend much on myself and give hardly anything to the neediest." For any such crazy remark as *that* to be correct, it is required, among other impossible things, that the remark be made in a context that is, at once, *both demanding and also not demanding*. Just as there can't ever be a context of *that* sort, so a remark of *that* sort can't ever be correct. To make such crazy remarks, or to think contextualism implies them, is to commit the fallacy of conflating contexts.[14]

## 5. Epistemological Skepticism and Epistemically Demanding Contexts

As I'll soon attempt to make plausible, there's an interesting parallel between the demanding *ethical* argumentation that we have encountered and, on the other side, certain demanding *epistemological* argument. For the attempt to make much sense, there's a central point about epistemological matters that we must keep in mind: Although only at a very much *more moderate level*, the same factors that find their epitome in our encounters with skeptical epistemological argument are also at work in many contexts of our lives.

As one conspicuous instance of this, what goes on in many American courts of law resembles, in this regard, what goes on in the

---

14. In his "Contextualism and Knowledge Attributions," *Philosophy and Phenomenological Research*, 1992, this fallacy is lucidly discussed by Keith DeRose. For this discussion, see part III of DeRose's paper, "The Objection to Contextualism".

writing and reading of certain philosophy books, and what goes on in many college classrooms. In those courts the attorney for the defense may use various rhetorical means to *elevate the epistemic standards* that are then in play with the jury members and that, as is the lawyer's hope, *will in consequence still be* in play, after he concludes his case and they convene for deliberation. This attorney's hope often may be reasonable, and may also be fulfilled. For, as is known, the jurors will convene only a day or so later, not a year or so hence. By drawing upon various dialectical considerations, the defense may sometimes get the jurors to have, for the meanwhile and relative to the case at hand, epistemic standards that are notably higher than is usual in such settings. When this is accomplished, then, even when there isn't even a small hole in the case against the defendant, still, the affected jury may accept that there *is* at least a *reasonable doubt* regarding whether it was the defendant who committed the crime in question.

On the other side, one thing that the prosecutor means to do, at least implicitly, is to keep the jurors *maintaining their more usual epistemic standards*.[15] When the prevailing epistemic standards are the appropriately more usual ones, as may rather often happen, and when a basis of very strong incriminating evidence is offered, then, even if the jurors might agree that there are some *extremely far-fetched* doubts as to whether the accused committed the crime, they will *not* hold that there is *any reasonable* doubt.

With these ideas in mind, we turn to discuss those contexts of ordinary life that involve certain philosophy books, and that obtain in many college classrooms. After all, at least during certain periods, philosophy is part of the life of very many quite ordinary people, in particular, many college freshmen and sophomores. Now, as must be sadly admitted, there are many very interesting, but rather abstruse, philosophic arguments whose impact most of these ordinary students never do feel. But happily, and in sharp contrast to that, the great majority of them do feel the impact of certain *skeptical epistemological arguments*.

According to these arguments, none of us ever knows anything to be so or, at the least, no one ever knows anything beyond his own present moment conscious thought and his own present existence. Now, as is familiar enough, the most widely *forceful* of these arguments involve the presentation of very far-fetched "skeptical hypotheses," or

---

15. As would be shameful, the prosecutor may try to get the jurors to have, for the meanwhile, uncommonly low epistemic standards. If she is successful, then even pretty skimpy evidence may be considered, by the jurors, as being enough to mean there is no reasonable doubt.

"skeptical alternatives," that contradict commonsense (explanatory) beliefs regarding one's experiences and (ostensible) memories. Vividly provided by Descartes, the most famous such hypothesis involves the postulation of an evil demon who might be responsible for all of one's experience and air one's ostensible memories.

Even if it may be only a *re*encounter, let's now encounter the forceful argumentation: For all you really know, all your experiences, and all your ostensible memories, are right now being caused in you by a powerful evil demon. And, for all you really know, this demon created you only a moment ago, complete with just these putative memories. If that is indeed the case, then absolutely everything *will appear* to you precisely as things actually *do appear* to you right now. Since this is so, and since you don't have any "over-arching" means to acquire knowledge, you *don't know whether or not* you are merely such a recently arrived, and such a perceptually blocked, being. Consequently, you *don't know that* you have existed for some years, or that there are any concrete things or people whose existence is independent of your own mind.

As familiar as they are forceful, arguments like these have, for centuries, received extensive discussion by philosophers. Many "refutations" of the arguments have been variously offered. As I suggested in an earlier essay, those responses badly misrepresent the import of the skeptic's moves.[16] There, I offered a different way to understand the challenges from skeptical argumentation, one that also helps in understanding the force of effective responses to that challenge. What did I say?

First, there was this suggestion, useful on a wide variety of views: Someone's knowing something to be so has (indefinitely) many *aspects*; not all of them, but many of these aspects are best understood as *matters of degree*, a good example being the aspect of how (close to being absolutely) certain of the thing is the person who might know. Second, and related, there was this widely useful idea: Only in the *absolutely perfect case* of knowledge—which case perhaps might never actually obtain—will it be that *all* of these aspects are *satisfied in the very highest degree.*[17]

---

16. See a lot of "The Cone."

17. As noted in "The Cone," *some* conditions of knowledge are *not* relevantly matters of degree. Nor are they relevantly sensitive to context. The most conspicuous of these are, first, that the being who is said to know must *exist* and, second, that what he is said to know to be so must *be so*. Does fictional discourse mean trouble for this idea? No; at the relevant level of interpretation, fiction must be understood as conforming to these conditions.

With these widely useful thoughts in mind, I then went contextual: When someone *attributes knowledge* to someone, be it to himself or to another, then the statement that he then makes is to be semantically evaluated with reference to that statement's context. So, suppose I standardly say, "You know you're wearing pants." Then, in attributing knowledge to you, my words are to be semantically evaluated along some such line as this: *In respect of the conditions for acceptability determined by this very context, you are (at least) close enough to the perfect case of knowing (that something is so) for you to satisfy these very conditions in regards to this very attribution to you of the knowledge that you are wearing pants.* In order to be as clear as I can about the matter, I'll add that the acceptability in question is the acceptability *to* the people who are in the indicated context *of* the indicated knowledge attribution *as* being *true*.

Even as our language itself does its part, and even as "the non-linguistic world" also serves, so I myself do my key part in contributing to the fact that, rather often, my knowledge attributions are indeed true: I create, or I maintain, contexts where there predominate just such epistemic interests as will serve to ensure obligingly low standards for *passing*, for being *close enough* to the perfect case of knowing.

All that being so, good contextualists can make most sense of the intriguing moves from the usual to the unusual: When engaged in his (overly) ambitious philosophical quest, Descartes did *not* have, as his dominant interests, the sort of interests that, even in his own life, were usually the dominant ones. For, at *these* times, the great thinker was fairly embroiled in a quest for complete, absolute and perfect objective certainty. At *these* times, Descartes's epistemic standards were *extraordinarily high* standards. As our account nicely has it, relative to such extraordinarily high standards, none of us will ever know (more than hardly) anything.

When someone (innocent of philosophy) first reads Descartes's passages, then, through the force of the encountered writing upon her, those high standards may then become her own standards. At *that* time, even if at hardly any other time, it may be very difficult for the reader *correctly to think* "I know a fair amount about the world." But, at ever so many *other* times, the same person has much lower standards in force. At these other times, it may be easy for her correctly to think "I know a fair amount about the world."

In a general way, the main points of the traditional dialectic have just been presented. As I trust, it will also be useful to encounter a few details: In advancing his argument, Descartes gets us strongly to fix on some such *complex aspect* of knowledge as this: An aspect to the effect that, at least in the perfect case of knowledge, the savvy subject should

(1) be in the *best possible* position to (2) *rule out as not so*—sure, should *know* to be *not* so, but, that's all right—(3) *any* proposition, or *any* situation, that is logically incompatible with the thing the subject is to know. By introducing his evil demon hypothesis, that's one crucial thing that he accomplishes.

With this aspect so strongly in mind, you may very quickly come to think you know nothing beyond your present moment thought and existence. For, jamming you up in three related ways at once, Descartes gets you into an enormously demanding context: As it then quickly appears, you can't rule out *any* of the *very far-fetched* competitors *at all*, let alone your ruling out any of them absolutely, let still further alone your so conclusively ruling out *all* of them. And, as it *then also comes* to seem, you are never in even a *modestly* good position for getting *any* competing hypotheses, whether very far-fetched or whether only quite mundane, to be even *the least bit less likely*. Just so, Descartes gets you into a context where epistemic standards are about as high as can be. So, at *this* point, it won't even be correct for you to say that you're *justified in believing* you're wearing pants.

Heaping one benefit on another, good contextualists can also make best sense of the most effective moves from the unusual back to the usual: Put down your Descartes, and close the book. Think *not* of evil demons, *nor of any other such far-fetched* scenarios, like brains in vats. Instead, think only of very much more *mundane* matters. Further, and somewhat in the manner of G. E. Moore, you may stoutly *state that* you're wearing pants, thus *representing yourself as knowing that* you're wearing pants.[18] Shortly, you may find yourself in a quite different context, where the standards for knowing are much lower. At this later time, it may be easy for you *correctly* to think that you know you're wearing pants, and it may be *very* easy for you to correctly think that, at the least, you're justified in believing you're wearing pants.[19]

Largely motivated by the idea that we be able to explain two closely related things, I've tried to make sense of the traditionally trying epistemological dialectic: (1) In a *certain way*, there's *something* right, or at least something *all right*, in what the skeptic does and, at times, gets us to do. (2) In a closely related but quite *opposite way*, there's *also something* right in our making *ordinary attributions* of knowledge. As was plain, in trying to make sense of this dialectic, I used a contextual account of

---

18. For an account of how our assertions involve us in representing ourselves as *knowing*, and not just as correctly believing, see chapter 6 of *Ignorance*.

19. In much more detail, this is discussed in section 3 of "The Cone."

epistemic terms. If I had some success, then, by now, there's fair support for a leading idea: Both in ethics and in epistemology, progress is made by way of the hypothesis that centrally useful normative terms have a contextually sensitive semantics.

## 6. The Parallel between the Two Domains

To help further this suggestion, it will be useful to make more explicit a rather extensive *parallel* between, on the one side, the *ethical* argumentation presented earlier in our essay and, on the other side, the *epistemological* discourse encountered in the just previous section.

First, just as certain ethically useful words, like "your buying those pants is all right," may be best understood in terms of the ideal of perfect conformity with absolutely all of ethics, so certain epistemically useful words, like "he knows he is buying those pants," may be best understood in terms of the ideal of perfect conformity with the absolutely perfect case of knowledge. Second, just as the ethically useful words are semantically sensitive to the context of their then current use or understanding, so the terms of knowledge are also sensitive to context. Following directly upon these two, there is this third point: On the one side, a given ethical judgment that is standardly made with the morally useful words requires, for its truth, or for its acceptability, that, as regards closeness to the *morally ideal* case, the subject be above (only) *whatever particular passing line* that judgment's own context then establishes. And, on the other side, a particular epistemic judgment requires, for *its* truth, or for *its* acceptability, that, as regards closeness to the *epistemologically ideal* case, the subject be above (only) whatever passing line *its* own context *then* establishes. From these three points, there arises the parallel between the dialectical situations.

Following Peter Singer and others, we may encounter *ethical argument* of the sort that, *in the very encountering of its typical instances, certain contexts are established **the very establishment of which** ensures that certain uncommonly high ethical standards are in force.* Now, when there *are* these encounters, then, generally, we correctly think that, *hardly ever*, or perhaps even *never*, are we close enough to perfect conformity with absolutely all of morality for us to behave in a way that is morally permissible.

Following Descartes, and a younger Peter Unger, we may encounter relevantly parallel *epistemological argument*. This will be argument of the sort that, in the very encountering of *its* typical instances, certain *other* contexts are established the very establishment of which *others* ensures that certain uncommonly high *epistemological* standards are in force. So, when there are these *other* encounters, then, generally, we *correctly* think that, *hardly ever*, or perhaps even *never*, are we close enough to perfect conformity with the absolutely perfect case of knowledge for us to know.

In both cases, the argumentation presented tends to elevate, in us who typically encounter and appreciate it, the standards in question. In both cases, the standards are raised to such uncommonly high levels that we never, or hardly ever, are up to those levels. According to our own then current judgment, and as we properly help to make so, in both cases we wind up getting a failing score. And, finally, all of this may be true even while, in both cases, something else also remains true: In the *absence* of any (currently still effective) encounter with the arguments, generally the *context will be quite different*. Just so, and as much more commonly happens, in both cases we may properly help to create, or help to maintain, contexts where the levels for passing are much lower. So, in both cases, *most commonly* our own *correct current judgments* are that we get *passing* scores with respect to the normative matters judged.

## 7. Multitude of Terms and Limits of Contextual Influence

Even placing to the side its obvious application to patently indexical expressions, like "here" and "last week," a contextual semantics is by no means confined to certain terms that are especially useful in ethical and in epistemological assessments. To the contrary, there's a *multitude* of contextually sensitive terms. Conspicuously, these include a large battery of "positive" adjectives to which, in some early work, I gave the name *absolute terms*.[20] Having often discussed positive absolute terms, like "flat" and "certain," it will be less tedious, and more instructive, to focus on a "comparative," or relational, absolute term. So, we'll briefly discuss when, in respect of various matters of degree, two items are *equal*, or the *same*.

For you and me to be *equal* in height, for instance, we must be *exactly* equal, and *absolutely* equal, in height. Being even *extremely* nearly equal in height will not do; indeed, our being so very nearly equal actually *entails* that we are *not* the same height. Rather, we must be a *perfect case* of two who are the same height.

As philosophers, we want to make good sense of our *flexibly instructive use* with these central comparative terms. And, as sensible

---

20. The first dubbing occurred in "A Defense of Skepticism," cited in note 2.

philosophers, we want to *count as true* many of the positive judgments that we make with the terms. In order to do both at once, we take a contextual approach to their semantics.

Consider a judgment standardly made with "This table is *the same weight as* that table." Now, as is pretty certain, one of the two tables has at least several more protons and neutrons than the other. So, as is pretty certain, any extremely high standard for sameness of weight will mean trouble for the truth of this ordinary judgment. But implicit reference to context saves the day: *According to the standards for sameness of weight determined by the context of this very judgment, the two indicated tables are close enough to* **the perfect case** *of two items being equal in weight.*

Similar remarks apply to the truth of, *and also to the relevant instructiveness of*, not only many ordinary judgments of sameness, but also many such *judgments of difference*. Regarding height, length, weight, age, and so on, the most basic point in the area is just this double-barrelled idea: If extremely high standards are always in force, then, first, judgments of *sameness* will (almost) always *be false* and, second, the corresponding judgments of *difference* will (almost) always be both *trivially* true and *hopelessly uninstructive*.

There are ever so many areas in which reference to context operates in various ways, including our two normative areas. Well enough, just one ethical case makes the point: From two seats in Shea Stadium, for example, select two typical citizens. As we suppose, in all *other* respects, these two people are morally fine and, to boot, they are equally so. At the same time, neither does much for those in direst need. Now, over their lives, there is *some* difference between them in this regard. But, in many contexts, the tiny difference may be ignored. In these contexts, you can correctly say that, morally, the behavior of each is, neither better nor worse, but is the *same* as the other.

As should be noted, there are *limits* to the range of situations for which contextual factors have a semantic impact: Suppose your shorter fence is just ten feet long while your longer fence is fully ten miles long. To make our point clearly, suppose we refer to the shorter fence with the relevantly neutral term, "this fence," and we refer to the longer fence with "that fence." This, then, is the point: Providing the lengths of the fences don't change, there is *no* context where you can *correctly* say that *this* fence is the same length as *that* fence.

The point about these limits is not itself limited to philosophically banal cases. As well, it applies to ethical and epistemological assessments. First, ethics: Take any gruesomely familiar case of cold-blooded killing for the sake only of, and resulting only in, the agent's own financial gain. There's *no* context in which we can *correctly* say that *such* behavior is morally permissible. Next, epistemology: Take your-average stranger from Peru, who hasn't the slightest idea even who you are, or where you are, much less any idea whether you're wearing pants. Then, there's *no* context in which we can *correctly* say that *such* a person knows that you're wearing pants.

## 8. Contextualism and the Feeling of "Too Much Subjectivity"

Even after familiarity with the foregoing discussion, some will feel that, in contextualism, there's something wildly too *subjective*, or *relative*. While I won't try fully to explain this persistent feeling, I think I can provide a pretty good explanation, good enough for contextual analysis in ethics to receive serious consideration. Making a reasonable division, there are three main parts to this.

The first part concerns a very wide variety of the terms that I've said have a contextually sensitive semantics. As the main point here pertains to all these terms, for the sake of clear exposition I'll discuss it with reference to a very simple and familiar instance: In the case of *sameness of length*, I believe, contextualism really does provide the truth of the matter. But that's certainly *not* how things *first appear*. Rather, the initial appearance is this: Because questions of length are entirely *objective* matters, completely *independent* of what anyone thinks or wants, the truth-value of *any* judgment to the effect that two physical objects are the *same length* is completely independent of what anyone wants or thinks. So, the truth, or the proper acceptability, of *any* such judgment will *never* depend on any speaker's interests or context.

We have a proclivity, I'm suggesting, to think that fully objective matters are somehow invulnerable to, and are not susceptible of, certain sorts of judgment. These are judgments that have, as factors appropriate to their semantic evaluation, what people may say or think about those matters. In other words: As we are prone confusedly to view the subject, the very objectivity of the matters renders them impervious to being judged in any even modestly subjective way.

Because we often think of ethical matters as fully objective, this proclivity may work, as well, in ethics. Just as it may create an unfavorable appearance for a contextual treatment of "This fence is *the same length* as that fence," so it may create a bad one, too, for our treatment of "What you are doing is *morally all right*." Wherever it's at work, this proclivity is to be resisted. With an injunction to be vigilant, the first part of my explanation is over.

The second part concerns what I take to be another sort of confusion. As some might think, our contextual account implies rampant relativity, and rampant subjectivity, with regard to factors that influence context and, thus, with regard to which contexts are most suitable for us: If someone strongly wants to make correct particular judgments of a lenient sort, for example, then, with nothing to stop him, he can just become most involved with those factors that will establish, for him, suitably lenient contexts. On the contextualist account, then, he will be correct in making those lenient judgments. But, surely, this is far too relative, and far too subjective, an account of the matter.

What is confused about this line of thinking? Perhaps there are two confusions here, one blatant and the other more subtle. The blatant confusion is this: As someone might think, if he can only get himself often to be in ethically more lenient contexts, then that will ensure that his rather uncaring behavior will, somehow, be ethically better behavior than it now is correctly judged to be. This can no more happen, of course, than someone can improve his behavior by having it called "extremely good" by people who do not know what he is doing, or by people who are very careless about the ethical judgments that they make. And, it can no more happen than the lengths of two objects can be made to converge by having them called "the same" by many people. In other words, this can never happen.

The more subtle confusion lies in the idea that contextualism entails that, regarding the factors that influence our contexts, there is nothing that can make it better for us to favor some and to avoid others. There is no such implication. Rather, just as we can make intelligent distinctions regarding other pervasive aspects of our lives, we can do that regarding the formation of, and the maintenance of, our contexts. As regards the *formation of our beliefs*, for example, we can distinguish between cogent arguments and merely rhetorical devices. And, in the beliefs that we form, we can allow ourselves to be influenced much more by the former than by the latter. In this way, we can, indirectly but intelligently, manage to foster behavior that's conducive to satisfying our desires and to promoting our values. Although the point is less familiar, it's just as true that we can distinguish intelligently with regard to the various factors that influence contexts and, thus, with regard to which contexts prevail in our lives. Contextualism or no contextualism, if you strongly care about being very ethical, then, as a sensible person, you'll take care more often to set for yourself ethically demanding contexts, and not allow yourself to be, so very often, in quite lenient contexts. In this way you can, even more indirectly but just as intelligently, manage to foster behavior that's conducive to satisfying your highly ethical desires and to promoting your highly ethical values. Of course, the main points here are scarcely confined to ethical matters; rather, they pertain to any area of concern.

Finally, I offer the third part of my explanation: Consider our thoughts about what things are *intrinsically important*, in any serious sense of the term. Surely, people's having long happy lives, rather than short miserable ones, is one of these things. Now, as I suggest, perhaps most of us have a certain psychological tendency: We tend to persist in taking a matter to be fully *independent*, or to be *in no wise dependent upon context*, in (rough) proportion to how *important* the matter *appears to be*. Perhaps, the *remaining* difficulty we are having about that same old feeling arises, in largest measure, from just such a tendency. If that is so, then, just as we should expect, this following will be our psychological situation: It may persistently appear to us that the statement that it is morally all right for you to do nothing to prevent those children's deaths *just cannot* be a judgment that, semantically, is properly evaluated with respect to the context in which it is made or grasped.

Though it may now be more intense, still, what we have here is just that same old feeling about dependence on context. And, as far as the mind's eye can see, for all its intensity, there's nothing much behind this feeling of too much subjectivity.

## 9. What Might This All Mean?

In closing let me offer a perspective that is hardly confined to philosophy, or to dialectical encounter, but that fully extends to the great bulk of our lives. Though philosophy is an important activity, there are certain other things that are much more important. Indeed, far more important than ever learning (more of) the truth about ethics, or about epistemology, is even this: There should *very generally and commonly prevail*, among us human beings, certain contexts that, as a sad matter of fact, are very uncommon. For, when these contexts prevail, we'll be living on a much higher moral plane.

Hand in hand with this, as we may hope, there will be what is so terribly important: Even according to the (contextually referenced) moral assessments of us who will be living on this decently high moral plane, and who will be applying such higher moral standards, our *behavior* should be morally all right. For, as we know all too well, the likely alternative to our living on such a decently high moral plane is not some close second best. Very far from that, the likely alternative is a lot like the present situation. And, this amounts to our living in a sort of moral swamp: As though we are all in a protective fog emanating from a swamp, we keep ourselves, and each other, largely indifferent to the widely known, but dimly seen and felt, suffering of others.

For this obfuscating fog, we can't see our way out of the swamp. Now, to get out of the swamp, we'll likely need breakthroughs in our social arrangements. But can *philosophy* be of any help here? My hope is that it can. When presented in an encouraging manner, perhaps contextual analysis will help not only some philosophers, but also some socially powerful people, to see clearly what's really so important. If this should happen, then, indirectly, philosophy will help to create, and to sustain, a reasonably decent world.[21,22]

---

21. Many people helped me with this paper. While I cannot mention them all, I should publicly give thanks to Jonathan Adler, John Carroll, Keith DeRose, Mark Johnston, Shelly Kagan, David Lewis, Heidi Malm, Michael Otsuka, John Richardson, Stephen Schiffer, Roy Sorensen and Robert Stalnaker.

22. Since this paper was accepted for publication, Keith DeRose's outstanding essay, "Solving the Skeptical Problem," has been published in the January 1995 issue of *Philosophical Review* (pp. 1 ff.). More than anything else I've seen, that brilliant paper shows how much progress can be made by working with a contextualist approach.

# PART IV

# Defending and Transcending
*Living High and Letting Die*

# 11

# PRÉCIS OF *LIVING HIGH AND LETTING DIE*

Because this Symposium's commentators so clearly indicate so much of the central content of my *Living High and Letting Die*, I'll provide only a skeletal Precis of the book. Reducing redundancy, this also will allow more space to develop this content, in response to questions from critics, so as to clarify what's in the book and, perhaps, its potential for helping us appreciate both morality itself and morally central facts of our current situation.[1]

After presenting central facts about easily preventable childhood death in most of the poorest places in the world, Chapter 1 observes that, intuitively, we judge leniently the conduct of those who never do anything toward lessening such suffering and loss, not even when confronting a vividly informative Envelope from the likes of UNICEF. It's noted that, in contrast with such lax judgment of such fatally unhelpful behavior, when responding to the fatally unhelpful conduct in Peter Singer's case of a child on the verge of drowning in a nearby Shallow Pond, our intuitive moral assessment is very severe. How best to account for this great disparity in our intuitive behavioral judgments? On the dominant approach of Preservationism, it's held that, as with almost all moral responses to cases, these divergent reactions reflect an

---

1. In writing these replies, I've been helped by judicious thoughts from Thomas Pogge, well beyond what's in his incisive published commentary. I'm thankful also to David Barnett for helpful comments.

important feature of our good Basic Moral Values and, perhaps at just a short remove, of morality itself. On the contrasting Liberationism featured in the book, our intuitions on very many cases, both hypothetical and even actual, do nothing toward reflecting these Values, as they're produced by powerfully Distortional Mental Tendencies that prevent us from responding in line with the Values. And, in the morally most meaningful respects, the conduct in the Envelope is at least as bad as that in the Shallow Pond.

By contrast with fatally unhelpful conduct that's still so widespread, Chapter 1 then discusses our intuitive moral judgment of the *total conduct* of folks, mainly merely hypothetical people, who behave in morally wanting ways that, by now, humanity has progressed beyond. Mainly, the focus is slaveholding behavior: If we assume that, in a few generally advanced societies today, there are "extremely benevolent" slaveholders whose conduct is, in other matters, morally exemplary, the intuitive judgment is that their total conduct is quite shabby. By contrast, with such long-ago less benevolent slaveholders as Washington and Jefferson, the intuitive judgment is that their total conduct was rather good. Why is there this disparity? Only after a Distortional Mental Tendency is hypothesized do we see a satisfactory explanation.

Chapter 2 offers a detailed examination of what seem the most promising differences between the Envelope and the Vintage Sedan, a case more "surprisingly" eliciting a strict judgment of unhelpful conduct than does the Shallow Pond, in an attempt to see whether, as Preservationism holds, there's a morally crucial difference between such cases. But, as it turns out, the difference most productive of such divergent responses can't carry much moral weight: By contrast with the Envelope, in the Sedan and the Pond there's someone whose dire need is highly conspicuous to the agent, and to us judges of her behavior. For more about the book's longest chapter, we may see Brad Hooker's admirably lucid comments.

To keep matters interesting, in Chapter 3 we expand our canvass, examining cases where, in the furtherance of lessening serious loss to folks, the agent takes a lot from the wealthy, and engages in other sorts of generally objectionable behavior, like lying, though she doesn't go so far as to impose truly serious losses on others. Now, with the Yacht, it appears morally good for you to take a billionaire's ship to save a nearby drowning person's life, even if that means damage to the extent of millions beyond what insurance will cover; with the Account, in contrast, it seems wrong to funnel a million from his huge account to a UNICEF account so that thousands fewer children die in the near future. Why the difference? First, as with the Envelope, with the Account there's nothing to break the grip of our fallacious futility thinking, which has it seem that the saving done means no more than removing just a drop of misery from a whole ocean of suffering. So, second, it then seems that there's no strong moral reason to contribute one's wealth to the cause, much less someone else's. But, third, with the Yacht there's a dire need that's highly conspicuous, enough to break the grip of futility thinking, as with the Pond and the Sedan. So, fourth, it then rightly seems that there is strong reason.

In Chapter 4, our canvass is extended still further, as we examine cases where, for the agent to engage in effectively saving some folks, she must bring serious losses to others, as with the loss of life or limb. With the Trolley, it seems good to switch a runaway tram from a track where it's set to kill six onto a track where one will be killed. With the Foot, it seems bad forcibly to take one guy's left foot to make a life-saving antidote for sixty, which can be gotten only from a foots-worth of that one, no matter how conspicuously needy the sixty may be. Why that difference? Mainly, it's this: With the Foot, we Projectively Separate the needy sixty from the one whose loss can save them; far from falling prey to that Distortional Tendency, with the Trolley we Projectively Group everyone together and, thus, nothing prevents us from responding in line with the Values. To evidence this explanation, I introduce a new technique to moral psychology and philosophy: Comparing our responses to two-option cases with our responses to "aptly inclusive" several-option cases. For more about this chapter, see Singer's informative comments.

In chapter 5, there's the book's main case for how very strong is the influence of Projective Separating on our moral responses to so many cases. For encounters with especially striking instances of such Separating, a devil of a figure is introduced, one Dr. Strangemind, who's as powerful as he's nutty. This short chapter is the most entertaining, and I won't risk spoiling anyone's fun by detailing it here.

Chapter 6 concerns the costs of leading a morally decent life for well-to-do folks, like us, in what's actually our current situation. At least twice over, I argue that, by any ordinary standard, the costs are enormous. First, there's an argument that proceeds mainly by way of a consideration of cases. Then, there's one that proceeds largely through what I call Principles of Ethical Integrity. Though they also treat material featured in other chapters, the lively comments from Thomas Pogge, and from Fred Feldman, address these Principles and the costly conclusions variously drawn in this chapter.

Finally, and perhaps inadvisably, in chapter 7 there's offered a complex contextualist account of many moral judgments. If this semantic account is on track, as well it might be, then there might not be any real conflict between the harsh judgment of the Envelope's conduct offered in the bulk of the book, where very demanding contexts prevail, and, on the other side, the lax judgments offered in everyday life, where much less demanding contexts prevail. While such a modest reconciliation may take a bit of the sting out of my main moral contentions, it is not, I now think, a part of the book on which folks should much focus.

# REPLIES

In this set of four Replies, I try both to support the central thoughts of *Living High and Letting Die* and to extend its approach into new areas of consideration. As is my hope, perhaps these extensions will make a contribution to moral philosophy and, maybe, to what might be even more important than any philosophy.

## 1. Reply to Brad Hooker: A Dilemma about Morality's Demands?

At the outset of his comments, Brad Hooker accurately observes that "the centerpiece of the book is definitely the question about sacrificing your own good" in order to lessen the "early death and pointless suffering" that will otherwise befall socially distant others. Further on, he observes that I've done a fair amount to motivate my costly Liberationist answer to this question: Morally, we well-off folks must sacrifice almost all our worldly goods, at least to the point where, by our rich society's standards, we are no more than very modestly well-off. Further still, he notes that, even after everything I've written, a much less demanding view is at least as credible as the tough line I go so far as to advocate. And, toward the end, he observes that I should think further about this "difficult dilemma in moral philosophy.... any line... short of the extremely demanding... can seem counterintuitively mean. On the other hand, Unger's line itself seems counterintuitively demanding."

In recent months, I've wrestled hard with this dilemma. While it's not surprising that my further thinking has mainly favored the hard line I've favored, nor that none of my new thoughts are conclusive, I'll suggest that some of these further thoughts may be surprisingly far-reaching.

Imagine that we are quite wealthy citizens of a very small wealthy country and that, increasingly in the most recent 6 months, our well-off compatriots have been contributing the great bulk of their assets and incomes to the world's most efficient relief and development agencies, so that by now about half are just so fully committed. Because our country is so small, this flow of money has not been too much for these groups to handle well. Because it's so wealthy, the money has enabled them to save, in this period, nearly twice as many lives as in the previous parallel period a year before.

For you and me, this question now vividly arises: Does morality require us, who've so far been giving little or nothing, to go about as far as they have? According to the committed half of our society, it does. By contrast, the uncommitted half, as well as the "outside world," take the "traditional" line: While it's morally better for us also to make such big commitments, morality can't really require that, for such distant strangers, we go anywhere near that far. Who's right here, about what morality requires, the committed, the uncommitted, or neither?

To my mind, it seems clear that the committed are right, and that, until we also start making just such sacrifices, our conduct will continue to be seriously wrong.

In the imagined circumstance, the knowledge that so many of our compatriots have become so committed to such great life-saving sacrifice provides us, I'll suggest, with a great deal of psychological help that, in the actual everyday circumstance, we're almost entirely lacking. In such a society, we'd have vivid knowledge that, for many people very like us and in our very neighborhoods, it's *psychologically pretty easy* to contribute a lot and make do on very modest means, which explains the commitment rate already achieved. And, with this vivid knowledge, it's *not terribly hard*, psychologically, for *us* to contribute a great deal.

In the actual circumstance, by contrast, it *is* just so terribly hard. That's because nothing gives us much help, actually, toward seeing what morality may require of us by way of aiding inconspicuous others. So, though it may really require a great deal of us, often morality won't seem to require much at all.

Can the fact that it's psychologically so hard for us to make costly sacrifices mean that it's perfectly all right for us not to make them? Further thought about such Morally Advanced Societies favors a negative answer.

Suppose that, after due deliberation, we join our committed countrymen and, toward saving distant children, regularly make costly sacrifices. Then, after some years of such deeply altruistic behavior, on the part of so many in our society, there is widespread moral regress. One after another, most of our compatriots stop making much of a contribution and, instead, give little more than a token. Among the 10% that are still sacrificing greatly, we are now deliberating whether to continue with our sacrificial ways. At this point, it may be very hard, psychologically, for us to keep on with our costly conduct. Can this mean that it's now all right for us to revert to so much fatally unhelpful behavior? Or, rather, does the great psychological difficulty mean that, though it will be badly wrong for us to have many more children suffer and die, it's in mitigating circumstances that we'll be engaging in what's still badly unhelpful conduct? While I don't doubt that many smart philosophers will hold that the first of these suggestions gives a more accurate moral sense of direction, I think that the second more nearly points to the heart of morality.

Rather than being specially selected just for use with the moral matters on which I've most focused, there seems to be relevantly wide application for these thoughts about Morally Advanced Societies. So, let's consider what seems another area needing much moral progress where, owing largely to the lack of concerned behavior by so many apparently decent people, not so much is being made. I refer to our continuing financial support of those who, in reaping riches from their provision of animal products for our employment or enjoyment, bring untold pain and suffering to hundreds of millions of nonhuman animals annually and, with chickens included, billions every year.

Suppose that, in a similar imagined wealthy country, and also increasingly in the past 6 months, our compatriots have been forswearing the consumption of animal products, so that now about half are quite fully committed: they've switched to a vegan diet; they've bought only such new shoes as are made of cloth or plastics; and so on. Now, as making such a radical behavioral change is usually unpleasantly difficult, for most of our fellows the change means a real cost. Yet, their sacrifice might well be very worthwhile: Because our country is so small, this has already had an enormous impact on our domestic agriculture, and our related industry, though it has had only a slight impact on the similar businesses of other countries. At the same time, because our country's so wealthy, it has had a somewhat significant impact even on those foreign businesses: those export industries make less with leather and more with plastics; those resorts and hotels feature more vegan dishes and sell less meat; and so on. So, both near and far, the morally better behavior of so many of our compatriots has been serving significantly to lessen serious suffering.

For you and me, this question now vividly arises: Does morality require us, who've so far been doing little or nothing, to go about as far as they have? According to them, it does. By contrast, the uncommitted half of our society, as well as the "outside world," take the "traditional" line: While it's morally better for us also to make such big commitments, morality can't really require that, for such mere animals, we go anywhere near that far. Who's right here, about what morality requires, the committed, the uncommitted, or neither?

To my mind, it seems clear that the committed are right, and that, until we also start making just such sacrifices, our conduct will continue to be seriously wrong.

In parallel with what we did before, we may extend this present exercise, so that it also will include salient backsliding. Then, much as before, there's again the very strong suggestion that the backsliders will behave quite wrongly when, for instance, they revert to eating carnivorously in foreign restaurants and hotels.

Does all this do nothing to show that, in what may be the most pressing areas for moral progress, we shouldn't think we're perennially saddled with philosophic dilemmas about what morality requires? Or, does it serve to show that, however lax our ordinary impressions, morality really requires quite a lot? While I don't doubt that many smart philosophers will hold that the first of these suggestions gives a more accurate sense of what we should think about how morality bears on our actual situation, I'll suggest that the second more nearly points to the truth of the matter.

## 2. Reply to Peter Singer: Psychology, Philosophy, New Work for Several-option Cases

In his beautifully clear and concise comments, Peter Singer focuses on the central cases in my book, my observation of our intuitive responses to these cases, and my explanation of many responses as being the product primarily of our Distortional Mental Tendencies. First, he considers my treatment of our lax response to unhelpful behavior in the Envelope, by contrast with our very negative response to much less horribly consequential conduct in the Vintage Sedan. Turning from such contrasting cases of failures to aid, he then considers my treatment of groups of cases where, while the agent always does provide greatly needed aid, she imposes serious harm on innocent others in the process: In a case where an agent's saving six requires that she kill someone who seems "Separate from the Problematic Situation," as with a heavy person on a bridge who's so seemingly Separate from the Situation of six below imperiled by a trolley, our intuitive response to the saving-and-killing conduct is quite negative. In an "Aptly Inclusive Several-option Case," where intermediate options help us see the one as on a par with the others, we make a positive response to (what even seems to us to be) morally identical killing-and-saving conduct.

In light of that, Singer correctly concludes that, though philosophers frequently endorse certain normative moral theories because they appear to *capture our moral intuitions* on many canvassed cases, and reject others because they apparently *fail to capture our intuitions*, they oughtn't make such moves even nearly so quickly or directly as so many have done.

Finally, while noting that my observations are impressionistic, he rightly issues a call for a scientific study of intuitive responses to interesting ethical examples.

In reply, I'll first note that, largely in response to Singer's call, in the fall of 1997 I began some scientific work in collaboration with an experimental psychologist who is, as far as a layman like me can tell, currently one of the abler senior investigators of human value judgment, Professor Jonathan Baron of the University of Pennsylvania. (Of course, what we can learn from psychological experiments will be limited. One thing we can't learn from them, of course, is how we ought to behave.) In the very early studies so far attempted, the experimental subjects have been presented only with relatively simple cases, and none presented with anything like a rich description. With these "bare bones" cases, we've found that there are small effects, but significant effects, paralleling the unscientifically obtained results that, with a fuller battery of more detailed cases, I reported in the book.

At all events, I think the reported observations give some interesting indications as to my own "moral psychology," and my similarly educated reader's. And, at least for us, it may be instructive now, in advance of further scientific study, to engage in some further "armchair" exploration. So, proceeding impressionistically, I'll construct a new pair of contrast cases that, between them, newly present main features of both sorts of case Singer's considered: On the one hand, all the agent's active options concern only aiding the greatly needy, whilst none, then, concern harming anyone at all. And, while one of the pair features just two such aiding options, the other is an Aptly Inclusive Several-option Case, with intermediate options that may help show the moral situation that, most plausibly, is common to both examples.

Suppose that you were faced with a true choice between taking our wounded trespasser to the hospital in your Sedan and saving his leg and, on the other side, sending an Envelope to UNICEF and having it that thirty fewer kids die in the next few months than would otherwise. What's the right thing to do? In an inchoate form, some such thoughts have occurred to many who've read the book's second chapter. But, how are we to make sense of the question just posed or, for that matter, the supposition it's meant to concern? In any *ordinary* case there *won't* truly be any such choice: After taking one person to the hospital, you can contribute money to help others. So, *what sort of extraordinary* case might I have asked you to suppose?

To proceed helpfully, we'll make these extraordinary suppositions: Our Dr. Strangemind has given you a Strictly Dated Check made out to UNICEF for $50,000, an amount far greater than you yourself will otherwise ever control. Almost in the middle of nowhere, maybe in the middle of Montana, your options are spread out before you: If you drive quickly to the nearest U.S. Postal Service Overnight Mail Box, you'll get there within the hour, in time for the next Pick-up, in time for a Prompt delivery to UNICEF, and in time for a Timely Deposit in their Account, before the check becomes a worthless piece of paper. So, if you so quickly drive to just that Box, then, but only then, will you have it be that, in the next few months, fifty less children will die than otherwise. As we'll also suppose, after driving toward the Box for 5 minutes you come to a crossroads, where you encounter a trespasser who needs you to take to him to a hospital, which is a 40 minute drive down a different road from the Box, for his leg to be saved. So, now, we have a true choice between helping to save one salient leg so soon and, on the other side, helping to save, not so soon, dozens more inconspicuous lives. And, so, now we can more sensibly ask, "What's the right thing to do?"

With this case of Two Possible Savings, our intuitive response is that taking the wounded trespasser to the hospital is the right thing; being badly cold-hearted conduct, it's wrong to take the Check to the Box. Does this intuition reflect our Moral Values? Or, is it, rather, the product of nothing so much as Distortional Mental Tendencies? Let's look at an Aptly Inclusive Several-option Case.

In addition to the previous case's two active options, and its horrid passive option, with this case of Four Possible Savings, there are two further true alternatives. One is this: If you drive quickly down still another road, in 40 minutes you'll come to a then-salient place where two innocents are chained to a bomb that, while it's easy for you to disarm, will blow them both sky high in an hour if you don't do that.

And, this is the other: In their suburban house two thousand miles away, Strangemind has locked up a mother, a father and their three kids. If you do nothing on their behalf, then bombs placed under their floorboards will explode a week from now, killing all five. But, in a Federal Express Package, Strangemind gives you a second Strictly Dated Check, made out to Suburban Cable TV for $5,000, with an order for them promptly to install their UltraSystem on the lawn of that house. Now, if you drive quickly down yet still another road, in 40 minutes you'll come to the nearest Fed Ex Box in time for *that* next Pick-up, in time for a Prompt delivery to Suburban Cable, in time for a Timely Deposit in *their* Account, and in time for them to make the installation within the week. Only in that event will radio-waves from the UltraSystem deactivate the bombs, and the family not be killed.

Intuitively, what's our assessment of the four helpful courses of conduct in the Four Possible Savings? Well, for one thing, it's morally better to save the lives of the two in such *dramatically imminent* danger, even if their need isn't so salient, than to save the leg of the one whose lesser great need is so conspicuous. For another, it's better to save the faraway five in dramatic danger, even if their danger is no more imminent than their need is salient, than to save the two. Third, it's better to help UNICEF save fifty very distant children, even if their danger is no more dramatic than it's imminent, than to save the five in dramatic trouble. And, fourth, it's better to help save such a distant fifty than to save the leg of the one nearby. So, we now respond that it's good to help the many very needy inconspicuous people.

Most credibly, those responses are morally correct responses. And, it's also most credible that, to the *Two* Possible Savings, we react incorrectly, in responding that it's wrong to rush the Check to UNICEF.

But, now, these thoughts occur: If it's morally so very important to send, so terribly promptly, a Very Large Strictly Dated Check to UNICEF for fifty lives, can it be morally quite optional to send, in a pretty prompt response to our knowledge of the world's readily preventable horrors, a Moderately Large ordinary check for saving five? With the realization that there's no enormous importance in whether the check you send is Strictly Dated or whether it's ordinary, we may realize it's morally required (not to ceaselessly procrastinate on the matter, but) to contribute to such vital work at least a fairly significant proportion of what we can afford. And, with the realizations arising in the reply to Hooker, we might see that we should give nearly all we can afford.

As with our Morally Advanced Societies, so Aptly Inclusive Several-option Cases also prove instructive in other ethically urgent areas. In this connection, let's again return to the manmade suffering of nonhuman animals. For the two-option case, our suppositions will now be these: On one of her active options, our agent will free an animal that's trapped under heavy logs, a creature that, visibly in agony across a deep moat that takes time to circumvent, will so terribly suffer unto its death unless it's helped by her. On her other active option, she'll rush a large Strictly Dated Check to a distant Overnight Mail Box in time for a timely delivery to its payee, the Society for Animals, who'll use the money to have it that some fifty fewer animals suffer terribly in the next few months. These options are genuine alternatives.

With just these options, and without being "tainted" by contact with seemingly similar cases, many may first respond that aiding the wounded animal is the right thing to do; they'll then think that, for being badly cold-hearted conduct, it's wrong to rush the Check to the Box and let the animal, in plain sight, suffer such agony. But, with the addition of just a couple of apt options, there'll be an Aptly Inclusive Several-option Case that's more suited for engagement with our Basic Moral Values, as you can readily confirm. And, with such a more Inclusive Case, there's a very different reaction.

## 3. Reply to Thomas Pogge: Sensible Moralizing and Silly Labeling

Though Thomas Pogge offers substantial criticism of my book, his complex comments help show my main arguments aren't "consequentialist" arguments. After a sensibly brief assessment of his criticism, I'll address related questions concerning such labels, first extending some quite general points in the book and then following the lead of more specific points Pogge suggests.

The chief target of the criticism is my employment of Principles of Ethical Integrity in an attempt to give substantially new arguments for the thought that we well-off folks must do a great deal for the greatly needy. So far are these principles from any ideas both morally substantial and usefully novel, he observes, that they do more to obscure than to clarify important moral relations. As I'm convinced, Pogge's criticism is correct.

Rather than trying to save face, I'll put forth some thoughts that moved me to formulate those Principles. As I think Pogge will agree, the moving thoughts may still be worth our attention. Then, I'll clarify the book's sensibly modest approach to moral principles, which has most of them qualified with, say, an "other things being equal clause." With that, it may then be clear that, among the moral principles the book offers, most fare far better than the aforementioned Principles of Ethical Integrity.

After reading many discussions of fatally endangering trolleys, I found myself with this thought: How can it be all right, really, for such a trolley-switcher to *kill* an innocent person whilst saving the lives of only a very few needy people when, as we tacitly but rightly also suppose, she never imposes on herself any significant loss, not even the loss of a significant fraction of her mere *money*, even when she knows that her losing only that much will mean (the moral equivalent of) saving the lives of *many* needy people? As it certainly seems, there's something badly amiss with any ethic that permits such enormous sacrifices of others while requiring so little of oneself. Not so unfairly, I think, may we call such a morality an "ethics of hypocrisy."

Of course, that's not the only thought that so sensibly occurs. As Pogge suggests, another is this: When it's permitted to take one other's life to save the lives of a few, can it really be that the two salient options here have anything like the same moral status, as they might with, say, choosing between taking a hike and reading a novel. If it's really all right for you to do something as seriously imposing as taking the other's life, then, very far beyond it's just being permitted, and even quite beyond it's just being morally good to do, it should be *morally required* to kill the one, and even *seriously wrong not* to do it, so that the few will be spared. To think any less than this is to take far too lightly, not just the few who might be *saved with* such great sacrifice, but *also the one slated for* such great sacrifice. A morality that treats taking people's lives much like taking pleasant hikes may be rejected as an "ethics of trivialization."

Already embraced by sensible consequentialists, that idea should be welcomed by good nonconsequentialists. Combining the points of the two prior paragraphs, this related thought also should be accepted just as much by those liking the latter label as by those liking the former: Even as it won't just be permitted to switch your exciting trolley and kill one to save just a few, but will also be strongly required, so it's also strongly required that you part with most of your mere money for the saving of many innocent lives, even if it be in much more boring circumstances. As will be agreed by sensible thinkers of both stripes, that's morality. In contrast with an ethics of hypocrisy and an ethics of trivialization, morality itself is an "ethics of deep integrity."

When making the previous paragraphs' general remarks, I offered moral claims so usefully pointed that they'll be contested by quite a few smart moral philosophers. As a matter of course, I made those substantial contentions by offering not any extremely general, but just fairly general propositions. So, against my fairly general suggestion that you shouldn't save a few by fatal trolley-switching unless you also save many by money-contributing, it's silly to complain that it won't hold, for instance, in a circumstance where, for every life your money-contributing will help save, it will cause a thousand people to lose their sight.

In these replies, my avoidance of extremely general moral propositions is the same as in the book. Accordingly, in the sense of the term generally accepted by philosophers, I nowhere advocate any *moral theory*. For, as philosophers generally understand it, such theories are supposed to hold for all possible cases. Rather, I continue to follow the book's working hypothesis, which I've never seen any reason to reject:

> Pitched at a level somewhere between the extremely general considerations dominating the tenets of traditional moral theories, on one hand, and the quite fine-grained ones often dominating the particular cases philosophers present, on the other, it's at this moderately general level of discursive thought, I commonsensibly surmise, that we'll most often respond in ways reflecting our Values and, less directly, morality itself. (Page 28)

This doesn't deny, of course, that there may be positive moral truths at once so perfectly general as to be immune from any conceivable counterexample and, as well, so relevantly substantial as to be suited for such combinations with nonmoral facts as to yield, with strictest logic, moral verdicts for all sorts of conduct, in all sorts of situation. Rather, I'm supposing only that, if there should be such terribly general and substantial truths, we merely human people don't know them, or even have much prospect of that in the not very distant future.

Because they recognize that our moral understanding is quite as limited as our nonmoral understanding, sensible human ethicists preface their generally useful moral formulations with something like an "other things being equal" clause, or they mean for such a qualification to be understood. In illustration, suppose I seriously enough say:

> If your behaving in a certain way will result in your killing little children, then it's wrong for you so to behave.

Then, even with it being understood that these children were little people, you'd still sensibly understand such a qualification to be in force. So, you wouldn't take it as seriously damaging to my merely pretty general moral claim that it may well be permissible to kill two little children, and might even be morally required, if that's the only way to prevent a runaway trolley from similarly squashing sixty kids to death. Rather, you'd understand that, in making such a claim, the main thought offered is much the same as when saying, for instance, there's very strong moral reason against your killing little children, even if not so absolutely overwhelming as to prevail in every possible circumstance.

By contrast with such only pretty general claims, when moral theories are sought by philosophers, it's extreme generalizations that are discussed, those without any qualification. But, without mentioning such "encompassing motivation" as to make it nearly useless, as with:

> If your behaving in a certain way has it that you kill little children just for the purpose of getting a thrill, then it's wrong for you so to behave,

what principle won't fall prey to counterexamples?

The only ones I've ever seen are so nebulous that, for this different reason, they're also nearly useless. So, this unqualified "utilitarian" claim might be free from counterexample:

> If your behaving in a certain way will result in your failing to promote the good, then it's wrong for you so to behave.

But, if it is, then that's largely because we must be very unclear, in very many cases, whether some considered conduct promotes the good, or fails to promote the good.

It's unfortunate how much writing on ethics greatly concerns itself with a few readily labeled moral views, and with which works might be characterized as advocating which labeled positions. Some of this writing may serve the good purpose of seeing how various authors may be variously influenced historically. But, as it seems, most is just some pigeonholing through which an unsettled writer seeks to discredit work she finds so unpleasantly unsettling. Apparently unsettled by my suggestion that we aren't helping enough for us to lead morally decent lives, already two writers have conveniently classified my book, in the popular press of the intelligentsia, as a *utilitarian* work, hoping to discredit the book by placing it in such a notoriously familiar pigeonhole.[1] For two quite different reasons, one more general than the other, it's badly inaccurate, at all events, to suggest this book is a utilitarian volume.

---

1. Colin McGinn, "Saint Elsewhere *Living High and Letting Die* by Peter Unger," *The New Republic*, October 16, 1996, 54–57, and Martha Nussbaum, "Philanthropic Twaddle *Living High and Letting Die: Our Illusion of Innocence* by Peter Unger," *London Review of Books*, L, 17, September 4, 1997, 18–19.

By contrast, even when writing for such a popular press, some other philosophers were more continent and cautious, and thus more accurate, in their discussions of my ethical views: See Brad Hooker "The limits of self-sacrifice: "Futility thinking" and the "Oxfam case," *The Times Literary Supplement*, 4896, January 31, 1996, 26; and see David Lewis, "Illusory Innocence?" *Eureka Street*, Vol.6, No. 10, December 1996, 35–36.

Motivated by the discussion that's just above, the more general reason is just this: As I don't advocate *any* ethical theory, neither in the book nor anywhere else, nor come close to advocating any, in particular I don't favor any that's utilitarian, or any consequentialist theory.

Less generally, and in line with observations from Pogge, I'll note just two of the ways my book's fairly general claims differ from the most salient sorts of utilitarianism, and most meaningful sorts of consequentialism.

First, as the book is an "anti-hypocritical" work, it comports with the nonutilitarian proposition that an agent may act so that only the interests of others, and not her own interests, are given much consideration.

Second, I'm very friendly to the thought that, quite beyond anything they must do toward lessening serious suffering overall, many people have very strong agent-relative duties. Thus, the mother of a child does badly wrong when, instead of making sure her child gets badly needed medical attention, she enables two other mothers to do that for their own endangered children. Especially as there's a section of the book detailing just that, "Special Obligations and Care for Dependents" (pages 149–50), it's hard to see how anyone wouldn't see how friendly I am to this "anti-consequentialist" idea.

## 4. Reply to Fred Feldman: Charity All Over Again?

Fred Feldman says much more that's critical of my book than any of the other commentators. Not so much for that reason as for what we may see to be another understandable reason, his central claims are, apparently, pretty silly suggestions. Here, I'll try to show why that's so. Toward the end of this reply's effort, I'll try to make good use of thoughts from the prior three.

As Hooker and others have also done, Feldman rightly observes that my book's most substantive message is that, for most well-off folks in our actual situation, morality requires that "we give quite a lot of our money to organizations such as Oxfam America, UNICEF, and CARE, to be used to prevent premature deaths among distant children."[2] Then, he

---

2. Page 195; henceforth, page references for Feldman's comments will be placed in brackets in the text.

In an equally peculiar but utterly different critical commentary, "Unger's Living High and Letting Die: Our Illusion of Innocence," *Nous*, XXXII, 1, March 1998, 138–47, Feldman apparently suggests that the book really doesn't have any most substantive message, since it's so largely consumed with making a case for a contextualist semantics

strangely states that it's "a bit fanatical to focus in this way on the suffering of distant dying children," as multiply opposed to people who (1) are teenagers, and (2) are nearby, and (3) are in less than vital need. (196) As I'm afraid, that's where the main difference between us lies.

Less strangely, in a complex sequence of comments his thought is this: *If* I showed how an injunction to engage in such seemingly "fanatical" conduct is *deducible* from the conjunction of *wholly unqualified, completely general, correct moral precepts* and "empirical facts about people like us" in our actual worldly situation, *then I might have* made something of a case for thinking it wrong for us not to help Oxfam, CARE and UNICEF save distant kids' lives. But, as I never did as much as that, I offered no good reason for thinking any such thing, by contrast with, say, thinking "my overriding obligation is to use my time and money to help immigrant Cambodians in Northampton learn to speak English." (198)

As I'll suggest, this may do nothing so much as show how very inappropriate, to our actual situation, is any such a "puristic" conception of what moral precepts, and what moral arguments, are worth our serious attention. Anyway, from the reply to Pogge, we readily recall our discussion of extremely general principles and, by contrast, the more restricted precepts that, for us humans, are much more useful. As the main points there are the main points here, that discussion here suffices.

Though a paralyzingly puristic conception of moral reasoning seems one motivating factor for Feldman's strange take on my work, the psychologically strongest motivation seems to flow from some thinking that's not particularly philosophical. This is our habitual thinking that most of what we might do to aid needy people is a question of nothing morally more momentous than charity, an habitual illusion about which Singer has been warning us for decades. Now, when we engage in this habitual thinking, then we fall prey to all sorts of silly thoughts about the morality of aiding behavior, as with several central in Feldman's commentary.

In some passages, Feldman isn't *wholly* absorbed in this habit, as when he suggests that I might behave quite well when, turning my back on UNICEF'S imperiled would-be clients, I make a huge contribution

---

and a relativistic metaethics. Even as my offering a contextualist semantics for moral discourse is confined to the book's last chapter, and there's really no offer of a relativistic metaethics anywhere in the work, that's one of the reasons, one of many, that, as observed in the Précis, I now think it may have been inadvisable for me to include that chapter.

toward having it that nearby immigrant Cambodians speak English better, or sooner, than if I make no such helpful contribution. But, in others, he seems to be wholly absorbed, as when he wonders whether we might not do quite well when, forsaking even such presumably healthy immigrants, we might make most of our greatest sacrifices toward the end of increasing "intellectual satisfactions among first world teenagers." (196) Sometimes more and sometimes a little less, I hypothesize, he's in a very common frame of mind, one that may be associated with our asking ourselves such a question as this: Is there, really, something morally *amiss* in the conduct of a Harvard alum who, even if he doesn't do anything much like saving poor kid's lives, freely gives $10,000 of his own money to (say) the Harvard Classics Club?

One way to get past the habit of viewing so much of what folks might do as just so many opportunities for nice charity is, I've found, to suppose that, on her deathbed, a dear old friend has gotten you to promise to use funds she's entrusted to you—it also might be $10,000—in a way that, as far as you can determine but as you really believe, isn't morally questionable, or at all objectionable. Because it's so inexpensive to have fewer distant tykes die painfully and prematurely, and have more tykes live long, you can have it that over 40 more kids' lives take the latter path. So, that's one thing you can do with the money. Alternatively, you can give it to the Metropolitan Museum of Art, or to the Boston Symphony. And, as we'll suppose, even though you're not a Harvard alum, you can give it to the Harvard Classics Club. Now, as it certainly seems, if you give the $10,000 to UNICEF for saving such tykes, then, even as you're keeping that solemn promise, there's nothing wrong with your behavior. And, as it equally appears, if you give the funds to the Museum, or to the Symphony, or to the Club, then, even as you're breaking that solemn promise, there's something wrong with your behavior. But, now, this thought also should occur: Unless we're thinking of all the behavioral possibilities as just so many chances for being charitable, we won't need any assumptions about a Solemn Promise to endorse such moral judgments. Thus freed from habitual "nice charity thinking," the most clearheaded among the morally concerned will donate to UNICEF, not to the Club.

In repeatedly recommending the likes of UNICEF, do I express a fanatical bias in favor of little kids over teenagers? Of course not. The point is that, since very many tykes are vulnerable to cheap-to-beat painful threats, and hardly any teenagers, with our limited resources we can do a very great deal more for tykes than teenagers. Do I express a fanatical bias in favor of the distant over the nearby? For a very similar reason, it's obvious that the answer is No. Finally, do I fanatically favor those who'll painfully lose their lives over those who'll just as painfully lose just their hearing? Though not quite as obvious, the main point here isn't any esoteric idea: As a matter of actual fact, it's generally much cheaper to save young kids from painfully dying than from painfully suffering a lesser loss; it's on top of this, so to speak, that the losses prevented are much greater losses.

Trying to be helpfully instructive, I'll complete this reply by extending some thoughts from my reply to Singer, and then from my reply to Hooker. Complementing the help we got with the Solemn Promise, we'll see two more ways of cracking our habitual "nice charity thinking," one with Aptly Inclusive Several-option Cases, the other with Morally Advanced Societies.

First, we consider a small variant of the Two Possible Savings, and a parallel small variant of the Four Possible Savings. With the former variant, the two active options are saving the trespasser's leg and, alternatively, rushing to the Overnight Mail Box with a Strictly Dated Check for $50,000 earmarked for the *Harvard Classics Club*. As most intuitively respond, it's wrong to rush the Check to the Box; what's right is to rush the wounded trespasser to the hospital. With the latter variant, there are, in addition to those active options, these others from the Four Possible Savings: Down another road, there are the two imperiled by a bomb that's set to kill in an hour, and whom only you can save; down yet another, there's the Fed Ex Box, and the way for you to save, from such explosive bomb death in a week, the family of five in the region served by Suburban Cable. With these additional options, is there much movement toward thinking that what's right is to rush to the Overnight Mail Box to benefit, not any distant kids in mortal peril, but members of the Club? I find none at all. How different this is from the result for the Four Possible Savings itself, with its option of rushing to that Box to benefit just such imperiled distant kids, not any intellectually thirsting teenagers. Why this great difference in response? For those most prone to engagement in "nice charity thinking," the answer may be nearly as helpful as it's obviously correct.

Now, Morally Advanced Societies. In my reply to Hooker, I had us imagine we were wealthy members of a small wealthy society, about half of whom recently gave most of their wealth toward lessening the most serious loss and suffering among the world's worst-off people, and who are continuing to give most of their income toward that vital end. And, we have not yet followed suit. In thinking of what we might next do, our also making great sacrifices seemed just the morally decent thing to do, not just very nice philanthropy.

For a parallel exercise, let's now suppose that, instead of ever doing anything much in that direction, what half our compatriots recently sacrificed so greatly for was to provide our county's youth, almost all of them already very well-off, with further benefits, and to provide similarly well-off youth, in quite a few wealthy neighboring nations, with such advanced benefits. Thus, while the more mature folk we've noted now live very modestly, all those younger folk have all sorts of advantages that, before, were enjoyed by only a few: Ever so many are offered excellent artistic opportunities; and so many are offered the chance to go on well-funded scientific expeditions; and so on. Now, as we're further imagining, the provision of all these benefits to so very many robustly appreciative youths means a small net gain in the well-being of all the world's people, even though there's a loss for quite a few of its more mature people. Yet, and at the same time, the wealthy sacrificers would do far more good, and apparently far more important good, were they to contribute, instead, to meeting the much more basic needs of so many of the world's worst-off children. As before, you and I haven't yet followed suit.

In thinking what we might do here, is our continuing with habitual behavior morally very wrong, whilst our also making great sacrifices is just the morally decent thing to do? Not by a long shot.

On the two sides of this parallel, why are there two such very different appearances? As I see it, the answer's pretty plain.

# INDEX OF NAMES

Adams, Robert, 190n8, 195n10
Adler, Jonathan, 218, 232, 235, 244, 248, 263n27, 292n21
Alston, William P., 68n19
Aristotle, 118
Ayer, Alfred Jules, 3n1, 28, 39, 39n1, 42, 95, 97, 211, 211n1

Barnett, David, 295n1
Baron, Jonathan, 303
Bonjour, Lawrence, 251n25
Brown, Peter M., 21n6
Brueckner, Anthony, 263n27

Cargile, James, 50n11, 76n3, 95
Carroll, John, 292n21
Cartwright, Richard, 21n7
Carville, James, vii
Chisholm, Roderick M., 3n1, 16n4, 29, 112n3
Clarke, Thompson, 249n23

Danto, Arthur C., 20n6
Dauer, Francis, 237–238, 241, 263n27
Davidson, Donald, 180n1
Delibovi, Dana, 186n6, 208n18
DeRose, Keith, 281n14, 292n21, 292n22

Descartes, René, 59, 63, 78–79, 97, 170, 176–177, 245, 265n2, 283–286
Donnellan, Keith, 118n3
Dretske, Fred I., 21n7, 265n4

Erwin, Edward, 59n15
Eubulides, 70, 70n1, 77
Euclid, 204, 222
Evans, Gareth, 150n19

Feldman, Fred, 297, 310n2, 310–311
Ferris, Timothy, 181n2
Field, Hartry, 21n7
Fishkin, James, 265n1
Fodor, Jerry, 164n5
Frankfurt, Harry G., 52n12
Freed, Bruce, 21n7

Gettier, Edmund L., 30n5, 229n11, 229–230
Ginet, Carl, 226n7
Goldman, Alvin, 251n25
Grice, H.P., 21n7

Hamburger, Robert, 21n7
Harman, Gilbert H., 20n6, 48n8, 68n19, 114n5, 226n7

# INDEX OF NAMES

Hazen, Allen, 160n23, 179n8, 179n9, 190n8, 208n18
Helmsley, Leona, 271
Hintikka, Jaakko, 39, 39n1, 43n2, 53–54
Hooker, Brad, 296, 299, 305, 309n1, 310, 313
Horowitz, Tamara, 179n9
Hume, David, 155, 192

Jefferson, Thomas, 296
Johnston, Mark, 292n21

Kagan, Shelly, 292n21
Katz, Jerrold J., 122n7, 123n9, 131n13, 165n6, 179n9
Klein, Peter, 212n3, 213n4, 263n27
Kneale, Martha, 95
Kneale, William, 95
Kripke, Saul A., 21n7, 22n, 48n9, 68n19, 118n1, 118–120, 119n4, 121n6, 126, 126n11, 126n12, 139n15, 139–140, 148, 150n19, 226n7

Lehrer, Keith, 20n6
Leibniz, Gottfried Wilhelm, 253
Leichti, Terence, 95n9
Lewis, C.I., 97n2
Lewis, David, 77n4, 164n4, 164n5, 179n9, 184–192, 184n4, 186n6, 186n7, 190n8, 192n9, 195n11, 195–196, 196n12, 198–199, 200–201n15, 202n17, 208n18, 246n21, 266n4, 274, 280n13, 292n21, 309n1
Lincoln, Abraham, 112–113
Locke, John, 118
Lockwood, Michael, 48n8
Luper-Foy, Steven, 263n27

Mackie, J.L., 20n6, 185, 185n5
Malcolm, Norman, 39, 39n1, 43n2, 46–47, 49n10, 53–54, 58, 60n16, 114n5
Malm, Heidi, 292n21
Martin, Steve, x
McGinn, Colin, 309n1
Moline, Jon, 95

Moore, G.E., 3n1, 16, 16n3, 39, 39n1, 53–55, 243n18, 243n19, 243–248, 248n22, 249n23, 285
Munitz, Milton, 190n8

Nagel, Thomas, 160n23, 208n18, 251n24
Nozick, Robert, 28n2, 211, 211n2, 251n25
Nussbaum, Martha, 309n1

Otsuka, Michael, 292n21

Parmenides, 161, 173
Paxson, Thomas, Jr., 20n6
Platinga, Alvin, 190n8
Pogge, Thomas, 295n1, 297, 306, 307, 309n, 310–311
Putnam, Hilary, 118, 121, 121n6, 122n7, 123, 123n8, 123n9, 130–132, 131n13, 135, 137, 139, 142–146, 142n16, 144n18, 148, 150, 162n3, 162–163, 164n5, 165n6, 166–168, 175, 177, 242n17
Putnam, Ruth Anna, 20n6

Quine, W.V., 177, 179, 179n7

Rachels, James, 114n5, 159n21
Radford, Colin, 16n5
Richardson, John, 208n18, 238, 241, 263n27, 292n21
Rockefeller, John D., Jr., 18
Rockefeller, Nelson, 18
Rockefeller, Winthrop, 18
Rosenthal, David, 160n23
Rozeboom, William W., 4n1
Russell, Bertrand, 30n5, 32, 62, 97n2, 229n10, 229–230, 243, 243n19, 245, 248

Sanford, David, 77n4
Schiffer, Stephen, 21n7, 179n9, 231n12, 292n21
Shakespeare, William, 121
Shoemaker, Sydney, 21n7
Singer, Peter, 264, 264n1, 265n2, 267, 286, 295, 297, 302–303, 311, 313

Skyrms, Brian, 4n1
Slote, Michael Anthony, 16n2, 21n7, 22n, 28n2, 60n16, 68n19, 114n5, 267n6
Sorensen, Roy, 292n21
Stalnaker, Robert, 185n5, 292n21
Stampe, Dennis W., 21n7
Stich, Stephen P., 160n22
Stroud, Barry, 249n23

Tienson, John, 263n27

Van Inwagen, Peter, 201n15, 208n18

Washington, George, 296
Weinberg, Julius, 21n7
Wheeler, Samuel C., III, 75n2, 95, 95n9
Wilson, Margaret, 21n7
Wittgenstein, Ludwig, 248n22, 248–249

Yagisawa, Tak, 227n8, 263n27

Zemach, Eddy M., 121n6, 122n7, 144n18
Zeno, 161, 173, 219
Ziff, Paul, 119n5

## ...mer Information

_____
_____
...act: _____  Technical Contact:_____
_____  Email:_____
_____  Fax: _____

## ...formation

_____  Pages: _____  Front Matter: _____
_____  Date Submitted to IBT: _____  Trim Size: _____

## ...nd File Information

### ...ormat
- ...ows (PC or DOS)   ☐ Macintosh   ☐ Other: _____

### ...t Files
...cation Name/Version: _____

**...hics / Artwork**

| | |
|---|---|
| ...ame/ Type: picture.eps (Illustrator EPS) | FileName/ Type: _____ |
| ...ame/ Type: _____ | FileName/ Type: _____ |
| ...ame/ Type: _____ | FileName/ Type: _____ |

### ...er Files
...cation Name/ Version: _____

**...hics / Artwork**

**Color Palette**

| Color | %C | %M | %Y | %K | Pantone Colors |
|---|---|---|---|---|---|
| ...ame/ Type: _____ | _____ | ☐ | ☐ | ☐ | _____ _____ |
| ...ame/ Type: _____ | _____ | ☐ | ☐ | ☐ | _____ _____ |
| ...ame/ Type: _____ | _____ | ☐ | ☐ | ☐ | |
| ...ame/ Type: _____ | _____ | ☐ | ☐ | ☐ | **Lamination** |
| ...ame/ Type: _____ | _____ | ☐ | ☐ | ☐ | ☐ Gloss |
| ...ame/ Type: _____ | _____ | ☐ | ☐ | ☐ | ☐ Matte |

### ...er Files
...cation Name/ Version: _____

**...hics / Artwork**

| | |
|---|---|
| ...ame/ Type: _____ | FileName/ Type: _____ |
| ...ame/ Type: _____ | FileName/ Type: _____ |
| ...ame/ Type: _____ | FileName/ Type: _____ |

## ...face Information

| ...ame (Variants) | Format (PS or TT) | Included on Disk? | Special Instructions |
|---|---|---|---|
| _____ | _____ | ☐ | _____ |
| _____ | _____ | ☐ | _____ |
| _____ | _____ | ☐ | _____ |
| _____ | _____ | ☐ | _____ |
| _____ | _____ | ☐ | _____ |
| _____ | _____ | ☐ | _____ |
| | | ☐ | |